T0143804

A Journal to Stella

A Journal to Stella

Jonathan Swift

MINT EDITIONS

A Journal to Stella was first published in 1766.

This edition published by Mint Editions 2020.

ISBN 9781513270296 | E-ISBN 9781513275475

Published by Mint Editions®

 MINT
EDITIONS

minteditionbooks.com

Publishing Director: Jennifer Newens
Design & Production: Rachel Lopez Metzger
Project Manager: Micaela Clark
Typesetting: Westchester Publishing Services

INTRODUCTION

When Swift began to write the letters known as the *Journal to Stella*, he was forty-two years of age, and Esther Johnson twenty-nine. Perhaps the most useful introduction to the correspondence will be a brief setting forth of what is known of their friendship from Stella's childhood, the more specially as the question has been obscured by many assertions and theories resting on a very slender basis of fact.

Jonathan Swift, born in 1667 after his father's death, was educated by his uncle Godwin, and after a not very successful career at Trinity College, Dublin, went to stay with his mother, Abigail Erick, at Leicester. Mrs. Swift feared that her son would fall in love with a girl named Betty Jones, but, as Swift told a friend, he had had experience enough "not to think of marriage till I settle my fortune in the world, which I am sure will not be in some years; and even then, I am so hard to please that I suppose I shall put it off to the other world." Soon afterwards an opening for Swift presented itself. Sir William Temple, now living in retirement at Moor Park, near Farnham, had been, like his father, Master of the Irish Rolls, and had thus become acquainted with Swift's uncle Godwin. Moreover, Lady Temple was related to Mrs. Swift, as Lord Orrery tells us. Thanks to these facts, the application to Sir William Temple was successful, and Swift went to live at Moor Park before the end of 1689. There he read to Temple, wrote for him, and kept his accounts, and growing into confidence with his employer, "was often trusted with matters of great importance." The story—afterwards improved upon by Lord Macaulay—that Swift received only £20 and his board, and was not allowed to sit at table with his master, is wholly untrustworthy. Within three years of their first intercourse, Temple had introduced his secretary to William the Third, and sent him to London to urge the King to consent to a bill for triennial Parliaments.

When Swift took up his residence at Moor Park he found there a little girl of eight, daughter of a merchant named Edward Johnson, who had died young. Swift says that Esther Johnson was born on March 18, 1681; in the parish register of Richmond, which shows that she was baptized on March 20, 1680–81, her name is given as Hester; but she signed her will "Esther," the name by which she was always known. Swift says, "Her father was a younger brother of a good family in Nottinghamshire, her mother of a lower degree; and indeed she had little to boast in her birth." Mrs. Johnson had two children, Esther and Ann, and lived at Moor Park as companion to Lady Giffard, Temple's widowed sister. Another member of the household, afterwards to be Esther's constant companion, was Rebecca Dingley, a relative of the Temple family. She was a year or two older than Swift.

The lonely young man of twenty-two was both playfellow and teacher of the delicate child of eight. How he taught her to write has been charmingly brought before us in the painting exhibited by Miss Dicksee at the Royal Academy a few years ago; he advised her what books to read, and instructed her, as he says, "in the principles of honour and virtue, from which she never swerved in any one action or moment of her life."

By 1694 Swift had grown tired of his position, and finding that Temple, who valued his services, was slow in finding him preferment, he left Moor Park in order to carry out his resolve to go into the Church. He was ordained, and obtained the prebend of Kilroot, near Belfast, where he carried on a flirtation with a Miss Waring, whom he called Varina. But in May 1696 Temple made proposals which induced Swift to return to Moor Park, where he was employed in preparing Temple's memoirs and correspondence for publication, and in supporting the side taken by Temple in the Letters of Phalaris controversy by writing *The Battle of the Books*, which was, however, not published until 1704. On his return to Temple's house, Swift found his old playmate grown from a sickly child into a girl of fifteen, in perfect health. She came, he says, to be "looked upon as one of the most beautiful, graceful, and agreeable young women in London, only a little too fat. Her hair was blacker than a raven, and every feature of her face in perfection."

On his death in January 1699, Temple left a will, dated 1694, directing the payment of £20 each, with half a year's wages, to Bridget Johnson "and all my other servants"; and leaving a lease of some land in Monistown, County Wicklow, to Esther Johnson, "servant to my sister Giffard." By a codicil of February 1698, Temple left £100 to "Mr. Jonathan Swift, now living with me." It may be added that by her will of 1722, proved in the following year, Lady Giffard gave £20 to Mrs. Moss—Mrs. Bridget Johnson, who had married Richard Mose or Moss, Lady Giffard's steward. The will proceeds: "To Mrs. Hester (*sic*) Johnson I give £10, with the £100 I put into the Exchequer for her life and my own, and declare the £100 to be hers which I am told is there in my name upon the survivorship, and for which she has constantly sent over her certificate and received the interest. I give her besides my two little silver candlesticks."

Temple left in Swift's hands the task of publishing his posthumous works, a duty which afterwards led to a quarrel with Lady Giffard and other members of the family. Many years later Swift told Lord Palmerston that he stopped at Moor Park solely for the benefit of Temple's conversation and advice, and the opportunity of pursuing his studies. At Temple's death he was "as far to seek as ever." In the summer of 1699, however, he was offered and accepted the post of secretary and chaplain to the Earl of Berkeley, one of the Lords Justices, but when he reached Ireland he found that the secretaryship had been given to another. He soon, however, obtained the living of Laracor, Agher, and Rathbeggan, and the prebend of Dunlavin in St. Patrick's Cathedral, Dublin. The total value of these preferments was about £230 a year, an income which Miss Waring seems to have thought enough to justify him in marrying. Swift's reply to the lady whom he had "singled out at first from the rest of women" could only have been written with the intention of breaking off the connection, and accordingly we hear no more of poor Varina.

At Laracor, a mile or two from Trim, and twenty miles from Dublin, Swift ministered to a congregation of about fifteen persons, and had abundant leisure for cultivating his garden, making a canal (after the Dutch fashion of Moor Park), planting willows, and rebuilding the vicarage. As chaplain to Lord Berkeley, he spent much of his time in Dublin. He was on intimate terms with Lady Berkeley and her daughters, one of whom is best known by her married name of Lady Betty Germaine; and through them he had access to the fashionable society of Dublin. When Lord Berkeley returned to England in April 1701, Swift, after taking his Doctor's degree at Dublin, went with him, and soon afterwards published, anonymously, a political pamphlet, *A Discourse on the Contests and Dissentions in Athens and Rome*. When he returned to Ireland in September he was accompanied by Stella—to give Esther Johnson the name by which she is best known—and her friend Mrs. Dingley. Stella's fortune was about £1500, and the property Temple had left her was in County Wicklow. Swift, very much for his "own satisfaction, who had few friends or acquaintance in Ireland," persuaded Stella— now twenty years old—that living was cheaper there than in England, and that a better return was obtainable on money. The ladies took his advice, and made Ireland their home. At first they felt themselves strangers in Dublin; "the adventure looked so like a frolic," Swift says, "the censure held for some time as if there were a secret history in such a removal: which however soon blew off by her excellent conduct." Swift took every step that was possible to avoid scandal. When he was away, the ladies occupied his rooms; when he returned, they went into their own lodgings. When he was absent, they often stopped at the vicarage at Laracor, but if he were there, they moved to Trim, where they visited the vicar, Dr. Raymond, or lived in lodgings in the town or neighbourhood. Swift was never with Stella except in the presence of a third person, and in 1726 he said that he had not seen her in a morning "these dozen years, except once or twice in a journey."

During a visit to England in the winter of 1703–4 we find Swift in correspondence with the Rev. William Tisdall, a Dublin incumbent whom he had formerly known at Belfast. Tisdall was on friendly terms with Stella and Mrs. Dingley, and Swift sent messages to them through him. "Pray put them upon reading," he wrote, "and be always teaching something to Mrs. Johnson, because she is good at comprehending, remembering and retaining." But the correspondence soon took a different turn. Tisdall paid his addresses to Stella, and charged Swift with opposing his suit. Tisdall's letters are missing, but Swift's reply of April 20, 1704, puts things sufficiently clearly. "My conjecture is," he says, "that you think I obstructed your inclinations to please my own, and that my intentions were the same with yours. In answer to all which I will, upon my conscience and honour, tell you the naked truth. First, I think I have said to you before that, if my fortunes and humour served me to think of that state, I should certainly, among all persons upon earth, make your choice; because I never saw that person whose conversation I entirely valued but hers; this was the utmost I ever gave way to. And secondly, I must assure you sincerely that this regard of mine never once entered into my head to be an impediment to you." He had thought Tisdall not rich enough to marry; "but the objection of your fortune being removed, I declare I have no other; nor shall any consideration of my own misfortune, in losing so good a friend and companion as her, prevail on me, against her interest and settlement in the world, since it is held so necessary and convenient a thing for ladies to marry, and that time takes off from the lustre of virgins in all other eyes but mine. I appeal to my letters to herself whether I was your friend or not in the whole concern, though the part I designed to act in it was purely passive." He had even thought "it could not be decently broken," without disadvantage to the lady's credit, since he supposed it was known to the town; and he had always spoken of her in a manner far from discouraging. Though he knew many ladies of rank, he had "nowhere met with an humour, a wit, or conversation so agreeable, a better portion of good sense, or a truer judgment of men or things." He envied Tisdall his prudence and temper, and love of peace and settlement, "the reverse of which has been the great uneasiness of my life, and is likely to continue so."

This letter has been quoted at some length because of its great importance. It is obviously capable of various interpretations, and some, like Dr. Johnson, have concluded that Swift was resolved to keep Stella in his power, and therefore prevented an advantageous match by making unreasonable demands. I cannot see any ground for this interpretation, though it is probable that Tisdall's appearance as a suitor was sufficiently annoying. There is no evidence that Stella viewed Tisdall's proposal with any favour, unless it can be held to be furnished by Swift's belief that the town thought—rightly or wrongly—that there was an engagement. In any case, there could be no mistake in future with regard to Swift's attitude towards Stella. She was dearer to him than anyone else, and his feeling for her would not change, but for marriage he had neither fortune nor humour. Tisdall consoled himself by marrying another lady two years afterwards; and though for a long time Swift entertained for him feelings of dislike, in later life their relations improved, and Tisdall was one of the witnesses to Swift's will.

The *Tale of a Tub* was published in 1704, and Swift was soon in constant intercourse with Addison and the other wits. While he was in England in 1705, Stella and Mrs. Dingley made a short visit to London. This and a similar visit in 1708 are the only occasions on which Stella is known to have left Ireland after taking up her residence in that country. Swift's influence over women was always very striking. Most of the toasts of the day were his friends, and he insisted that any lady of wit and quality who desired his acquaintance should make the first advances. This, he says—writing in 1730—had been an established rule for over twenty years. In 1708 a dispute on this question with one toast, Mrs. Long, was referred for settlement to Ginckel Vanhomrigh, the son of the house where it was proposed that the meeting should take place; and by the decision—which was in Swift's favour—"Mrs. Vanhomrigh and her fair daughter Hessy" were forbidden to aid Mrs. Long in her disobedience for the future. This is the first that we hear of Hester or

Esther Vanhomrigh, who was afterwards to play so marked a part in the story of Swift's life. Born on February 14, 1690, she was now eighteen. Her father, Bartholomew Vanhomrigh, a Dublin merchant of Dutch origin, had died in 1703, leaving his wife a fortune of some sixteen thousand pounds. On the income from this money Mrs. Vanhomrigh, with her two daughters, Hester and Mary, were able to mix in fashionable society in London. Swift was introduced to them by Sir Andrew Fountaine early in 1708, but evidently Stella did not make their acquaintance, nor indeed hear much, if anything, of them until the time of the *Journal*.

Swift's visit to London in 1707–9 had for its object the obtaining for the Irish Church of the surrender by the Crown of the First-Fruits and Twentieths, which brought in about £2500 a year. Nothing came of Swift's interviews with the Whig statesmen, and after many disappointments he returned to Laracor (June 1709), and conversed with none but Stella and her card-playing friends, and Addison, now secretary to Lord Wharton. Next year came the fall of the Whigs, and a request to Swift from the Irish bishops that he would renew the application for the First-Fruits, in the hope that there would be greater success with the Tories. Swift reached London in September 1710, and began the series of letters, giving details of the events of each day, which now form the *Journal to Stella*. "I will write something every day to MD," he says, "and make it a sort of journal; and when it is full I will send it, whether MD writes or no; and so that will be pretty; and I shall always be in conversation with MD, and MD with Presto." It is interesting to note that by way of caution these letters were usually addressed to Mrs. Dingley, and not to Stella.

The story of Swift's growing intimacy with the Tory leaders, of the success of his mission, of the increasing coolness towards older acquaintances, and of his services to the Government, can best be read in the *Journal* itself. In the meantime the intimacy with the Vanhomrighs grew rapidly. They were near neighbours of Swift's, and in a few weeks after his arrival in town we find frequent allusions to the dinners at their house (where he kept his best gown and periwig), sometimes with the explanation that he went there "out of mere listlessness," or because it was wet, or because another engagement had broken down. Only thrice does he mention the "eldest daughter": once on her birthday; once on the occasion of a trick played him, when he received a message that she was suddenly very ill ("I rattled off the daughter"); and once to state that she was come of age, and was going to Ireland to look after her fortune. There is evidence that "Miss Essy," or Vanessa, to give her the name by which she will always be known, was in correspondence with Swift in July 1710—while he was still in Ireland—and in the spring of 1711; and early in 1711 Stella seems to have expressed surprise at Swift's intimacy with the family, for in February he replied, "You say they are of no consequence; why, they keep as good female company as I do male; I see all the drabs of quality at this end of the town with them." In the autumn Swift seems to have thought that Vanessa was keeping company with a certain Hatton, but Mrs. Long—possibly meaning to give him a warning hint—remarked that if this were so "she is not the girl I took her for; but to me she seems melancholy."

In 1712 occasional letters took the place of the daily journal to "MD," but there is no change in the affectionate style in which Swift wrote. In the spring he had a long illness, which affected him, indeed, throughout the year. Other reasons which he gives for the falling off in his correspondence are his numerous business engagements, and the hope of being able to send some good news of an appointment for himself. There is only one letter to Stella between July 19 and September 15, and Dr. Birkbeck Hill argues that the poem "Cadenus and Vanessa" was composed at that time. If this be so, it must have been altered next year, because it was not until 1713 that Swift was made a Dean. Writing on April 19, 1726, Swift said that the poem "was written at Windsor near fourteen years ago, and dated: it was a task performed on a frolic among some ladies, and she it was addressed to died some time ago in Dublin, and on her death the copy shewn by her executor." Several copies were in circulation, and he was indifferent what was done with it; it was "only a cavalier business," and if those who would not give allowances were malicious, it was only what he had long expected.

From this letter it would appear that this remarkable poem was written in the summer of 1712; whereas the title-page of the pamphlet says it was "written at Windsor, 1713." Swift visited Windsor in both years, but he had more leisure in 1712, and we know that Vanessa was also at Windsor in that year. In that year, too, he was forty-four, the age mentioned in the poem. Neither Swift nor Vanessa forgot this intercourse: years afterwards Swift wrote to her, "Go over the scenes of Windsor. . . Cad thinks often of these"; and again, "Remember the indisposition at Windsor." We know that this poem was revised in 1719, when in all probability Swift added the lines to which most exception can be taken. Cadenus was to be Vanessa's instructor:—

> *"His conduct might have made him styled*
> *A father, and the nymph his child."*

He had "grown old in politics and wit," and "in every scene had kept his heart," so that he now "understood not what was love." But he had written much, and Vanessa admired his wit. Cadenus found that her thoughts wandered—

> *"Though she seemed to listen more*
> *To all he spoke than e'er before."*

When she confessed her love, he was filled with "shame, disappointment, guilt, surprise." He had aimed only at cultivating the mind, and had hardly known whether she was young or old. But he was flattered, and though he could not give her love, he offered her friendship, "with gratitude, respect, esteem." Vanessa took him at his word, and said she would now be tutor, though he was not apt to learn:—

> *"But what success Vanessa met*
> *Is to the world a secret yet.*
> *Whether the nymph to please her swain*
> *Talks in a high romantic strain;*
> *Or whether he at last descends*
> *To act with less seraphic ends;*
> *Or, to compound the business, whether*
> *They temper love and books together,*
> *Must never to mankind be told,*
> *Nor shall the conscious Muse unfold."*

Such is the poem as we now have it, written, it must be remembered, for Vanessa's private perusal. It is to be regretted, for her own sake, that she did not destroy it.

Swift received the reward of his services to the Government—the Deanery of St. Patrick's, Dublin—in April 1713. Disappointed at what he regarded as exile, he left London in June. Vanessa immediately began to send him letters which brought home to him the extent of her passion; and she hinted at jealousy in the words, "If you are very happy, it is ill-natured of you not to tell me so, except 'tis what is inconsistent with my own." In his reply Swift dwelt upon the dreariness of his surroundings at Laracor, and reminded her that he had said he would endeavour to forget everything in England, and would write as seldom as he could.

Swift was back again in the political strife in London in September, taking Oxford's part in the quarrel between that statesman and Bolingbroke. On the fall of the Tories at the death of Queen Anne, he saw that all was over, and retired to Ireland, not to return again for twelve years. In the meantime the intimacy with Vanessa had been renewed. Her mother had died, leaving debts, and she pressed Swift for advice in the management of her affairs. When she suggested coming to Ireland, where she had property, he told her that if she took this step he would "see her very seldom." However, she took up her abode at Celbridge, only a few miles from Dublin. Swift gave her many cautions, out of "the perfect esteem and friendship" he felt for her, but he often visited her. She was dissatisfied, however, begging him to speak kindly, and at least to counterfeit his former indulgent friendship. "What can be wrong," she wrote, "in seeing and advising an unhappy young woman? You cannot but know that your frowns make my life unsupportable." Sometimes he treated the matter lightly; sometimes he showed annoyance; sometimes he assured her of his esteem and love, but urged her not to make herself or him "unhappy by imaginations." He was uniformly unsuccessful in stopping Vanessa's importunity. He endeavoured, she said, by severities to force her from him; she knew she was the cause of uneasy reflections to him; but nothing would lessen her "inexpressible passion."

Unfortunately he failed—partly no doubt from mistaken considerations of kindness, partly because he shrank from losing her affection—to take effective steps to put an end to Vanessa's hopes. It would have been better if he had unhesitatingly made it clear to her that he could not return her passion, and that if she could not be satisfied with friendship the intimacy must cease. To quote Sir Henry Craik, "The friendship had begun in literary guidance: it was strengthened by flattery: it lived on a cold and almost stern repression, fed by confidences as to literary schemes, and by occasional literary compliments: but it never came to have a real hold over Swift's heart."

With 1716 we come to the alleged marriage with Stella. In 1752, seven years after Swift's death, Lord Orrery, in his *Remarks* on Swift, said that Stella was "the concealed, but undoubted, wife of Dr. Swift. . . If my informations are right, she was married to Dr. Swift in the year 1716, by Dr. Ashe, then Bishop of Clogher." Ten years earlier, in 1742, in a letter to Deane Swift which I have not seen quoted before, Orrery spoke of the advantage of a wife to a man in his declining years; "nor had the Dean felt a blow, or wanted a companion, had he been married, or, in other words, had Stella lived." What this means is not at all clear. In 1754, Dr. Delany, an old friend of Swift's, wrote, in comment upon Orrery's *Remarks*, "Your account of his marriage is, I am satisfied, true." In 1789, George Monck Berkeley, in his *Literary Relics*, said that Swift and Stella were married by Dr. Ashe, "who himself related the circumstances to Bishop Berkeley, by whose relict the story was communicated to me." Dr. Ashe cannot have told Bishop Berkeley by word of mouth, because Ashe died in 1717, the year after the supposed marriage, and Berkeley was then still abroad. But Berkeley was at the time tutor to Ashe's son, and may therefore have been informed by letter, though it is difficult to believe that Ashe would write about such a secret so soon after the event. Thomas Sheridan, on information received from his father, Dr. Sheridan, Swift's friend, accepted the story of the marriage in his book (1784), adding particulars which are of very doubtful authenticity; and Johnson, in his *Lives of the Poets*, says that Dr. Madden told him that Stella had related her "melancholy story" to Dr. Sheridan before her death. On the other hand, Dr. Lyon, Swift's attendant in his later years, disbelieved the story of the marriage, which was, he said, "founded only on hearsay"; and Mrs. Dingley "laughed at it as an idle tale," founded on suspicion.

Sir Henry Craik is satisfied with the evidence for the marriage. Mr. Leslie Stephen is of opinion that it is inconclusive, and Forster could find no evidence that is at all reasonably sufficient; while Mr. Stanley Lane-Poole, Mr. Churton Collins, and others are strongly of opinion that no such marriage ever took place. A full discussion of the evidence would involve the consideration of the reliability of the witnesses, and the probability of their having authentic information, and would be out of place here. My own opinion is that the evidence for the marriage is very far from convincing, and this view seems to be confirmed by all that we know from his own letters of Swift's relations with Stella. It has been suggested that she was pained by reports of

Swift's intercourse with Vanessa, and felt that his feelings towards herself were growing colder; but this is surmise, and no satisfactory explanation has been given to account for a form of marriage being gone through after so many years of the closest friendship. There is no reason to suppose that there was at the time any gossip in circulation about Stella, and if her reputation was in question, a marriage of which the secret was carefully kept would obviously be of no benefit to her. Moreover, we are told that there was no change in their mode of life; if they were married, what reason could there be for keeping it a secret, or for denying themselves the closer relationship of marriage? The only possible benefit to Stella was that Swift would be prevented marrying anyone else. It is impossible, of course, to disprove a marriage which we are told was secretly performed, without banns or licence or witnesses; but we may reasonably require strong evidence for so startling a step. If we reject the tale, the story of Swift's connection with Stella is at least intelligible; while the acceptance of this marriage introduces many puzzling circumstances, and makes it necessary to believe that during the remainder of Stella's life Swift repeatedly spoke of his wife as a friend, and of himself as one who had never married. What right have we to put aside Swift's plain and repeated statements? Moreover, his attitude towards Vanessa for the remaining years of her life becomes much more culpable if we are to believe that he had given Stella the claim of a wife upon him.

From 1719 onwards we have a series of poems to Stella, written chiefly in celebration of her birthday. She was now thirty-eight (Swift says, "Thirty-four—we shan't dispute a year or more"), and the verses abound in laughing allusions to her advancing years and wasting form. Hers was "an angel's face a little cracked," but all men would crowd to her door when she was fourscore. His verses to her had always been

> "Without one word of Cupid's darts,
> Of killing eyes, or bleeding hearts;
> With friendship and esteem possessed,
> I ne'er admitted Love a guest."

Her only fault was that she could not bear the lightest touch of blame. Her wit and sense, her loving care in illness—to which he owed that fact that he was alive to say it—made her the "best pattern of true friends." She replied, in lines written on Swift's birthday in 1721, that she was his pupil and humble friend. He had trained her judgment and refined her fancy and taste:—

> *"You taught how I might youth prolong*
> *By knowing what was right and wrong;*
> *How from my heart to bring supplies*
> *Of lustre to my fading eyes;*
> *How soon a beauteous mind repairs*
> *The loss of changed or falling hairs;*
> *How wit and virtue from within*
> *Send out a smoothness o'er the skin*
> *Your lectures could my fancy fix,*
> *And I can please at thirty-six."*

In 1723 Vanessa is said to have written to Stella or to Swift—there are discrepancies in the versions given by Sheridan and Lord Orrery, both of whom are unreliable—asking whether the report that they were married was true. Swift, we are told, rode to Celbridge, threw down Vanessa's letter in a great rage, and left without speaking a word. Vanessa, whose health had been failing for some time, died shortly afterwards, having cancelled a will in Swift's favour. She left "Cadenus and Vanessa" for publication, and when someone said that she must have been a remarkable woman to inspire such a poem, Stella replied that it was well known that the Dean could write finely upon a broomstick.

Soon after this tragedy Swift became engrossed in the Irish agitation which led to the publication of the *Drapier's Letters*, and in 1726 he paid a long-deferred visit to London, taking with him the manuscript of *Gulliver's Travels*. While in England he was harassed by bad news of Stella, who had been in continued ill-health for some years. His letters to friends in Dublin show how greatly he suffered. To the Rev. John Worrall he wrote, in a letter which he begged him to burn, "What you tell me of Mrs. Johnson I have long expected with great oppression and heaviness of heart. We have been perfect friends these thirty-five years. Upon my advice they both came to Ireland, and have been ever since my constant companions; and the remainder of my life will be a very melancholy scene, when one of them is gone, whom I most esteemed, upon the score of every good quality that can possibly recommend a human creature." He would not for the world be present at her death: "I should be a trouble to her, and a torment to myself." If Stella came to

Dublin, he begged that she might be lodged in some airy, healthy part, and not in the Deanery, where too it would be improper for her to die. "There is not a greater folly," he thinks, "than to contract too great and intimate a friendship, which must always leave the survivor miserable." To Dr. Stopford he wrote in similar terms of the "younger of the two" "oldest and dearest friends I have in the world." "This was a person of my own rearing and instructing from childhood, who excelled in every good quality that can possibly accomplish a human creature. . . I know not what I am saying; but believe me that violent friendship is much more lasting and as much engaging as violent love." To Dr. Sheridan he said, "I look upon this to be the greatest event that can ever happen to me; but all my preparation will not suffice to make me bear it like a philosopher nor altogether like a Christian. There hath been the most intimate friendship between us from our childhood, and the greatest merit on her side that ever was in one human creature towards another." Pope alludes in a letter to Sheridan to the illness of Swift's "particular friend," but with the exception of another reference by Pope, and of a curiously flippant remark by Bolingbroke, the subject is nowhere mentioned in Swift's correspondence with his literary and fashionable friends in London.

Swift crossed to Ireland in August, fearing the worst; but Stella rallied, and in the spring of 1727 he returned to London. In August, however, there came alarming news, when Swift was himself suffering from giddiness and deafness. To Dr. Sheridan he wrote that the last act of life was always a tragedy at best: "it is a bitter aggravation to have one's best friend go before one." Life was indifferent to him; if he recovered from his disorder it would only be to feel the loss of "that person for whose sake only life was worth preserving. I brought both those friends over that we might be happy together as long as God should please; the knot is broken, and the remaining person you know has ill answered the end; and the other, who is now to be lost, is all that was valuable." To Worrall he again wrote (in Latin) that Stella ought not to be lodged at the Deanery; he had enemies who would place a bad interpretation upon it if she died there.

Swift left London for Dublin in September; he was detained some days at Holyhead by stress of weather, and in the private journal which he kept during that time he speaks of the suspense he was in about his "dearest friend." In December Stella made a will—signed "Esther Johnson, spinster"—disposing of her property in the manner Swift had suggested. Her allusions to Swift are incompatible with any such feeling of resentment as is suggested by Sheridan. She died on January 28, 1728. Swift could not bear to be present, but on the night of her death he began to write his very interesting *Character of Mrs. Johnson*, from which passages have already been quoted. He there calls her "the truest, most virtuous and valuable friend that I, or perhaps any other person, was ever blessed with." Combined with excellent gifts of the mind, "she had a gracefulness, somewhat more than human, in every motion, word, and action. Never was so happy a conjunction of civility, freedom, easiness, and sincerity." Everyone treated her with marked respect, yet everyone was at ease in her society. She preserved her wit, judgment, and vivacity to the last, but often complained of her memory. She chose men rather than women for her companions, "the usual topic of ladies' discourse being such as she had little knowledge of and less relish." "Honour, truth, liberality, good nature, and modesty were the virtues she chiefly possessed, and most valued in her acquaintance." In some Prayers used by Swift during her last sickness, he begged for pity for "the mournful friends of Thy distressed servant, who sink under the weight of her present condition, and the fear of losing the most valuable of our friends." He was too ill to be present at the funeral at St. Patrick's. Afterwards, we are told, a lock of her hair was found in his desk, wrapped in a paper bearing the words, "Only a woman's hair."

Swift continued to produce pamphlets manifesting growing misanthropy, though he showed many kindnesses to people who stood in need of help. He seems to have given Mrs. Dingley fifty guineas a year, pretending that it came from a fund for which he was trustee. The mental decay which he had always feared—"I shall be like that tree," he once said, "I shall die at the top"—became marked about 1738. Paralysis was followed by aphasia, and after acute pain, followed by a long period of apathy, death relieved him in October 1745. He was buried by Stella's side, in accordance with his wishes. The bulk of his fortune was left to found a hospital for idiots and lunatics.

There has been much rather fruitless discussion respecting the reason or reasons why Swift did not marry Stella; for if there was any marriage, it was nothing more than a form. Some have supposed that Swift resolved to remain unmarried because the insanity of an uncle and the fits and giddiness to which he was always subject led him to fear insanity in his own case. Others, looking rather to physical causes, have dwelt upon his coldness of temperament and indisposition to love;

upon the repugnance he often showed towards marriage, and the tone of some of the verses on the subject written in his later years. Others, again, have found a cause in his parsimonious habits, in his dread of poverty, the effects of which he had himself felt, and in the smallness of his income, at least until he was middle-aged. It may well be that one or all of these things influenced Swift's action. We cannot say more. He himself, as we have seen, said, as early as 1704, that if his humour and means had permitted him to think of marriage, his choice would have been Stella. Perhaps, however, there is not much mystery in the matter. Swift seems to have been wanting in passion; probably he was satisfied with the affection which Stella gave him, and did not wish for more. Such an attachment as his usually results in marriage, but not necessarily. It is not sufficiently remembered that the affection began in Stella's childhood. They were "perfect friends" for nearly forty years, and her advancing years in no way lessened his love, which was independent of beauty. Whether Stella was satisfied, who shall say? Mrs. Oliphant thought that few women would be disposed to pity Stella, or think her life one of blight or injury. Mr. Leslie Stephen says, "She might and probably did regard his friendship as a full equivalent for the sacrifice. . . Is it better to be the most intimate friend of a man of genius or the wife of a commonplace Tisdall?" Whatever we may surmise, there is nothing to prove that she was disappointed. She was the one star which brightened Swift's storm-tossed course; it is well that she was spared seeing the wreck at the end.

THE *JOURNAL TO STELLA* is interesting from many points of view: for its bearing upon Swift's relations with Stella and upon his own character; for the light which it throws upon the history of the time and upon prominent men of the day; and for the illustrations it contains of the social life of people of various classes in London and elsewhere. The fact that it was written without any thought of publication is one of its greatest attractions. Swift jotted down his opinions, his hopes, his disappointments, without thought of their being seen by anybody but his correspondents. The letters are transparently natural. It has been said more than once that the *Journal*, by the nature of the case, contains no full-length portraits, and hardly any sketches. Swift mentions the people he met, but rarely stops to draw a picture of them. But though this is true, the casual remarks which he makes often give a vivid impression of what he thought of the person of whom he is speaking, and in many cases those few words form a chief part of our general estimate of the man. There are but few people of note at the time who are not mentioned in these pages. We see Queen Anne holding a Drawing-room in her bedroom: "she looked at us round with her fan in her mouth, and once a minute said about three words to some that were nearest her." We see Harley, afterwards the Earl of Oxford, "a pure trifler," who was always putting off important business; Bolingbroke, "a thorough rake"; the prudent Lord Dartmouth, the other Secretary of State, from whom Swift could never "work out a dinner." There is Marlborough, "covetous as Hell, and ambitious as the prince of it," yet a great general and unduly pressed by the Tories; and the volatile Earl of Peterborough, "above fifty, and as active as one of five-and-twenty"— "the ramblingest lying rogue on earth." We meet poor Congreve, nearly blind, and in fear of losing his commissionership; the kindly Arbuthnot, the Queen's physician; Addison, whom Swift met more and more rarely, busy with the preparation and production of *Cato*; Steele, careless as ever, neglecting important appointments, and "governed by his wife most abominably"; Prior, poet and diplomatist, with a "lean carcass"; and young Berkeley of Trinity College, Dublin, "a very ingenious man and great philosopher," whom Swift determined to favour as much as he could. Mrs. Masham, the Duchess of Somerset, the Duchess of Shrewsbury, the Duchess of Hamilton, Lady Betty Germaine, and many other ladies appear with more or less distinctness; besides a host of people of less note, of whom we often know little but what Swift tells us.

Swift throws much light, too, on the daily life of his time. The bellman on his nightly rounds, calling "Paaast twelvvve o'clock"; the dinner at three, or at the latest, four; the meetings at coffee-houses; the book-sales; the visit to the London sights—the lions at the Tower, Bedlam, the tombs in Westminster Abbey, and the puppet-show; the terrible Mohocks, of whom Swift stood in so much fear; the polite "howdees" sent to friends by footmen; these and more are all described in the *Journal*. We read of curious habits and practices of fashionable ladies; of the snuff used by Mrs. Dingley and others; of the jokes— "bites," puns, and the like—indulged in by polite persons. When Swift lodged at Chelsea, he reached London either by boat, or by coach,— which was sometimes full when he wanted it,—or by walking across the "Five Fields," not without fear of robbers at night. The going to or from Ireland was a serious matter; after the long journey by road came the voyage (weather permitting) of some fifteen hours, with the risk of being seized or pursued by French privateers; and when Ireland was reached the roads were of the worst. We have glimpses of fashionable society in Dublin, of the quiet life at Laracor and Trim, and of the drinking of the waters at Wexford, where visitors had to put up with primitive arrangements: "Mrs. Dingley never saw such a place in her life."

Swift's own characteristics come out in the clearest manner in the *Journal*, which gives all his hopes and fears during three busy years. He was pleased to find on his arrival in London how great a value was set on his friendship by both political parties: "The Whigs were ravished to see me, and would lay hold on me as a twig while they are drowning;" but Godolphin's coldness enraged him, so that he was "almost vowing vengeance." Next day he talked treason heartily against the Whigs, their baseness and ingratitude, and went home full of schemes of revenge. "The Tories drily tell me I may make my fortune, if I please; but I do not understand them, or rather, I *do* understand them." He realised that the Tories might not be more grateful than others, but he thought they were pursuing the true interests of the public, and was glad to contribute what was in his power. His vanity was gratified by Harley inviting him to the private dinners with St. John and Harcourt which were given on Saturdays, and by their calling him Jonathan; but he did not hope too much from their friendship: "I said I believed they would leave me Jonathan, as they found me. . . but I care not."

Of Swift's frugal habits there is abundant evidence in the *Journal*. When he came to town he took rooms on a first floor, "a dining-room and bed-chamber, at eight shillings a week; plaguy dear, but I spend nothing for eating, never go to a tavern, and very seldom in a coach; yet after all it will be expensive." In November he mentions that he had a fire: "I am spending my second half-bushel of coals." In another place he says, "People have so left the town, that I am at a loss for a dinner. . . It cost me eighteenpence in coach-hire before I could find a place to dine in." Elsewhere we find: "This paper does not cost me a farthing: I have it from the Secretary's office." He often complains of having to take a coach owing to the dirty condition of the streets: "This rain ruins me in coach-hire; I walked away sixpennyworth, and came within a shilling length, and then took a coach, and got a lift back for nothing."

Swift's arrogance—the arrogance, sometimes, of a man who is morbidly suspicious that he may be patronised—is shown in the manner in which he speaks of the grand ladies with whom he came in contact.

He calls the Duke of Ormond's daughters "insolent drabs," and talks of his "mistress, Ophy Butler's wife, who is grown a little charmless." When the Duchess of Shrewsbury reproached him for not dining with her, Swift said that was not so soon done; he expected more advances from ladies, especially duchesses. On another occasion he was to have supped at Lady Ashburnham's, "but the drab did not call for us in her coach, as she promised, but sent for us, and so I sent my excuses." The arrogance was, however, often only on the surface. It is evident that Swift was very kind in many cases. He felt deeply for Mrs. Long in her misfortunes, living and dying in an obscure country town. On the last illness of the poet Harrison he says, "I am very much afflicted for him, as he is my own creature. . . I was afraid to knock at the door; my mind misgave me." He was "heartily sorry for poor Mrs. Parnell's death; she seemed to be an excellent good-natured young woman, and I believe the poor lad is much afflicted; they appeared to live perfectly well together." Afterwards he helped Parnell by introducing him to Bolingbroke and Oxford. He found kind words for Mrs. Manley in her illness, and Lady Ashburnham's death was "extremely moving. . . She was my greatest favourite, and I am in excessive concern for her loss." Lastly, he was extraordinarily patient towards his servant Patrick, who drank, stopped out at night, and in many ways tried Swift's temper. There were good points about Patrick, but no doubt the great consideration which Swift showed him was due in part to the fact that he was a favourite of the ladies in Dublin, and had Mrs. Vanhomrigh to intercede for him.

But for the best example of the kindly side of Swift's nature, we must turn to what he tells us in the *Journal* about Stella herself. The "little language" which Swift used when writing to her was the language he employed when playing with Stella as a little child at Moor Park. Thackeray, who was not much in sympathy with Swift, said that he knew of "nothing more manly, more tender, more exquisitely touching, than some of these notes." Swift says that when he wrote plainly, he felt as if they were no longer alone, but "a bad scrawl is so snug it looks like a PMD." In writing his fond and playful prattle, he made up his mouth "just as if he were speaking it."

Though Mrs. Dingley is constantly associated with Stella in the affectionate greetings in the *Journal*, she seems to have been included merely as a cloak to enable him to express the more freely his affection for her companion. Such phrases as "saucy girls," "sirrahs," "sauceboxes," and the like, are often applied to both; and sometimes Swift certainly writes as if the one were as dear to him as the other; thus we find, "Farewell, my dearest lives and delights, I love you better than ever, if possible, as hope saved, I do, and ever will. . . I can count upon nothing, nor will, but upon MD's love and kindness. . . And so farewell, dearest MD, Stella, Dingley, Presto, all together, now and for ever, all together." But as a rule, notwithstanding Swift's caution, the greetings intended for Stella alone are easily distinguishable in tone. He often refers to her weak eyes and delicate health. Thus he writes, "The chocolate is a present, madam, for Stella. Don't read this, you little rogue, with your little eyes; but give it to Dingley, pray now; and I will write as plain as the skies." And again, "God Almighty bless poor Stella, and her eyes and head: what shall we do to cure them, poor dear life?" Or, "Now to Stella's little postscript; and I am almost crazed that you vex yourself for not writing. Can't you dictate to Dingley, and not strain your dear little eyes? I am sure 'tis the grief of my soul to think you are out of order." They had been keeping his birthday; Swift wished he had been with them, rather than in London, where he had no manner of pleasure: "I say Amen with all my heart and vitals, that we may never be asunder again ten days together while poor Presto lives." A few days later he says, "I wish I were at Laracor, with dear charming MD," and again, "Farewell, dearest beloved MD, and love poor poor Presto, who has not had one happy day since he left you." "I will say no more, but beg you to be easy till Fortune takes his course, and to believe MD's felicity is the great goal I aim at in all my pursuits." "How does Stella look, Madam Dingley?" he asks; "pretty well, a handsome young woman still? Will she pass in a crowd? Will she make a figure in a country church?" Elsewhere he writes, on receipt of a letter, "God Almighty bless poor dear Stella, and send her a great many birthdays, all happy and healthy and wealthy, and with me ever together, and never asunder again, unless by chance. . . I can hardly imagine you absent when I am reading your letter or writing to you. No, faith, you are just here upon this little paper, and therefore I see and talk with you every evening constantly, and sometimes in the morning." The letters lay under Swift's pillow, and he fondled them as if he were caressing Stella's hand.

Of Stella herself we naturally have no direct account in the *Journal*, but we hear a good deal of her life in Ireland, and can picture what she was. Among her friends in and about Trim and Laracor were Dr. Raymond, the vicar of Trim, and his wife, the Garret Wesleys, the Percevals, and Mr. Warburton, Swift's curate. At Dublin there were

Archdeacon Walls and his family; Alderman Stoyte, his wife and sister-in-law; Dean Sterne and the Irish Postmaster-General, Isaac Manley. For years these friends formed a club which met in Dublin at each other's houses, to sup and play cards ("ombre and claret, and toasted oranges"), and we have frequent allusions to Stella's indifferent play, and the money which she lost, much to Mrs. Dingley's chagrin: "Poor Dingley fretted to see Stella lose that four and elevenpence t'other night." Mrs. Dingley herself could hardly play well enough to hold the cards while Stella went into the next room. If at dinner the mutton was underdone, and "poor Stella cannot eat, poor dear rogue," then "Dingley is so vexed." Swift was for ever urging Stella to walk and ride; she was "naturally a stout walker," and "Dingley would do well enough if her petticoats were pinned up." And we see Stella setting out on and returning from her ride, with her riband and mask: "Ah, that riding to Laracor gives me short sighs as well as you," he says; "all the days I have passed here have been dirt to those."

If the *Journal* shows us some of Swift's less attractive qualities, it shows still more how great a store of humour, tenderness, and affection there was in him. In these letters we see his very soul; in his literary work we are seldom moved to anything but admiration of his wit and genius. Such daily outpourings could never have been written for publication, they were meant only for one who understood him perfectly; and everything that we know of Stella—her kindliness, her wit, her vivacity, her loyalty—shows that she was worthy of the confidence.

LETTER I

Joe will give you an account of me till I got into the boat; after which the rogues made a new bargain, and forced me to give them two crowns, and talked as if we should not be able to overtake any ship: but in half an hour we got to the yacht; for the ships lay by (to) wait for my Lord Lieutenant's steward. We made our voyage in fifteen hours just. Last night I came to this town, and shall leave it, I believe, on Monday. The first man I met in Chester was Dr. Raymond. He and Mrs. Raymond were here about levying a fine, in order to have power to sell their estate. They have found everything answer very well. They both desire to present their humble services to you: they do not think of Ireland till next year. I got a fall off my horse, riding here from Parkgate, but no hurt; the horse understanding falls very well, and lying quietly till I get up. My duty to the Bishop of Clogher. I saw him returning from Dunleary; but he saw not me. I take it ill he was not at Convocation, and that I have not his name to my powers. I beg you will hold your resolution of going to Trim, and riding there as much as you can. Let the Bishop of Clogher remind the Bishop of Killala to send me a letter, with one enclosed to the Bishop of Lichfield. Let all who write to me, enclose to Richard Steele, Esq., at his office at the Cockpit, near Whitehall. But not MD; I will pay for their letters at St. James's Coffee-house, that I may have them the sooner. My Lord Mountjoy is now in the humour that we should begin our journey this afternoon; so that I have stole here again to finish this letter, which must be short or long accordingly. I write this post to Mrs. Wesley, and will tell her, that I have taken care she may have her bill of one hundred and fifteen pounds whenever she pleases to send for it; and in that case I desire you will send it her enclosed and sealed, and have it ready so, in case she should send for it: otherwise keep it. I will say no more till I hear whether I go to-day or no: if I do, the letter is almost at an end. My cozen Abigail is grown prodigiously old. God Almighty bless poo dee richar MD; and, for God's sake, be merry, and get oo health. I am perfectly resolved to return as soon as I have done my commission, whether it succeeds or no. I never went to England with so little desire in my life. If Mrs. Curry makes any difficulty about the lodgings, I will quit them and pay her from July 9 last, and Mrs. Brent must write to Parvisol with orders accordingly. The post is come from London, and just going out; so I have only time to pray God to bless poor richr MD FW FW MD MD ME ME ME.

Letter II

I got here last Thursday, after five days' travelling, weary the first, almost dead the second, tolerable the third, and well enough the rest; and am now glad of the fatigue, which has served for exercise; and I am at present well enough. The Whigs were ravished to see me, and would lay hold on me as a twig while they are drowning, and the great men making me their clumsy apologies, etc. But my Lord Treasurer received me with a great deal of coldness, which has enraged me so, I am almost vowing revenge. I have not yet gone half my circle; but I find all my acquaintance just as I left them. I hear my Lady Giffard is much at Court, and Lady Wharton was ridiculing it t'other day; so I have lost a friend there. I have not yet seen her, nor intend it; but I will contrive to see Stella's mother some other way. I writ to the Bishop of Clogher from Chester; and I now write to the Archbishop of Dublin. Everything is turning upside down; every Whig in great office will, to a man, be infallibly put out; and we shall have such a winter as hath not been seen in England. Everybody asks me, how I came to be so long in Ireland, as naturally as if here were my being; but no soul offers to make it so: and I protest I shall return to Dublin, and the Canal at Laracor, with more satisfaction than ever I did in my life. The Tatler expects every day to be turned out of his employment; and the Duke of Ormond, they say, will be Lieutenant of Ireland. I hope you are now peaceably in Presto's lodgings; but I resolve to turn you out by Christmas; in which time I shall either do my business, or find it not to be done. Pray be at Trim by the time this letter comes to you; and ride little Johnson, who must needs be now in good case. I have begun this letter unusually, on the post-night, and have already written to the Archbishop; and cannot lengthen this. Henceforth I will write something every day to MD, and make it a sort of journal; and when it is full, I will send it, whether MD writes or no; and so that will be pretty: and I shall always be in conversation with MD, and MD with Presto. Pray make Parvisol pay you the ten pounds immediately; so I ordered him. They tell me I am grown fatter, and look better; and, on Monday, Jervas is to retouch my picture. I thought I saw Jack Temple and his wife pass by me to-day in their coach; but I took no notice of them. I am glad I have wholly shaken off that family. Tell the Provost, I have obeyed his commands to the Duke of Ormond; or let it alone, if you please. I saw Jemmy Leigh just now at the Coffee-house, who asked after you with great kindness: he talks of going in a fortnight to Ireland. My service to the Dean, and Mrs. Walls, and her Archdeacon. Will Frankland's wife is near bringing to-bed, and I have promised to christen the child. I fancy you had my Chester letter the Tuesday after I writ. I presented Dr. Raymond to Lord Wharton at Chester. Pray let me know when Joe gets his money. It is near ten, and I hate to send by the bellman. MD shall have a longer letter in a week, but I send this only to tell I am safe in London; and so farewell, etc.

Letter III

London, *Sept.* 9, 1710

After seeing the Duke of Ormond, dining with Dr. Cockburn, passing some part of the afternoon with Sir Matthew Dudley and Will Frankland, the rest at St. James's Coffee-house, I came home, and writ to the Archbishop of Dublin and MD, and am going to bed. I forgot to tell you, that I begged Will Frankland to stand Manley's friend with his father in this shaking season for places. He told me, his father was in danger to be out; that several were now soliciting for Manley's place; that he was accused of opening letters; that Sir Thomas Frankland would sacrifice everything to save himself; and in that, I fear, Manley is undone, etc.

10. To-day I dined with Lord Mountjoy at Kensington; saw my mistress, Ophy Butler's wife, who is grown a little charmless. I sat till ten in the evening with Addison and Steele: Steele will certainly lose his Gazetteer's place, all the world detesting his engaging in parties. At ten I went to the Coffee-house, hoping to find Lord Radnor, whom I had not seen. He was there; and for an hour and a half we talked treason heartily against the Whigs, their baseness and ingratitude. And I am come home, rolling resentments in my mind, and framing schemes of revenge: full of which (having written down some hints) I go to bed. I am afraid MD dined at home, because it is Sunday; and there was the little half-pint of wine: for God's sake, be good girls, and all will be well. Ben Tooke was with me this morning.

11. Seven, morning. I am rising to go to Jervas to finish my picture, and 'tis shaving-day, so good-morrow MD; but don't keep me now, for I can't stay; and pray dine with the Dean, but don't lose your money. I long to hear from you, etc.—Ten at night. I sat four hours this morning to Jervas, who has given my picture quite another turn, and now approves it entirely; but we must have the approbation of the town. If I were rich enough, I would get a copy of it, and bring it over. Mr. Addison and I dined together at his lodgings, and I sat with him part of this evening; and I am now come home to write an hour. Patrick observes, that the rabble here are much more inquisitive in politics than in Ireland. Every day we expect changes, and the Parliament to be dissolved. Lord

Wharton expects every day to be out: he is working like a horse for elections; and, in short, I never saw so great a ferment among all sorts of people. I had a miserable letter from Joe last Saturday, telling me Mr. Pratt refuses payment of his money. I have told it Mr. Addison, and will to Lord Wharton; but I fear with no success. However, I will do all I can.

12. To-day I presented Mr. Ford to the Duke of Ormond; and paid my first visit to Lord President, with whom I had much discourse; but put him always off when he began to talk of Lord Wharton in relation to me, till he urged it: then I said, he knew I never expected anything from Lord Wharton, and that Lord Wharton knew that I understood it so. He said that he had written twice to Lord Wharton about me, who both times said nothing at all to that part of his letter. I am advised not to meddle in the affair of the First-Fruits, till this hurry is a little over, which still depends, and we are all in the dark. Lord President told me he expects every day to be out, and has done so these two months. I protest, upon my life, I am heartily weary of this town, and wish I had never stirred.

13. I went this morning to the city, to see Mr. Stratford the Hamburg merchant, my old schoolfellow; but calling at Bull's on Ludgate Hill, he forced me to his house at Hampstead to dinner among a great deal of ill company; among the rest Mr. Hoadley, the Whig clergyman, so famous for acting the contrary part to Sacheverell: but to-morrow I design again to see Stratford. I was glad, however, to be at Hampstead, where I saw Lady Lucy and Moll Stanhope. I hear very unfortunate news of Mrs. Long; she and her comrade have broke up house, and she is broke for good and all, and is gone to the country: I should be extremely sorry if this be true.

14. To-day, I saw Patty Rolt, who heard I was in town; and I dined with Stratford at a merchant's in the city, where I drank the first Tokay wine I ever saw; and it is admirable, yet not to the degree I expected. Stratford is worth a plum, and is now lending the Government forty thousand pounds; yet we were educated together at the same school and university. We hear the Chancellor is to be suddenly out, and Sir Simon Harcourt to succeed him: I am come early home, not caring for the Coffee-house.

15. To-day Mr. Addison, Colonel Freind, and I, went to see the million lottery drawn at Guildhall. The jackanapes of bluecoat boys gave themselves such airs in pulling out the tickets, and showed white hands open to the company, to let us see there was no cheat. We dined at a country-house near Chelsea, where Mr. Addison often retires; and tonight, at the Coffee-house, we hear Sir Simon Harcourt is made Lord Keeper; so that now we expect every moment the Parliament will be dissolved; but I forgot that this letter will not go in three or four days, and that my news will be stale, which I should therefore put in the last paragraph. Shall I send this letter before I hear from MD, or shall I keep it to lengthen? I have not yet seen Stella's mother, because I will not see Lady Giffard; but I will contrive to go there when Lady Giffard is abroad. I forgot to mark my two former letters; but I remember this is Number 3, and I have not yet had Number 1 from MD; but I shall by Monday, which I reckon will be just a fortnight after you had my first. I am resolved to bring over a great deal of china. I loved it mightily today. What shall I bring?

16. Morning. Sir John Holland, Comptroller of the Household, has sent to desire my acquaintance: I have a mind to refuse him, because he is a Whig, and will, I suppose, be out among the rest; but he is a man of worth and learning. Tell me, do you like this journal way of writing? Is it not tedious and dull?

Night. I dined to-day with a cousin, a printer, where Patty Rolt lodges, and then came home, after a visit or two; and it has been a very insipid day. Mrs. Long's misfortune is confirmed to me; bailiffs were in her house; she retired to private lodgings; thence to the country, nobody knows where: her friends leave letters at some inn, and they are carried to her; and she writes answers without dating them from any place. I swear, it grieves me to the soul.

17. To-day I dined six miles out of town, with Will Pate, the learned woollen-draper; Mr. Stratford went with me; six miles here is nothing: we left Pate after sunset, and were here before it was dark. This letter shall go on Tuesday, whether I hear from MD or no. My health continues pretty well; pray God Stella may give me a good account of hers! and I hope you are now at Trim, or soon designing it. I was disappointed to-night: the fellow gave me a letter, and I hoped to see little MD's hand; and it was only to invite me to a venison pasty

to-day: so I lost my pasty into the bargain. Pox on these declining courtiers! Here is Mr. Brydges, the Paymaster-General, desiring my acquaintance; but I hear the Queen sent Lord Shrewsbury to assure him he may keep his place; and he promises me great assistance in the affair of the First-Fruits. Well, I must turn over this leaf to-night, though the side would hold another line; but pray consider this is a whole sheet; it holds a plaguy deal, and you must be content to be weary; but I'll do so no more. Sir Simon Harcourt is made Attorney-General, and not Lord Keeper.

18. To-day I dined with Mr. Stratford at Mr. Addison's retirement near Chelsea; then came to town; got home early, and began a letter to the *Tatler*, about the corruptions of style and writing, etc., and, having not heard from you, am resolved this letter shall go to-night. Lord Wharton was sent for to town in mighty haste, by the Duke of Devonshire: they have some project in hand; but it will not do, for every hour we expect a thorough revolution, and that the Parliament will be dissolved. When you see Joe, tell him Lord Wharton is too busy to mind any of his affairs; but I will get what good offices I can from Mr. Addison, and will write to-day to Mr. Pratt; and bid Joe not to be discouraged, for I am confident he will get the money under any Government; but he must have patience.

19. I have been scribbling this morning, and I believe shall hardly fill this side to-day, but send it as it is; and it is good enough for naughty girls that won't write to a body, and to a good boy like Presto. I thought to have sent this to-night, but was kept by company, and could not; and, to say the truth, I had a little mind to expect one post more for a letter from MD. Yesterday at noon died the Earl of Anglesea, the great support of the Tories; so that employment of Vice-Treasurer of Ireland is again vacant. We were to have been great friends, and I could hardly have a loss that could grieve me more. The Bishop of Durham died the same day. The Duke of Ormond's daughter was to visit me to-day at a third place by way of advance, and I am to return it to-morrow. I have had a letter from Lady Berkeley, begging me for charity to come to Berkeley Castle, for company to my lord, who has been ill of a dropsy; but I cannot go, and must send my excuse to-morrow. I am told that in a few hours there will be more removals.

20. To-day I returned my visits to the Duke's daughters; the insolent drabs came up to my very mouth to salute me. Then I heard the report confirmed of removals; my Lord President Somers; the Duke of Devonshire, Lord Steward; and Mr. Boyle, Secretary of State, are all turned out to-day. I never remember such bold steps taken by a Court: I am almost shocked at it, though I did not care if they were all hanged. We are astonished why the Parliament is not yet dissolved, and why they keep a matter of that importance to the last. We shall have a strange winter here, between the struggles of a cunning provoked discarded party, and the triumphs of one in power; of both which I shall be an indifferent spectator, and return very peaceably to Ireland, when I have done my part in the affair I am entrusted with, whether it succeeds or no. To-morrow I change my lodgings in Pall Mall for one in Bury Street, where I suppose I shall continue while I stay in London. If anything happens to-morrow, I will add it.—Robin's Coffee-house. We have great news just now from Spain; Madrid taken, and Pampeluna. I am here ever interrupted.

21. I have just received your letter, which I will not answer now; God be thanked all things are so well. I find you have not yet had my second: I had a letter from Parvisol, who tells me he gave Mrs. Walls a bill of twenty pounds for me, to be given to you; but you have not sent it. This night the Parliament is dissolved: great news from Spain; King Charles and Stanhope are at Madrid, and Count Staremberg has taken Pampeluna. Farewell. This is from St. James's Coffee-house. I will begin my answer to your letter to-night, but not send it this week. Pray tell me whether you like this journal way of writing.—I don't like your reasons for not going to Trim. Parvisol tells me he can sell your horse. Sell it, with a pox? Pray let him know that he shall sell his soul as soon. What? sell anything that Stella loves, and may sometimes ride? It is hers, and let her do as she pleases: pray let him know this by the first that you know goes to Trim. Let him sell my grey, and be hanged.

Letter IV

Here must I begin another letter, on a whole sheet, for fear saucy little MD should be angry, and think *much* that the paper is too *little*. I had your letter this night, as told you just and no more in my last; for this must be taken up in answering yours, saucebox. I believe I told you where I dined to-day; and to-morrow I go out of town for two days to dine with the same company on Sunday; Molesworth the Florence Envoy, Stratford, and some others. I heard to-day that a gentlewoman from Lady Giffard's house had been at the Coffee-house to inquire for me. It was Stella's mother, I suppose. I shall send her a penny-post letter to-morrow, and contrive to see her without hazarding seeing Lady Giffard, which I will not do until she begs my pardon.

22. I dined to-day at Hampstead with Lady Lucy, etc., and when I got home found a letter from Joe, with one enclosed to Lord Wharton, which I will send to his Excellency, and second it as well as I can; but to talk of getting the Queen's order is a jest. Things are in such a combustion here, that I am advised not to meddle yet in the affair I am upon, which concerns the clergy of a whole kingdom; and does he think anybody will trouble the Queen about Joe? We shall, I hope, get a recommendation from the Lord Lieutenant to the trustees for the linen business, and I hope that will do; and so I will write to him in a few days, and he must have patience. This is an answer to part of your letter as well as his. I lied; it is to-morrow I go to the country, and I won't answer a bit more of your letter yet.

23. Here is such a stir and bustle with this little MD of ours; I must be writing every night; I can't go to bed without a word to them; I can't put out my candle till I have bid them good-night: O Lord, O Lord! Well, I dined the first time to-day, with Will Frankland and his fortune: she is not very handsome. Did I not say I would go out of town to-day? I hate lying abroad and clutter; I go to-morrow in Frankland's chariot, and come back at night. Lady Berkeley has invited me to Berkeley Castle, and Lady Betty Germaine to Drayton in Northamptonshire; and I'll go to neither. Let me alone, I must finish my pamphlet. I have sent a long letter to Bickerstaff: let the Bishop of Clogher smoke it if he can. Well,

I'll write to the Bishop of Killala; but you might have told him how sudden and unexpected my journey was though. Deuce take Lady S—; and if I know D—y, he is a rawboned-faced fellow, not handsome, nor visibly so young as you say: she sacrifices two thousand pounds a year, and keeps only six hundred. Well, you have had all my land journey in my second letter, and so much for that. So, you have got into Presto's lodgings; very fine, truly! We have had a fortnight of the most glorious weather on earth, and still continues: I hope you have made the best of it. Ballygall will be a pure good place for air, if Mrs. Ashe makes good her promise. Stella writes like an emperor: I am afraid it hurts your eyes; take care of that pray, pray, Mrs. Stella. Can't you do what you will with your own horse? Pray don't let that puppy Parvisol sell him. Patrick is drunk about three times a week, and I bear it, and he has got the better of me; but one of these days I will positively turn him off to the wide world, when none of you are by to intercede for him.—Stuff—how can I get her husband into the Charter-house? get a—into the Charter-house.—Write constantly! Why, sirrah, don't I write every day, and sometimes twice a day to MD? Now I have answered all your letter, and the rest must be as it can be: send me my bill. Tell Mrs. Brent what I say of the Charter-house. I think this enough for one night; and so farewell till this time to-morrow.

24. To-day I dined six miles out of town at Will Pate's, with Stratford, Frankland, and the Molesworths, and came home at night, and was weary and lazy. I can say no more now, but good-night.

25. I was so lazy to-day that I dined at next door, and have sat at home since six, writing to the Bishop of Clogher, Dean Sterne, and Mr. Manley: the last, because I am in fear for him about his place, and have sent him my opinion, what I and his other friends here think he ought to do. I hope he will take it well. My advice was, to keep as much in favour as possible with Sir Thomas Frankland, his master here.

26. Smoke how I widen the margin by lying in bed when I write. My bed lies on the wrong side for me, so that I am forced often to write when I am up. Manley, you must know, has had people putting in for his place already; and has been complained of for opening letters. Remember that last Sunday, September 24, 1710, was as hot as midsummer. This was written in the morning; it is now night, and Presto in bed. Here's

a clutter, I have gotten MD's second letter, and I must answer it here. I gave the bill to Tooke, and so—Well, I dined to-day with Sir John Holland the Comptroller, and sat with him till eight; then came home, and sent my letters, and writ part of a lampoon, which goes on very slow: and now I am writing to saucy MD; no wonder, indeed, good boys must write to naughty girls. I have not seen your mother yet; my penny-post letter, I suppose, miscarried: I will write another. Mr. S— came to see me; and said M—was going to the country next morning with her husband (who I find is a surly brute); so I could only desire my service to her.

27. To-day all our company dined at Will Frankland's, with Steele and Addison too. This is the first rainy day since I came to town; I cannot afford to answer your letter yet. Morgan, the puppy, writ me a long letter, to desire I would recommend him for purse-bearer or secretary to the next Lord Chancellor that would come with the next Governor. I will not answer him; but beg you will say these words to his father Raymond, or anybody that will tell him: That Dr. Swift has received his letter; and would be very ready to serve him, but cannot do it in what he desires, because he has no sort of interest in the persons to be applied to. These words you may write, and let Joe, or Mr. Warburton, give them to him: a pox on him! However, it is by these sort of ways that fools get preferment. I must not end yet, because I cannot say good-night without losing a line, and then MD would scold; but now, good-night.

28. I have the finest piece of Brazil tobacco for Dingley that ever was born. You talk of Leigh; why, he won't be in Dublin these two months: he goes to the country, then returns to London, to see how the world goes here in Parliament. Good-night, sirrahs; no, no, not night; I writ this in the morning, and looking carelessly I thought it had been of last night. I dined to-day with Mrs. Barton alone at her lodgings; where she told me for certain, that Lady S—was with child when she was last in England, and pretended a tympany, and saw everybody; then disappeared for three weeks, her tympany was gone, and she looked like a ghost, etc. No wonder she married when she was so ill at containing. Connolly is out; and Mr. Roberts in his place, who loses a better here, but was formerly a Commissioner in Ireland. That employment cost Connolly three thousand pounds to Lord Wharton; so he has made one ill bargain in his life.

29. I wish MD a merry Michaelmas. I dined with Mr. Addison, and Jervas the painter, at Addison's country place; and then came home, and writ more to my lampoon. I made a *Tatler* since I came: guess which it is, and whether the Bishop of Clogher smokes it. I saw Mr. Sterne to-day: he will do as you order, and I will give him chocolate for Stella's health. He goes not these three weeks. I wish I could send it some other way. So now to your letter, brave boys. I don't like your way of saving shillings: nothing vexes me but that it does not make Stella a coward in a coach. I don't think any lady's advice about my ear signifies twopence: however I will, in compliance to you, ask Dr. Cockburn. Radcliffe I know not, and Barnard I never see. Walls will certainly be stingier for seven years, upon pretence of his robbery. So Stella puns again; why, 'tis well enough; but I'll not second it, though I could make a dozen: I never thought of a pun since I left Ireland.—Bishop of Clogher's bill? Why, he paid it to me; do you think I was such a fool to go without it? As for the four shillings, I will give you a bill on Parvisol for it on t'other side of this paper; and pray tear off the two letters I shall write to him and Joe, or let Dingley transcribe and send them; though that to Parvisol, I believe, he must have my hand for. No, no, I'll eat no grapes; I ate about six the other day at Sir John Holland's; but would not give sixpence for a thousand, they are so bad this year. Yes, faith, I hope in God Presto and MD will be together this time twelvemonth. What then? Last year I suppose I was at Laracor; but next I hope to eat my Michaelmas goose at my two little gooses' lodgings. I drink no *aile* (I suppose you mean *ale*); but yet good wine every day, of five and six shillings a bottle. O Lord, how much Stella writes! pray don't carry that too far, young women, but be temperate, to hold out. To-morrow I go to Mr. Harley. Why, small hopes from the Duke of Ormond: he loves me very well, I believe, and would, in my turn, give me something to make me easy; and I have good interest among his best friends. But I don't think of anything further than the business I am upon. You see I writ to Manley before I had your letter, and I fear he will be out. Yes, Mrs. Owl, Bligh's corpse came to Chester when I was there; and I told you so in my letter, or forgot it. I lodge in Bury Street, where I removed a week ago. I have the first floor, a dining-room, and bed-chamber, at eight shillings a week; plaguy deep, but I spend nothing for eating, never go to a tavern, and very seldom in a coach; yet after all it will be expensive. Why do you trouble yourself, Mistress Stella, about my instrument? I have the same the Archbishop gave me; and it is as

good now the bishops are away. The Dean friendly! the Dean be poxed: a great piece of friendship indeed, what you heard him tell the Bishop of Clogher; I wonder he had the face to talk so: but he lent me money, and that's enough. Faith, I would not send this these four days, only for writing to Joe and Parvisol. Tell the Dean that when the bishops send me any packets, they must not write to me at Mr. Steele's; but direct for Mr. Steele, at his office at the Cockpit, and let the enclosed be directed for me: that mistake cost me eighteenpence the other day.

30. I dined with Stratford to-day, but am not to see Mr. Harley till Wednesday: it is late, and I send this before there is occasion for the bell; because I would have Joe have his letter, and Parvisol too; which you must so contrive as not to cost them double postage. I can say no more, but that I am, etc.

LETTER V

LONDON, *Sept.* 30, 1710

Han't I brought myself into a fine *præmunire*, to begin writing letters in whole sheets? and now I dare not leave it off. I cannot tell whether you like these journal letters: I believe they would be dull to me to read them over; but, perhaps, little MD is pleased to know how Presto passes his time in her absence. I always begin my last the same day I ended my former. I told you where I dined to-day at a tavern with Stratford: Lewis, who is a great favourite of Harley's, was to have been with us; but he was hurried to Hampton Court, and sent his excuse; and that next Wednesday he would introduce me to Harley. 'Tis good to see what a lamentable confession the Whigs all make me of my ill usage: but I mind them not. I am already represented to Harley as a discontented person, that was used ill for not being Whig enough; and I hope for good usage from him. The Tories drily tell me, I may make my fortune, if I please; but I do not understand them—or rather, I do understand them.

Oct. 1. To-day I dined at Molesworth's, the Florence Envoy; and sat this evening with my friend Darteneuf, whom you have heard me talk of; the greatest punner of this town next myself. Have you smoked the *Tatler* that I writ? It is much liked here, and I think it a pure one. To-morrow I go with Delaval, the Portugal Envoy, to dine with Lord Halifax near Hampton Court. Your Manley's brother, a Parliament-man here, has gotten an employment; and I am informed uses much interest to preserve his brother: and, to-day, I spoke to the elder Frankland to engage his father (Postmaster here); and I hope he will be safe, although he is cruelly hated by all the Tories of Ireland. I have almost finished my lampoon, and will print it for revenge on a certain great person. It has cost me but three shillings in meat and drink since I came here, as thin as the town is. I laugh to see myself so disengaged in these revolutions. Well, I must leave off, and go write to Sir John Stanley, to desire him to engage Lady Hyde as my mistress to engage Lord Hyde in favour of Mr. Pratt.

2. Lord Halifax was at Hampton Court at his lodgings, and I dined with him there with Methuen, and Delaval, and the late Attorney-General.

A JOURNAL TO STELLA   39

I went to the Drawing-room before dinner (for the Queen was at Hampton Court), and expected to see nobody; but I met acquaintance enough. I walked in the gardens, saw the cartoons of Raphael, and other things; and with great difficulty got from Lord Halifax, who would have kept me to-morrow to show me his house and park, and improvements. We left Hampton Court at sunset, and got here in a chariot and two horses time enough by starlight. That's something charms me mightily about London; that you go dine a dozen miles off in October, stay all day, and return so quickly: you cannot do anything like this in Dublin. I writ a second penny post letter to your mother, and hear nothing of her. Did I tell you that Earl Berkeley died last Sunday was se'nnight, at Berkeley Castle, of a dropsy? Lord Halifax began a health to me to-day; it was the Resurrection of the Whigs, which I refused unless he would add their Reformation too and I told him he was the only Whig in England I loved, or had any good opinion of.

3. This morning Stella's sister came to me with a letter from her mother, who is at Sheen; but will soon be in town, and will call to see me: she gave me a bottle of palsy water, a small one, and desired I would send it you by the first convenience, as I will; and she promises a quart bottle of the same: your sister looked very well, and seems a good modest sort of girl. I went then to Mr. Lewis, first secretary to Lord Dartmouth, and favourite to Mr. Harley, who is to introduce me to-morrow morning. Lewis had with him one Mr. Dyot, a Justice of Peace, worth twenty thousand pounds, a Commissioner of the Stamp Office, and married to a sister of Sir Philip Meadows, Envoy to the Emperor. I tell you this, because it is odds but this Mr. Dyot will be hanged; for he is discovered to have counterfeited stamped paper, in which he was a Commissioner; and, with his accomplices, has cheated the Queen of a hundred thousand pounds. You will hear of it before this come to you, but may be not so particularly; and it is a very odd accident in such a man. Smoke Presto writing news to MD. I dined to-day with Lord Mountjoy at Kensington, and walked from thence this evening to town like an emperor. Remember that yesterday, October 2, was a cruel hard frost, with ice; and six days ago I was dying with heat. As thin as the town is, I have more dinners than ever; and am asked this month by some people, without being able to come for pre-engagements. Well, but I should write plainer, when I consider Stella cannot read, and Dingley is not so skilful at my ugly hand. I had to-night a letter from

Mr. Pratt, who tells me Joe will have his money when there are trustees appointed by the Lord Lieutenant for receiving and disposing the linen fund; and whenever those trustees are appointed, I will solicit whoever is Lord Lieutenant, and am in no fear of succeeding. So pray tell or write him word, and bid him not be cast down; for Ned Southwell and Mr. Addison both think Pratt in the right. Don't lose your money at Manley's to-night, sirrahs.

4. After I had put out my candle last night, my landlady came into my room, with a servant of Lord Halifax, to desire I would go dine with him at his house near Hampton Court; but I sent him word, I had business of great importance that hindered me, etc. And to-day I was brought privately to Mr. Harley, who received me with the greatest respect and kindness imaginable: he has appointed me an hour on Saturday at four, afternoon, when I will open my business to him; which expression I would not use if I were a woman. I know you smoked it; but I did not till I writ it. I dined to-day at Mr. Delaval's, the Envoy for Portugal, with Nic Rowe the poet, and other friends; and I gave my lampoon to be printed. I have more mischief in my heart; and I think it shall go round with them all, as this hits, and I can find hints. I am certain I answered your 2d letter, and yet I do not find it here. I suppose it was in my 4th: and why N. 2d, 3d; is it not enough to say, as I do, 1, 2, 3? etc. I am going to work at another *Tatler*: I'll be far enough but I say the same thing over two or three times, just as I do when I am talking to little MD; but what care I? they can read it as easily as I can write it: I think I have brought these lines pretty straight again. I fear it will be long before I finish two sides at this rate. Pray, dear MD, when I occasionally give you any little commission mixed with my letters, don't forget it, as that to Morgan and Joe, etc., for I write just as I can remember, otherwise I would put them all together. I was to visit Mr. Sterne to-day, and give him your commission about handkerchiefs: that of chocolate I will do myself, and send it him when he goes, and you'll pay me when *the giver's bread*, etc. To-night I will read a pamphlet, to amuse myself. God preserve your dear healths!

5. This morning Delaval came to see me, and we went together to Kneller's, who was not in town. In the way we met the electors for Parliament-men: and the rabble came about our coach, crying, "A Colt, a Stanhope," etc. We were afraid of a dead cat, or our glasses broken,

and so were always of their side. I dined again at Delaval's; and in the evening, at the Coffee-house, heard Sir Andrew Fountaine was come to town. This has been but an insipid sort of day, and I have nothing to remark upon it worth threepence: I hope MD had a better, with the Dean, the Bishop, or Mrs. Walls. Why, the reason you lost four and eightpence last night but one at Manley's was, because you played bad games: I took notice of six that you had ten to one against you: Would any but a mad lady go out twice upon Manilio; Basto, and two small diamonds? Then in that game of spades, you blundered when you had ten-ace; I never saw the like of you: and now you are in a huff because I tell you this. Well, here's two and eightpence halfpenny towards your loss.

6. Sir Andrew Fountaine came this morning, and caught me writing in bed. I went into the city with him; and we dined at the Chop-house with Will Pate, the learned woollen-draper: then we sauntered at China-shops and booksellers; went to the tavern, drank two pints of white wine, and never parted till ten: and now I am come home, and must copy out some papers I intend for Mr. Harley, whom I am to see, as I told you, to-morrow afternoon; so that this night I shall say little to MD, but that I heartily wish myself with them, and will come as soon as I either fail, or compass my business. We now hear daily of elections; and, in a list I saw yesterday of about twenty, there are seven or eight more Tories than in the last Parliament; so that I believe they need not fear a majority, with the help of those who will vote as the Court pleases. But I have been told that Mr. Harley himself would not let the Tories be too numerous, for fear they should be insolent, and kick against him; and for that reason they have kept several Whigs in employments, who expected to be turned out every day; as Sir John Holland the Comptroller, and many others. And so get you gone to your cards, and your claret and orange, at the Dean's; and I'll go write.

7. I wonder when this letter will be finished: it must go by Tuesday, that's certain; and if I have one from MD before, I will not answer it, that's as certain too. 'Tis now morning, and I did not finish my papers for Mr. Harley last night; for you must understand Presto was sleepy, and made blunders and blots. Very pretty that I must be writing to young women in a morning fresh and fasting, faith. Well, good-morrow to you; and so I go to business, and lay aside this paper till night, sirrahs.—

At night. Jack How told Harley that if there were a lower place in hell than another, it was reserved for his porter, who tells lies so gravely, and with so civil a manner. This porter I have had to deal with, going this evening at four to visit Mr. Harley, by his own appointment. But the fellow told me no lie, though I suspected every word he said. He told me his master was just gone to dinner, with much company, and desired I would come an hour hence: which I did, expecting to hear Mr. Harley was gone out; but they had just done dinner. Mr. Harley came out to me, brought me in, and presented to me his son-in-law Lord Doblane (or some such name) and his own son, and, among others, Will Penn the Quaker: we sat two hours drinking as good wine as you do; and two hours more he and I alone; where he heard me tell my business; entered into it with all kindness; asked for my powers, and read them; and read likewise a memorial I had drawn up, and put it in his pocket to show the Queen; told me the measures he would take; and, in short, said everything I could wish: told me, he must bring Mr. St. John (Secretary of State) and me acquainted; and spoke so many things of personal kindness and esteem for me, that I am inclined half to believe what some friends have told me, that he would do everything to bring me over. He has desired to dine with me (what a comical mistake was that!). I mean he has desired me to dine with him on Tuesday; and after four hours being with him, set me down at St. James's Coffee-house in a hackney-coach. All this is odd and comical, if you consider him and me. He knew my Christian name very well. I could not forbear saying thus much upon this matter, although you will think it tedious. But I'll tell you; you must know, 'tis fatal to me to be a scoundrel and a prince the same day: for, being to see him at four, I could not engage myself to dine at any friend's; so I went to Tooke, to give him a ballad, and dine with him; but he was not at home: so I was forced to go to a blind chop-house, and dine for tenpence upon gill-ale, bad broth, and three chops of mutton; and then go reeking from thence to the First Minister of State. And now I am going in charity to send Steele a *Tatler*, who is very low of late. I think I am civiller than I used to be; and have not used the expression of "you in Ireland" and "we in England" as I did when I was here before, to your great indignation.—They may talk of the you know what; but, gad, if it had not been for that, I should never have been able to get the access I have had; and if that helps me to succeed, then that same thing will be serviceable to the Church. But how far we must depend upon new friends, I have learnt by long practice, though I think among great Ministers, they are just as good as old ones. And so I think this important day has made a great hole in this side of the paper; and the fiddle-faddles of to-morrow and Monday will make up the rest; and, besides, I shall see Harley on Tuesday before this letter goes.

8. I must tell you a great piece of refinement of Harley. He charged me to come to him often: I told him I was loth to trouble him in so much business as he had, and desired I might have leave to come at his levee; which he immediately refused, and said, that was not a place for friends to come to. 'Tis now but morning; and I have got a foolish trick, I must say something to MD when I wake, and wish them a good-morrow; for this is not a shaving-day, Sunday, so I have time enough: but get you gone, you rogues, I must go write: Yes, 'twill vex me to the blood if any of these long letters should miscarry: if they do, I will shrink to half-sheets again; but then what will you do to make up the journal? there will be ten days of Presto's life lost; and that will be a sad thing, faith and troth.—At night. I was at a loss to-day for a dinner, unless I would have gone a great way, so I dined with some friends that board hereabout, as a spunger; and this evening Sir Andrew Fountaine would needs have me go to the tavern; where, for two bottles of wine, Portugal and Florence, among three of us, we had sixteen shillings to pay; but if ever he catches me so again, I'll spend as many pounds: and therefore I have it among my extraordinaries but we had a neck of mutton dressed *à la Maintenon*, that the dog could not eat: and it is now twelve o'clock, and I must go sleep. I hope this letter will go before I have MD's third. Do you believe me? and yet, faith, I long for MD's third too and yet I would have it to say, that I writ five for two. I am not fond at all of St. James's Coffee-house, as I used to be. I hope it will mend in winter; but now they are all out of town at elections, or not come from their country houses. Yesterday I was going with Dr. Garth to dine with Charles Main, near the Tower, who has an employment there: he is of Ireland; the Bishop of Clogher knows him well: an honest, good-natured fellow, a thorough hearty laugher, mightily beloved by the men of wit: his mistress is never above a cook-maid. And so, good-night, etc.

9. I dined to-day at Sir John Stanley's; my Lady Stanley is one of my favourites: I have as many here as the Bishop of Killala has in Ireland. I am thinking what scurvy company I shall be to MD when I come back:

they know everything of me already: I will tell you no more, or I shall have nothing to say, no story to tell, nor any kind of thing. I was very uneasy last night with ugly, nasty, filthy wine, that turned sour on my stomach. I must go to the tavern: oh, but I told you that before. To-morrow I dine at Harley's, and will finish this letter at my return; but I can write no more now, because of the Archbishop: faith, 'tis true; for I am going now to write to him an account of what I have done in the business with Harley: and, faith, young women, I'll tell you what you must count upon, that I never will write one word on the third side in these long letters.

10. Poor MD's letter was lying so huddled up among papers, I could not find it: I mean poor Presto's letter. Well, I dined with Mr. Harley to-day, and hope some things will be done; but I must say no more: and this letter must be sent to the post-house, and not by the bellman. I am to dine again there on Sunday next; I hope to some good issue. And so now, soon as ever I can in bed, I must begin my 6th to MD as gravely as if I had not written a word this month: fine doings, faith! Methinks I don't write as I should, because I am not in bed: see the ugly wide lines. God Almighty ever bless you, etc.

Faith, this is a whole treatise; I'll go reckon the lines on the other sides. I've reckoned them.

Letter VI

So, as I told you just now in the letter I sent half an hour ago, I dined with Mr. Harley to-day, who presented me to the Attorney-General, Sir Simon Harcourt, with much compliment on all sides, etc. Harley told me he had shown my memorial to the Queen, and seconded it very heartily; and he desires me to dine with him again on Sunday, when he promises to settle it with Her Majesty, before she names a Governor: and I protest I am in hopes it will be done, all but the forms, by that time; for he loves the Church. This is a popular thing, and he would not have a Governor share in it; and, besides, I am told by all hands, he has a mind to gain me over. But in the letter I writ last post (yesterday) to the Archbishop, I did not tell him a syllable of what Mr. Harley said to me last night, because he charged me to keep it secret; so I would not tell it to you, but that, before this goes, I hope the secret will be over. I am now writing my poetical "Description of a Shower in London," and will send it to the *Tatler*. This is the last sheet of a whole quire I have written since I came to town. Pray, now it comes into my head, will you, when you go to Mrs. Walls, contrive to know whether Mrs. Wesley be in town, and still at her brother's, and how she is in health, and whether she stays in town. I writ to her from Chester, to know what I should do with her note; and I believe the poor woman is afraid to write to me: so I must go to my business, etc.

11. To-day at last I dined with Lord Mountrath, and carried Lord Mountjoy, and Sir Andrew Fountaine with me; and was looking over them at ombre till eleven this evening like a fool: they played running ombre half-crowns; and Sir Andrew Fountaine won eight guineas of Mr. Coote; so I am come home late, and will say but little to MD this night. I have gotten half a bushel of coals, and Patrick, the extravagant whelp, had a fire ready for me; but I picked off the coals before I went to bed. It is a sign London is now an empty place, when it will not furnish me with matter for above five or six lines in a day. Did you smoke in my last how I told you the very day and the place you were playing at ombre? But I interlined and altered a little, after I had received a letter from Mr. Manley, that said you were at it in his house, while he was writing to me; but without his help I guessed within one day. Your town

is certainly much more sociable than ours. I have not seen your mother yet, etc.

12. I dined to-day with Dr. Garth and Mr. Addison, at the Devil Tavern by Temple Bar, and Garth treated; and 'tis well I dine every day, else I should be longer making out my letters: for we are yet in a very dull state, only inquiring every day after new elections, where the Tories carry it among the new members six to one. Mr. Addison's election has passed easy and undisputed; and I believe if he had a mind to be chosen king, he would hardly be refused. An odd accident has happened at Colchester: one Captain Lavallin, coming from Flanders or Spain, found his wife with child by a clerk of Doctors' Commons, whose trade, you know, it is to prevent fornications: and this clerk was the very same fellow that made the discovery of Dyot's counterfeiting the stamp-paper. Lavallin has been this fortnight hunting after the clerk, to kill him; but the fellow was constantly employed at the Treasury, about the discovery he made: the wife had made a shift to patch up the business, alleging that the clerk had told her her husband was dead and other excuses; but t'other day somebody told Lavallin his wife had intrigues before he married her: upon which he goes down in a rage, shoots his wife through the head, then falls on his sword; and, to make the matter sure, at the same time discharges a pistol through his own head, and died on the spot, his wife surviving him about two hours, but in what circumstances of mind and body is terrible to imagine. I have finished my poem on the "Shower," all but the beginning; and am going on with my *Tatler*. They have fixed about fifty things on me since I came: I have printed but three. One advantage I get by writing to you daily, or rather you get, is, that I shall remember not to write the same things twice; and yet, I fear, I have done it often already: but I will mind and confine myself to the accidents of the day; and so get you gone to ombre, and be good girls, and save your money, and be rich against Presto comes, and write to me now and then: I am thinking it would be a pretty thing to hear sometimes from saucy MD; but do not hurt your eyes, Stella, I charge you.

13. O Lord, here is but a trifle of my letter written yet; what shall Presto do for prattle-prattle, to entertain MD? The talk now grows fresher of the Duke of Ormond for Ireland; though Mr. Addison says he hears it will be in commission, and Lord Galway one. These letters of mine

are a sort of journal, where matters open by degrees; and, as I tell true or false, you will find by the event whether my intelligence be good; but I do not care twopence whether it be or no.—At night. To-day I was all about St. Paul's, and up at the top like a fool, with Sir Andrew Fountaine and two more; and spent seven shillings for my dinner like a puppy: this is the second time he has served me so; but I will never do it again, though all mankind should persuade me, unconsidering puppies! There is a young fellow here in town we are all fond of, and about a year or two come from the University, one Harrison, a little pretty fellow, with a great deal of wit, good sense, and good nature; has written some mighty pretty things; that in your 6th *Miscellanea*, about the Sprig of an Orange, is his: he has nothing to live on but being governor to one of the Duke of Queensberry's sons for forty pounds a year. The fine fellows are always inviting him to the tavern, and make him pay his club. Henley is a great crony of his: they are often at the tavern at six or seven shillings reckoning, and he always makes the poor lad pay his full share. A colonel and a lord were at him and me the same way to-night: I absolutely refused, and made Harrison lag behind, and persuaded him not to go to them. I tell you this, because I find all rich fellows have that humour of using all people without any consideration of their fortunes; but I will see them rot before they shall serve me so. Lord Halifax is always teasing me to go down to his country house, which will cost me a guinea to his servants, and twelve shillings coach-hire; and he shall be hanged first. Is not this a plaguy silly story? But I am vexed at the heart; for I love the young fellow, and am resolved to stir up people to do something for him: he is a Whig, and I will put him upon some of my cast Whigs; for I have done with them; and they have, I hope, done with this kingdom for our time. They were sure of the four members for London above all places, and they have lost three in the four. Sir Richard Onslow, we hear, has lost for Surrey; and they are overthrown in most places. Lookee, gentlewomen, if I write long letters, I must write you news and stuff, unless I send you my verses; and some I dare not; and those on the "Shower in London" I have sent to the *Tatler*, and you may see them in Ireland. I fancy you will smoke me in the *Tatler* I am going to write; for I believe I have told you the hint. I had a letter sent me to-night from Sir Matthew Dudley, and found it on my table when I came in. Because it is extraordinary, I will transcribe it from beginning to end. It is as follows: "Is the Devil in you? Oct. 13, 1710." I would have answered every particular passage in it, only I wanted time. Here is enough for to-night, such as it is, etc.

14. Is that tobacco at the top of the paper, or what? I do not remember I slobbered. Lord, I dreamt of Stella, etc., so confusedly last night, and that we saw Dean Bolton and Sterne go into a shop: and she bid me call them to her, and they proved to be two parsons I know not; and I walked without till she was shifting, and such stuff, mixed with much melancholy and uneasiness, and things not as they should be, and I know not how: and it is now an ugly gloomy morning.—At night. Mr. Addison and I dined with Ned Southwell, and walked in the Park; and at the Coffee-house I found a letter from the Bishop of Clogher, and a packet from MD. I opened the Bishop's letter; but put up MD's, and visited a lady just come to town; and am now got into bed, and going to open your little letter: and God send I may find MD well, and happy, and merry, and that they love Presto as they do fires. Oh, I will not open it yet! yes I will! no I will not! I am going; I cannot stay till I turn over. What shall I do? My fingers itch; and now I have it in my left hand; and now I will open it this very moment.—I have just got it, and am cracking the seal, and cannot imagine what is in it; I fear only some letter from a bishop, and it comes too late; I shall employ nobody's credit but my own. Well, I see though—Pshaw, 'tis from Sir Andrew Fountaine. What, another! I fancy that's from Mrs. Barton; she told me she would write to me; but she writes a better hand than this: I wish you would inquire; it must be at Dawson's office at the Castle. I fear this is from Patty Rolt, by the scrawl. Well, I will read MD's letter. Ah, no; it is from poor Lady Berkeley, to invite me to Berkeley Castle this winter; and now it grieves my heart: she says, she hopes my lord is in a fair way of recovery; poor lady! Well, now I go to MD's letter: faith, it is all right; I hoped it was wrong. Your letter, N. 3, that I have now received, is dated Sept. 26; and Manley's letter, that I had five days ago, was dated Oct. 3, that's a fortnight difference: I doubt it has lain in Steele's office, and he forgot. Well, there's an end of that: he is turned out of his place; and you must desire those who send me packets, to enclose them in a paper directed to Mr. Addison, at St. James's Coffee-house: not common letters, but packets: the Bishop of Clogher may mention it to the Archbishop when he sees him. As for your letter, it makes me mad: slidikins, I have been the best boy in Christendom, and you come with your two eggs a penny.—Well; but stay, I will look

over my book: adad, I think there was a chasm between my N. 2 and N. 3. Faith, I will not promise to write to you every week; but I will write every night, and when it is full I will send it; that will be once in ten days, and that will be often enough: and if you begin to take up the way of writing to Presto, only because it is Tuesday, a Monday bedad it will grow a task; but write when you have a mind.—No, no, no, no, no, no, no, no—Agad, agad, agad, agad, agad, agad; no, poor Stellakins. Slids, I would the horse were in your—chamber! Have not I ordered Parvisol to obey your directions about him? And han't I said in my former letters that you may pickle him, and boil him, if you will? What do you trouble me about your horses for? Have I anything to do with them?—Revolutions a hindrance to me in my business? Revolutions to me in my business? If it were not for the revolutions, I could do nothing at all; and now I have all hopes possible, though one is certain of nothing; but to-morrow I am to have an answer, and am promised an effectual one. I suppose I have said enough in this and a former letter how I stand with new people; ten times better than ever I did with the old; forty times more caressed. I am to dine to-morrow at Mr. Harley's; and if he continues as he has begun, no man has been ever better treated by another. What you say about Stella's mother, I have spoken enough to it already. I believe she is not in town; for I have not yet seen her. My lampoon is cried up to the skies; but nobody suspects me for it, except Sir Andrew Fountaine: at least they say nothing of it to me. Did not I tell you of a great man who received me very coldly? That's he; but say nothing; 'twas only a little revenge. I will remember to bring it over. The Bishop of Clogher has smoked my *Tatler*, about shortening of words, etc. But, God So! etc.

15. I will write plainer if I can remember it; for Stella must not spoil her eyes, and Dingley can't read my hand very well; and I am afraid my letters are too long: then you must suppose one to be two, and read them at twice. I dined to-day with Mr. Harley: Mr. Prior dined with us. He has left my memorial with the Queen, who has consented to give the First-Fruits and Twentieth Parts, and will, we hope, declare it to-morrow in the Cabinet. But I beg you to tell it to no person alive; for so I am ordered, till in public: and I hope to get something of greater value. After dinner came in Lord Peterborow: we renewed our acquaintance, and he grew mightily fond of me. They began to talk of a paper of verses called "Sid Hamet." Mr. Harley repeated part, and then pulled them

out, and gave them to a gentleman at the table to read, though they had all read them often. Lord Peterborow would let nobody read them but himself: so he did; and Mr. Harley bobbed me at every line, to take notice of the beauties. Prior rallied Lord Peterborow for author of them; and Lord Peterborow said he knew them to be his; and Prior then turned it upon me, and I on him. I am not guessed at all in town to be the author; yet so it is: but that is a secret only to you. Ten to one whether you see them in Ireland; yet here they run prodigiously. Harley presented me to Lord President of Scotland, and Mr. Benson, Lord of the Treasury. Prior and I came away at nine, and sat at the Smyrna till eleven, receiving acquaintance.

16. This morning early I went in a chair, and Patrick before it, to Mr. Harley, to give him another copy of my memorial, as he desired; but he was full of business, going to the Queen, and I could not see him; but he desired I would send up the paper, and excused himself upon his hurry. I was a little baulked; but they tell me it is nothing. I shall judge by next visit. I tipped his porter with half a crown; and so I am well there for a time at least. I dined at Stratford's in the City, and had Burgundy and Tokay: came back afoot like a scoundrel: then went with Mr. Addison and supped with Lord Mountjoy, which made me sick all night. I forgot that I bought six pounds of chocolate for Stella, and a little wooden box; and I have a great piece of Brazil tobacco for Dingley, and a bottle of palsy-water for Stella: all which, with the two handkerchiefs that Mr. Sterne has bought, and you must pay him for, will be put in the box, directed to Mrs. Curry's, and sent by Dr. Hawkshaw, whom I have not seen; but Sterne has undertaken it. The chocolate is a present, madam, for Stella. Don't read this, you little rogue, with your little eyes; but give it to Dingley, pray now; and I will write as plain as the skies: and let Dingley write Stella's part, and Stella dictate to her, when she apprehends her eyes, etc.

17. This letter should have gone this post, if I had not been taken up with business, and two nights being late out; so it must stay till Thursday. I dined to-day with your Mr. Sterne, by invitation, and drank Irish wine; but, before we parted, there came in the prince of puppies, Colonel Edgworth; so I went away. This day came out the *Tatler*, made up wholly of my "Shower," and a preface to it. They say it is the best thing I ever writ, and I think so too. I suppose the Bishop of Clogher

will show it you. Pray tell me how you like it. Tooke is going on with my *Miscellany*. I'd give a penny the letter to the Bishop of Killaloe was in it: 'twould do him honour. Could not you contrive to say, you hear they are printing my things together; and that you with the bookseller had that letter among the rest: but don't say anything of it as from me. I forget whether it was good or no; but only having heard it much commended, perhaps it may deserve it. Well, I have to-morrow to finish this letter in, and then I will send it next day. I am so vexed that you should write your third to me, when you had but my second, and I had written five, which now I hope you have all: and so I tell you, you are saucy, little, pretty, dear rogues, etc.

18. To-day I dined, by invitation, with Stratford and others, at a young merchant's in the City, with Hermitage and Tokay, and stayed till nine, and am now come home. And that dog Patrick is abroad, and drinking, and I cannot I get my night-gown. I have a mind to turn that puppy away: he has been drunk ten times in three weeks. But I han't time to say more; so good-night, etc.

19. I am come home from dining in the city with Mr. Addison, at a merchant's; and just now, at the Coffee-house, we have notice that the Duke of Ormond was this day declared Lord Lieutenant at Hampton Court, in Council. I have not seen Mr. Harley since; but hope the affair is done about First-Fruits. I will see him, if possible, to-morrow morning; but this goes to-night. I have sent a box to Mr. Sterne, to send to you by some friend: I have directed it for Mr. Curry, at his house; so you have warning when it comes, as I hope it will soon. The handkerchiefs will be put in some friend's pocket, not to pay custom. And so here ends my sixth, sent when I had but three of MD's: now I am beforehand, and will keep so; and God Almighty bless dearest MD, etc.

LETTER VII

Faith, I am undone! this paper is larger than the other, and yet I am condemned to a sheet; but, since it is MD, I did not value though I were condemned to a pair. I told you in my letter to-day where I had been, and how the day passed; and so, etc.

20. To-day I went to Mr. Lewis, at the Secretary's office, to know when I might see Mr. Harley; and by and by comes up Mr. Harley himself, and appoints me to dine with him to-morrow. I dined with Mrs. Vanhomrigh, and went to wait on the two Lady Butlers; but the porter answered they were not at home: the meaning was, the youngest, Lady Mary, is to be married to-morrow to Lord Ashburnham, the best match now in England, twelve thousand pounds a year, and abundance of money. Tell me how my "Shower" is liked in Ireland: I never knew anything pass better here. I spent the evening with Wortley Montagu and Mr. Addison, over a bottle of Irish wine. Do they know anything in Ireland of my greatness among the Tories? Everybody reproaches me of it here; but I value them not. Have you heard of the verses about the "Rod of Sid Hamet"? Say nothing of them for your life. Hardly anybody suspects me for them; only they think nobody but Prior or I could write them. But I doubt they have not reached you. There is likewise a ballad full of puns on the Westminster Election, that cost me half an hour: it runs, though it be good for nothing. But this is likewise a secret to all but MD. If you have them not, I will bring them over.

21. I got MD's fourth to-day at the Coffee-house. God Almighty bless poor, dear Stella, and her eyes and head! What shall we do to cure them? poor, dear life! Your disorders are a pull-back for your good qualities. Would to Heaven I were this minute shaving your poor, dear head, either here or there! Pray do not write, nor read this letter, nor anything else; and I will write plainer for Dingley to read from henceforward, though my pen is apt to ramble when I think whom I am writing to. I will not answer your letter until I tell you that I dined this day with Mr. Harley, who presented me to the Earl of Stirling, a Scotch lord; and in the evening came in Lord Peterborow. I stayed till nine before Mr. Harley would let me go, or tell me anything of my affair. He says

the Queen has now granted the First-Fruits and Twentieth Parts; but he will not give me leave to write to the Archbishop, because the Queen designs to signify it to the Bishops in Ireland in form; and to take notice, that it was done upon a memorial from me; which, Mr. Harley tells me he does to make it look more respectful to me, etc.; and I am to see him on Tuesday. I know not whether I told you that, in my memorial which was given to the Queen, I begged for two thousand pounds a year more, though it was not in my commission; but that, Mr. Harley says, cannot yet be done, and that he and I must talk of it further: however, I have started it, and it may follow in time. Pray say nothing of the First-Fruits being granted, unless I give leave at the bottom of this. I believe never anything was compassed so soon, and purely done by my personal credit with Mr. Harley, who is so excessively obliging, that I know not what to make of it, unless to show the rascals of the other party that they used a man unworthily who had deserved better. The memorial given to the Queen from me speaks with great plainness of Lord Wharton. I believe this business is as important to you as the Convocation disputes from Tisdall. I hope in a month or two all the forms of settling this matter will be over; and then I shall have nothing to do here. I will only add one foolish thing more, because it is just come into my head. When this thing is made known, tell me impartially whether they give any of the merit to me, or no; for I am sure I have so much, that I will never take it upon me.—Insolent sluts! because I say Dublin, Ireland, therefore you must say London, England: that is Stella's malice.—Well, for that I will not answer your letter till to-morrow-day, and so and so: I will go write something else, and it will not be much; for 'tis late.

22. I was this morning with Mr. Lewis, the under-secretary to Lord Dartmouth, two hours, talking politics, and contriving to keep Steele in his office of stamped paper: he has lost his place of Gazetteer, three hundred pounds a year, for writing a *Tatler*, some months ago, against Mr. Harley, who gave it him at first, and raised the salary from sixty to three hundred pounds. This was devilish ungrateful; and Lewis was telling me the particulars: but I had a hint given me, that I might save him in the other employment: and leave was given me to clear matters with Steele. Well, I dined with Sir Matthew Dudley, and in the evening went to sit with Mr. Addison, and offer the matter at distance to him, as the discreeter person; but found party had so possessed him, that he talked as if he suspected me, and would not fall in with anything I said.

So I stopped short in my overture, and we parted very drily; and I shall say nothing to Steele, and let them do as they will; but, if things stand as they are, he will certainly lose it, unless I save him; and therefore I will not speak to him, that I may not report to his disadvantage. Is not this vexatious? and is there so much in the proverb of proffered service? When shall I grow wise? I endeavour to act in the most exact points of honour and conscience; and my nearest friends will not understand it so. What must a man expect from his enemies? This would vex me, but it shall not; and so I bid you good-night, etc.

23. I know 'tis neither wit nor diversion to tell you every day where I dine; neither do I write it to fill my letter; but I fancy I shall, some time or other, have the curiosity of seeing some particulars how I passed my life when I was absent from MD this time; and so I tell you now that I dined to-day at Molesworth's, the Florence Envoy, then went to the Coffee-house, where I behaved myself coldly enough to Mr. Addison, and so came home to scribble. We dine together to-morrow and next day by invitation; but I shall alter my behaviour to him, till he begs my pardon, or else we shall grow bare acquaintance. I am weary of friends; and friendships are all monsters, but MD's.

24. I forgot to tell you, that last night I went to Mr. Harley's, hoping— faith, I am blundering, for it was this very night at six; and I hoped he would have told me all things were done and granted: but he was abroad, and came home ill, and was gone to bed, much out of order, unless the porter lied. I dined to-day at Sir Matthew Dudley's, with Mr. Addison, etc.

25. I was to-day to see the Duke of Ormond; and, coming out, met Lord Berkeley of Stratton, who told me that Mrs. Temple, the widow, died last Saturday, which, I suppose, is much to the outward grief and inward joy of the family. I dined to-day with Addison and Steele, and a sister of Mr. Addison, who is married to one Mons. Sartre, a Frenchman, prebendary of Westminster, who has a delicious house and garden; yet I thought it was a sort of monastic life in those cloisters, and I liked Laracor better. Addison's sister is a sort of a wit, very like him. I am not fond of her, etc.

26. I was to-day to see Mr. Congreve, who is almost blind with cataracts growing on his eyes; and his case is, that he must wait two or three

years, until the cataracts are riper, and till he is quite blind, and then he must have them couched; and, besides, he is never rid of the gout, yet he looks young and fresh, and is as cheerful as ever. He is younger by three years or more than I; and I am twenty years younger than he. He gave me a pain in the great toe, by mentioning the gout. I find such suspicions frequently, but they go off again. I had a second letter from Mr. Morgan, for which I thank you: I wish you were whipped, for forgetting to send him that answer I desired you in one of my former, that I could do nothing for him of what he desired, having no credit at all, etc. Go, be far enough, you negligent baggages. I have had also a letter from Parvisol, with an account how my livings are set; and that they are fallen, since last year, sixty pounds. A comfortable piece of news! He tells me plainly that he finds you have no mind to part with the horse, because you sent for him at the same time you sent him my letter; so that I know not what must be done. It is a sad thing that Stella must have her own horse, whether Parvisol will or no. So now to answer your letter that I had three or four days ago. I am not now in bed, but am come home by eight; and, it being warm, I write up. I never writ to the Bishop of Killala, which, I suppose, was the reason he had not my letter. I have not time, there is the short of it.—As fond as the Dean is of my letter, he has not written to me. I would only know whether Dean Bolton paid him the twenty pounds; and for the rest, he may kiss—And that you may ask him, because I am in pain about it, that Dean Bolton is such a whipster. 'Tis the most obliging thing in the world in Dean Sterne to be so kind to you. I believe he knows it will please me, and makes up, that way, his other usage. No, we have had none of your snow, but a little one morning; yet I think it was great snow for an hour or so, but no longer. I had heard of Will Crowe's death before, but not the foolish circumstance that hastened his end. No, I have taken care that Captain Pratt shall not suffer by Lord Anglesea's death. I will try some contrivance to get a copy of my picture from Jervas. I will make Sir Andrew Fountaine buy one as for himself, and I will pay him again, and take it, that is, provided I have money to spare when I leave this.— Poor John! is he gone? and Madam Parvisol has been in town! Humm. Why, Tighe and I, when he comes, shall not take any notice of each other; I would not do it much in this town, though we had not fallen out.—I was to-day at Mr. Sterne's lodging: he was not within; and Mr. Leigh is not come to town; but I will do Dingley's errand when I see him. What do I know whether china be dear or no? I once took a fancy of resolving to grow mad for it, but now it is off; I suppose I told you in some former letter. And so you only want some salad-dishes, and plates, and etc. Yes, yes, you shall. I suppose you have named as much as will cost five pounds.—Now to Stella's little postscript; and I am almost crazed that you vex yourself for not writing. Cannot you dictate to Dingley, and not strain your little, dear eyes? I am sure it is the grief of my soul to think you are out of order. Pray be quiet; and, if you will write, shut your eyes, and write just a line, and no more, thus, "How do you do, Mrs. Stella?" That was written with my eyes shut. Faith, I think it is better than when they are open: and then Dingley may stand by, and tell you when you go too high or too low.—My letters of business, with packets, if there be any more occasion for such, must be enclosed to Mr. Addison, at St. James's Coffee-house: but I hope to hear, as soon as I see Mr. Harley, that the main difficulties are over, and that the rest will be but form.—Take two or three nutgalls, take two or three—galls, stop your receipt in your—I have no need on't. Here is a clutter! Well, so much for your letter, which I will now put up in my letter-partition in my cabinet, as I always do every letter as soon as I answer it. Method is good in all things. Order governs the world. The Devil is the author of confusion. A general of an army, a minister of state; to descend lower, a gardener, a weaver, etc. That may make a fine observation, if you think it worth finishing; but I have not time. Is not this a terrible long piece for one evening? I dined to-day with Patty Rolt at my cousin Leach's, with a pox, in the City: he is a printer, and prints the *Postman*, oh hoo, and is my cousin, God knows how, and he married Mrs. Baby Aires of Leicester; and my cousin Thomson was with us: and my cousin Leach offers to bring me acquainted with the author of the *Postman*; and says he does not doubt but the gentleman will be glad of my acquaintance; and that he is a very ingenious man, and a great scholar, and has been beyond sea. But I was modest and said, may be the gentleman was shy, and not fond of new acquaintance; and so put it off: and I wish you could hear me repeating all I have said of this in its proper tone, just as I am writing it. It is all with the same cadence with "Oh hoo," or as when little girls say, "I have got an apple, miss, and I won't give you some." It is plaguy twelvepenny weather this last week, and has cost me ten shillings in coach and chair hire. If the fellow that has your money will pay it, let me beg you to buy Bank Stock with it, which is fallen near thirty per cent. and pays eight pounds per cent. and you have the principal when you please: it will certainly soon rise. I would to God

Lady Giffard would put in the four hundred pounds she owes you, and take the five per cent. common interest, and give you the remainder. I will speak to your mother about it when I see her. I am resolved to buy three hundred pounds of it for myself, and take up what I have in Ireland; and I have a contrivance for it, that I hope will do, by making a friend of mine buy it as for himself, and I will pay him when I can get in my money. I hope Stratford will do me that kindness. I'll ask him to-morrow or next day.

27. Mr. Rowe the poet desired me to dine with him to-day. I went to his office (he is under-secretary in Mr. Addison's place that he had in England), and there was Mr. Prior; and they both fell commending my "Shower" beyond anything that has been written of the kind: there never was such a "Shower" since Danae's, etc. You must tell me how it is liked among you. I dined with Rowe; Prior could not come: and after dinner we went to a blind tavern, where Congreve, Sir Richard Temple, Estcourt, and Charles Main, were over a bowl of bad punch. The knight sent for six flasks of his own wine for me, and we stayed till twelve. But now my head continues pretty well; I have left off my drinking, and only take a spoonful mixed with water, for fear of the gout, or some ugly distemper; and now, because it is late, I will, etc.

28. Garth and Addison and I dined to-day at a hedge tavern; then I went to Mr. Harley, but he was denied, or not at home: so I fear I shall not hear my business is done before this goes. Then I visited Lord Pembroke, who is just come to town; and we were very merry talking of old things; and I hit him with one pun. Then I went to see the Ladies Butler, and the son of a whore of a porter denied them: so I sent them a threatening message by another lady, for not excepting me always to the porter. I was weary of the Coffee-house, and Ford desired me to sit with him at next door; which I did, like a fool, chatting till twelve, and now am got into bed. I am afraid the new Ministry is at a terrible loss about money: the Whigs talk so, it would give one the spleen; and I am afraid of meeting Mr. Harley out of humour. They think he will never carry through this undertaking. God knows what will come of it. I should be terribly vexed to see things come round again: it will ruin the Church and clergy for ever; but I hope for better. I will send this on Tuesday, whether I hear any further news of my affair or not.

29. Mr. Addison and I dined to-day with Lord Mountjoy; which is all the adventures of this day.—I chatted a while to-night in the Coffee-house, this being a full night; and now am come home, to write some business.

30. I dined to-day at Mrs. Vanhomrigh's, and sent a letter to poor Mrs. Long, who writes to us, but is God knows where, and will not tell anybody the place of her residence. I came home early, and must go write.

31. The month ends with a fine day; and I have been walking, and visiting Lewis, and concerting where to see Mr. Harley. I have no news to send you. Aire, they say, is taken, though the Whitehall letters this morning say quite the contrary: 'tis good, if it be true. I dined with Mr. Addison and Dick Stewart, Lord Mountjoy's brother; a treat of Addison's. They were half-fuddled, but not I; for I mixed water with my wine, and left them together between nine and ten; and I must send this by the bellman, which vexes me, but I will put it off no longer. Pray God it does not miscarry. I seldom do so; but I can put off little MD no longer. Pray give the under note to Mrs. Brent.

I am a pretty gentleman; and you lose all your money at cards, sirrah Stella. I found you out; I did so.

I am staying before I can fold up this letter, till that ugly D is dry in the last line but one. Do not you see it? O Lord, I am loth to leave you, faith—but it must be so, till the next time. Pox take that D; I will blot it, to dry it.

LETTER VIII

LONDON, *Oct.* 31, 1710

So, now I have sent my seventh to your fourth, young women; and now I will tell you what I would not in my last, that this morning, sitting in my bed, I had a fit of giddiness: the room turned round for about a minute, and then it went off, leaving me sickish, but not very: and so I passed the day as I told you; but I would not end a letter with telling you this, because it might vex you: and I hope in God I shall have no more of it. I saw Dr. Cockburn to-day, and he promises to send me the pills that did me good last year; and likewise has promised me an oil for my ear, that he has been making for that ailment for somebody else.

Nov. 1. I wish MD a merry new year. You know this is the first day of it with us. I had no giddiness to-day; but I drank brandy, and have bought a pint for two shillings. I sat up the night before my giddiness pretty late, and writ very much; so I will impute it to that. But I never eat fruit, nor drink ale; but drink better wine than you do, as I did to-day with Mr. Addison at Lord Mountjoy's: then went at five to see Mr. Harley, who could not see me for much company; but sent me his excuse, and desired I would dine with him on Friday; and then I expect some answer to this business, which must either be soon done, or begun again; and then the Duke of Ormond and his people will interfere for their honour, and do nothing. I came home at six, and spent my time in my chamber, without going to the Coffee-house, which I grow weary of; and I studied at leisure, writ not above forty lines, some inventions of my own, and some hints, and read not at all, and this because I would take care of Presto, for fear little MD should be angry.

2. I took my four pills last night, and they lay an hour in my throat, and so they will do to-night. I suppose I could swallow four affronts as easily. I dined with Dr. Cockburn to-day, and came home at seven; but Mr. Ford has been with me till just now, and it is near eleven. I have had no giddiness to-day. Mr. Dopping I have seen; and he tells me coldly, my "Shower" is liked well enough; there's your Irish judgment! I writ this post to the Bishop of Clogher. It is now just a fortnight since I heard from you. I must have you write once a fortnight, and then I will allow for wind and weather. How goes ombre? Does Mrs. Walls win

60   JONATHAN SWIFT

constantly, as she used to do? And Mrs. Stoyte; I have not thought of her this long time: how does she? I find we have a cargo of Irish coming for London: I am sorry for it; but I never go near them. And Tighe is landed; but Mrs. Wesley, they say, is going home to her husband, like a fool. Well, little monkeys mine, I must go write; and so good-night.

3. I ought to read these letters I write, after I have done; for, looking over thus much, I found two or three literal mistakes, which should not be when the hand is so bad. But I hope it does not puzzle little Dingley to read, for I think I mend: but methinks, when I write plain, I do not know how, but we are not alone, all the world can see us. A bad scrawl is so snug, it looks like a PMD. We have scurvy *Tatlers* of late: so pray do not suspect me. I have one or two hints I design to send him, and never any more: he does not deserve it. He is governed by his wife most abominably, as bad as—. I never saw her since I came; nor has he ever made me an invitation: either he dares not, or is such a thoughtless Tisdall fellow, that he never minds it. So what care I for his wit? for he is the worst company in the world, till he has a bottle of wine in his head. I cannot write straighter in bed, so you must be content.—At night in bed. Stay, let me see where's this letter to MD among these papers? Oh! here. Well, I will go on now; but I am very busy (smoke the new pen.) I dined with Mr. Harley to-day, and am invited there again on Sunday. I have now leave to write to the Primate and Archbishop of Dublin, that the Queen has granted the First-Fruits; but they are to take no notice of it, till a letter is sent them by the Queen's orders from Lord Dartmouth, Secretary of State, to signify it. The bishops are to be made a corporation, to dispose of the revenue, etc.; and I shall write to the Archbishop of Dublin to-morrow (I have had no giddiness to-day). I know not whether they will have any occasion for me longer to be here; nor can I judge till I see what letter the Queen sends to the bishops, and what they will do upon it. If despatch be used, it may be done in six weeks; but I cannot judge. They sent me to-day a new Commission, signed by the Primate and Archbishop of Dublin, and promise me letters to the two archbishops here; but mine a—for it all. The thing is done, and has been so these ten days; though I had only leave to tell it to-day. I had this day likewise a letter from the Bishop of Clogher, who complains of my not writing; and, what vexes me, says he knows you have long letters from me every week. Why do you tell him so? 'Tis not right, faith: but I won't be angry with MD at

distance. I writ to him last post, before I had his; and will write again soon, since I see he expects it, and that Lord and Lady Mountjoy put him off upon me, to give themselves ease. Lastly, I had this day a letter from a certain naughty rogue called MD, and it was N. 5; which I shall not answer to-night, I thank you. No, faith, I have other fish to fry; but to-morrow or next day will be time enough. I have put MD's commissions in a memorandum paper. I think I have done all before, and remember nothing but this to-day about glasses and spectacles and spectacle cases. I have no commission from Stella, but the chocolate and handkerchiefs; and those are bought, and I expect they will be soon sent. I have been with, and sent to, Mr. Sterne, two or three times to know; but he was not within. Odds my life, what am I doing? I must go write and do business.

4. I dined to-day at Kensington, with Addison, Steele, etc., came home, and writ a short letter to the Archbishop of Dublin, to let him know the Queen has granted the thing, etc. I writ in the Coffee-house, for I stayed at Kensington till nine, and am plaguy weary; for Colonel Proud was very ill company, and I will never be of a party with him again; and I drank punch, and that and ill company has made me hot.

5. I was with Mr. Harley from dinner to seven this night, and went to the Coffee-house, where Dr. Davenant would fain have had me gone and drink a bottle of wine at his house hard by, with Dr. Chamberlen, but the puppy used so many words, that I was afraid of his company; and though we promised to come at eight, I sent a messenger to him, that Chamberlen was going to a patient, and therefore we would put it off till another time: so he, and the Comptroller, and I, were prevailed on by Sir Matthew Dudley to go to his house, where I stayed till twelve, and left them. Davenant has been teasing me to look over some of his writings that he is going to publish; but the rogue is so fond of his own productions, that I hear he will not part with a syllable; and he has lately put out a foolish pamphlet, called *The Third Part of Tom Double*; to make his court to the Tories, whom he had left.

6. I was to-day gambling in the City to see Patty Rolt, who is going to Kingston, where she lodges; but, to say the truth, I had a mind for a walk to exercise myself, and happened to be disengaged: for dinners are ten times more plentiful with me here than ever, or than in Dublin.

I won't answer your letter yet, because I am busy. I hope to send this before I have another from MD: it would be a sad thing to answer two letters together, as MD does from Presto. But when the two sides are full, away the letter shall go, that is certain, like it or not like it; and that will be about three days hence, for the answering-night will be a long one.

7. I dined to-day at Sir Richard Temple's, with Congreve, Vanbrugh, Lieutenant-General Farrington, etc. Vanbrugh, I believe I told you, had a long quarrel with me about those verses on his house; but we were very civil and cold. Lady Marlborough used to tease him with them, which had made him angry, though he be a good-natured fellow. It was a Thanksgiving-day, and I was at Court, where the Queen passed us by with all Tories about her; not one Whig: Buckingham, Rochester, Leeds, Shrewsbury, Berkeley of Stratton, Lord Keeper Harcourt, Mr. Harley, Lord Pembroke, etc.; and I have seen her without one Tory. The Queen made me a curtsey, and said, in a sort of familiar way to Presto, "How does MD?" I considered she was a Queen, and so excused her. I do not miss the Whigs at Court; but have as many acquaintance there as formerly.

8. Here's ado and a clutter! I must now answer MD's fifth; but first you must know I dined at the Portugal Envoy's to-day, with Addison, Vanbrugh, Admiral Wager, Sir Richard Temple, Methuen, etc. I was weary of their company, and stole away at five, and came home like a good boy, and studied till ten, and had a fire, O ho! and now am in bed. I have no fireplace in my bed-chamber; but 'tis very warm weather when one's in bed. Your fine cap, Madam Dingley, is too little, and too hot: I will have that fur taken off; I wish it were far enough; and my old velvet cap is good for nothing. Is it velvet under the fur? I was feeling, but cannot find: if it be, 'twill do without it else I will face it; but then I must buy new velvet: but may be I may beg a piece. What shall I do? Well, now to rogue MD's letter. God be thanked for Stella's eyes mending; and God send it holds; but faith you writ too much at a time: better write less, or write it at ten times. Yes, faith, a long letter in a morning from a dear friend is a dear thing. I smoke a compliment, little mischievous girls, I do so. But who are those *Wiggs* that think I am turned Tory? Do you mean Whigs? Which *Wiggs* and *wat* do you mean? I know nothing of Raymond, and only had one letter from him

a little after I came here. (Pray remember Morgan.) Raymond is indeed like to have much influence over me in London, and to share much of my conversation. I shall, no doubt, introduce him to Harley, and Lord Keeper, and the Secretary of State. The *Tatler* upon Ithuriel's spear is not mine, madam. What a puzzle there is betwixt you and your judgment! In general you may be sometimes sure of things, as that about *style*, because it is what I have frequently spoken of; but guessing is mine a—, and I defy mankind, if I please. Why, I writ a pamphlet when I was last in London, that you and a thousand have seen, and never guessed it to be mine. Could you have guessed the "Shower in Town" to be mine? How chance you did not see that before your last letter went? but I suppose you in Ireland did not think it worth mentioning. Nor am I suspected for the lampoon; only Harley said he smoked me; (have I told you so before?) and some others knew it. 'Tis called "The Rod of Sid Hamet." And I have written several other things that I hear commended, and nobody suspects me for them; nor you shall not know till I see you again. What do you mean, "That boards near me, that I dine with now and then?" I know no such person: I do not dine with boarders. What the pox! You know whom I have dined with every day since I left you, better than I do. What do you mean, sirrah? Slids, my ailment has been over these two months almost. Impudence, if you vex me, I will give ten shillings a week for my lodging; for I am almost st—k out of this with the sink, and it helps me to verses in my "Shower." Well, Madam Dingley, what say you to the world to come? What ballad? Why go look, it was not good for much: have patience till I come back: patience is a gay thing as, etc. I hear nothing of Lord Mountjoy's coming for Ireland. When is Stella's birthday? in March? Lord bless me, my turn at Christ Church; it is so natural to hear you write about that, I believe you have done it a hundred times; it is as fresh in my mind, the verger coming to you; and why to you? Would he have you preach for me? O, pox on your spelling of Latin, *Johnsonibus atque*, that is the way. How did the Dean get that name by the end? 'Twas you betrayed me: not I, faith; I'll not break his head. Your mother is still in the country, I suppose; for she promised to see me when she came to town. I writ to her four days ago, to desire her to break it to Lady Giffard, to put some money for you in the Bank, which was then fallen thirty per cent. Would to God mine had been here, I should have gained one hundred pounds, and got as good interest as in Ireland, and much securer. I would fain have borrowed three hundred pounds; but money is so scarce here, there is

no borrowing, by this fall of stocks. 'Tis rising now, and I knew it would: it fell from one hundred and twenty-nine to ninety-six. I have not heard since from your mother. Do you think I would be so unkind not to see her, that you desire me in a style so melancholy? Mrs. Raymond, you say, is with child: I am sorry for it; and so is, I believe, her husband. Mr. Harley speaks all the kind things to me in the world; and, I believe, would serve me, if I were to stay here; but I reckon in time the Duke of Ormond may give me some addition to Laracor. Why should the Whigs think I came to England to leave them? Sure my journey was no secret. I protest sincerely, I did all I could to hinder it, as the Dean can tell you, although now I do not repent it. But who the Devil cares what they think? Am I under obligations in the least to any of them all? Rot 'em, for ungrateful dogs; I will make them repent their usage before I leave this place. They say here the same thing of my leaving the Whigs; but they own they cannot blame me, considering the treatment I have had. I will take care of your spectacles, as I told you before, and of the Bishop of Killala's; but I will not write to him, I have not time. What do you mean by my fourth, Madam Dinglibus? Does not Stella say you have had my fifth, Goody Blunder? You frighted me till I looked back. Well, this is enough for one night. Pray give my humble service to Mrs. Stoyte and her sister, Kate is it, or Sarah? I have forgot her name, faith. I think I will even (and to Mrs. Walls and the Archdeacon) send this to-morrow: no, faith, that will be in ten days from the last. I will keep it till Saturday, though I write no more. But what if a letter from MD should come in the meantime? Why then I would only say, "Madam, I have received your sixth letter; your most humble servant to command, Presto"; and so conclude. Well, now I will write and think a little, and so to bed, and dream of MD.

9. I have my mouth full of water, and was going to spit it out, because I reasoned with myself, how could I write when my mouth was full? Han't you done things like that, reasoned wrong at first thinking? Well, I was to see Mr. Lewis this morning, and am to dine a few days hence, as he tells me, with Mr. Secretary St. John; and I must contrive to see Harley soon again, to hasten this business from the Queen. I dined to-day at Lord Mountrath's, with Lord Mountjoy, etc.; but the wine was not good, so I came away, stayed at the Coffee-house till seven, then came home to my fire, the maidenhead of my second half-bushel, and am now in bed at eleven, as usual. 'Tis mighty warm; yet I fear I should

catch cold this wet weather, if I sat an evening in my room after coming from warm places: and I must make much of myself, because MD is not here to take care of Presto; and I am full of business, writing, etc., and do not care for the Coffee-house; and so this serves for all together, not to tell it you over and over, as silly people do; but Presto is a wiser man, faith, than so, let me tell you, gentlewomen. See, I am got to the third side; but, faith, I will not do that often; but I must say something early to-day, till the letter is done, and on Saturday it shall go; so I must leave something till to-morrow, till to-morrow and next day.

10. O Lord, I would this letter was with you with all my heart! If it should miscarry, what a deal would be lost! I forgot to leave a gap in the last line but one for the seal, like a puppy; but I should have allowed for night, good-night; but when I am taking leave, I cannot leave a bit, faith; but I fancy the seal will not come there. I dined to-day at Lady Lucy's, where they ran down my "Shower"; and said, "Sid Hamet" was the silliest poem they ever read; and told Prior so, whom they thought to be author of it. Don't you wonder I never dined there before? But I am too busy, and they live too far off; and, besides, I do not like women so much as I did. (MD, you must know, are not women.) I supped to-night at Addison's, with Garth, Steele, and Mr. Dopping; and am come home late. Lewis has sent to me to desire I will dine with some company I shall like. I suppose it is Mr. Secretary St. John's appointment. I had a letter just now from Raymond, who is at Bristol, and says he will be at London in a fortnight, and leave his wife behind him; and desires any lodging in the house where I am: but that must not be. I shall not know what to do with him in town: to be sure, I will not present him to any acquaintance of mine; and he will live a delicate life, a parson and a perfect stranger! Paaast twelvvve o'clock, and so good-night, etc. Oh! but I forgot, Jemmy Leigh is come to town; says he has brought Dingley's things, and will send them with the first convenience. My parcel, I hear, is not sent yet. He thinks of going for Ireland in a month, etc. I cannot write to-morrow, because—what, because of the Archbishop; because I will seal my letter early; because I am engaged from noon till night; because of many kind of things; and yet I will write one or two words to-morrow morning, to keep up my journal constant, and at night I will begin my ninth.

11. Morning by candlelight. You must know that I am in my nightgown every morning between six and seven, and Patrick is forced to ply me

fifty times before I can get on my nightgown; and so now I will take my leave of my own dear MD for this letter, and begin my next when I come home at night. God Almighty bless and protect dearest MD. Farewell, etc.

This letter's as long as a sermon, faith.

Letter IX

London, *Nov.* 11, 1710

I dined to-day, by invitation, with the Secretary of State, Mr. St. John. Mr. Harley came in to us before dinner, and made me his excuses for not dining with us, because he was to receive people who came to propose advancing money to the Government: there dined with us only Mr. Lewis, and Dr. Freind (that writ "Lord Peterborow's Actions in Spain"). I stayed with them till just now between ten and eleven, and was forced again to give my eighth to the bellman, which I did with my own hands, rather than keep it till next post. The Secretary used me with all the kindness in the world. Prior came in after dinner; and, upon an occasion, he (the Secretary) said, "The best thing I ever read is not yours, but Dr. Swift's on Vanbrugh"; which I do not reckon so very good neither. But Prior was damped, until I stuffed him with two or three compliments. I am thinking what a veneration we used to have for Sir William Temple, because he might have been Secretary of State at fifty; and here is a young fellow, hardly thirty, in that employment. His father is a man of pleasure, that walks the Mall, and frequents St. James's Coffee-house, and the chocolate-houses; and the young son is principal Secretary of State. Is there not something very odd in that? He told me, among other things, that Mr. Harley complained he could keep nothing from me, I had the way so much of getting into him. I knew that was a refinement; and so I told him, and it was so: indeed, it is hard to see these great men use me like one who was their betters, and the puppies with you in Ireland hardly regarding me: but there are some reasons for all this, which I will tell you when we meet. At coming home, I saw a letter from your mother, in answer to one I sent her two days ago. It seems she is in town; but cannot come out in a morning, just as you said; and God knows when I shall be at leisure in an afternoon: for if I should send her a penny-post letter, and afterwards not be able to meet her, it would vex me; and, besides, the days are short, and why she cannot come early in a morning, before she is wanted, I cannot imagine. I will desire her to let Lady Giffard know that she hears I am in town; and that she would go to see me, to inquire after you. I wonder she will confine herself so much to that old beast's humour. You know I cannot in honour see Lady Giffard, and consequently not go into her house. This I think is enough for the first time.

12. And how could you write with such thin paper? (I forgot to say this in my former.) Cannot you get thicker? Why, that's a common caution that writing-masters give their scholars; you must have heard it a hundred times. 'Tis this:

> *"If paper be thin,*
> *Ink will slip in;*
> *But, if it be thick,*
> *You may write with a stick."*

I had a letter to-day from poor Mrs. Long, giving me an account of her present life, obscure in a remote country town, and how easy she is under it. Poor creature! 'tis just such an alteration in life, as if Presto should be banished from MD, and condemned to converse with Mrs. Raymond. I dined to-day with Ford, Sir Richard Levinge, etc., at a place where they board, hard by. I was lazy, and not very well, sitting so long with company yesterday. I have been very busy writing this evening at home, and had a fire: I am spending my second half-bushel of coals; and now am in bed, and 'tis late.

13. I dined to-day in the City, and then went to christen Will Frankland's child; and Lady Falconbridge was one of the godmothers: this is a daughter of Oliver Cromwell, and extremely like him by his pictures that I have seen. I stayed till almost eleven, and am now come home and gone to bed. My business in the City was, to thank Stratford for a kindness he has done me, which now I will tell you. I found Bank Stock was fallen thirty-four in the hundred, and was mighty desirous to buy it; but I was a little too late for the cheapest time, being hindered by business here; for I was so wise to guess to a day when it would fall. My project was this: I had three hundred pounds in Ireland; and so I writ to Mr. Stratford in the City, to desire he would buy me three hundred pounds in Bank Stock, and that he should keep the papers, and that I would be bound to pay him for them; and, if it should rise or fall, I would take my chance, and pay him interest in the meantime. I showed my letter to one or two people who understand those things; and they said money was so hard to be got here, that no man would do it for me. However, Stratford, who is the most generous man alive, has done it: but it costs one hundred pounds and a half, that is, ten shillings; so that three hundred pounds cost me three hundred pounds

and thirty shillings. This was done about a week ago, and I can have five pounds for my bargain already. Before it fell, it was one hundred and thirty pounds; and we are sure it will be the same again. I told you I writ to your mother, to desire that Lady Giffard would do the same with what she owes you; but she tells your mother she has no money. I would to God all you had in the world was there. Whenever you lend money, take this rule, to have two people bound, who have both visible fortunes; for they will hardly die together; and, when one dies, you fall upon the other, and make him add another security: and if Rathburn (now I have his name) pays you in your money, let me know, and I will direct Parvisol accordingly: however, he shall wait on you and know. So, ladies, enough of business for one night. Paaaaast twelvvve o'clock. I must only add, that, after a long fit of rainy weather, it has been fair two or three days, and is this day grown cold and frosty; so that you must give poor little Presto leave to have a fire in his chamber morning and evening too; and he will do as much for you.

14. What, has your Chancellor lost his senses, like Will Crowe? I forgot to tell Dingley that I was yesterday at Ludgate, bespeaking the spectacles at the great shop there, and shall have them in a day or two. This has been an insipid day. I dined with Mrs. Vanhomrigh, and came gravely home, after just visiting the Coffee-house. Sir Richard Cox, they say, is sure of going over Lord Chancellor, who is as arrant a puppy as ever ate bread: but the Duke of Ormond has a natural affection to puppies; which is a thousand pities, being none himself. I have been amusing myself at home till now, and in bed bid you good-night.

15. I have been visiting this morning, but nobody was at home, Secretary St. John, Sir Thomas Hanmer, Sir Chancellor Cox-comb, etc. I attended the Duke of Ormond with about fifty other Irish gentlemen at Skinners' Hall, where the Londonderry Society laid out three hundred pounds to treat us and his Grace with a dinner. Three great tables with the dessert laid in mighty figure. Sir Richard Levinge and I got discreetly to the head of the second table, to avoid the crowd at the first: but it was so cold, and so confounded a noise with the trumpets and hautboys, that I grew weary, and stole away before the second course came on; so I can give you no account of it, which is a thousand pities. I called at Ludgate for Dingley's glasses, and shall have them in a day or two; and I doubt it will cost me thirty shillings for a microscope, but not without Stella's

permission; for I remember she is a virtuoso. Shall I buy it or no? 'Tis not the great bulky ones, nor the common little ones, to impale a louse (saving your presence) upon a needle's point; but of a more exact sort, and clearer to the sight, with all its equipage in a little trunk that you may carry in your pocket. Tell me, sirrah, shall I buy it or not for you? I came home straight, etc.

16. I dined to-day in the city with Mr. Manley, who invited Mr. Addison and me, and some other friends, to his lodging, and entertained us very handsomely. I returned with Mr. Addison, and loitered till nine in the Coffee-house, where I am hardly known, by going so seldom. I am here soliciting for Trounce; you know him: he was gunner in the former yacht, and would fain be so in the present one if you remember him, a good, lusty, fresh-coloured fellow. Shall I stay till I get another letter from MD before I close up this? Mr. Addison and I meet a little seldomer than formerly, although we are still at bottom as good friends as ever, but differ a little about party.

17. To-day I went to Lewis at the Secretary's office; where I saw and spoke to Mr. Harley, who promised, in a few days, to finish the rest of my business. I reproached him for putting me on the necessity of minding him of it, and rallied him, etc., which he took very well. I dined to-day with one Mr. Gore, elder brother to a young merchant of my acquaintance; and Stratford and my other friend merchants dined with us, where I stayed late, drinking claret and burgundy; and am just got to bed, and will say no more, but that it now begins to be time to have a letter from my own little MD; for the last I had above a fortnight ago, and the date was old too.

18. To-day I dined with Lewis and Prior at an eating-house, but with Lewis's wine. Lewis went away, and Prior and I sat on, where we complimented one another for an hour or two upon our mutual wit and poetry. Coming home at seven, a gentleman unknown stopped me in the Pall Mall, and asked my advice; said he had been to see the Queen (who was just come to town), and the people in waiting would not let him see her; that he had two hundred thousand men ready to serve her in the war; that he knew the Queen perfectly well, and had an apartment at Court, and if she heard he was there, she would send for him immediately; that she owed him two hundred thousand

pounds, etc., and he desired my opinion, whether he should go try again whether he could see her; or because, perhaps, she was weary after her journey, whether he had not better stay till to-morrow. I had a mind to get rid of my companion, and begged him of all love to go and wait on her immediately; for that, to my knowledge, the Queen would admit him; that this was an affair of great importance, and required despatch: and I instructed him to let me know the success of his business, and come to the Smyrna Coffee-house, where I would wait for him till midnight; and so ended this adventure. I would have fain given the man half a crown; but was afraid to offer it him, lest he should be offended; for, beside his money, he said he had a thousand pounds a year. I came home not early; and so, madams both, good-night, etc.

19. I dined to-day with poor Lord Mountjoy, who is ill of the gout; and this evening I christened our coffee-man Elliot's child, where the rogue had a most noble supper, and Steele and I sat among some scurvy company over a bowl of punch; so that I am come home late, young women, and can't stay to write to little rogues.

20. I loitered at home, and dined with Sir Andrew Fountaine at his lodging, and then came home: a silly day.

21. I was visiting all this morning, and then went to the Secretary's office, and found Mr. Harley, with whom I dined; and Secretary St. John, etc., and Harley promised in a very few days to finish what remains of my business. Prior was of the company, and we all dine at the Secretary's to-morrow. I saw Stella's mother this morning: she came early, and we talked an hour. I wish you would propose to Lady Giffard to take the three hundred pounds out of her hands, and give her common interest for life, and security that you will pay her: the Bishop of Clogher, or any friend, would be security for you, if you gave them counter-security; and it may be argued that it will pass better to be in your hands than hers, in case of mortality, etc. Your mother says, if you write, she will second it; and you may write to your mother, and then it will come from her. She tells me Lady Giffard has a mind to see me, by her discourse; but I told her what to say, with a vengeance. She told Lady Giffard she was going to see me: she looks extremely well. I am writing in my bed like a tiger; and so good-night, etc.

22. I dined with Secretary St. John; and Lord Dartmouth, who is t'other Secretary, dined with us, and Lord Orrery and Prior, etc. Harley called, but could not dine with us, and would have had me away while I was at dinner; but I did not like the company he was to have. We stayed till eight, and I called at the Coffee-house, and looked where the letters lie; but no letter directed for Mr. Presto: at last I saw a letter to Mr. Addison, and it looked like a rogue's hand; so I made the fellow give it me, and opened it before him, and saw three letters all for myself: so, truly, I put them in my pocket, and came home to my lodging. Well, and so you shall hear: well, and so I found one of them in Dingley's hand, and t'other in Stella's, and the third in Domville's. Well, so you shall hear; so, said I to myself, What now, two letters from MD together? But I thought there was something in the wind; so I opened one, and I opened t'other; and so you shall hear, one was from Walls. Well, but t'other was from our own dear MD; yes it was. O faith, have you received my seventh, young women, already? Then I must send this to-morrow, else there will be old doings at our house, faith.—Well, I won't answer your letter in this: no, faith, catch me at that, and I never saw the like. Well; but as to Walls, tell him (with service to him and wife, etc.) that I have no imagination of Mr. Pratt's losing his place: and while Pratt continues, Clements is in no danger; and I have already engaged Lord Hyde he speaks of, for Pratt and twenty others; but, if such a thing should happen, I will do what I can. I have above ten businesses of other people's now on my hands, and, I believe, shall miscarry in half. It is your sixth I now have received. I writ last post to the Bishop of Clogher again. Shall I send this to-morrow? Well, I will, to oblige MD. Which would you rather, a short letter every week, or a long one every fortnight? A long one; well, it shall be done, and so good-night. Well, but is this a long one? No, I warrant you: too long for naughty girls.

23. I only ask, have you got both the ten pounds, or only the first; I hope you mean both. Pray be good housewives; and I beg you to walk when you can, for health. Have you the horse in town? and do you ever ride him? how often? Confess. Ahhh, sirrah, have I caught you? Can you contrive to let Mrs. Fenton know, that the request she has made me in her letter I will use what credit I have to bring about, although I hear it is very difficult, and I doubt I shall not succeed? Cox is not to be your Chancellor: all joined against him. I have been supping with Lord Peterborow at his house, with Prior, Lewis, and Dr. Freind. 'Tis

the ramblingest lying rogue on earth. Dr. Raymond is come to town: 'tis late, and so I bid you good-night.

24. I tell you, pretty management! Ned Southwell told me the other day he had a letter from the bishops of Ireland, with an address to the Duke of Ormond, to intercede with the Queen to take off the First-Fruits. I dined with him to-day, and saw it, with another letter to him from the Bishop of Kildare, to call upon me for the papers, etc.; and I had last post one from the Archbishop of Dublin, telling me the reason of this proceeding; that, upon hearing the Duke of Ormond was declared Lord Lieutenant, they met; and the bishops were for this project, and talked coldly of my being solicitor, as one that was favoured by t'other party, etc., but desired that I would still solicit. Now the wisdom of this is admirable; for I had given the Archbishop an account of my reception from Mr. Harley, and how he had spoken to the Queen, and promised it should be done; but Mr. Harley ordered me to tell no person alive. Some time after, he gave me leave to let the Primate and Archbishop know that the Queen had remitted the First-Fruits; and that in a short time they should have an account of it in form from Lord Dartmouth, Secretary of State. So while their letter was on the road to the Duke of Ormond and Southwell, mine was going to them with an account of the thing being done. I writ a very warm answer to the Archbishop immediately; and showed my resentments, as I ought, against the bishops; only, in good manners, excepting himself. I wonder what they will say when they hear the thing is done. I was yesterday forced to tell Southwell so, that the Queen had done it, etc.; for he said, my Lord Duke would think of it some months hence, when he was going for Ireland; and he had it three years in doing formerly, without any success. I give you free leave to say, on occasion, that it is done; and that Mr. Harley prevailed on the Queen to do it, etc., as you please. As I hope to live, I despise the credit of it, out of an excess of pride; and desire you will not give me the least merit when you talk of it; but I would vex the bishops, and have it spread that Mr. Harley had done it: pray do so. Your mother sent me last night a parcel of wax candles, and a bandbox full of small plumcakes. I thought it had been something for you; and, without opening them, sent answer by the maid that brought them, that I would take care to send the things, etc.; but I will write her thanks. Is this a long letter, sirrahs? Now, are you satisfied? I have had no fit since the first: I drink brandy every morning, and take pills every

night. Never fear, I an't vexed at this puppy business of the bishops, although I was a little at first. I will tell you my reward: Mr. Harley will think he has done me a favour; the Duke of Ormond, perhaps, that I have put a neglect on him; and the bishops in Ireland, that I have done nothing at all. So goes the world. But I have got above all this, and, perhaps, I have better reason for it than they know: and so you shall hear no more of First-Fruits, dukes, Harleys, archbishops, and Southwells.

I have slipped off Raymond upon some of his countrymen, to show him the town, etc., and I lend him Patrick. He desires to sit with me in the evenings; upon which I have given Patrick positive orders that I am not within at evenings.

I will tell you something that's plaguy silly: I had forgot to say on the 23d in my last, where I dined; and because I had done it constantly, I thought it was a great omission, and was going to interline it; but at last the silliness of it made me cry, Pshah, and I let it alone. I was to-day to see the Parliament meet; but only saw a great crowd; and Ford and I went to see the tombs at Westminster, and sauntered so long I was forced to go to an eating-house for my dinner. Bromley is chosen Speaker, *nemine contradicente*: Do you understand those two words? And Pompey, Colonel Hill's black, designs to stand Speaker for the footmen. I am engaged to use my interest for him, and have spoken to Patrick to get him some votes. We are now all impatient for the Queen's speech, what she will say about removing the Ministry, etc. I have got a cold, and I don't know how; but got it I have, and am hoarse: I don't know whether it will grow better or worse. What's that to you? I won't answer your letter to-night. I'll keep you a little longer in suspense: I can't send it. Your mother's cakes are very good, and one of them serves me for a breakfast, and so I'll go sleep like a good boy.

26. I have got a cruel cold, and stayed within all this day in my nightgown, and dined on sixpennyworth of victuals, and read and writ, and was denied to everybody. Dr. Raymond called often, and I was denied; and at last, when I was weary, I let him come up, and asked him, without consequence, how Patrick denied me, and whether he had the art of it? So by this means he shall be used to have me denied to him; otherwise he would be a plaguy trouble and hindrance to me: he has sat with me two hours, and drank a pint of ale cost me fivepence, and smoked his pipe, and it is now past eleven that he is just gone. Well, my eighth is with you now, young women; and your seventh to me is somewhere in a post-boy's bag; and so go to your gang of deans, and Stoytes, and Walls, and lose your money; go, sauceboxes: and so good-night, and be happy, dear rogues. Oh, but your box was sent to Dr. Hawkshaw by Sterne, and you will have it with Hawkshaw, and spectacles, etc., etc.

27. To-day Mr. Harley met me in the Court of Requests, and whispered me to dine with him. At dinner I told him what those bishops had

done, and the difficulty I was under. He bid me never trouble myself; he would tell the Duke of Ormond the business was done, and that he need not concern himself about it. So now I am easy, and they may hang themselves for a parcel of insolent, ungrateful rascals. I suppose I told you in my last, how they sent an address to the Duke of Ormond, and a letter to Southwell, to call on me for the papers, after the thing was over; but they had not received my letter, though the Archbishop might, by what I writ to him, have expected it would be done. Well, there is an end of that; and in a little time the Queen will send them notice, etc. And so the methods will be settled; and then I shall think of returning, although the baseness of those bishops makes me love Ireland less than I did.

28. Lord Halifax sent to invite me to dinner; where I stayed till six, and crossed him in all his Whig talk, and made him often come over to me. I know he makes court to the new men, although he affects to talk like a Whig. I had a letter to-day from the Bishop of Clogher; but I writ to him lately, that I would obey his commands to the Duke of Ormond. He says I bid him read the London "Shaver," and that you both swore it was "Shaver," and not "Shower." You all lie, and you are puppies, and can't read Presto's hand. The Bishop is out entirely in his conjectures of my share in the *Tatlers*.—I have other things to mind, and of much greater importance; else I have little to do to be acquainted with a new Ministry, who consider me a little more than Irish bishops do.

29. Now for your saucy, good dear letter: let me see, what does it say? come then. I dined to-day with Ford, and went home early; he debauched me to his chamber again with a bottle of wine till twelve: so good-night. I cannot write an answer now, you rogues.

30. To-day I have been visiting, which I had long neglected; and I dined with Mrs. Barton alone; and sauntered at the Coffee-house till past eight, and have been busy till eleven, and now I'll answer your letter, saucebox. Well, let me see now again. My wax candle's almost out, but however I'll begin. Well then, do not be so tedious, Mr. Presto; what can you say to MD's letter? Make haste, have done with your preambles— Why, I say I am glad you are so often abroad; your mother thinks it is want of exercise hurts you, and so do I. (She called here to-night, but I was not within, that's by the bye.) Sure you do not deceive me, Stella, when you say you are in better health than you were these three weeks;

for Dr. Raymond told me yesterday, that Smyth of the Blind Quay had been telling Mr. Leigh that he left you extremely ill; and in short, spoke so, that he almost put poor Leigh into tears, and would have made me run distracted; though your letter is dated the 11th instant, and I saw Smyth in the city above a fortnight ago, as I passed by in a coach. Pray, pray, don't write, Stella, until you are mighty, mighty, mighty, mighty well in your eyes, and are sure it won't do you the least hurt. Or come, I'll tell you what; you, Mistress Stella, shall write your share at five or six sittings, one sitting a day; and then comes Dingley all together, and then Stella a little crumb towards the end, to let us see she remembers Presto; and then conclude with something handsome and genteel, as your most humblecumdumble, or, etc. O Lord! does Patrick write word of my not coming till spring? Insolent man! he know my secrets? No; as my Lord Mayor said, No; if I thought my shirt knew, etc. Faith, I will come as soon as it is any way proper for me to come; but, to say the truth, I am at present a little involved with the present Ministry in some certain things (which I tell you as a secret); and soon as ever I can clear my hands, I will stay no longer; for I hope the First-Fruit business will be soon over in all its forms. But, to say the truth, the present Ministry have a difficult task, and want me, etc. Perhaps they may be just as grateful as others: but, according to the best judgment I have, they are pursuing the true interest of the public; and therefore I am glad to contribute what is in my power. For God's sake, not a word of this to any alive.—Your Chancellor? Why, madam, I can tell you he has been dead this fortnight. Faith, I could hardly forbear our little language about a nasty dead Chancellor, as you may see by the blot. Ploughing? A pox plough them; they'll plough me to nothing. But have you got your money, both the ten pounds? How durst he pay you the second so soon? Pray be good huswifes. Ay, well, and Joe, why, I had a letter lately from Joe, desiring I would take some care of their poor town, who, he says, will lose their liberties. To which I desired Dr. Raymond would return answer, that the town had behaved themselves so ill to me, so little regarded the advice I gave them, and disagreed so much among themselves, that I was resolved never to have more to do with them; but that whatever personal kindness I could do to Joe, should be done. Pray, when you happen to see Joe, tell him this, lest Raymond should have blundered or forgotten—Poor Mrs. Wesley!—Why these poligyes for being abroad? Why should you be at home at all, until Stella is quite well?—So, here is Mistress Stella again, with her two eggs, etc.

My "Shower" admired with you; why, the Bishop of Clogher says, he has seen something of mine of the same sort, better than the "Shower." I suppose he means "The Morning"; but it is not half so good. I want your judgment of things, and not your country's. How does MD like it? and do they taste it *all*? etc. I am glad Dean Bolton has paid the twenty pounds. Why should not I chide the Bishop of Clogher for writing to the Archbishop of Cashel, without sending the letter first to me? It does not signify a—; for he has no credit at Court. Stuff—they are all puppies. I will break your head in good earnest, young woman, for your nasty jest about Mrs. Barton. Unlucky sluttikin, what a word is there! Faith, I was thinking yesterday, when I was with her, whether she could break them or no, and it quite spoilt my imagination. "Mrs. Walls, does Stella win as she pretends?" "No indeed, Doctor; she loses always, and will play so *ventersomely*, how can she win?" See here now; an't you an impudent lying slut? Do, open Domville's letter; what does it signify, if you have a mind? Yes, faith, you write smartly with your eyes shut; all was well but the *n*. See how I can do it; *Madam Stella, your humble servant*. O, but one may look whether one goes crooked or no, and so write on. I will tell you what you may do; you may write with your eyes half shut, just as when one is going to sleep: I have done so for two or three lines now; it is but just seeing enough to go straight.—Now, Madam Dingley, I think I bid you tell Mr. Walls that, in case there be occasion, I will serve his friend as far as I can; but I hope there will be none. Yet I believe you will have a new Parliament; but I care not whether you have or no a better. You are mistaken in all your conjectures about the *Tatlers*. I have given him one or two hints, and you have heard me talk about the Shilling. Faith, these answering letters are very long ones: you have taken up almost the room of a week in journals; and I will tell you what, I saw fellows wearing crosses to-day, and I wondered what was the matter; but just this minute I recollect it is little Presto's birthday; and I was resolved these three days to remember it when it came, but could not. Pray, drink my health to-day at dinner; do, you rogues. Do you like "Sid Hamet's Rod"? Do you understand it all? Well, now at last I have done with your letter, and so I will lay me down to sleep, and about, fair maids; and I hope merry maids all.

Dec. 1. Morning. I wish Smyth were hanged. I was dreaming the most melancholy things in the world of poor Stella, and was grieving and crying all night.—Pshah, it is foolish: I will rise and divert myself; so good-morrow; and God of His infinite mercy keep and protect you! The Bishop of Clogher's letter is dated Nov. 21. He says you thought of going with him to Clogher. I am heartily glad of it, and wish you would ride there, and Dingley go in a coach. I have had no fit since my first, although sometimes my head is not quite in good order.—At night. I was this morning to visit Mr. Pratt, who is come over with poor, sick Lord Shelburne: they made me dine with them; and there I stayed, like a booby, till eight, looking over them at ombre, and then came home. Lord Shelburne's giddiness is turned into a colic, and he looks miserably.

2. Steele, the rogue, has done the imprudentest thing in the world: he said something in a *Tatler*, that we ought to use the word Great Britain, and not England, in common conversation, as, "The finest lady in Great Britain," etc. Upon this, Rowe, Prior, and I sent him a letter, turning this into ridicule. He has to-day printed the letter, and signed it J.S., M.P., and N.R., the first letters of all our names. Congreve told me to-day, he smoked it immediately. Congreve and I, and Sir Charles Wager, dined to-day at Delaval's, the Portugal Envoy; and I stayed there till eight, and came home, and am now writing to you before I do business, because that dog Patrick is not at home, and the fire is not made, and I am not in my gear. Pox take him!—I was looking by chance at the top of this side, and find I make plaguy mistakes in words; so that you must fence against that as well as bad writing. Faith, I can't nor won't read what I have written. (Pox of this puppy!) Well, I'll leave you till I am got to bed, and then I will say a word or two.—Well, 'tis now almost twelve, and I have been busy ever since, by a fire too (I have my coals by half a bushel at a time, I'll assure you), and now I am got to bed. Well, and what have you to say to Presto now he is abed? Come now, let us hear your speeches. No, 'tis a lie; I an't sleepy yet. Let us sit up a little longer, and talk. Well, where have you been to-day, that you are but just this minute come home in a coach? What have you lost? Pay the coachman, Stella. No, faith, not I, he'll grumble.—What new acquaintance have you got? come, let us hear. I have made Delaval promise to send me some Brazil tobacco from Portugal for you, Madam Dingley. I hope you will have your chocolate and spectacles before this comes to you.

3. Pshaw, I must be writing to these dear saucy brats every night, whether I will or no, let me have what business I will, or come home ever so late, or be ever so sleepy; but an old saying, and a true one,

> *"Be you lords, or be you earls,*
> *You must write to naughty girls."*

I was to-day at Court, and saw Raymond among the Beefeaters, staying to see the Queen: so I put him in a better station, made two or three dozen of bows, and went to church, and then to Court again, to pick up a dinner, as I did with Sir John Stanley; and then we went to visit Lord Mountjoy, and just now left him; and 'tis near eleven at night, young women; and methinks this letter comes pretty near to the bottom, and 'tis but eight days since the date, and don't think I'll write on the other side, I thank you for nothing. Faith, if I would use you to letters on sheets as broad as this room, you would always expect them from me. O, faith, I know you well enough; but an old saying, etc.,

> *"Two sides in a sheet,*
> *And one in a street."*

I think that's but a silly old saying; and so I'll go to sleep, and do you so too.

4. I dined to-day with Mrs. Vanhomrigh, and then came home, and studied till eleven. No adventure at all to-day.

5. So I went to the Court of Requests (we have had the Devil and all of rain by the bye) to pick up a dinner; and Henley made me go dine with him and one Colonel Bragg at a tavern; cost me money, faith. Congreve was to be there, but came not. I came with Henley to the Coffee-house, where Lord Salisbury seemed mighty desirous to talk with me; and, while he was wriggling himself into my favour, that dog Henley asked me aloud, whether I would go to see Lord Somers as I had promised (which was a lie); and all to vex poor Lord Salisbury, who is a high Tory. He played two or three other such tricks; and I was forced to leave my lord, and I came home at seven, and have been writing ever since, and will now go to bed. The other day I saw Jack Temple in the Court of Requests: it was the first time of seeing him; so we talked two or three careless words, and parted. Is it true that your Recorder and Mayor, and fanatic aldermen, a month or two ago, at a solemn feast, drank Mr. Harley's, Lord Rochester's, and other Tory healths? Let me know; it was confidently said here.—The scoundrels! It shan't do, Tom.

6. When is this letter to go, I wonder? harkee, young women, tell me that. Saturday next for certain, and not before: then it will be just a fortnight; time enough for naughty girls, and long enough for two letters, faith. Congreve and Delaval have at last prevailed on Sir Godfrey Kneller to entreat me to let him draw my picture for nothing; but I know not yet when I shall sit.—It is such monstrous rainy weather, that there is no doing with it. Secretary St. John sent to me this morning, that my dining with him to-day was put off till to-morrow; so I peaceably sat with my neighbour Ford, dined with him, and came home at six, and am now in bed as usual; and now it is time to have another letter from MD, yet I would not have it till this goes; for that would look like two letters for one. Is it not whimsical that the Dean has never once written to me? And I find the Archbishop very silent to that letter I sent him with an account that the business was done. I believe he knows not what to write or say; and I have since written twice to him, both times with a vengeance. Well, go to bed, sirrahs, and so will I. But have you lost to-day? Three shillings! O fie, O fie!

7. No, I won't send this letter to-day, nor till Saturday, faith; and I am so afraid of one from MD between this and that; if it comes, I will just say I received a letter, and that is all. I dined to-day with Mr. Secretary St. John, where were Lord Anglesea, Sir Thomas Hanmer, Prior, Freind, etc., and then made a debauch after nine at Prior's house, and have eaten cold pie, and I hate the thoughts of it, and I am full, and I don't like it, and I will go to bed, and it is late, and so good-night.

8. To-day I dined with Mr. Harley and Prior; but Mr. St. John did not come, though he promised: he chid me for not seeing him oftener. Here is a damned, libellous pamphlet come out against Lord Wharton, giving the character first, and then telling some of his actions: the character is very well, but the facts indifferent. It has been sent by dozens to several gentlemen's lodgings, and I had one or two of them; but nobody knows the author or printer. We are terribly afraid of the plague; they say it is at Newcastle. I begged Mr. Harley for the love of God to take some care about it, or we are all ruined. There have been orders for all ships from the Baltic to pass their quarantine before they land; but they neglect it. You remember I have been afraid these two years.

9. O, faith, you are a saucy rogue. I have had your sixth letter just now, before this is gone; but I will not answer a word of it, only that I never was giddy since my first fit; but I have had a cold just a fortnight, and cough with it still morning and evening; but it will go off. It is, however, such abominable weather that no creature can walk. They say here three of your Commissioners will be turned out, Ogle, South, and St. Quintin; and that Dick Stewart and Ludlow will be two of the new ones. I am a little soliciting for another: it is poor Lord Abercorn, but that is a secret; I mean, that I befriend him is a secret; but I believe it is too late, by his own fault and ill fortune. I dined with him to-day. I am heartily sorry you do not go to Clogher, faith, I am; and so God Almighty protect poor, dear, dear, dear, dearest MD. Farewell till to-night. I'll begin my eleventh to-night; so I am always writing to little MD.

Letter XI

So, young women, I have just sent my tenth to the post-office, and, as I told you, have received your seventh (faith, I am afraid I mistook, and said your sixth, and then we shall be all in confusion this month.) Well, I told you I dined with Lord Abercorn to-day; and that is enough till by and bye; for I must go write idle things, and twittle twattle. What's here to do with your little MD's? and so I put this by for a while. 'Tis now late, and I can only say MD is a dear, saucy rogue, and what then? Presto loves them the better.

10. This son of a b— Patrick is out of the way, and I can do nothing; am forced to borrow coals: 'tis now six o'clock, and I am come home after a pure walk in the park; delicate weather, begun only to-day. A terrible storm last night: we hear one of your packet-boats is cast away, and young Beau Swift in it, and General Sankey: I know not the truth; you will before me. Raymond talks of leaving the town in a few days, and going in a month to Ireland, for fear his wife should be too far gone, and forced to be brought to bed here. I think he is in the right; but perhaps this packet-boat will fright him. He has no relish for London; and I do not wonder at it. He has got some Templars from Ireland that show him the town. I do not let him see me above twice a week, and that only while I am dressing in the morning.—So, now the puppy's come in, and I have got my own ink, but a new pen; and so now you are rogues and sauceboxes till I go to bed; for I must go study, sirrahs. Now I think of it, tell the Bishop of Clogher, he shall not cheat me of one inch of my bell metal. You know it is nothing but to save the town money; and Enniskillen can afford it better than Laracor: he shall have but one thousand five hundred weight. I have been reading, etc., as usual, and am now going to bed; and I find this day's article is long enough: so get you gone till to-morrow, and then. I dined with Sir Matthew Dudley.

11. I am come home again as yesterday, and the puppy had again locked up my ink, notwithstanding all I said to him yesterday; but he came home a little after me, so all is well: they are lighting my fire, and I'll go study. The fair weather is gone again, and it has rained all day. I do

not like this open weather, though some say it is healthy. They say it is a false report about the plague at Newcastle. I have no news to-day: I dined with Mrs. Vanhomrigh, to desire them to buy me a scarf; and Lady Abercorn is to buy me another, to see who does best: mine is all in rags. I saw the Duke of Richmond yesterday at Court again, but would not speak to him: I believe we are fallen out. I am now in bed; and it has rained all this evening, like wildfire: have you so much rain in your town? Raymond was in a fright, as I expected, upon the news of this shipwreck; but I persuaded him, and he leaves this town in a week. I got him acquainted with Sir Robert Raymond, the Solicitor-General, who owns him to be of his family; and I believe it may do him a kindness, by being recommended to your new Lord Chancellor.—I had a letter from Mrs. Long, that has quite turned my stomach against her: no less than two nasty jests in it, with dashes to suppose them. She is corrupted in that country town with vile conversation.—I will not answer your letter till I have leisure: so let this go on as it will, what care I? what cares saucy Presto?

12. I was to-day at the Secretary's office with Lewis, and in came Lord Rivers; who took Lewis out and whispered him; and then came up to me to desire my acquaintance, etc., so we bowed and complimented a while, and parted and I dined with Phil. Savage and his Irish Club, at their boarding-place; and, passing an evening scurvily enough, did not come home till eight. Mr. Addison and I hardly meet once a fortnight; his Parliament and my different friendships keep us asunder. Sir Matthew Dudley turned away his butler yesterday morning; and at night the poor fellow died suddenly in the streets: was not it an odd event? But what care you? But then I knew the butler.—Why, it seems your packet-boat is not lost: psha, how silly that is, when I had already gone through the forms, and said it was a sad thing, and that I was sorry for it! But when must I answer this letter of our MD's? Here it is, it lies between this paper on t'other side of the leaf: one of these odd-come-shortly's I'll consider, and so good-night.

13. Morning. I am to go trapesing with Lady Kerry and Mrs. Pratt to see sights all this day: they engaged me yesterday morning at tea. You hear the havoc making in the army: Meredith, Maccartney, and Colonel Honeywood are obliged to sell their commands at half-value, and leave the army, for drinking destruction to the present Ministry,

and dressing up a hat on a stick, and calling it Harley; then drinking a glass with one hand, and discharging a pistol with the other at the maukin, wishing it were Harley himself; and a hundred other such pretty tricks, as inflaming their soldiers, and foreign Ministers, against the late changes at Court. Cadogan has had a little paring: his mother told me yesterday he had lost the place of Envoy; but I hope they will go no further with him, for he was not at those mutinous meetings.—Well, these saucy jades take up so much of my time with writing to them in a morning; but, faith, I am glad to see you whenever I can: a little snap and away; and so hold your tongue, for I must rise: not a word, for your life. How nowww? So, very well; stay till I come home, and then, perhaps, you may hear further from me. And where will you go to-day, for I can't be with you for these ladies? It is a rainy, ugly day. I'd have you send for Walls, and go to the Dean's; but don't play small games when you lose. You'll be ruined by Manilio, Basto, the queen, and two small trumps, in red. I confess 'tis a good hand against the player: but then there are Spadilio, Punto, the king, strong trumps, against you, which, with one trump more, are three tricks ten ace: for, suppose you play your Manilio—Oh, silly, how I prate, and can't get away from this MD in a morning! Go, get you gone, dear naughty girls, and let me rise. There, Patrick locked up my ink again the third time last night: the rogue gets the better of me; but I will rise in spite of you, sirrahs.—At night. Lady Kerry, Mrs. Pratt, Mrs. Cadogan, and I, in one coach; Lady Kerry's son and his governor, and two gentlemen, in another; maids, and misses and little master (Lord Shelburne's children), in a third, all hackneys, set out at ten o'clock this morning from Lord Shelburne's house in Piccadilly to the Tower, and saw all the sights, lions, etc.; then to Bedlam; then dined at the chop-house behind the Exchange; then to Gresham College (but the keeper was not at home); and concluded the night at the Puppet-show, whence we came home safe at eight, and I left them. The ladies were all in mobs (how do you call it?), undrest; and it was the rainiest day that ever dripped; and I am weary; and it is now past eleven.

14. Stay, I'll answer some of your letter this morning in bed: let me see; come and appear, little letter. Here I am, says he: and what say you to Mrs. MD this morning fresh and fasting? Who dares think MD negligent? I allow them a fortnight; and they give it me. I could fill a letter in a week; but it is longer every day; and so I keep it a fortnight,

and then 'tis cheaper by one half. I have never been giddy, dear Stella, since that morning: I have taken a whole box of pills, and kecked at them every night, and drank a pint of brandy at mornings.—Oh then, you kept Presto's little birthday: would to God I had been with you! I forgot it, as I told you before. R*e*diculous, madam? I suppose you mean r*i*diculous: let me have no more of that; 'tis the author of the *Atalantis's* spelling. I have mended it in your letter. And can Stella read this writing without hurting her dear eyes? O, faith, I am afraid not. Have a care of those eyes, pray, pray, pretty Stella.—'Tis well enough what you observe, that, if I writ better, perhaps you would not read so well, being used to this manner; 'tis an alphabet you are used to: you know such a pot-hook makes a letter; and you know what letter, and so and so.—I'll swear he told me so, and that they were long letters too; but I told him it was a gasconnade of yours, etc. I am talking of the Bishop of Clogher, how he forgot. Turn over. I had not room on t'other side to say that, so I did it on this: I fancy that's a good Irish blunder. Ah, why do not you go down to Clogher, nautinautinautideargirls; I dare not say *nauti* without *dear*: O, faith, you govern me. But, seriously, I'm sorry you don't go, as far as I can judge at this distance. No, we would get you another horse; I will make Parvisol get you one. I always doubted that horse of yours: prythee sell him, and let it be a present to me. My heart aches when I think you ride him. Order Parvisol to sell him, and that you are to return me the money: I shall never be easy until he is out of your hands. Faith, I have dreamt five or six times of horses stumbling since I had your letter. If he can't sell him, let him run this winter. Faith, if I was near you, I would whip your—to some tune, for your grave, saucy answer about the Dean and *Johnsonibus*; I would, young women. And did the Dean preach for me? Very well. Why, would they have me stand here and preach to them? No, the *Tatler* of the Shilling was not mine, more than the hint, and two or three general heads for it. I have much more important business on my hands; and, besides, the Ministry hate to think that I should help him, and have made reproaches on it; and I frankly told them I would do it no more. This is a secret though, Madam Stella. You win eight shillings? you win eight fiddlesticks. Faith, you say nothing of what you lose, young women.—I hope Manley is in no great danger; for Ned Southwell is his friend, and so is Sir Thomas Frankland; and his brother John Manley stands up heartily for him. On t'other side, all the gentlemen of Ireland here are furiously against him. Now, Mistress Dingley, an't you an impudent slut, to expect a letter next packet from Presto, when you confess yourself that you had so lately two letters in four days? Unreasonable baggage! No, little Dingley, I am always in bed by twelve; I mean my candle is out by twelve, and I take great care of myself. Pray let everybody know, upon occasion, that Mr. Harley got the First-Fruits from the Queen for the clergy of Ireland, and that nothing remains but the forms, etc. So you say the Dean and you dined at Stoyte's, and Mrs. Stoyte was in raptures that I remembered her. I must do it but seldom, or it will take off her rapture. But what now, you saucy sluts? all this written in a morning, and I must rise and go abroad. Pray stay till night: do not think I will squander mornings upon you, pray, good madam. Faith, if I go on longer in this trick of writing in the morning, I shall be afraid of leaving it off, and think you expect it, and be in awe. Good-morrow, sirrahs, I will rise.— At night. I went to-day to the Court of Requests (I will not answer the rest of your letter yet, that by the way), in hopes to dine with Mr. Harley: but Lord Dupplin, his son-in-law, told me he did not dine at home; so I was at a loss, until I met with Mr. Secretary St. John, and went home and dined with him, where he told me of a good bite. Lord Rivers told me two days ago, that he was resolved to come Sunday fortnight next to hear me preach before the Queen. I assured him the day was not yet fixed, and I knew nothing of it. To-day the Secretary told me that his father, Sir Harry St. John, and Lord Rivers were to be at St. James's Church, to hear me preach there; and were assured I was to preach: so there will be another bite; for I know nothing of the matter, but that Mr. Harley and St. John are resolved I must preach before the Queen; and the Secretary of State has told me he will give me three weeks' warning; but I desired to be excused, which he will not. St. John, "You shall not be excused": however, I hope they will forget it; for if it should happen, all the puppies hereabouts will throng to hear me, and expect something wonderful, and be plaguily baulked; for I shall preach plain honest stuff. I stayed with St. John till eight, and then came home; and Patrick desired leave to go abroad, and by and by comes up the girl to tell me, a gentleman was below in a coach, who had a bill to pay me; so I let him come up, and who should it be but Mr. Addison and Sam Dopping, to haul me out to supper, where I stayed till twelve. If Patrick had been at home, I should have 'scaped this; for I have taught him to deny me almost as well as Mr. Harley's porter.—Where did I leave off in MD's letter? let me see. So, now I have it. You are pleased to say, Madam Dingley, that those who go for England can never tell when to come back. Do you mean this as a reflection upon Presto, madam? Sauceboxes, I will come back as soon as I can, as hope saved, and I hope with some advantage, unless all Ministries be alike, as perhaps they may. I hope Hawkshaw is in Dublin before now, and that you have your things, and like your spectacles: if you do not, you shall have better. I hope Dingley's tobacco did not spoil Stella's chocolate, and that all is safe: pray let me know. Mr. Addison and I are different as black and white, and I believe our friendship will go off, by this damned business of party: he cannot bear seeing me fall in so with this Ministry: but I love him still as well as ever, though we seldom meet.—Hussy, Stella, you jest about poor Congreve's eyes; you do so, hussy; but I'll bang your bones, faith.—Yes, Steele was a little while in prison, or at least in a spunging-house, some time before I came, but not since.—Pox on your convocations, and your Lamberts; they write with a vengeance! I suppose you think it a piece of affectation in me to wish your Irish folks would not like my "Shower,"; but you are mistaken. I should be glad to have the general applause there as I have here (though I say it); but I have only that of one or two, and therefore I would have none at all, but let you all be in the wrong. I don't know, this is not what I would say; but I am so tosticated with supper and stuff, that I can't express myself.—What you say of "Sid Hamet" is well enough; that an enemy should like it, and a friend not; and that telling the author would make both change their opinions. Why did you not tell Griffyth that you fancied there was something in it of my manner; but first spur up his commendation to the height, as we served my poor uncle about the sconce that I mended? Well, I desired you to give what I intended for an answer to Mrs. Fenton, to save her postage, and myself trouble; and I hope I have done it, if you han't.

15. Lord, what a long day's writing was yesterday's answer to your letter, sirrahs! I dined to-day with Lewis and Ford, whom I have brought acquainted. Lewis told me a pure thing. I had been hankering with Mr. Harley to save Steele his other employment, and have a little mercy on him; and I had been saying the same thing to Lewis, who is Mr. Harley's chief favourite. Lewis tells Mr. Harley how kindly I should take it, if he would be reconciled to Steele, etc. Mr. Harley, on my account, falls in with it, and appoints Steele a time to let him attend him, which Steele accepts with great submission, but never comes, nor sends any excuse. Whether it was blundering, sullenness, insolence, or

rancour of party, I cannot tell; but I shall trouble myself no more about him. I believe Addison hindered him out of mere spite, being grated to the soul to think he should ever want my help to save his friend; yet now he is soliciting me to make another of his friends Queen's Secretary at Geneva; and I'll do it if I can; it is poor Pastoral Philips.

16. O, why did you leave my picture behind you at t'other lodgings? Forgot it? Well; but pray remember it now, and don't roll it up, d'ye hear; but hang it carefully in some part of your room, where chairs and candles and mop-sticks won't spoil it, sirrahs. No, truly, I will not be godfather to Goody Walls this bout, and I hope she will have no more. There will be no quiet nor cards for this child. I hope it will die the day after the christening. Mr. Harley gave me a paper, with an account of the sentence you speak of against the lads that defaced the statue, and that Ingoldsby reprieved that part of it of standing before the statue. I hope it was never executed. We have got your Broderick out; Doyne is to succeed him, and Cox Doyne. And so there's an end of your letter; 'tis all answered; and now I must go on upon my own stock. Go on, did I say? Why, I have written enough; but this is too soon to send it yet, young women; faith, I dare not use you to it, you'll always expect it; what remains shall be only short journals of a day, and so I'll rise for this morning.—At night. I dined with my opposite neighbour, Darteneuf; and I was soliciting this day to present the Bishop of Clogher Vice-Chancellor; but it won't do; they are all set against him, and the Duke of Ormond, they say, has resolved to dispose of it somewhere else. Well; little saucy rogues, do not stay out too late to-night, because it is Saturday night, and young women should come home soon then.

17. I went to Court to seek a dinner: but the Queen was not at church, she has got a touch of the gout; so the Court was thin, and I went to the Coffee-house; and Sir Thomas Frankland and his eldest son and I went and dined with his son William. I talked a great deal to Sir Thomas about Manley; and find he is his good friend, and so has Ned Southwell been, and I hope he will be safe, though all the Irish folks here are his mortal enemies. There was a devilish bite to-day. They had it, I know not how, that I was to preach this morning at St. James's Church; an abundance went, among the rest Lord Radnor, who never is abroad till three in the afternoon. I walked all the way home from Hatton Garden at six, by moonlight, a delicate night. Raymond called at nine, but I was

denied; and now I am in bed between eleven and twelve, just going to sleep, and dream of my own dear roguish impudent pretty MD.

18. You will now have short days' works, just a few lines to tell you where I am, and what I am doing; only I will keep room for the last day to tell you news, if there be any worth sending. I have been sometimes like to do it at the top of my letter, until I remark it would be old before it reached you. I was hunting to dine with Mr. Harley to-day, but could not find him; and so I dined with honest Dr. Cockburn, and came home at six, and was taken out to next door by Dopping and Ford, to drink bad claret and oranges; and we let Raymond come to us, who talks of leaving the town to-morrow, but I believe will stay a day or two longer. It is now late, and I will say no more, but end this line with bidding my own dear saucy MD good-night, etc.

19. I am come down proud stomach in one instance, for I went to-day to see the Duke of Buckingham, but came too late: then I visited Mrs. Barton, and thought to have dined with some of the Ministry; but it rained, and Mrs. Vanhomrigh was nigh, and I took the opportunity of paying her for a scarf she bought me, and dined there; at four I went to congratulate with Lord Shelburne, for the death of poor Lady Shelburne dowager; he was at his country house, and returned while I was there, and had not heard of it, and he took it very well. I am now come home before six, and find a packet from the Bishop of Clogher, with one enclosed to the Duke of Ormond, which is ten days earlier dated than another I had from Parvisol; however, 'tis no matter, for the Duke has already disposed of the Vice-Chancellorship to the Archbishop of Tuam, and I could not help it, for it is a thing wholly you know in the Duke's power; and I find the Bishop has enemies about the Duke. I write this while Patrick is folding up my scarf, and doing up the fire (for I keep a fire, it costs me twelvepence a week); and so be quiet till I am gone to bed, and then sit down by me a little, and we will talk a few words more. Well; now MD is at my bedside; and now what shall we say? How does Mrs. Stoyte? What had the Dean for supper? How much did Mrs. Walls win? Poor Lady Shelburne: well, go get you to bed, sirrahs.

20. Morning. I was up this morning early, and shaved by candlelight, and write this by the fireside. Poor Raymond just came in and took his

leave of me; he is summoned by high order from his wife, but pretends he has had enough of London. I was a little melancholy to part with him; he goes to Bristol, where they are to be with his merchant brother, and now thinks of staying till May; so she must be brought to bed in England. He was so easy and manageable, that I almost repent I suffered him to see me so seldom. But he is gone, and will save Patrick some lies in a week: Patrick is grown admirable at it, and will make his fortune. How now, sirrah, must I write in a morning to your impudence?

Stay till night,
And then I'll write,
In black and white,
By candlelight,
Of wax so bright,
It helps the sight—
A bite, a bite!

Marry come up, Mistress Boldface.—At night. Dr. Raymond came back, and goes to-morrow. I did not come home till eleven, and found him here to take leave of me. I went to the Court of Requests, thinking to find Mr. Harley and dine with him, and refused Henley, and everybody, and at last knew not where to go, and met Jemmy Leigh by chance, and he was just in the same way, so I dined at his lodgings on a beef-steak, and drank your health; then left him and went to the tavern with Ben Tooke and Portlack, the Duke of Ormond's secretary, drinking nasty white wine till eleven. I am sick, and ashamed of it, etc.

21. I met that beast Ferris, Lord Berkeley's steward formerly; I walked with him a turn in the Park, and that scoundrel dog is as happy as an emperor, has married a wife with a considerable estate in land and houses about this town, and lives at his ease at Hammersmith. See your confounded sect! Well; I had the same luck to-day with Mr. Harley; 'twas a lovely day, and went by water into the City, and dined with Stratford at a merchant's house, and walked home with as great a dunce as Ferris, I mean honest Colonel Caulfeild, and came home by eight, and now am in bed, and going to sleep for a wager, and will send this letter on Saturday, and so; but first I will wish you a merry Christmas and a happy New Year, and pray God we may never keep them asunder again.

22. Morning. I am going now to Mr. Harley's levee on purpose to vex him; I will say I had no other way of seeing him, etc. Patrick says it is a dark morning, and that the Duke of Argyle is to be knighted to-day; the booby means installed at Windsor. But I must rise, for this is a shaving-day, and Patrick says there is a good fire; I wish MD were by it, or I by MD's.—At night. I forgot to tell you, Madam Dingley, that I paid nine shillings for your glass and spectacles, of which three were for the Bishop's case: I am sorry I did not buy you such another case; but if you like it, I will bring one over with me; pray tell me: the glass to read was four shillings, the spectacles two. And have you had your chocolate? Leigh says he sent the petticoat by one Mr. Spencer. Pray have you no further commissions for me? I paid the glass-man but last night, and he would have made me a present of the microscope worth thirty shillings, and would have sent it home along with me; I thought the deuce was in the man: he said I could do him more service than that was worth, etc. I refused his present, but promised him all service I could do him; and so now I am obliged in honour to recommend him to everybody.—At night. I went to Mr. Harley's levee; he came and asked me what I had to do there, and bid me come and dine with him on a family dinner; which I did, and it was the first time I ever saw his lady and daughter; at five my Lord Keeper came in: I told Mr. Harley, he had formerly presented me to Sir Simon Harcourt, but now must to my Lord Keeper; so he laughed, etc.

23. Morning. This letter goes to-night without fail; I hope there is none from you yet at the Coffee-house; I will send and see by and by, and let you know, and so and so. Patrick goes to see for a letter: what will you lay, is there one from MD or no? No, I say; done for sixpence. Why has the Dean never once written to me? I won sixpence; I won sixpence; there is not one letter to Presto. Good-morrow, dear sirrahs: Stratford and I dine to-day with Lord Mountjoy. God Almighty preserve and bless you; farewell, etc.

I have been dining at Lord Mountjoy's; and am come to study; our news from Spain this post takes off some of our fears. The Parliament is prorogued to-day, or adjourned rather till after the holidays. Bank Stock is 105, so I may get 12 shillings for my bargain already. Patrick, the puppy, is abroad, and how shall I send this letter? Good-night, little dears both, and be happy; and remember your poor Presto, that wants you sadly, as hope saved. Let me go study, naughty girls, and don't keep me at the bottom of the paper. O, faith, if you knew what lies on my hands constantly, you would wonder to see how I could write such long letters; but we'll talk of that some other time. Good-night again, and God bless dear MD with His best blessings, yes, yes, and Dingley and Stella and me too, etc.

Ask the Bishop of Clogher about the pun I sent him of Lord Stawel's brother; it will be a pure bite. This letter has 199 lines in it, beside all postscripts; I had a curiosity to reckon.

There is a long letter for you.

It is longer than a sermon, faith.

I had another letter from Mrs. Fenton, who says you were with her; I hope you did not go on purpose. I will answer her letter soon; it is about some money in Lady Giffard's hands.

They say you have had eight packets due to you; so pray, madams, do not blame Presto, but the wind.

My humble service to Mrs. Walls and Mrs. Stoyte; I missed the former a good while.

London, *Dec.* 23, 1710

I have sent my 11th to-night as usual, and begin the dozenth, and I told you I dined with Stratford at Lord Mountjoy's, and I will tell you no more at present, guess for why; because I am going to mind things, and mighty affairs, not your nasty First-Fruits—I let them alone till Mr. Harley gets the Queen's letter—but other things of greater moment, that you shall know one day, when the ducks have eaten up all the dirt. So sit still a while just by me, while I am studying, and don't say a word, I charge you, and when I am going to bed, I will take you along, and talk with you a little while, so there, sit there.—Come then, let us see what we have to say to these saucy brats, that will not let us go sleep at past eleven. Why, I am a little impatient to know how you do; but that I take it for a standing maxim, that when you are silent, all is pretty well, because that is the way I will deal with you; and if there was anything you ought to know now, I would write by the first post, although I had written but the day before. Remember this, young women; and God Almighty preserve you both, and make us happy together; and tell me how accompts stand between us, that you may be paid long before it is due, not to want. I will return no more money while I stay, so that you need not be in pain to be paid; but let me know at least a month before you can want. Observe this, d'ye hear, little dear sirrahs, and love Presto, as Presto loves MD, etc.

24. You will have a merrier Christmas Eve than we here. I went up to Court before church; and in one of the rooms, there being but little company, a fellow in a red coat without a sword came up to me, and, after words of course, asked me how the ladies did? I asked, "What ladies?" He said, "Mrs. Dingley and Mrs. Johnson." "Very well," said I, "when I heard from them last: and pray when came you from thence, sir?" He said, "I never was in Ireland"; and just at that word Lord Winchelsea comes up to me, and the man went off: as I went out I saw him again, and recollected him, it was Vedeau with a pox: I then went and made my apologies, that my head was full of something I had to say to Lord Winchelsea, etc., and I asked after his wife, and so all was well; and he inquired after my lodging, because he had some favour to desire of me in Ireland, to recommend somebody to somebody, I know

not what it is. When I came from church, I went up to Court again, where Sir Edmond Bacon told me the bad news from Spain, which you will hear before this reaches you; as we have it now, we are undone there, and it was odd to see the whole countenances of the Court changed so in two hours. Lady Mountjoy carried me home to dinner, where I stayed not long after, and came home early, and now am got into bed, for you must always write to your MD's in bed, that is a maxim.

> *Mr. White and Mr. Red,*
> *Write to MD when abed;*
> *Mr. Black and Mr. Brown,*
> *Write to MD when you're down;*
> *Mr. Oak and Mr. Willow,*
> *Write to MD on your pillow.—*

What is this? faith, I smell fire; what can it be? this house has a thousand stinks in it. I think to leave it on Thursday, and lodge over the way. Faith, I must rise, and look at my chimney, for the smell grows stronger, stay—I have been up, and in my room, and found all safe, only a mouse within the fender to warm himself, which I could not catch. I smelt nothing there, but now in my bed-chamber I smell it again; I believe I have singed the woollen curtain, and that is all, though I cannot smoke it. Presto is plaguy silly to-night, an't he? Yes, and so he be. Ay, but if I should wake and see fire. Well; I will venture; so good-night, etc.

25. Pray, young women, if I write so much as this every day, how will this paper hold a fortnight's work, and answer one of yours into the bargain? You never think of this, but let me go on like a simpleton. I wish you a merry Christmas, and many, many a one with poor Presto at some pretty place. I was at church to-day by eight, and received the Sacrament, and came home by ten; then went to Court at two: it was a Collar-day, that is, when the Knights of the Garter wear their collars; but the Queen stayed so late at Sacrament, that I came back, and dined with my neighbour Ford, because all people dine at home on this day. This is likewise a Collar-day all over England in every house, at least where there is *brawn*: that's very well.—I tell you a good pun; a fellow hard by pretends to cure agues, and has set out a sign, and spells it *egoes*; a gentleman and I observing it, he said, "How does that fellow pretend

to cure *agues*?" I said I did not know; but I was sure it was not by a *spell*. That is admirable. And so you asked the Bishop about that pun of Lord Stawel's brother. Bite! Have I caught you, young women? Must you pretend to ask after roguish puns, and Latin ones too? Oh but you smoked me, and did not ask the Bishop. Oh but you are a fool, and you did. I met Vedeau again at Court to-day, and I observed he had a sword on; I fancy he was broke, and has got a commission, but I never asked him. Vedeau I think his name is, yet Parvisol's man is Vedel, that is true. Bank Stock will fall like stock-fish by this bad news, and two days ago I could have got twelve pounds by my bargain; but I do not intend to sell, and in time it will rise. It is odd that my Lord Peterborow foretold this loss two months ago, one night at Mr. Harley's, when I was there; he bid us count upon it, that Stanhope would lose Spain before Christmas; that he would venture his head upon it, and gave us reasons; and though Mr. Harley argued the contrary, he still held to his opinion. I was telling my Lord Angelsea this at Court this morning; and a gentleman by said he had heard my Lord Peterborow affirm the same thing. I have heard wise folks say, "An ill tongue may do much." And 'tis an odd saying,

> "Once I guessed right,
> And I got credit by't;
> Thrice I guessed wrong,
> And I kept my credit on."

No, it is you are sorry, not I.

26. By the Lord Harry, I shall be undone here with Christmas boxes. The rogues of the Coffee-house have raised their tax, everyone giving a crown; and I gave mine for shame, besides a great many half-crowns to great men's porters, etc. I went to-day by water into the city, and dined with no less a man than the City Printer. There is an intimacy between us, built upon reasons that you shall know when I see you; but the rain caught me within twelvepenny length of home. I called at Mr. Harley's, who was not within, dropped my half-crown with his porter, drove to the Coffee-house, where the rain kept me till nine. I had letters to-day from the Archbishop of Dublin and Mr. Bernage; the latter sends me a melancholy account of Lady Shelburne's death, and his own disappointments, and would gladly be a captain; if I can help him, I will.

27. Morning. I bespoke a lodging over the way for to-morrow, and the dog let it yesterday to another; I gave him no earnest, so it seems he could do it; Patrick would have had me give him earnest to bind him; but I would not. So I must go saunter to-day for a lodging somewhere else. Did you ever see so open a winter in England? We have not had two frosty days; but it pays it off in rain: we have not had three fair days these six weeks. O, faith, I dreamt mightily of MD last night; but so confused, I cannot tell a word. I have made Ford acquainted with Lewis; and to-day we dined together: in the evening I called at one or two neighbours, hoping to spend a Christmas evening; but none were at home, they were all gone to be merry with others. I have often observed this, that in merry times everybody is abroad; where the deuce are they? So I went to the Coffee-house, and talked with Mr. Addison an hour, who at last remembered to give me two letters, which I cannot answer to-night, nor to-morrow neither, I can assure you, young women, count upon that. I have other things to do than to answer naughty girls, an old saying and true,

Letters from MD's
Must not be answered in ten days:

it is but bad rhyme, etc.

28. To-day I had a message from Sir Thomas Hanmer, to dine with him; the famous Dr. Smalridge was of the company, and we sat till six; and I came home to my new lodgings in St. Albans Street, where I pay the same rent (eight shillings a week) for an apartment two pair of stairs; but I have the use of the parlour to receive persons of quality, and I am got into my new bed, etc.

29. Sir Andrew Fountaine has been very ill this week; and sent to me early this morning to have prayers, which you know is the last thing. I found the doctors and all in despair about him. I read prayers to him, found he had settled all things; and, when I came out, the nurse asked me whether I thought it possible he could live; for the doctors thought not. I said, I believed he would live; for I found the seeds of life in him, which I observe seldom fail (and I found them in poor, dearest Stella, when she was ill many years ago); and to-night I was with him again, and he was mightily recovered, and I hope he will

do well, and the doctor approved my reasons; but, if he should die, I should come off scurvily. The Secretary of State (Mr. St. John) sent to me to dine with him; Mr. Harley and Lord Peterborow dined there too; and at night came Lord Rivers. Lord Peterborow goes to Vienna in a day or two: he has promised to make me write to him. Mr. Harley went away at six; but we stayed till seven. I took the Secretary aside, and complained to him of Mr. Harley, that he had got the Queen to grant the First-Fruits, promised to bring me to her, and get her letter to the bishops of Ireland; but the last part he had not done in six weeks, and I was in danger to lose reputation, etc. He took the matter right, desired me to be with him on Sunday morning, and promises me to finish the affair in four days; so I shall know in a little time what I have to trust to.—It is nine o'clock, and I must go study, you little rogues; and so good-night, etc.

30. Morning. The weather grows cold, you sauceboxes. Sir Andrew Fountaine, they bring me word, is better. I will go rise, for my hands are starving while I write in bed. Night. Now Sir Andrew Fountaine is recovering, he desires to be at ease; for I called in the morning to read prayers, but he had given orders not to be disturbed. I have lost a legacy by his living; for he told me he had left me a picture and some books, etc. I called to see my quondam neighbour Ford (do you know what *quondam* is, though?), and he engaged me to dine with him; for he always dines at home on Opera-days. I came home at six, writ to the Archbishop, then studied till past eleven, and stole to bed, to write to MD these few lines, to let you know I am in good health at the present writing hereof, and hope in God MD is so too. I wonder I never write politics to you: I could make you the profoundest politician in all the lane.—Well, but when shall we answer this letter, No. 8 of MD's? Not till next year, faith. O Lord—bo—but that will be a Monday next. Cod's-so, is it? and so it is: never saw the like.—I made a pun t'other day to Ben Portlack about a pair of drawers. Poh, said he, that's mine a—all over. Pray, pray, Dingley, let me go sleep; pray, pray, Stella, let me go slumber; and put out my wax-candle.

31. Morning. It is now seven, and I have got a fire, but am writing abed in my bed-chamber. 'Tis not shaving-day, so I shall be ready early to go before church to Mr. St. John; and to-morrow I will answer our MD's letter.

Would you answer MD's letter,
On New Year's Day you'll do it better;
For, when the year with MD 'gins,
It without MD never lins.

(These proverbs have always old words in them; lins is leave off.)

But, if on New Year you write nones,
MD then will bang your bones.

But Patrick says I must rise.—Night. I was early this morning with Secretary St. John, and gave him a memorial to get the Queen's letter for the First-Fruits, who has promised to do it in a very few days. He told me he had been with the Duke of Marlborough, who was lamenting his former wrong steps in joining with the Whigs, and said he was worn out with age, fatigues, and misfortunes. I swear it pitied me; and I really think they will not do well in too much mortifying that man, although indeed it is his own fault. He is covetous as hell, and ambitious as the Prince of it: he would fain have been General for life, and has broken all endeavours for peace, to keep his greatness and get money. He told the Queen he was neither covetous nor ambitious. She said if she could have conveniently turned about, she would have laughed, and could hardly forbear it in his face. He fell in with all the abominable measures of the late Ministry, because they gratified him for their own designs. Yet he has been a successful General, and I hope he will continue his command. O Lord, smoke the politics to MD! Well; but, if you like them, I will scatter a little now and then, and mine are all fresh from the chief hands. Well, I dined with Mr. Harley, and came away at six: there was much company, and I was not merry at all. Mr. Harley made me read a paper of verses of Prior's. I read them plain, without any fine manner; and Prior swore, I should never read any of his again; but he would be revenged, and read some of mine as bad. I excused myself, and said I was famous for reading verses the worst in the world; and that everybody snatched them from me when I offered to begin. So we laughed.—Sir Andrew Fountaine still continues ill. He is plagued with some sort of bile.

Jan. 1. Morning. I wish my dearest, pretty Dingley and Stella a happy New Year, and health, and mirth, and good stomachs, and Fr's company.

Faith, I did not know how to write Fr. I wondered what was the matter; but now I remember I always write Pdfr. Patrick wishes me a happy New Year, and desires I would rise, for it is a good fire, and faith 'tis cold. I was so politic last night with MD, never saw the like. Get the *Examiners*, and read them; the last nine or ten are full of the reasons for the late change, and of the abuses of the last Ministry; and the great men assure me they are all true. They are written by their encouragement and direction. I must rise and go see Sir Andrew Fountaine; but perhaps to-night I may answer MD's letter: so good-morrow, my mistresses all, good-morrow.

> *I wish you both a merry New Year,*
> *Roast beef, minced pies, and good strong beer,*
> *And me a share of your good cheer,*
> *That I was there, or you were here;*
> *And you're a little saucy dear.*

Good-morrow again, dear sirrahs; one cannot rise for your play.—At night. I went this morning to visit Lady Kerry and Lord Shelburne; and they made me dine with them. Sir Andrew Fountaine is better. And now let us come and see what this saucy, dear letter of MD says. Come out, letter, come out from between the sheets; here it is underneath, and it will not come out. Come out again, I say: so there. Here it is. What says Presto to me, pray? says it. Come, and let me answer for you to your ladies. Hold up your head then, like a good letter. There. Pray, how have you got up with Presto, Madam Stella? You write your eighth when you receive mine: now I write my twelfth when I receive your eighth. Do not you allow for what are upon the road, simpleton? What say you to that? And so you kept Presto's little birthday, I warrant: would to God I had been at the health rather than here, where I have no manner of pleasure, nothing but eternal business upon my hands. I shall grow wise in time; but no more of that: only I say Amen with my heart and vitals, that we may never be asunder again ten days together while poor Presto lives.—I can't be merry so near any splenetic talk; so I made that long line, and now all's well again. Yes, you are a pretending slut, indeed, with your fourth and fifth in the margin, and your journal, and everything. Wind—we saw no wind here, nothing at all extraordinary at any time. We had it once when you had it not. But an old saying and a true:

> *"I hate all wind,*
> *Before and behind,*
> *From cheeks with eyes,*
> *Or from blind.—"*

Your chimney fall down! God preserve you. I suppose you only mean a brick or two: but that's a d—ned lie of your chimney being carried to the next house with the wind. Don't put such things upon us; those matters will not pass here: keep a little to possibilities. My Lord Hertford would have been ashamed of such a stretch. You should take care of what company you converse with: when one gets that faculty, 'tis hard to break one's self of it. Jemmy Leigh talks of going over; but *quando*? I do not know when he will go. Oh, now you have had my ninth, now you are come up with me; marry come up with you, indeed. I know all that business of Lady S—. Will nobody cut that D—y's throat? Five hundred pounds do you call poor pay for living three months the life of a king? They say she died with grief, partly, being forced to appear as a witness in court about some squabble among their servants.—The Bishop of Clogher showed you a pamphlet. Well, but you must not give your mind to believe those things; people will say anything. The *Character* is here reckoned admirable, but most of the facts are trifles. It was first printed privately here; and then some bold cur ventured to do it publicly, and sold two thousand in two days: who the author is must remain uncertain. Do you pretend to know, impudence? How durst you think so? Pox on your Parliaments: the Archbishop has told me of it; but we do not vouchsafe to know anything of it here. No, no, no more of your giddiness yet; thank you, Stella, for asking after it; thank you; God Almighty bless you for your kindness to poor Presto. You write to Lady Giffard and your mother upon what I advise when it is too late. But yet I fancy this bad news will bring down stocks so low, that one might buy to great advantage. I design to venture going to see your mother some day when Lady Giffard is abroad. Well, keep your Rathburn and stuff. I thought he was to pay in your money upon his houses to be flung down about the what do you call it.—Well, Madam Dingley, I sent your enclosed to Bristol, but have not heard from Raymond since he went. Come, come, young women, I keep a good fire; it costs me twelvepence a week, and I fear something more; vex me, and I will have one in my bed-chamber too. No, did not I tell you but just now, we have no high winds here? Have you forgot already?—Now you're at it again, silly

JONATHAN SWIFT

Stella; why does your mother say my candles are scandalous? They are good sixes in the pound, and she said I was extravagant enough to burn them by daylight. I never burn fewer at a time than one. What would people have? The D—burst Hawkshaw. He told me he had not the box; and the next day Sterne told me he had sent it a fortnight ago. Patrick could not find him t'other day, but he shall to-morrow. Dear life and heart, do you tease me? does Stella tease Presto? That palsy-water was in the box; it was too big for a packet, and I was afraid of its breaking. Leigh was not in town then; or I would not have trusted it to Sterne, whom yet I have befriended enough to do me more kindness than that. I'll never rest till you have it, or till it is in a way for you to have it. Poor dear rogue, naughty to think it teases me; how could I ever forgive myself for neglecting anything that related to your health? Sure I were a Devil if I did.—See how far I am forced to stand from Stella, because I am afraid she thinks poor Presto has not been careful about her little things; I am sure I bought them immediately according to order, and packed them up with my own hands, and sent them to Sterne, and was six times with him about sending them away. I am glad you are pleased with your glasses. I have got another velvet cap; a new one Lord Herbert bought and presented me one morning I was at breakfast with him, where he was as merry and easy as ever I saw him, yet had received a challenge half an hour before, and half an hour after fought a duel. It was about ten days ago. You are mistaken in your guesses about *Tatlers*: I did neither write that on Noses nor Religion, nor do I send him of late any hints at all.—Indeed, Stella, when I read your letter, I was not uneasy at all; but when I came to answer the particulars, and found that you had not received your box, it grated me to the heart, because I thought, through your little words, that you imagined I had not taken the care I ought. But there has been some blunder in this matter, which I will know to-morrow, and write to Sterne, for fear he should not be within.—And pray, pray, Presto, pray now do.—No, Raymond was not above four times with me while he stayed, and then only while I was dressing. Mrs. Fenton has written me another letter about some money of hers in Lady Giffard's hands, that is entrusted to me by my mother, not to come to her husband. I send my letters constantly every fortnight, and, if you will have them oftener, you may, but then they will be the shorter. Pray, let Parvisol sell the horse. I think I spoke to you of it in a former letter: I am glad you are rid of him, and was in pain while I thought you rode him; but, if he would buy you another, or anybody else, and that you could be often able to ride, why do not you do it?

2. I went this morning early to the Secretary of State, Mr. St. John; and he told me from Mr. Harley that the warrant was now drawn, in order for a patent for the First-Fruits: it must pass through several offices, and take up some time, because in things the Queen gives they are always considerate; but that, he assures me, 'tis granted and done, and past all dispute, and desires I will not be in any pain at all. I will write again to the Archbishop to-morrow, and tell him this, and I desire you will say it on occasion. From the Secretary I went to Mr. Sterne, who said he would write to you to-night; and that the box must be at Chester; and that some friend of his goes very soon, and will carry it over. I dined with Mr. Secretary St. John, and at six went to Darteneufs house to drink punch with him, and Mr. Addison, and little Harrison, a young poet, whose fortune I am making. Steele was to have been there, but came not, nor never did twice, since I knew him, to any appointment. I stayed till past eleven, and am now in bed. Steele's last *Tatler* came out to-day. You will see it before this comes to you, and how he takes leave of the world. He never told so much as Mr. Addison of it, who was surprised as much as I; but, to say the truth, it was time, for he grew cruel dull and dry. To my knowledge he had several good hints to go upon; but he was so lazy and weary of the work that he would not improve them. I think I will send this after to-morrow: shall I before 'tis full, Dingley?

3. Lord Peterborow yesterday called me into a barber's shop, and there we talked deep politics: he desired me to dine with him to-day at the Globe in the Strand; he said he would show me so clearly how to get Spain, that I could not possibly doubt it. I went to-day accordingly, and saw him among half a dozen lawyers and attorneys and hang-dogs, signing of deeds and stuff before his journey; for he goes to-morrow to Vienna. I sat among that scurvy company till after four, but heard nothing of Spain; only I find, by what he told me before, that he fears he shall do no good in his present journey. We are to be mighty constant correspondents. So I took my leave of him, and called at Sir Andrew Fountaine's, who mends much. I came home, an't please you, at six, and have been studying till now past eleven.

4. Morning. Morrow, little dears. O, faith, I have been dreaming; I was to be put in prison. I do not know why, and I was so afraid of a black dungeon; and then all I had been inquiring yesterday of Sir Andrew Fountaine's sickness I thought was of poor Stella. The worst of dreams is, that one wakes just in the humour they leave one. Shall I send this to-day? With all my heart: it is two days within the fortnight; but may be MD are in haste to have a round dozen: and then how are you come up to me with your eighth, young women? But you indeed ought to write twice slower than I, because there are two of you; I own that. Well then, I will seal up this letter by my morning candle, and carry it into the city with me, where I go to dine, and put it into the post-office with my own fair hands. So, let me see whether I have any news to tell MD. They say they will very soon make some inquiries into the corruptions of the late Ministry; and they must do it, to justify their turning them out. Atterbury, we think, is to be Dean of Christ Church in Oxford; but the College would rather have Smalridge—What's all this to you? What care you for Atterburys and Smalridges? No, you care for nothing but Presto, faith. So I will rise, and bid you farewell; yet I am loth to do so, because there is a great bit of paper yet to talk upon; but Dingley will have it so: "Yes," says she, "make your journals shorter, and send them oftener;" and so I will. And I have cheated you another way too; for this is clipped paper, and holds at least six lines less than the former ones. I will tell you a good thing I said to my Lord Carteret. "So," says he, "my Lord came up to me, and asked me," etc. "No," said I, "my Lord never did, nor ever can come up to you." We all pun here sometimes. Lord Carteret set down Prior t'other day in his chariot; and Prior thanked him for his *charity*; that was fit for Dilly. I do not remember I heard one good one from the Ministry; which is really a shame. Henley is gone to the country for Christmas. The puppy comes here without his wife, and keeps no house, and would have me dine with him at eating-houses; but I have only done it once, and will do it no more. He had not seen me for some time in the Coffee-house, and asking after me, desired Lord Herbert to tell me I was a beast for ever, after the order of Melchisedec. Did you ever read the Scripture? It is only changing the word priest to beast.—I think I am bewitched, to write so much in a morning to you, little MD. Let me go, will you? and I'll come again to-night in a fine clean sheet of paper; but I can nor will stay no longer now; no, I won't, for all your wheedling: no, no, look off, do not smile at me, and say, "Pray, pray, Presto, write a little more." Ah! you are a wheedling slut, you

be so. Nay, but prithee turn about, and let me go, do; 'tis a good girl, and do. O, faith, my morning candle is just out, and I must go now in spite of my teeth; for my bed-chamber is dark with curtains, and I am at the wrong side. So farewell, etc. etc.

I am in the dark almost: I must have another candle, when I am up, to seal this; but I will fold it up in the dark, and make what you can of this, for I can only see this paper I am writing upon. Service to Mrs. Walls and Mrs. Stoyte.

God Almighty bless you, etc. What I am doing I can't see; but I will fold it up, and not look on it again.

LETTER XIII

I was going into the City (where I dined) and put my 12th, with my own fair hands, into the post-office as I came back, which was not till nine this night. I dined with people that you never heard of, nor is it worth your while to know; an authoress and a printer. I walked home for exercise, and at eleven got to bed; and, all the while I was undressing myself, there was I speaking monkey things in air, just as if MD had been by, and did not recollect myself till I got into bed. I writ last night to the Archbishop, and told him the warrant was drawn for the First-Fruits; and I told him Lord Peterborow was set out for his journey to Vienna; but it seems the Lords have addressed to have him stay, to be examined about Spanish affairs, upon this defeat there, and to know where the fault lay, etc. So I writ to the Archbishop a lie; but I think it was not a sin.

5. Mr. Secretary St. John sent for me this morning so early, that I was forced to go without shaving, which put me quite out of method. I called at Mr. Ford's, and desired him to lend me a shaving; and so made a shift to get into order again. Lord! here is an impertinence: Sir Andrew Fountaine's mother and sister are come above a hundred miles, from Worcester, to see him before he died. They got here but yesterday; and he must have been past hopes, or past fears, before they could reach him. I fell a scolding when I heard they were coming; and the people about him wondered at me, and said what a mighty content it would be on both sides to die when they were with him! I knew the mother; she is the greatest Overdo upon earth; and the sister, they say, is worse; the poor man will relapse again among them. Here was the scoundrel brother always crying in the outer room till Sir Andrew was in danger; and the dog was to have all his estate if he died; and it is an ignorant, worthless, scoundrel-rake: and the nurses were comforting him, and desiring he would not take on so. I dined to-day the first time with Ophy Butler and his wife; and you supped with the Dean, and lost two-and-twenty pence at cards. And so Mrs. Walls is brought to bed of a girl, who died two days after it was christened; and, betwixt you and me, she is not very sorry: she loves her ease and diversions too well to be troubled with children. I will go to bed.

6. Morning. I went last night to put some coals on my fire after Patrick was gone to bed; and there I saw in a closet a poor linnet he has bought to bring over to Dingley: it cost him sixpence, and is as tame as a dormouse. I believe he does not know he is a bird: where you put him, there he stands, and seems to have neither hope nor fear; I suppose in a week he will die of the spleen. Patrick advised with me before he bought him. I laid fairly before him the greatness of the sum, and the rashness of the attempt; showed how impossible it was to carry him safe over the salt sea: but he would not take my counsel; and he will repent it. 'Tis very cold this morning in bed; and I hear there is a good fire in the room without (what do you call it?), the dining-room. I hope it will be good weather, and so let me rise, sirrahs, do so.—At night. I was this morning to visit the Dean, or Mr. Prolocutor, I think you call him, don't you? Why should not I go to the Dean's as well as you? A little, black man, of pretty near fifty? Ay, the same. A good, pleasant man? Ay, the same. Cunning enough? Yes. One that understands his own interests? As well as anybody. How comes it MD and I don't meet there sometimes? A very good face, and abundance of wit? Do you know his lady? O Lord! whom do you mean? I mean Dr. Atterbury, Dean of Carlisle and Prolocutor. Pshaw, Presto, you are a fool: I thought you had meant our Dean of St. Patrick's.—Silly, silly, silly, you are silly, both are silly, every kind of thing is silly. As I walked into the city I was stopped with clusters of boys and wenches buzzing about the cake-shops like flies. There had the fools let out their shops two yards forward into the streets, all spread with great cakes frothed with sugar, and stuck with streamers of tinsel. And then I went to Bateman's the bookseller, and laid out eight-and-forty shillings for books. I bought three little volumes of Lucian in French for our Stella, and so and so. Then I went to Garraway's to meet Stratford and dine with him; but it was an idle day with the merchants, and he was gone to our end of the town: so I dined with Sir Thomas Frankland at the Post Office, and we drank your Manley's health. It was in a newspaper that he was turned out; but Secretary St. John told me it was false: only that newswriter is a plaguy Tory. I have not seen one bit of Christmas merriment.

7. Morning. Your new Lord Chancellor sets out to-morrow for Ireland: I never saw him. He carries over one Trapp a parson as his chaplain, a sort of pretender to wit, a second-rate pamphleteer for the cause, whom they pay by sending him to Ireland. I never saw Trapp neither. I met

Tighe and your Smyth of Lovet's yesterday by the Exchange. Tighe and I took no notice of each other; but I stopped Smyth, and told him of the box that lies for you at Chester, because he says he goes very soon to Ireland, I think this week: and I will send this morning to Sterne, to take measures with Smyth; so good-morrow, sirrahs, and let me rise, pray. I took up this paper when I came in at evening, I mean this minute, and then said I, "No, no, indeed, MD, you must stay"; and then was laying it aside, but could not for my heart, though I am very busy, till I just ask you how you do since morning; by and by we shall talk more, so let me leave you: softly down, little paper, till then; so there—now to business; there, I say, get you gone; no, I will not push you neither, but hand you on one side—So—Now I am got into bed, I'll talk with you. Mr. Secretary St. John sent for me this morning in all haste; but I would not lose my shaving, for fear of missing church. I went to Court, which is of late always very full; and young Manley and I dined at Sir Matthew Dudley's.—I must talk politics. I protest I am afraid we shall all be embroiled with parties. The Whigs, now they are fallen, are the most malicious toads in the world. We have had now a second misfortune, the loss of several Virginia ships. I fear people will begin to think that nothing thrives under this Ministry: and if the Ministry can once be rendered odious to the people, the Parliament may be chosen Whig or Tory as the Queen pleases. Then I think our friends press a little too hard on the Duke of Marlborough. The country members are violent to have past faults inquired into, and they have reason; but I do not observe the Ministry to be very fond of it. In my opinion we have nothing to save us but a Peace; and I am sure we cannot have such a one as we hoped; and then the Whigs will bawl what they would have done had they continued in power. I tell the Ministry this as much as I dare; and shall venture to say a little more to them, especially about the Duke of Marlborough, who, as the Whigs give out, will lay down his command; and I question whether ever any wise State laid aside a general who had been successful nine years together, whom the enemy so much dread, and his own soldiers cannot but believe must always conquer; and you know that in war opinion is nine parts in ten. The Ministry hear me always with appearance of regard, and much kindness; but I doubt they let personal quarrels mingle too much with their proceedings. Meantime, they seem to value all this as nothing, and are as easy and merry as if they had nothing in their hearts or upon their shoulders; like physicians, who endeavour to cure, but feel no grief, whatever the patient suffers.—Pshaw, what is all this? Do you know one thing, that I find I can write politics to you much easier than to anybody alive? But I swear my head is full; and I wish I were at Laracor, with dear, charming MD, etc.

8. Morning. Methinks, young women, I have made a great progress in four days, at the bottom of this side already, and no letter yet come from MD (that word interlined is morning). I find I have been writing State affairs to MD. How do they relish it? Why, anything that comes from Presto is welcome; though really, to confess the truth, if they had their choice, not to disguise the matter, they had rather, etc. Now, Presto, I must tell you, you grow silly, says Stella. That is but one body's opinion, madam. I promised to be with Mr. Secretary St. John this morning; but I am lazy, and will not go, because I had a letter from him yesterday, to desire I would dine there to-day. I shall be chid; but what care I?—Here has been Mrs. South with me, just come from Sir Andrew Fountaine, and going to market. He is still in a fever, and may live or die. His mother and sister are now come up, and in the house; so there is a lurry. I gave Mrs. South half a pistole for a New Year's gift. So good-morrow, dears both, till anon.—At night. Lord! I have been with Mr. Secretary from dinner till eight; and, though I drank wine and water, I am so hot! Lady Stanley came to visit Mrs. St. John, and sent up for me to make up a quarrel with Mrs. St. John, whom I never yet saw; and do you think that devil of a Secretary would let me go, but kept me by main force, though I told him I was in love with his lady, and it was a shame to keep back a lover, etc.? But all would not do; so at last I was forced to break away, but never went up, it was then too late; and here I am, and have a great deal to do to-night, though it be nine o'clock; but one must say something to these naughty MD's, else there will be no quiet.

9. To-day Ford and I set apart to go into the City to buy books; but we only had a scurvy dinner at an alehouse; and he made me go to the tavern and drink Florence, four and sixpence a flask; damned wine! so I spent my money, which I seldom do, and passed an insipid day, and saw nobody, and it is now ten o'clock, and I have nothing to say, but that 'tis a fortnight to-morrow since I had a letter from MD; but if I have it time enough to answer here, 'tis well enough, otherwise woe betide you, faith. I will go to the toyman's, here just in Pall Mall, and he sells great

hugeous battoons; yes, faith, and so he does. Does not he, Dingley? Yes, faith. Don't lose your money this Christmas.

10. I must go this morning to Mr. Secretary St. John. I promised yesterday, but failed, so can't write any more till night to poor, dear MD.—At night. O, faith, Dingley. I had company in the morning, and could not go where I designed; and I had a basket from Raymond at Bristol, with six bottles of wine and a pound of chocolate, and some tobacco to snuff; and he writ under, the carriage was paid; but he lied, or I am cheated, or there is a mistake; and he has written to me so confusedly about some things, that Lucifer could not understand him. This wine is to be drunk with Harley's brother and Sir Robert Raymond, Solicitor-General, in order to recommend the Doctor to your new Lord Chancellor, who left this place on Monday; and Raymond says he is hasting to Chester, to go with him.—I suppose he leaves his wife behind; for when he left London he had no thoughts of stirring till summer. So I suppose he will be with you before this. Ford came and desired I would dine with him, because it was Opera-day; which I did, and sent excuses to Lord Shelburne, who had invited me.

11. I am setting up a new Tatler, little Harrison, whom I have mentioned to you. Others have put him on it, and I encourage him; and he was with me this morning and evening, showing me his first, which comes out on Saturday. I doubt he will not succeed, for I do not much approve his manner; but the scheme is Mr. Secretary St. John's and mine, and would have done well enough in good hands. I recommended him to a printer, whom I sent for, and settled the matter between them this evening. Harrison has just left me, and I am tired with correcting his trash.

12. I was this morning upon some business with Mr. Secretary St. John, and he made me promise to dine with him; which otherwise I would have done with Mr. Harley, whom I have not been with these ten days. I cannot but think they have mighty difficulties upon them; yet I always find them as easy and disengaged as schoolboys on a holiday. Harley has the procuring of five or six millions on his shoulders, and the Whigs will not lend a groat; which is the only reason of the fall of stocks: for they are like Quakers and fanatics, that will only deal among themselves, while all others deal indifferently with them. Lady Marlborough offers,

if they will let her keep her employments, never to come into the Queen's presence. The Whigs say the Duke of Marlborough will serve no more; but I hope and think otherwise. I would to Heaven I were this minute with MD at Dublin; for I am weary of politics, that give me such melancholy prospects.

13. O, faith, I had an ugly giddy fit last night in my chamber, and I have got a new box of pills to take, and hope I shall have no more this good while. I would not tell you before, because it would vex you, little rogues; but now it is over. I dined to-day with Lord Shelburne; and to-day little Harrison's new *Tatler* came out: there is not much in it, but I hope he will mend. You must understand that, upon Steele's leaving off, there were two or three scrub *Tatlers* came out, and one of them holds on still, and to-day it advertised against Harrison's; and so there must be disputes which are genuine, like the strops for razors. I am afraid the little toad has not the true vein for it. I will tell you a copy of verses. When Mr. St. John was turned out from being Secretary at War, three years ago, he retired to the country: there he was talking of something he would have written over his summer-house, and a gentleman gave him these verses—

> *From business and the noisy world retired,*
> *Nor vexed by love, nor by ambition fired;*
> *Gently I wait the call of Charon's boat,*
> *Still drinking like a fish, and—like a stoat.*

He swore to me he could hardly bear the jest; for he pretended to retire like a philosopher, though he was but twenty-eight years old: and I believe the thing was true: for he had been a thorough rake. I think the three grave lines do introduce the last well enough. Od so, but I will go sleep; I sleep early now.

14. O, faith, young women, I want a letter from MD; 'tis now nineteen days since I had the last: and where have I room to answer it, pray? I hope I shall send this away without any answer at all; for I'll hasten it, and away it goes on Tuesday, by which time this side will be full. I will send it two days sooner on purpose out of spite; and the very next day after, you must know, your letter will come, and then 'tis too late, and I will so laugh, never saw the like! 'Tis spring with us already. I

ate asparagus t'other day. Did you ever see such a frostless winter? Sir Andrew Fountaine lies still extremely ill; it costs him ten guineas a day to doctors, surgeons, and apothecaries, and has done so these three weeks. I dined to-day with Mr. Ford; he sometimes chooses to dine at home, and I am content to dine with him; and at night I called at the Coffee-house, where I had not been in a week, and talked coldly a while with Mr. Addison. All our friendship and dearness are off: we are civil acquaintance, talk words of course, of when we shall meet, and that is all. I have not been at any house with him these six weeks: t'other day we were to have dined together at the Comptroller's; but I sent my excuses, being engaged to the Secretary of State. Is not it odd? But I think he has used me ill; and I have used him too well, at least his friend Steele.

15. It has cost me three guineas to-day for a periwig. I am undone! It was made by a Leicester lad, who married Mr. Worrall's daughter, where my mother lodged; so I thought it would be cheap, and especially since he lives in the city. Well, London lickpenny: I find it true. I have given Harrison hints for another *Tatler* to-morrow. The jackanapes wants a right taste: I doubt he won't do. I dined with my friend Lewis of the Secretary's office, and am got home early, because I have much business to do; but before I begin, I must needs say something to MD, faith—No, faith, I lie, it is but nineteen days to-day since my last from MD. I have got Mr. Harley to promise that whatever changes are made in the Council, the Bishop of Clogher shall not be removed, and he has got a memorial accordingly. I will let the Bishop know so much in a post or two. This is a secret; but I know he has enemies, and they shall not be gratified, if they designed any such thing, which perhaps they might; for some changes there will be made. So drink up your claret, and be quiet, and do not lose your money.

16. Morning. Faith, I will send this letter to-day to shame you, if I han't one from MD before night, that's certain. Won't you grumble for want of the third side, pray now? Yes, I warrant you; yes, yes, you shall have the third, you shall so, when you can catch it, some other time; when you be writing girls.—O, faith, I think I won't stay till night, but seal up this just now, and carry it in my pocket, and whip it into the post-office as I come home at evening. I am going out early this morning.—Patrick's bills for coals and candles, etc., come sometimes

to three shillings a week; I keep very good fires, though the weather be warm. Ireland will never be happy till you get small coal likewise; nothing so easy, so convenient, so cheap, so pretty, for lighting a fire. My service to Mrs. Stoyte and Walls; has she a boy or a girl? A girl, hum; and died in a week, humm; and was poor Stella forced to stand for godmother?—Let me know how accompts stand, that you may have your money betimes. There's four months for my lodging, that must be thought on too: and so go dine with Manley, and lose your money, do, extravagant sluttikin, but don't fret.—It will be just three weeks when I have the next letter, that's to-morrow. Farewell, dearest beloved MD; and love poor, poor Presto, who has not had one happy day since he left you, as hope saved.—It is the last sally I will ever make, but I hope it will turn to some account. I have done more for these, and I think they are more honest than the last; however, I will not be disappointed. I would make MD and me easy; and I never desired more.—Farewell, etc. etc.

Letter XIV

O faith, young women, I have sent my letter N. 13 without one crumb of an answer to any of MD's, there's for you now; and yet Presto ben't angry, faith, not a bit, only he will begin to be in pain next Irish post, except he sees MD's little handwriting in the glass-frame at the bar of St. James's Coffee-house, where Presto would never go but for that purpose. Presto is at home, God help him, every night from six till bed-time, and has as little enjoyment or pleasure in life at present as anybody in the world, although in full favour with all the Ministry. As hope saved, nothing gives Presto any sort of dream of happiness but a letter now and then from his own dearest MD. I love the expectation of it; and when it does not come, I comfort myself that I have it yet to be happy with. Yes, faith, and when I write to MD, I am happy too; it is just as if methinks you were here, and I prating to you, and telling you where I have been: "Well," says you, "Presto, come, where have you been to-day? come, let's hear now." And so then I answer: "Ford and I were visiting Mr. Lewis and Mr. Prior; and Prior has given me a fine Plautus; and then Ford would have had me dine at his lodgings, and so I would not; and so I dined with him at an eating-house, which I have not done five times since I came here; and so I came home, after visiting Sir Andrew Fountaine's mother and sister, and Sir Andrew Fountaine is mending, though slowly."

17. I was making, this morning, some general visits, and at twelve I called at the Coffee-house for a letter from MD; so the man said he had given it to Patrick. Then I went to the Court of Requests and Treasury, to find Mr. Harley, and, after some time spent in mutual reproaches, I promised to dine with him. I stayed there till seven, then called at Sterne's and Leigh's to talk about your box, and to have it sent by Smyth. Sterne says he has been making inquiries, and will set things right as soon as possible. I suppose it lies at Chester, at least I hope so, and only wants a lift over to you. Here has little Harrison been to complain that the printer I recommended to him for his *Tatler* is a coxcomb; and yet to see how things will happen; for this very printer is my cousin, his name is Dryden Leach; did you never hear of Dryden Leach, he that prints the *Postman*? He acted Oroonoko; he's in love

with Miss Cross.—Well, so I came home to read my letter from Stella, but the dog Patrick was abroad; at last he came, and I got my letter. I found another hand had superscribed it; when I opened it, I found it written all in French, and subscribed Bernage: faith, I was ready to fling it at Patrick's head. Bernage tells me he had been to desire your recommendation to me, to make him a captain; and your cautious answer, that he had as much power with me as you, was a notable one; if you were here, I would present you to the Ministry as a person of ability. Bernage should let me know where to write to him; this is the second letter I have had without any direction; however, I beg I may not have a third, but that you will ask him, and send me how I shall direct to him. In the meantime, tell him that if regiments are to be raised here, as he says, I will speak to George Granville, Secretary at War, to make him a captain; and use what other interest I conveniently can. I think that is enough, and so tell him, and do not trouble me with his letters, when I expect them from MD; do you hear, young women? write to Presto.

18. I was this morning with Mr. Secretary St. John, and we were to dine at Mr. Harley's alone, about some business of importance; but there were two or three gentlemen there. Mr. Secretary and I went together from his office to Mr. Harley's, and thought to have been very wise; but the deuce a bit, the company stayed, and more came, and Harley went away at seven, and the Secretary and I stayed with the rest of the company till eleven; I would then have had him come away; but he was in for't; and though he swore he would come away at that flask, there I left him. I wonder at the civility of these people; when he saw I would drink no more, he would always pass the bottle by me, and yet I could not keep the toad from drinking himself, nor he would not let me go neither, nor Masham, who was with us. When I got home, I found a parcel directed to me; and opening it, I found a pamphlet written entirely against myself, not by name, but against something I writ: it is pretty civil, and affects to be so, and I think I will take no notice of it; 'tis against something written very lately; and indeed I know not what to say, nor do I care. And so you are a saucy rogue for losing your money to-day at Stoyte's; to let that bungler beat you, fie, Stella, an't you ashamed? Well, I forgive you this once, never do so again; no, noooo. Kiss and be friends, sirrah.—Come, let me go sleep, I go earlier to bed than formerly; and have not been out so late these two

months; but the Secretary was in a drinking humour. So good-night, myownlittledearsaucyinsolentrogues.

19. Then you read that long word in the last line; no, faith, han't you. Well, when will this letter come from our MD? to-morrow or next day without fail; yes, faith, and so it is coming. This was an insipid snowy day, no walking day, and I dined gravely with Mrs. Vanhomrigh, and came home, and am now got to bed a little after ten; I remember old Culpepper's maxim:

> *"Would you have a settled head,*
> *You must early go to bed:*
> *I tell you, and I tell't again,*
> *You must be in bed at ten."*

20. And so I went to-day with my new wig, o hoao, to visit Lady Worsley, whom I had not seen before, although she was near a month in town. Then I walked in the Park to find Mr. Ford, whom I had promised to meet; and coming down the Mall, who should come towards me but Patrick, and gives me five letters out of his pocket. I read the superscription of the first, "Pshoh," said I; of the second, "Pshoh" again; of the third, "Pshah, pshah, pshah"; of the fourth, "A gad, a gad, a gad, I'm in a rage"; of the fifth and last, "O hoooa; ay marry this is something, this is our MD"; so truly we opened it, I think immediately, and it began the most impudently in the world, thus: "Dear Presto, We are even thus far." "Now we are even," quoth Stephen, when he gave his wife six blows for one. I received your ninth four days after I had sent my thirteenth. But I'll reckon with you anon about that, young women. Why did not you recant at the end of your letter, when you got my eleventh, tell me that, huzzies base? were we even then, were we, sirrah? But I won't answer your letter now, I'll keep it for another time. We had a great deal of snow to-day, and 'tis terrible cold. I dined with Ford, because it was his Opera-day and snowed, so I did not care to stir farther. I will send to-morrow to Smyth.

21. Morning. It has snowed terribly all night, and is vengeance cold. I am not yet up, but cannot write long; my hands will freeze. "Is there a good fire, Patrick?" "Yes, sir." "Then I will rise; come, take away the candle." You must know I write on the dark side of my bed-chamber, and am forced to have a candle till I rise, for the bed stands between

me and the window, and I keep the curtains shut this cold weather. So pray let me rise; and Patrick, here, take away the candle.—At night. We are now here in high frost and snow, the largest fire can hardly keep us warm. It is very ugly walking; a baker's boy broke his thigh yesterday. I walk slow, make short steps, and never tread on my heel. 'Tis a good proverb the Devonshire people have:

> *"Walk fast in snow,*
> *In frost walk slow;*
> *And still as you go,*
> *Tread on your toe.*
> *When frost and snow are both together,*
> *Sit by the fire, and spare shoe-leather."*

I dined to-day with Dr. Cockburn, but will not do so again in haste, he has generally such a parcel of Scots with him.

22. Morning. Starving, starving, uth, uth, uth, uth, uth.—Don't you remember I used to come into your chamber, and turn Stella out of her chair, and rake up the fire in a cold morning, and cry Uth, uth, uth? etc. O, faith, I must rise, my hand is so cold I can write no more. So good-morrow, sirrahs.—At night. I went this morning to Lady Giffard's house, and saw your mother, and made her give me a pint bottle of palsy-water, which I brought home in my pocket; and sealed and tied up in a paper, and sent it to Mr. Smyth, who goes to-morrow for Ireland, and sent a letter to him to desire his care of it, and that he would inquire at Chester about the box. He was not within: so the bottle and letter were left for him at his lodgings, with strict orders to give them to him; and I will send Patrick in a day or two, to know whether it was given, etc. Dr. Stratford and I dined to-day with Mr. Stratford in the City, by appointment; but I chose to walk there, for exercise in the frost. But the weather had given a little, as you women call it, so it was something slobbery. I did not get home till nine.

> *And now I'm in bed,*
> *To break your head.*

23. Morning. They tell me it freezes again, but it is not so cold as yesterday: so now I will answer a bit of your letter.—At night. O, faith,

I was just going to answer some of our MD's letter this morning, when a printer came in about some business, and stayed an hour; so I rose, and then came in Ben Tooke, and then I shaved and scribbled; and it was such a terrible day, I could not stir out till one, and then I called at Mrs. Barton's, and we went to Lady Worsley's, where we were to dine by appointment. The Earl of Berkeley is going to be married to Lady Louisa Lennox, the Duke of Richmond's daughter. I writ this night to Dean Sterne, and bid him tell you all about the bottle of palsy-water by Smyth; and to-morrow morning I will say something to your letter.

24. Morning. Come now to your letter. As for your being even with me, I have spoken to that already. So now, my dearly beloved, let us proceed to the next. You are always grumbling that you han't letters fast enough; "surely we shall have your tenth;" and yet, before you end your letter, you own you have my eleventh.—And why did not MD go into the country with the Bishop of Clogher? faith, such a journey would have done you good; Stella should have rode, and Dingley gone in the coach. The Bishop of Kilmore I know nothing of; he is old, and may die; he lives in some obscure corner, for I never heard of him. As for my old friends, if you mean the Whigs, I never see them, as you may find by my journals, except Lord Halifax, and him very seldom; Lord Somers never since the first visit, for he has been a false, deceitful rascal. My new friends are very kind, and I have promises enough, but I do not count upon them, and besides my pretences are very young to them. However, we will see what may be done; and if nothing at all, I shall not be disappointed; although perhaps poor MD may, and then I shall be sorrier for their sakes than my own.—Talk of a merry Christmas (why do you write it so then, young women? sauce for the goose is sauce for the gander), I have wished you all that two or three letters ago. Good lack; and your news, that Mr. St. John is going to Holland; he has no such thoughts, to quit the great station he is in; nor, if he had, could I be spared to go with him. So, faith, politic Madam Stella, you come with your two eggs a penny, etc. Well, Madam Dingley, and so Mrs. Stoyte invites you, and so you stay at Donnybrook, and so you could not write. You are plaguy exact in your journals, from Dec. 25 to Jan. 4. Well, Smyth and the palsy-water I have handled already, and he does not lodge (or rather did not, for, poor man, now he is gone) at Mr. Jesse's, and all that stuff; but we found his lodging, and I went to Stella's mother on my own head, for I

never remembered it was in the letter to desire another bottle; but I was so fretted, so tosticated, and so impatient that Stella should have her water (I mean decently, do not be rogues), and so vexed with Sterne's carelessness.—Pray God, Stella's illness may not return! If they come seldom, they begin to be weary; I judge by myself; for when I seldom visit, I grow weary of my acquaintance.—Leave a good deal of my tenth unanswered! Impudent slut, when did you ever answer my tenth, or ninth, or any other number? or who desires you to answer, provided you write? I defy the D—to answer my letters: sometimes there may be one or two things I should be glad you would answer; but I forget them, and you never think of them. I shall never love answering letters again, if you talk of answering. Answering, quotha! pretty answerers truly.—As for the pamphlet you speak of, and call it scandalous, and that one Mr. Presto is said to write it, hear my answer. Fie, child, you must not mind what every idle body tells you—I believe you lie, and that the dogs were not crying it when you said so; come, tell truth. I am sorry you go to St. Mary's so soon, you will be as poor as rats; that place will drain you with a vengeance: besides, I would have you think of being in the country in summer. Indeed, Stella, pippins produced plentifully; Parvisol could not send from Laracor: there were about half a score, I would be glad to know whether they were good for anything.—Mrs. Walls at Donnybrook with you; why is not she brought to bed? Well, well, well, Dingley, pray be satisfied; you talk as if you were angry about the Bishop's not offering you conveniences for the journey; and so he should.—What sort of Christmas? Why, I have had no Christmas at all; and has it really been Christmas of late? I never once thought of it. My service to Mrs. Stoyte, and Catherine; and let Catherine get the coffee ready against I come, and not have so much care on her countenance; for all will go well.—Mr. Bernage, Mr. Bernage, Mr. Fiddlenage, I have had three letters from him now successively; he sends no directions, and how the D—shall I write to him? I would have burnt his last, if I had not seen Stella's hand at the bottom: his request is all nonsense. How can I assist him in buying? and if he be ordered to go to Spain, go he must, or else sell, and I believe one can hardly sell in such a juncture. If he had stayed, and new regiments raised, I would have used my endeavour to have had him removed; although I have no credit that way, or very little: but, if the regiment goes, he ought to go too; he has had great indulgence, and opportunities of saving; and I have urged him to it a hundred times.

JONATHAN SWIFT

What can I do? whenever it lies in my power to do him a good office, I will do it. Pray draw up this into a handsome speech, and represent it to him from me, and that I would write, if I knew where to direct to him; and so I have told you, and desired you would tell him, fifty times. Yes, Madam Stella, I think I can read your long concluding word, but you can't read mine after bidding you good-night. And yet methinks, I mend extremely in my writing; but when Stella's eyes are well, I hope to write as bad as ever.—So now I have answered your letter, and mine is an answer; for I lay yours before me, and I look and write, and write and look, and look and write again.—So good-morrow, madams both, and I will go rise, for I must rise; for I take pills at night, and so I must rise early, I don't know why.

25. Morning. I did not tell you how I passed my time yesterday, nor bid you good-night, and there was good reason. I went in the morning to Secretary St. John about some business; he had got a great Whig with him; a creature of the Duke of Marlborough, who is a go-between to make peace between the Duke and the Ministry: so he came out of his closet, and, after a few words, desired I would dine with him at three; but Mr. Lewis stayed till six before he came; and there we sat talking, and the time slipped so, that at last, when I was positive to go, it was past two o'clock; so I came home, and went straight to bed. He would never let me look at his watch, and I could not imagine it above twelve when we went away. So I bid you good-night for last night, and now I bid you good-morrow, and I am still in bed, though it be near ten, but I must rise.

26, 27, 28, 29, 30. I have been so lazy and negligent these last four days that I could not write to MD. My head is not in order, and yet is not absolutely ill, but giddyish, and makes me listless; I walk every day, and take drops of Dr. Cockburn, and I have just done a box of pills; and to-day Lady Kerry sent me some of her bitter drink, which I design to take twice a day, and hope I shall grow better. I wish I were with MD; I long for spring and good weather, and then I will come over. My riding in Ireland keeps me well. I am very temperate, and eat of the easiest meats as I am directed, and hope the malignity will go off; but one fit shakes me a long time. I dined to-day with Lord Mountjoy, yesterday at Mr. Stone's, in the City, on Sunday at Vanhomrigh's, Saturday with Ford, and Friday I think at Vanhomrigh's; and that is all the journal I can send MD, for I was so lazy while I was well, that I could not write. I thought to have sent this to-night, but 'tis ten, and I'll go to bed, and write on t'other side to Parvisol to-morrow, and send it on Thursday; and so good-night, my dears; and love Presto, and be healthy, and Presto will be so too, etc.

Cut off these notes handsomely, d'ye hear, sirrahs, and give Mrs. Brent hers, and keep yours till you see Parvisol, and then make up the letter to him, and send it him by the first opportunity; and so God Almighty bless you both, here and ever, and poor Presto.

What, I warrant you thought at first that these last lines were another letter.

Dingley, Pray pay Stella six fishes, and place them to the account of your humble servant, Presto.

Stella, Pray pay Dingley six fishes, and place them to the account of your humble servant, Presto.

There are bills of exchange for you.

Letter XV

I am to send you my fourteenth to-morrow; but my head, having some little disorders, confounds all my journals. I was early this morning with Mr. Secretary St. John about some business, so I could not scribble my morning lines to MD. They are here intending to tax all little printed penny papers a halfpenny every half-sheet, which will utterly ruin Grub Street, and I am endeavouring to prevent it. Besides, I was forwarding an impeachment against a certain great person; that was two of my businesses with the Secretary, were they not worthy ones? It was Ford's birthday, and I refused the Secretary, and dined with Ford. We are here in as smart a frost for the time as I have seen; delicate walking weather, and the Canal and Rosamond's Pond full of the rabble sliding and with skates, if you know what those are. Patrick's bird's water freezes in the gallipot, and my hands in bed.

Feb. 1. I was this morning with poor Lady Kerry, who is much worse in her head than I. She sends me bottles of her bitter; and we are so fond of one another, because our ailments are the same; don't you know that, Madam Stella? Han't I seen you conning ailments with Joe's wife, and some others, sirrah? I walked into the City to dine, because of the walk, for we must take care of Presto's health, you know, because of poor little MD. But I walked plaguy carefully, for fear of sliding against my will; but I am very busy.

2. This morning Mr. Ford came to me to walk into the City, where he had business, and then to buy books at Bateman's; and I laid out one pound five shillings for a Strabo and Aristophanes, and I have now got books enough to make me another shelf, and I will have more, or it shall cost me a fall; and so as we came back, we drank a flask of right French wine at Ben Tooke's chamber; and when I got home, Mrs. Vanhomrigh sent me word her eldest daughter was taken suddenly very ill, and desired I would come and see her. I went, and found it was a silly trick of Mrs. Armstrong, Lady Lucy's sister, who, with Moll Stanhope, was visiting there: however, I rattled off the daughter.

3. To-day I went and dined at Lady Lucy's, where you know I have not been this long time. They are plaguy Whigs, especially the sister

Armstrong, the most insupportable of all women, pretending to wit, without any taste. She was running down the last *Examiner*, the prettiest I had read, with a character of the present Ministry.—I left them at five, and came home. But I forgot to tell you, that this morning my cousin Dryden Leach, the printer, came to me with a heavy complaint, that Harrison the new Tatler had turned him off, and taken the last Tatler's printers again. He vowed revenge; I answered gravely, and so he left me, and I have ordered Patrick to deny me to him from henceforth: and at night comes a letter from Harrison, telling me the same thing, and excused his doing it without my notice, because he would bear all the blame; and in his *Tatler* of this day he tells you the story, how he has taken his old officers, and there is a most humble letter from Morphew and Lillie to beg his pardon, etc. And lastly, this morning Ford sent me two letters from the Coffee-house (where I hardly ever go), one from the Archbishop of Dublin, and t'other from—Who do you think t'other was from?—I'll tell you, because you are friends; why, then it was, faith, it was from my own dear little MD, N. 10. Oh, but will not answer it now, no, noooooh, I'll keep it between the two sheets; here it is, just under; oh, I lifted up the sheet and saw it there: lie still, you shan't be answered yet, little letter; for I must go to bed, and take care of my head.

4. I avoid going to church yet, for fear of my head, though it has been much better these last five or six days, since I have taken Lady Kerry's bitter. Our frost holds like a dragon. I went to Mr. Addison's, and dined with him at his lodgings; I had not seen him these three weeks, we are grown common acquaintance; yet what have not I done for his friend Steele? Mr. Harley reproached me the last time I saw him, that to please me he would be reconciled to Steele, and had promised and appointed to see him, and that Steele never came. Harrison, whom Mr. Addison recommended to me, I have introduced to the Secretary of State, who has promised me to take care of him; and I have represented Addison himself so to the Ministry, that they think and talk in his favour, though they hated him before.—Well, he is now in my debt, and there's an end; and I never had the least obligation to him, and there's another end. This evening I had a message from Mr. Harley, desiring to know whether I was alive, and that I would dine with him to-morrow. They dine so late, that since my head has been wrong I have avoided being with them.—Patrick has been out of favour these ten days; I talk dry

and cross to him, and have called him "friend" three or four times. But, sirrahs, get you gone.

5. Morning. I am going this morning to see Prior, who dines with me at Mr. Harley's; so I can't stay fiddling and talking with dear little brats in a morning, and 'tis still terribly cold.—I wish my cold hand was in the warmest place about you, young women, I'd give ten guineas upon that account with all my heart, faith; oh, it starves my thigh; so I'll rise and bid you good-morrow, my ladies both, good-morrow. Come, stand away, let me rise: Patrick, take away the candle. Is there a good fire?— So—up-a-dazy.—At night. Mr. Harley did not sit down till six, and I stayed till eleven; henceforth I will choose to visit him in the evenings, and dine with him no more if I can help it. It breaks all my measures, and hurts my health; my head is disorderly, but not ill, and I hope it will mend.

6. Here has been such a hurry with the Queen's Birthday, so much fine clothes, and the Court so crowded that I did not go there. All the frost is gone. It thawed on Sunday, and so continues, yet ice is still on the Canal (I did not mean that of Laracor, but St. James's Park) and boys sliding on it. Mr. Ford pressed me to dine with him in his chamber.—Did not I tell you Patrick has got a bird, a linnet, to carry over to Dingley? It was very tame at first, and 'tis now the wildest I ever saw. He keeps it in a closet, where it makes a terrible litter; but I say nothing: I am as tame as a clout. When must we answer our MD's letter? One of these odd-come-shortlies. This is a week old, you see, and no farther yet. Mr. Harley desired I would dine with him again to-day; but I refused him, for I fell out with him yesterday, and will not see him again till he makes me amends: and so I go to bed.

7. I was this morning early with Mr. Lewis of the Secretary's office, and saw a letter Mr. Harley had sent to him, desiring to be reconciled; but I was deaf to all entreaties, and have desired Lewis to go to him, and let him know I expect further satisfaction. If we let these great Ministers pretend too much, there will be no governing them. He promises to make me easy, if I will but come and see him; but I won't, and he shall do it by message, or I will cast him off. I'll tell you the cause of our quarrel when I see you, and refer it to yourselves. In that he did something, which he intended for a favour; and I have taken it

quite otherwise, disliking both the thing and the manner, and it has heartily vexed me, and all I have said is truth, though it looks like jest; and I absolutely refused to submit to his intended favour, and expect further satisfaction. Mr. Ford and I dined with Mr. Lewis. We have a monstrous deal of snow, and it has cost me two shillings to-day in chair and coach, and walked till I was dirty besides. I know not what it is now to read or write after I am in bed. The last thing I do up is to write something to our MD, and then get into bed, and put out my candle, and so go sleep as fast as ever I can. But in the mornings I do write sometimes in bed, as you know.

8. Morning. *I have desired Apronia to be always careful, especially about the legs*. Pray, do you see any such great wit in that sentence? I must freely own that I do not. But party carries everything nowadays, and what a splutter have I heard about the wit of that saying, repeated with admiration above a hundred times in half an hour! Pray read it over again this moment, and consider it. I think the word is *advised*, and not *desired*. I should not have remembered it if I had not heard it so often. Why—ay—You must know I dreamed it just now, and waked with it in my mouth. Are you bit, or are you not, sirrahs? I met Mr. Harley in the Court of Requests, and he asked me how long I had learnt the trick of writing to myself? He had seen your letter through the glass case at the Coffee-house, and would swear it was my hand; and Mr. Ford, who took and sent it me, was of the same mind. I remember others have formerly said so too. I think I was little MD's writing-master.—But come, what is here to do, writing to young women in a morning? I have other fish to fry; so good-morrow, my ladies all, good-morrow. Perhaps I'll answer your letter to-night, perhaps I won't; that's as saucy little Presto takes the humour.—At night. I walked in the Park to-day in spite of the weather, as I do always when it does not actually rain. Do you know what it has gone and done? We had a thaw for three days, then a monstrous dirt and snow, and now it freezes, like a pot-lid, upon our snow. I dined with Lady Betty Germaine, the first time since I came for England; and there did I sit, like a booby, till eight, looking over her and another lady at piquet, when I had other business enough to do. It was the coldest day I felt this year.

9. Morning. After I had been abed an hour last night, I was forced to rise and call to the landlady and maid to have the fire removed in a chimney

below stairs, which made my bed-chamber smoke, though I had no fire in it. I have been twice served so. I never lay so miserable an hour in my life. Is it not plaguy vexatious?—It has snowed all night, and rains this morning.—Come, where's MD's letter? Come, Mrs. Letter, make your appearance. Here am I, says she, answer me to my face.—O, faith, I am sorry you had my twelfth so soon; I doubt you will stay longer for the rest. I'm so 'fraid you have got my fourteenth while I am writing this; and I would always have one letter from Presto reading, one travelling, and one writing. As for the box, I now believe it lost. It is directed for Mr. Curry, at his house in Capel Street, etc. I had a letter yesterday from Dr. Raymond in Chester, who says he sent his man everywhere, and cannot find it; and God knows whether Mr. Smyth will have better success. Sterne spoke to him, and I writ to him with the bottle of palsy-water; that bottle, I hope, will not miscarry: I long to hear you have it. O, faith, you have too good an opinion of Presto's care. I am negligent enough of everything but MD, and I should not have trusted Sterne.— But it shall not go so: I will have one more tug for it.—As to what you say of Goodman Peasly and Isaac, I answer as I did before. Fie, child, you must not give yourself the way to believe any such thing: and afterwards, only for curiosity, you may tell me how these things are approved, and how you like them; and whether they instruct you in the present course of affairs, and whether they are printed in your town, or only sent from hence.—Sir Andrew Fountaine is recovered; so take your sorrow again, but don't keep it, fling it to the dogs. And does little MD walk indeed?—I'm glad of it at heart.—Yes, we have done with the plague here: it was very saucy in you to pretend to have it before your betters. Your intelligence that the story is false about the officers forced to sell, is admirable. You may see them all three here every day, no more in the army than you. Twelve shillings for mending the strong box; that is, for putting a farthing's worth of iron on a hinge, and gilding it; give him six shillings, and I'll pay it, and never employ him or his again.— No indeed, I put off preaching as much as I can. I am upon another foot: nobody doubts here whether I can preach, and you are fools.—The account you give of that weekly paper agrees with us here. Mr. Prior was like to be insulted in the street for being supposed the author of it; but one of the last papers cleared him. Nobody knows who it is, but those few in the secret, I suppose the Ministry and the printer.—Poor Stella's eyes! God bless them, and send them better. Pray spare them, and write not above two lines a day in broad daylight. How does Stella look,

Madam Dingley? Pretty well, a handsome young woman still. Will she pass in a crowd? Will she make a figure in a country church?—Stay a little, fair ladies. I this minute sent Patrick to Sterne: he brings back word that your box is very safe with one Mr. Earl's sister in Chester, and that Colonel Edgworth's widow goes for Ireland on Monday next, and will receive the box at Chester, and deliver it you safe: so there are some hopes now.—Well, let us go on to your letter.—The warrant is passed for the First-Fruits. The Queen does not send a letter; but a patent will be drawn here, and that will take up time. Mr. Harley of late has said nothing of presenting me to the Queen: I was overseen when I mentioned it to you. He has such a weight of affairs on him, that he cannot mind all; but he talked of it three or four times to me, long before I dropped it to you. What, is not Mrs. Walls' business over yet? I had hopes she was up and well, and the child dead before this time.— You did right, at last, to send me your accompts; but I did not stay for them, I thank you. I hope you have your bill sent in my last, and there will be eight pounds' interest soon due from Hawkshaw: pray look at his bond. I hope you are good managers; and that, when I say so, Stella won't think I intend she should grudge herself wine. But going to those expensive lodgings requires some fund. I wish you had stayed till I came over, for some reasons. That Frenchwoman will be grumbling again in a little time: and if you are invited anywhere to the country, it will vex you to pay in absence; and the country may be necessary for poor Stella's health: but do as you like, and do not blame Presto.—Oh, but you are telling your reasons.—Well, I have read them; do as you please.—Yes, Raymond says he must stay longer than he thought, because he cannot settle his affairs. M—is in the country at some friend's, comes to town in spring, and then goes to settle in Herefordshire. Her husband is a surly, ill-natured brute, and cares not she should see anybody. O Lord, see how I blundered, and left two lines short; it was that ugly score in the paper that made me mistake.—I believe you lie about the story of the fire, only to make it more odd. Bernage must go to Spain; and I will see to recommend him to the Duke of Argyle, his General, when I see the Duke next: but the officers tell me it would be dishonourable in the last degree for him to sell now, and he would never be preferred in the army; so that, unless he designs to leave it for good and all, he must go. Tell him so, and that I would write if I knew where to direct to him; which I have said fourscore times already. I had rather anything almost than that you should strain yourselves to send a letter when it is inconvenient; we have settled that matter already. I'll write when I can, and so shall MD; and upon occasions extraordinary I will write, though it be a line; and when we have not letters soon, we agree that all things are well; and so that's settled for ever, and so hold your tongue.— Well, you shall have your pins; but for candles' ends, I cannot promise, because I burn them to the stumps; besides, I remember what Stella told Dingley about them many years ago, and she may think the same thing of me.—And Dingley shall have her hinged spectacles.—Poor dear Stella, how durst you write those two lines by candlelight? bang your bones! Faith, this letter shall go to-morrow, I think, and that will be in ten days from the last, young women; that's too soon of all conscience: but answering yours has filled it up so quick, and I do not design to use you to three pages in folio, no, nooooh. All this is one morning's work in bed;—and so good-morrow, little sirrahs; that's for the rhyme. You want politics: faith, I can't think of any; but may be at night I may tell you a passage. Come, sit off the bed, and let me rise, will you?—At night. I dined to-day with my neighbour Vanhomrigh; it was such dismal weather I could not stir further. I have had some threatenings with my head, but no fits. I still drink Dr. Radcliffe's bitter, and will continue it.

10. I was this morning to see the Secretary of State, and have engaged him to give a memorial from me to the Duke of Argyle in behalf of Bernage. The Duke is a man that distinguishes people of merit, and I will speak to him myself; but the Secretary backing it will be very effectual, and I will take care to have it done to purpose. Pray tell Bernage so, and that I think nothing can be luckier for him, and that I would have him go by all means. I will order it that the Duke shall send for him when they are in Spain; or, if he fails, that he shall receive him kindly when he goes to wait on him. Can I do more? Is not this a great deal?—I now send away this letter, that you may not stay.—I dined with Ford upon his Opera-day, and am now come home, and am going to study; do not you presume to guess, sirrahs, impudent saucy dear boxes. Towards the end of a letter I could not say saucy boxes without putting dear between. An't that right now? Farewell. *This* should *be* longer, *but* that *I* send *it* to-*night*.

O silly, silly loggerhead!

I send a letter this post to one Mr. Staunton, and I direct it to Mr. Acton's in St. Michael's Lane. He formerly lodged there, but he has not told me where to direct. Pray send to that Acton, whether the letter is come there, and whether he has sent it to Staunton.

If Bernage designs to sell his commission and stay at home, pray let him tell me so, that my recommendation to the Duke of Argyle may not be in vain.

Letter XVI

I have just despatched my fifteenth to the post; I tell you how things will be, after I have got a letter from MD. I am in furious haste to finish mine, for fear of having two of MD's to answer in one of Presto's, which would be such a disgrace, never saw the like; but, before you write to me, I write at my leisure, like a gentleman, a little every day, just to let you know how matters go, and so and so; and I hope before this comes to you, you'll have got your box and chocolate, and Presto will take more care another time.

11. Morning. I must rise and go see my Lord Keeper, which will cost me two shillings in coach-hire. Don't you call them two thirteens?—At night. It has rained all day, and there was no walking. I read prayers to Sir Andrew Fountaine in the forenoon, and I dined with three Irishmen, at one Mr. Cope's lodgings; the other two were one Morris an archdeacon, and Mr. Ford. When I came home this evening, I expected that little jackanapes Harrison would have come to get help about his *Tatler* for Tuesday: I have fixed two evenings in the week which I allow him to come. The toad never came, and I expecting him fell a reading, and left off other business.—Come, what are you doing? How do you pass your time this ugly weather? Gaming and drinking, I suppose: fine diversions for young ladies, truly! I wish you had some of our Seville oranges, and we some of your wine. We have the finest oranges for twopence apiece, and the basest wine for six shillings a bottle. They tell me wine grows cheap with you. I am resolved to have half a hogshead when I get to Ireland, if it be good and cheap, as it used to be; and I will treat MD at my table in an evening, oh hoa, and laugh at great Ministers of State.

12. The days are grown fine and long,—be thanked. O, faith, you forget all our little sayings, and I am angry. I dined to-day with Mr. Secretary St. John: I went to the Court of Requests at noon, and sent Mr. Harley into the House to call the Secretary, to let him know I would not dine with him if he dined late. By good luck the Duke of Argyle was at the lobby of the House too, and I kept him in talk till the Secretary came out; then told them I was glad to meet them together, and that I had a

request to the Duke, which the Secretary must second, and his Grace must grant. The Duke said he was sure it was something insignificant, and wished it was ten times greater. At the Secretary's house I writ a memorial, and gave it to the Secretary to give the Duke, and shall see that he does it. It is, that his Grace will please to take Mr. Bernage into his protection; and if he finds Bernage answers my character, to give him all encouragement. Colonel Masham and Colonel Hill (Mrs. Masham's) brother tell me my request is reasonable, and they will second it heartily to the Duke too: so I reckon Bernage is on a very good foot when he goes to Spain. Pray tell him this, though perhaps I will write to him before he goes; yet where shall I direct? for I suppose he has left Connolly's.

13. I have left off Lady Kerry's bitter, and got another box of pills. I have no fits of giddiness, but only some little disorders towards it; and I walk as much as I can. Lady Kerry is just as I am, only a great deal worse: I dined to-day at Lord Shelburne's, where she is, and we con ailments, which makes us very fond of each other. I have taken Mr. Harley into favour again, and called to see him, but he was not within; I will use to visit him after dinner, for he dines too late for my head: then I went to visit poor Congreve, who is just getting out of a severe fit of the gout; and I sat with him till near nine o'clock. He gave me a *Tatler* he had written out, as blind as he is, for little Harrison. It is about a scoundrel that was grown rich, and went and bought a coat of arms at the Herald's, and a set of ancestors at Fleet Ditch; 'tis well enough, and shall be printed in two or three days, and if you read those kind of things, this will divert you. It is now between ten and eleven, and I am going to bed.

14. This was Mrs. Vanhomrigh's daughter's birthday, and Mr. Ford and I were invited to dinner to keep it, and we spent the evening there, drinking punch. That was our way of beginning Lent; and in the morning Lord Shelburne, Lady Kerry, Mrs. Pratt, and I, went to Hyde Park, instead of going to church; for, till my head is a little settled, I think it better not to go; it would be so silly and troublesome to go out sick. Dr. Duke died suddenly two or three nights ago; he was one of the wits when we were children, but turned parson, and left it, and never writ farther than a prologue or recommendatory copy of verses. He had a fine living given him by the Bishop of Winchester about three months ago; he got his living suddenly, and he got his dying so too.

JONATHAN SWIFT

15. I walked purely to-day about the Park, the rain being just over, of which we have had a great deal, mixed with little short frosts. I went to the Court of Requests, thinking, if Mr. Harley dined early, to go with him. But meeting Leigh and Sterne, they invited me to dine with them, and away we went. When we got into his room, one H—, a worthless Irish fellow, was there, ready to dine with us; so I stepped out, and whispered them, that I would not dine with that fellow: they made excuses, and begged me to stay; but away I went to Mr. Harley's, and he did not dine at home; and at last I dined at Sir John Germaine's, and found Lady Betty but just recovered of a miscarriage. I am writing an inscription for Lord Berkeley's tomb; you know the young rake his son, the new Earl, is married to the Duke of Richmond's daughter, at the Duke's country house, and are now coming to town. She will be fluxed in two months, and they'll be parted in a year. You ladies are brave, bold, venturesome folks; and the chit is but seventeen, and is ill-natured, covetous, vicious, and proud in extremes. And so get you gone to Stoyte to-morrow.

16. Faith, this letter goes on but slow; 'tis a week old, and the first side not written. I went to-day into the City for a walk, but the person I designed to dine with was not at home; so I came back, and called at Congreve's, and dined with him and Estcourt, and laughed till six; then went to Mr. Harley's, who was not gone to dinner; there I stayed till nine, and we made up our quarrel, and he has invited me to dinner to-morrow, which is the day of the week (Saturday) that Lord Keeper and Secretary St. John dine with him privately, and at last they have consented to let me among them on that day. Atterbury and Prior went to bury poor Dr. Duke. Congreve's nasty white wine has given me the heart-burn.

17. I took some good walks in the Park to-day, and then went to Mr. Harley. Lord Rivers was got there before me, and I chid him for presuming to come on a day when only Lord Keeper and the Secretary and I were to be there; but he regarded me not; so we all dined together, and sat down at four; and the Secretary has invited me to dine with him to-morrow. I told them I had no hopes they could ever keep in, but that I saw they loved one another so well, as indeed they seem to do. They call me nothing but Jonathan; and I said I believed they would leave me Jonathan as they found me; and that I never knew a Ministry do

anything for those whom they make companions of their pleasures; and I believe you will find it so; but I care not. I am upon a project of getting five hundred pounds, without being obliged to anybody; but that is a secret, till I see my dearest MD; and so hold your tongue, and do not talk, sirrahs, for I am now about it.

18. My head has no fits, but a little disordered before dinner; yet I walk stoutly, and take pills, and hope to mend. Secretary St. John would needs have me dine with him to-day; and there I found three persons I never saw, two I had no acquaintance with, and one I did not care for: so I left them early and came home, it being no day to walk, but scurvy rain and wind. The Secretary tells me he has put a cheat on me; for Lord Peterborow sent him twelve dozen flasks of burgundy, on condition that I should have my share; but he never was quiet till they were all gone, so I reckon he owes me thirty-six pounds. Lord Peterborow is now got to Vienna, and I must write to him to-morrow. I begin now to be towards looking for a letter from some certain ladies of Presto's acquaintance, that live at St. Mary's, and are called in a certain language, our little MD. No, stay, I don't expect one these six days, that will be just three weeks; an't I a reasonable creature? We are plagued here with an October Club, that is, a set of above a hundred Parliament men of the country, who drink October beer at home, and meet every evening at a tavern near the Parliament to consult affairs, and drive things on to extremes against the Whigs, to call the old Ministry to account, and get off five or six heads. The Ministry seem not to regard them; yet one of them in confidence told me that there must be something thought on, to settle things better. I'll tell you one great State secret: the Queen, sensible how much she was governed by the late Ministry, runs a little into t'other extreme, and is jealous in that point, even of those who got her out of the others' hands. The Ministry is for gentler measures, and the other Tories for more violent. Lord Rivers, talking to me the other day, cursed the paper called the *Examiner*, for speaking civilly of the Duke of Marlborough; this I happened to talk of to the Secretary, who blamed the warmth of that lord and some others, and swore that if their advice were followed they would be blown up in twenty-four hours. And I have reason to think that they will endeavour to prevail on the Queen to put her affairs more in the hands of a Ministry than she does at present; and there are, I believe, two men thought on, one of them you have often met the name of in my letters. But so much for politics.

19. This proved a terrible rainy day, which prevented my walk into the City, and I was only able to run and dine with my neighbour Vanhomrigh, where Sir Andrew Fountaine dined too, who has just began to sally out, and has shipped his mother and sister, who were his nurses, back to the country. This evening was fair, and I walked a little in the Park, till Prior made me go with him to the Smyrna Coffee-house, where I sat a while, and saw four or five Irish persons, who are very handsome, genteel fellows; but I know not their names. I came away at seven, and got home. Two days ago I writ to Bernage, and told him what I had done, and directed the letter to Mr. Curry's, to be left with Dingley. Brigadiers Hill and Masham, brother and husband to Mrs. Masham, the Queen's favourite, Colonel Disney, and I, have recommended Bernage to the Duke of Argyle; and Secretary St. John has given the Duke my memorial; and, besides, Hill tells me, that Bernage's colonel, Fielding, designs to make him his captain-lieutenant: but I believe I said this to you before, and in this letter; but I will not look.

20. Morning. It snows terribly again; and 'tis mistaken, for I now want a little good weather. I bid you good-morrow; and, if it clear up, get you gone to poor Mrs. Walls, who has had a hard time of it, but is now pretty well again. I am sorry it is a girl: the poor Archdeacon too, see how simply he looked when they told him: what did it cost Stella to be gossip? I'll rise; so, d'ye hear, let me see you at night; and do not stay late out, and catch cold, sirrahs.—At night. It grew good weather, and I got a good walk, and dined with Ford upon his Opera-day; but, now all his wine is gone, I shall dine with him no more. I hope to send this letter before I hear from MD, methinks there is—something great in doing so, only I can't express where it lies; and, faith, this shall go by Saturday, as sure as you're a rogue. Mrs. Edgworth was to set out but last Monday; so you won't have your box so soon perhaps as this letter; but Sterne told me since that it is safe at Chester, and that she will take care of it. I'd give a guinea you had it.

21. Morning. Faith, I hope it will be fair for me to walk into the City; for I take all occasions of walking.—I should be plaguy busy at Laracor if I were there now, cutting down willows, planting others, scouring my canal, and every kind of thing. If Raymond goes over this summer, you must submit, and make them a visit, that we may have another eel and trout fishing; and that Stella may ride by, and see Presto in

his morning-gown in the garden, and so go up with Joe to the Hill of Bree, and round by Scurlock's Town. O Lord, how I remember names! faith, it gives me short sighs; therefore no more of that, if you love me. Good-morrow, I will go rise like a gentleman; my pills say I must.—At night. Lady Kerry sent to desire me to engage some lords about an affair she has in their house here: I called to see her, but found she had already engaged every lord I knew, and that there was no great difficulty in the matter; and it rained like a dog; so I took coach, for want of better exercise, and dined privately with a hang-dog in the City, and walked back in the evening. The days are now long enough to walk in the Park after dinner; and so I do whenever it is fair. This walking is a strange remedy: Mr. Prior walks, to make himself fat, and I to bring myself down; he has generally a cough, which he only calls a cold; we often walk round the Park together. So I'll go sleep.

22. It snowed all this morning prodigiously, and was some inches thick in three or four hours. I dined with Mr. Lewis of the Secretary's office at his lodgings: the chairmen that carried me squeezed a great fellow against a wall, who wisely turned his back, and broke one of the side-glasses in a thousand pieces. I fell a scolding, pretended I was like to be cut to pieces, and made them set down the chair in the Park, while they picked out the bits of glasses; and, when I paid them, I quarrelled still; so they dared not grumble, and I came off for my fare; but I was plaguily afraid they would have said, "God bless your honour, won't you give us something for our glass?" Lewis and I were forming a project how I might get three or four hundred pounds, which I suppose may come to nothing. I hope Smyth has brought you your palsy-drops. How does Stella do? I begin more and more to desire to know. The three weeks since I had your last is over within two days, and I will allow three for accidents.

23. The snow is gone every bit, except the remainder of some great balls made by the boys. Mr. Sterne was with me this morning about an affair he has before the Treasury. That drab Mrs. Edgworth is not yet set out, but will infallibly next Monday: and this is the third infallible Monday, and pox take her! So you will have this letter first; and this shall go to-morrow; and, if I have one from MD in that time, I will not answer it till my next; only I will say, "Madam, I received your letter, and so, and so." I dined to-day with my Mistress Butler, who grows very disagreeable.

24. Morning. This letter certainly goes this evening, sure as you're alive, young women, and then you will be so shamed that I have had none from you; and, if I was to reckon like you, I would say, I were six letters before you, for this is N. 16, and I have had your N. 10. But I reckon you have received but fourteen, and have sent eleven. I think to go to-day a Minister-of-State-hunting in the Court of Requests; for I have something to say to Mr. Harley. And it is fine, cold, sunshiny weather; I wish dear MD would walk this morning in your Stephen's Green; 'tis as good as our Park, but not so large. Faith, this summer we'll take a coach for sixpence to the Green Well, the two walks, and thence all the way to Stoyte's. My hearty service to Goody Stoyte and Catherine; and I hope Mrs. Walls had a good time. How inconstant I am! I can't imagine I was ever in love with her. Well, I'm going; what have you to say? *I do not care how I write now.* I don't design to write on this side; these few lines are but so much more than your due; so I will write *large* or small as I please. O, faith, my hands are starving in bed; I believe it is a hard frost. I must rise, and bid you good-bye, for I'll seal this letter immediately, and carry it in my pocket, and put it into the post-office with my own fair hands. Farewell.

This letter is just a fortnight's journal to-day. Yes, and so it is, I'm sure, says you, with your two eggs a penny.

Lele, lele, lele.

O Lord, I am saying lele, lele, to myself, in all our little keys: and, now you talk of keys, that dog Patrick broke the key-general of the chest of drawers with six locks, and I have been so plagued to get a new one, besides my good two shillings!

Letter XVII

Now, young women, I gave in my sixteenth this evening. I dined with Ford (it was his Opera-day) as usual; it is very convenient to me to do so, for coming home early after a walk in the Park, which now the days will allow. I called on the Secretary at his office, and he had forgot to give the memorial about Bernage to the Duke of Argyle; but, two days ago, I met the Duke, who desired I would give it him myself, which should have more power with him than all the Ministry together, as he protested solemnly, repeated it two or three times, and bid me count upon it. So that I verily believe Bernage will be in a very good way to establish himself. I think I can do no more for him at present, and there's an end of that; and so get you gone to bed, for it is late.

25. The three weeks are out yesterday since I had your last, and so now I will be expecting every day a pretty dear letter from my own MD, and hope to hear that Stella has been much better in her head and eyes: my head continues as it was, no fits, but a little disorder every day, which I can easily bear, if it will not grow worse. I dined to-day with Mr. Secretary St. John, on condition I might choose my company, which were Lord Rivers, Lord Carteret, Sir Thomas Mansel, and Mr. Lewis; I invited Masham, Hill, Sir John Stanley, and George Granville, but they were engaged; and I did it in revenge of his having such bad company when I dined with him before; so we laughed, etc. And I ventured to go to church to-day, which I have not done this month before. Can you send me such a good account of Stella's health, pray now? Yes, I hope, and better too. We dined (says you) at the Dean's, and played at cards till twelve, and there came in Mr. French, and Dr. Travors, and Dr. Whittingham, and Mr. (I forget his name, that I always tell Mrs. Walls of) the banker's son, a pox on him. And we were so merry; I vow they are pure good company. But I lost a crown; for you must know I had always hands tempting me to go out, but never took in anything, and often two black aces without a manilio; was not that hard, Presto? Hold your tongue, etc.

26. I was this morning with Mr. Secretary about some business, and he tells me that Colonel Fielding is now going to make Bernage his

captain-lieutenant, that is, a captain by commission, and the perquisites of the company; but not captain's pay, only the first step to it. I suppose he will like it; and the recommendation to the Duke of Argyle goes on. And so trouble me no more about your Bernage; the jackanapes understands what fair solicitors he has got, I warrant you. Sir Andrew Fountaine and I dined, by invitation, with Mrs. Vanhomrigh. You say they are of no consequence: why, they keep as good female company as I do male; I see all the drabs of quality at this end of the town with them: I saw two Lady Bettys there this afternoon; the beauty of one, the good-breeding and nature of t'other, and the wit of neither, would have made a fine woman. Rare walking in the Park now: why don't you walk in the Green of St. Stephen? The walks there are finer gravelled than the Mall. What beasts the Irish women are, never to walk!

27. Darteneuf and I, and little Harrison the new Tatler, and Jervas the painter, dined to-day with James, I know not his other name, but it is one of Darteneuf's dining-places, who is a true epicure. James is clerk of the kitchen to the Queen, and has a little snug house at St. James's; and we had the Queen's wine, and such very fine victuals that I could not eat it. Three weeks and three days since my last letter from MD; rare doings! why, truly we were so busy with poor Mrs. Walls, that indeed, Presto, we could not write, we were afraid the poor woman would have died; and it pitied us to see the Archdeacon, how concerned he was. The Dean never came to see her but once; but now she is up again, and we go and sit with her in the evenings. The child died the next day after it was born; and I believe, between friends, she is not very sorry for it.—Indeed, Presto, you are plaguy silly to-night, and han't guessed one word right; for she and the child are both well, and it is a fine girl, likely to live; and the Dean was godfather, and Mrs. Catherine and I were godmothers; I was going to say Stoyte, but I think I have heard they don't put maids and married women together; though I know not why I think so, nor I don't care; what care I? but I must prate, etc.

28. I walked to-day into the City for my health, and there dined; which I always do when the weather is fair, and business permits, that I may be under a necessity of taking a good walk, which is the best thing I can do at present for my health. Some bookseller has raked up everything I writ, and published it t'other day in one volume; but I know nothing of it, 'twas without my knowledge or consent: it makes a four-shilling

book, and is called *Miscellanies in Prose and Verse*. Tooke pretends he knows nothing of it; but I doubt he is at the bottom. One must have patience with these things; the best of it is, I shall be plagued no more. However, I will bring a couple of them over with me for MD; perhaps you may desire to see them. I hear they sell mightily.

March 1. Morning. I have been calling to Patrick to look in his almanac for the day of the month; I did not know but it might be leap-year. The almanac says 'tis the third after leap-year; and I always thought till now, that every third year was leap-year. I am glad they come so seldom; but I'm sure 'twas otherwise when I was a young man; I see times are mightily changed since then.—Write to me, sirrahs; be sure do by the time this side is done, and I'll keep t'other side for the answer: so I'll go write to the Bishop of Clogher; good-morrow, sirrahs.—Night. I dined to-day at Mrs. Vanhomrigh's, being a rainy day; and Lady Betty Butler, knowing it, sent to let me know she expected my company in the evening, where the Vans (so we call them) were to be. The Duchess and they do not go over this summer with the Duke; so I go to bed.

2. This rainy weather undoes me in coaches and chairs. I was traipsing to-day with your Mr. Sterne, to go along with them to Moore, and recommend his business to the Treasury. Sterne tells me his dependence is wholly on me; but I have absolutely refused to recommend it to Mr. Harley, because I have troubled him lately so much with other folks' affairs; and besides, to tell the truth, Mr. Harley told me he did not like Sterne's business: however, I will serve him, because I suppose MD would have me. But, in saying his dependence lies wholly on me, he lies, and is a fool. I dined with Lord Abercorn, whose son Peasley will be married at Easter to ten thousand pounds.

3. I forgot to tell you that yesterday morning I was at Mr. Harley's levee: he swore I came in spite, to see him among a parcel of fools. My business was to desire I might let the Duke of Ormond know how the affair stood of the First-Fruits. He promised to let him know it, and engaged me to dine with him to-day. Every Saturday, Lord Keeper, Secretary St. John, and I dine with him, and sometimes Lord Rivers; and they let in none else. Patrick brought me some letters into the Park; among which one was from Walls; and t'other, yes, faith, t'other was from our little MD, N. 11. I read the rest in the Park, and MD's

in a chair as I went from St. James's to Mr. Harley; and glad enough I was, faith, to read it, and see all right. Oh, but I won't answer it these three or four days at least, or may be sooner. An't I silly? faith, your letters would make a dog silly, if I had a dog to be silly, but it must be a little dog.—I stayed with Mr. Harley till past nine, where we had much discourse together after the rest were gone; and I gave him very truly my opinion where he desired it. He complained he was not very well, and has engaged me to dine with him again on Monday. So I came home afoot, like a fine gentleman, to tell you all this.

4. I dined to-day with Mr. Secretary St. John; and after dinner he had a note from Mr. Harley, that he was much out of order. Pray God preserve his health! everything depends upon it. The Parliament at present cannot go a step without him, nor the Queen neither. I long to be in Ireland; but the Ministry beg me to stay: however, when this Parliament lurry is over, I will endeavour to steal away; by which time I hope the First-Fruit business will be done. This kingdom is certainly ruined as much as was ever any bankrupt merchant. We must have peace, let it be a bad or a good one, though nobody dares talk of it. The nearer I look upon things, the worse I like them. I believe the confederacy will soon break to pieces, and our factions at home increase. The Ministry is upon a very narrow bottom, and stand like an isthmus, between the Whigs on one side, and violent Tories on the other. They are able seamen; but the tempest is too great, the ship too rotten, and the crew all against them. Lord Somers has been twice in the Queen's closet, once very lately; and your Duchess of Somerset, who now has the key, is a most insinuating woman; and I believe they will endeavour to play the same game that has been played against them.—I have told them of all this, which they know already, but they cannot help it. They have cautioned the Queen so much against being governed, that she observes it too much. I could talk till to-morrow upon these things, but they make me melancholy. I could not but observe that lately, after much conversation with Mr. Harley, though he is the most fearless man alive, and the least apt to despond, he confessed to me that uttering his mind to me gave him ease.

5. Mr. Harley continues out of order, yet his affairs force him abroad: he is subject to a sore throat, and was cupped last night: I sent and called two or three times. I hear he is better this evening. I dined to-day in

the City with Dr. Freind at a third body's house, where I was to pass for somebody else; and there was a plaguy silly jest carried on, that made me sick of it. Our weather grows fine, and I will walk like camomile. And pray walk you to your Dean's, or your Stoyte's, or your Manley's, or your Walls'. But your new lodgings make you so proud, you will walk less than ever. Come, let me go to bed, sirrahs.

6. Mr. Harley's going out yesterday has put him a little backwards. I called twice, and sent, for I am in pain for him. Ford caught me, and made me dine with him on his Opera-day; so I brought Mr. Lewis with me, and sat with him till six. I have not seen Mr. Addison these three weeks; all our friendship is over. I go to no Coffee-house. I presented a parson of the Bishop of Clogher's, one Richardson, to the Duke of Ormond to-day: he is translating prayers and sermons into Irish, and has a project about instructing the Irish in the Protestant religion.

7. Morning. Faith, a little would make me, I could find in my heart, if it were not for one thing, I have a good mind, if I had not something else to do, I would answer your dear saucy letter. O, Lord, I am going awry with writing in bed. O, faith, but I must answer it, or I shan't have room, for it must go on Saturday; and don't think I will fill the third side, I an't come to that yet, young women. Well then, as for your Bernage, I have said enough: I writ to him last week.—Turn over that leaf. Now, what says MD to the world to come? I tell you, Madam Stella, my head is a great deal better, and I hope will keep so. How came yours to be fifteen days coming, and you had my fifteenth in seven? Answer me that, rogues. Your being with Goody Walls is excuse enough: I find I was mistaken in the sex, 'tis a boy. Yes, I understand your cypher, and Stella guesses right, as she always does. He gave me al bsadnuk lboinlpl dfaonr ufainf btoy dpionufnad, which I sent him again by Mr. Lewis, to whom I writ a very complaining letter that was showed him; and so the matter ended. He told me he had a quarrel with me; I said I had another with him, and we returned to our friendship, and I should think he loves me as well as a great Minister can love a man in so short a time. Did not I do right? I am glad at heart you have got your palsy-water; pray God Almighty it may do my dearest little Stella good! I suppose Mrs. Edgworth set out last Monday se'ennight. Yes, I do read the *Examiners*, and they are written very finely, as you judge. I do not

think they are too severe on the Duke; they only tax him of avarice, and his avarice has ruined us. You may count upon all things in them to be true. The author has said it is not Prior, but perhaps it may be Atterbury.—Now, Madam Dingley, says she, 'tis fine weather, says she; yes, says she, and we have got to our new lodgings. I compute you ought to save eight pounds by being in the others five months; and you have no more done it than eight thousand. I am glad you are rid of that squinting, blinking Frenchman. I will give you a bill on Parvisol for five pounds for the half-year. And must I go on at four shillings a week, and neither eat nor drink for it? Who the Devil said Atterbury and your Dean were alike? I never saw your Chancellor, nor his chaplain. The latter has a good deal of learning, and is a well-wisher to be an author: your Chancellor is an excellent man. As for Patrick's bird, he bought him for his tameness, and is grown the wildest I ever saw. His wings have been quilled thrice, and are now up again: he will be able to fly after us to Ireland, if he be willing.—Yes, Mrs. Stella, Dingley writes more like Presto than you; for all you superscribed the letter, as who should say, Why should not I write like our Presto as well as Dingley? You with your awkward SS; cannot you write them thus, SS? No, but always SSS. Spiteful sluts, to affront Presto's writing; as that when you shut your eyes you write most like Presto. I know the time when I did not write to you half so plain as I do now; but I take pity on you both. I am very much concerned for Mrs. Walls's eyes. Walls says nothing of it to me in his letter dated after yours. You say, "If she recovers, she may lose her sight." I hope she is in no danger of her life. Yes, Ford is as sober as I please: I use him to walk with me as an easy companion, always ready for what I please, when I am weary of business and Ministers. I don't go to a Coffee-house twice a month. I am very regular in going to sleep before eleven.—And so you say that Stella is a pretty girl; and so she be, and methinks I see her just now as handsome as the day is long. Do you know what? when I am writing in our language, I make up my mouth just as if I was speaking it. I caught myself at it just now. And I suppose Dingley is so fair and so fresh as a lass in May, and has her health, and no spleen.—In your account you sent do you reckon as usual from the 1st of November was twelvemonth? Poor Stella, will not Dingley leave her a little daylight to write to Presto? Well, well, we'll have daylight shortly, spite of her teeth; and zoo must cly Lele and Hele, and Hele aden. Must loo mimitate Pdfr, pay? Iss, and so la shall. And so lele's fol ee rettle. Dood-mollow.—At night. Mrs. Barton sent this morning to invite me to dinner; and there I dined, just in that genteel manner that MD used when they would treat some better sort of body than usual.

8. O dear MD, my heart is almost broken. You will hear the thing before this comes to you. I writ a full account of it this night to the Archbishop of Dublin; and the Dean may tell you the particulars from the Archbishop. I was in a sorry way to write, but thought it might be proper to send a true account of the fact; for you will hear a thousand lying circumstances. It is of Mr. Harley's being stabbed this afternoon, at three o'clock, at a Committee of the Council. I was playing Lady Catharine Morris's cards, where I dined, when young Arundel came in with the story. I ran away immediately to the Secretary, which was in my way: no one was at home. I met Mrs. St. John in her chair; she had heard it imperfectly. I took a chair to Mr. Harley, who was asleep, and they hope in no danger; but he has been out of order, and was so when he came abroad to-day, and it may put him in a fever: I am in mortal pain for him. That desperate French villain, Marquis de Guiscard, stabbed Mr. Harley. Guiscard was taken up by Mr. Secretary St. John's warrant for high treason, and brought before the Lords to be examined; there he stabbed Mr. Harley. I have told all the particulars already to the Archbishop. I have now, at nine, sent again, and they tell me he is in a fair way. Pray pardon my distraction; I now think of all his kindness to me.—The poor creature now lies stabbed in his bed by a desperate French Popish villain. Good-night, and God preserve you both, and pity me; I want it.

9. Morning; seven, in bed. Patrick is just come from Mr. Harley's. He slept well till four; the surgeon sat up with him: he is asleep again: he felt a pain in his wound when he waked: they apprehend him in no danger. This account the surgeon left with the porter, to tell people that send. Pray God preserve him. I am rising, and going to Mr. Secretary St. John. They say Guiscard will die with the wounds Mr. St. John and the rest gave him. I shall tell you more at night.—Night. Mr. Harley still continues on the mending hand; but he rested ill last night, and felt pain. I was early with the Secretary this morning, and I dined with him, and he told me several particularities of this accident, too long to relate now. Mr. Harley is still mending this evening, but not at all out of danger; and till then I can have no peace. Good-night, etc., and pity Presto.

10. Mr. Harley was restless last night; but he has no fever, and the hopes of his mending increase. I had a letter from Mr. Walls, and one from Mr. Bernage. I will answer them here, not having time to write. Mr. Walls writes about three things. First, about a hundred pounds from Dr. Raymond, of which I hear nothing, and it is now too late. Secondly, about Mr. Clements: I can do nothing in it, because I am not to mention Mr. Pratt; and I cannot recommend without knowing Mr. Pratt's objections, whose relation Clements is, and who brought him into the place. The third is about my being godfather to the child: that is in my power, and (since there is no remedy) will submit. I wish you could hinder it; but if it can't be helped, pay what you think proper, and get the Provost to stand for me, and let his Christian name be Harley, in honour of my friend, now lying stabbed and doubtful of his life. As for Bernage, he writes me word that his colonel has offered to make him captain-lieutenant for a hundred pounds. He was such a fool to offer him money without writing to me till it was done, though I have had a dozen letters from him; and then he desires I would say nothing of this, for fear his colonel should be angry. People are mad. What can I do? I engaged Colonel Disney, who was one of his solicitors to the Secretary, and then told him the story. He assured me that Fielding (Bernage's colonel) said he might have got that sum; but, on account of those great recommendations he had, would give it him for nothing: and I would have Bernage write him a letter of thanks, as of a thing given him for nothing, upon recommendations, etc. Disney tells me he will again speak to Fielding, and clear up this matter; then I will write to Bernage. A pox on him for promising money till I had it promised to me; and then making it such a ticklish point, that one cannot expostulate with the colonel upon it: but let him do as I say, and there is an end. I engaged the Secretary of State in it; and am sure it was meant a kindness to me, and that no money should be given, and a hundred pounds is too much in a Smithfield bargain, as a major-general told me, whose opinion I asked. I am now hurried, and can say no more. Farewell, etc. etc.

How shall I superscribe to your new lodgings, pray, madams? Tell me but that, impudence and saucy-face.

Are not you sauceboxes to write "lele" like Presto? O poor Presto!

Mr. Harley is better to-night, that makes me so pert, you saucy Gog and Magog.

Letter XVIII

Pretty little MD must expect little from me till Mr. Harley is out of danger. We hope he is so now; but I am subject to fear for my friends. He has a head full of the whole business of the nation, was out of order when the villain stabbed him, and had a cruel contusion by the second blow. But all goes on well yet. Mr. Ford and I dined with Mr. Lewis, and we hope the best.

11. This morning Mr. Secretary and I met at Court, where he went to the Queen, who is out of order, and aguish: I doubt the worse for this accident to Mr. Harley. We went together to his house, and his wound looks well, and he is not feverish at all, and I think it is foolish in me to be so much in pain as I am. I had the penknife in my hand, which is broken within a quarter of an inch of the handle. I have a mind to write and publish an account of all the particularities of this fact: it will be very curious, and I would do it when Mr. Harley is past danger.

12. We have been in terrible pain to-day about Mr. Harley, who never slept last night, and has been very feverish. But this evening I called there; and young Mr. Harley (his only son) tells me he is now much better, and was then asleep. They let nobody see him, and that is perfectly right. The Parliament cannot go on till he is well, and are forced to adjourn their money businesses, which none but he can help them in. Pray God preserve him.

13. Mr. Harley is better to-day, slept well all night, and we are a little out of our fears. I send and call three or four times every day. I went into the City for a walk, and dined there with a private man; and coming home this evening, broke my shin in the Strand over a tub of sand left just in the way. I got home dirty enough, and went straight to bed, where I have been cooking it with gold-beater's skin, and have been peevish enough with Patrick, who was near an hour bringing a rag from next door. It is my right shin, where never any humour fell when t'other used to swell; so I apprehend it less: however, I shall not stir till 'tis well, which I reckon will be in a week. I am very careful in these sort of things; but I wish I had Mrs. J—'s water: she is out of town, and I must

make a shift with alum. I will dine with Mrs. Vanhomrigh till I am well, who lives but five doors off; and that I may venture.

14. My journals are like to be very diverting, now I cannot stir abroad, between accounts of Mr. Harley's mending, and of my broken shin. I just walked to my neighbour Vanhomrigh at two, and came away at six, when little Harrison the Tatler came to me, and begged me to dictate a paper to him, which I was forced in charity to do. Mr. Harley still mends; and I hope in a day or two to trouble you no more with him, nor with my shin. Go to bed and sleep, sirrahs, that you may rise to-morrow and walk to Donnybrook, and lose your money with Stoyte and the Dean; do so, dear little rogues, and drink Presto's health. O pray, don't you drink Presto's health sometimes with your deans, and your Stoytes, and your Walls, and your Manleys, and your everybodies, pray now? I drink MD's to myself a hundred thousand times.

15. I was this morning at Mr. Secretary St. John's for all my shin; and he has given me for young Harrison the Tatler the prettiest employment in Europe; secretary to my Lord Raby, who is to be Ambassador Extraordinary at the Hague, where all the great affairs will be concerted; so we shall lose the *Tatlers* in a fortnight. I will send Harrison to-morrow morning to thank the Secretary. Poor Biddy Floyd has got the smallpox. I called this morning to see Lady Betty Germaine, and when she told me so, I fairly took my leave. I have the luck of it; for about ten days ago I was to see Lord Carteret; and my lady was entertaining me with telling of a young lady, a cousin, who was then ill in the house of the smallpox, and is since dead: it was near Lady Betty's, and I fancy Biddy took the fright by it. I dined with Mr. Secretary; and a physician came in just from Guiscard, who tells us he is dying of his wounds, and can hardly live till to-morrow. A poor wench that Guiscard kept, sent him a bottle of sack; but the keeper would not let him touch it, for fear it was poison. He had two quarts of old clotted blood come out of his side to-day, and is delirious. I am sorry he is dying; for they had found out a way to hang him. He certainly had an intention to murder the Queen.

16. I have made but little progress in this letter for so many days, thanks to Guiscard and Mr. Harley; and it would be endless to tell you all the particulars of that odious fact. I do not yet hear that Guiscard is dead, but they say 'tis impossible he should recover. I walked too much

yesterday for a man with a broken shin; to-day I rested, and went no farther than Mrs. Vanhomrigh's, where I dined; and Lady Betty Butler coming in about six, I was forced in good manners to sit with her till nine; then I came home, and Mr. Ford came in to visit my shin, and sat with me till eleven: so I have been very idle and naughty. It vexes me to the pluck that I should lose walking this delicious day. Have you seen the *Spectator* yet, a paper that comes out every day? 'Tis written by Mr. Steele, who seems to have gathered new life, and have a new fund of wit; it is in the same nature as his *Tatlers*, and they have all of them had something pretty. I believe Addison and he club. I never see them; and I plainly told Mr. Harley and Mr. St. John, ten days ago, before my Lord Keeper and Lord Rivers, that I had been foolish enough to spend my credit with them in favour of Addison and Steele; but that I would engage and promise never to say one word in their behalf, having been used so ill for what I had already done.—So, now I am got into the way of prating again, there will be no quiet for me.

> *When Presto begins to prate,*
> *Give him a rap upon the pate.*

O Lord, how I blot! it is time to leave off, etc.

17. Guiscard died this morning at two; and the coroner's inquest have found that he was killed by bruises received from a messenger, so to clear the Cabinet Councillors from whom he received his wounds. I had a letter from Raymond, who cannot hear of your box; but I hope you have it before this comes to your hands. I dined to-day with Mr. Lewis of the Secretary's office. Mr. Harley has abundance of extravasated blood comes from his breast out of his wound, and will not be well so soon as we expected. I had something to say, but cannot call it to mind. (What was it?)

18. I was to-day at Court to look for the Duke of Argyle, and gave him the memorial about Bernage. The Duke goes with the first fair wind. I could not find him, but I have given the memorial to another to give him; and, however, it shall be sent after him. Bernage has made a blunder in offering money to his colonel without my advice; however, he is made captain-lieutenant, only he must recruit the company, which will cost him forty pounds, and that is cheaper than an hundred. I

dined to-day with Mr. Secretary St. John, and stayed till seven, but would not drink his champagne and burgundy, for fear of the gout. My shin mends, but is not well. I hope it will by the time I send this letter, next Saturday.

19. I went to-day into the City, but in a coach, and sossed up my leg on the seat; and as I came home, I went to see poor Charles Barnard's books, which are to be sold by auction, and I itch to lay out nine or ten pounds for some fine editions of fine authors. But 'tis too far, and I shall let it slip, as I usually do all such opportunities. I dined in a coffee-house with Stratford upon chops and some of his wine. Where did MD dine? Why, poor MD dined at home to-day, because of the Archbishop, and they could not go abroad, and had a breast of mutton and a pint of wine. I hope Mrs. Walls mends; and pray give me an account what sort of godfather I made, and whether I behaved myself handsomely. The Duke of Argyle is gone; and whether he has my memorial, I know not, till I see Dr. Arbuthnot, to whom I gave it. That hard name belongs to a Scotch doctor, an acquaintance of the Duke's and me; Stella can't pronounce it. Oh that we were at Laracor this fine day! the willows begin to peep, and the quicks to bud. My dream is out: I was a-dreamed last night that I ate ripe cherries.—And now they begin to catch the pikes, and will shortly the trouts (pox on these Ministers!)—and I would fain know whether the floods were ever so high as to get over the holly bank or the river walk; if so, then all my pikes are gone; but I hope not. Why don't you ask Parvisol these things, sirrahs? And then my canal, and trouts, and whether the bottom be fine and clear? But harkee, ought not Parvisol to pay in my last year's rents and arrears out of his hands? I am thinking, if either of you have heads to take his accounts, it should be paid in to you; otherwise to Mr. Walls. I will write an order on t'other side; and do as you will. Here's a world of business; but I must go sleep, I'm drowsy; and so good-night, etc.

20. This sore shin ruins me in coach-hire; no less than two shillings to-day going and coming from the City, where I dined with one you never heard of, and passed an insipid day. I writ this post to Bernage, with the account I told you above. I hope he will like it; 'tis his own fault, or it would have been better. I reckon your next letter will be full of Mr. Harley's stabbing. He still mends, but abundance of extravasated blood has come out of the wound: he keeps his bed, and sees nobody.

The Speaker's eldest son is just dead of the smallpox, and the House is adjourned a week, to give him time to wipe off his tears. I think it very handsomely done; but I believe one reason is, that they want Mr. Harley so much. Biddy Floyd is like to do well: and so go to your Dean's, and roast his oranges, and lose your money, do so, you saucy sluts. Stella, you lost three shillings and fourpence t'other night at Stoyte's, yes, you did, and Presto stood in a corner, and saw you all the while, and then stole away. I dream very often I am in Ireland, and that I have left my clothes and things behind me, and have not taken leave of anybody; and that the Ministry expect me to-morrow, and such nonsense.

21. I would not for a guinea have a letter from you till this goes; and go it shall on Saturday, faith. I dined with Mrs. Vanhomrigh, to save my shin, and then went on some business to the Secretary, and he was not at home.

22. Yesterday was a short day's journal: but what care I? what cares saucy Presto? Darteneuf invited me to dinner to-day. Do not you know Darteneuf? That's the man that knows everything, and that everybody knows; and that knows where a knot of rabble are going on a holiday, and when they were there last: and then I went to the Coffee-house. My shin mends, but is not quite healed: I ought to keep it up, but I don't; I e'en let it go as it comes. Pox take Parvisol and his watch! If I do not receive the ten-pound bill I am to get towards it, I will neither receive watch nor chain; so let Parvisol know.

23. I this day appointed the Duke of Ormond to meet him at Ned Southwell's, about an affair of printing Irish Prayer-Books, etc., but the Duke never came. There Southwell had letters that two packets are taken; so if MD writ then, the letters are gone; for they are packets coming hither. Mr. Harley is not yet well, but his extravasated blood continues, and I doubt he will not be quite well in a good while: I find you have heard of the fact by Southwell's letters from Ireland: what do you think of it? I dined with Sir John Perceval, and saw his lady sitting in the bed, in the forms of a lying-in woman; and coming home my sore shin itched, and I forgot what it was, and rubbed off the scab, and blood came; but I am now got into bed, and have put on alum curd, and it is almost well. Lord Rivers told me yesterday a piece of bad news, as a secret, that the Pretender is going to be married to the Duke of Savoy's

daughter. 'Tis very bad if it be true. We were walking in the Mall with some Scotch lords, and he could not tell it until they were gone, and he bade me tell it to none but the Secretary of State and MD. This goes to-morrow, and I have no room but to bid my dearest little MD good-night.

24. I will now seal up this letter, and send it; for I reckon to have none from you ('tis morning now) between this and night; and I will put it in the post with my own hands. I am going out in great haste; so farewell, etc.

Letter XIX

It was a little cross in Presto not to send to-day to the Coffee-house to see whether there was a letter from MD before I sent away mine; but, faith, I did it on purpose, because I would scorn to answer two letters of yours successively. This way of journal is the worst in the world for writing of news, unless one does it the last day; and so I will observe henceforward, if there be any politics or stuff worth sending. My shin mends in spite of the scratching last night. I dined to-day at Ned Southwell's with the Bishop of Ossory and a parcel of Irish gentlemen. Have you yet seen any of the *Spectators*? Just three weeks to-day since I had your last, N. 11. I am afraid I have lost one by the packet that was taken; that will vex me, considering the pains MD take to write, especially poor pretty Stella, and her weak eyes. God bless them and the owner, and send them well, and little me together, I hope ere long. This illness of Mr. Harley puts everything backwards, and he is still down, and like to be so, by that extravasated blood which comes from his breast to the wound: it was by the second blow Guiscard gave him after the penknife was broken. I am shocked at that villainy whenever I think of it. Biddy Floyd is past danger, but will lose all her beauty: she had them mighty thick, especially about her nose.

25. Morning. I wish you a merry New Year; this is the first day of the year, you know, with us, and 'tis Lady-day. I must rise and go to my Lord Keeper: it is not shaving-day to-day, so I shall be early. I am to dine with Mr. Secretary St. John. Good-morrow, my mistresses both, good-morrow. Stella will be peeping out of her room at Mrs. De Caudres' down upon the folks as they come from church; and there comes Mrs. Proby, and that is my Lady Southwell, and there is Lady Betty Rochfort. I long to hear how you are settled in your new lodgings. I wish I were rid of my old ones, and that Mrs. Brent could contrive to put up my books in boxes, and lodge them in some safe place, and you keep my papers of importance. But I must rise, I tell you.—At night. So I visited and dined as I told you, and what of that? We have let Guiscard be buried at last, after showing him pickled in a trough this fortnight for twopence apiece: and the fellow that showed would point to his body, and, "See, gentlemen, this is the wound that was given him by

his Grace the Duke of Ormond; and this is the wound," etc., and then the show was over, and another set of rabble came in. 'Tis hard our laws would not suffer us to hang his body in chains, because he was not tried; and in the eye of our law every man is innocent till then.—Mr. Harley is still very weak, and never out of bed.

26. This was a most delicious day; and my shin being past danger, I walked like lightning above two hours in the Park. We have generally one fair day, and then a great deal of rain for three or four days together. All things are at a stop in Parliament for want of Mr. Harley; they cannot stir an inch without him in their most material affairs: and we fear, by the caprice of Radcliffe, who will admit none but his own surgeon, he has not been well looked after. I dined at an alehouse with Mr. Lewis, but had his wine. Don't you begin to see the flowers and blossoms of the field? How busy should I be now at Laracor! No news of your box? I hope you have it, and are this minute drinking the chocolate, and that the smell of the Brazil tobacco has not affected it. I would be glad to know whether you like it, because I would send you more by people that are now every day thinking of going to Ireland; therefore pray tell me, and tell me soon: and I will have the strong box.

27. A rainy, wretched, scurvy day from morning till night: and my neighbour Vanhomrigh invited me to dine with them and this evening I passed at Mr. Prior's with Dr. Freind; and 'tis now past twelve, so I must go sleep.

28. Morning. O, faith, you're an impudent saucy couple of sluttikins for presuming to write so soon, said I to myself this morning; who knows but there may be a letter from MD at the Coffee-house? Well, you must know, and so, I just now sent Patrick, and he brought me three letters, but not one from MD, no indeed, for I read all the superscriptions; and not one from MD. One I opened, it was from the Archbishop; t'other I opened, it was from Staunton; the third I took, and looked at the hand. Whose hand is this? says I; yes, says I, whose hand is this? Then there was wax between the folds; then I began to suspect; then I peeped; faith, it was Walls's hand after all: then I opened it in a rage, and then it was little MD's hand, dear, little, pretty, charming MD's sweet hand again. O Lord, an't here a clutter and a stir, and a bustle? never saw the like. Faith, I believe yours lay some

days at the post-office, and that it came before my eighteenth went, but that I did not expect it, and I hardly ever go there. Well, and so you think I'll answer this letter now; no, faith, and so I won't. I'll make you wait, young women; but I'll inquire immediately about poor Dingley's exchequer trangum. What, is that Vedel again a soldier? was he broke? I'll put it in Ben Tooke's hand. I hope Vedel could not sell it.—At night. Vedel, Vedel, poh, pox, I think it is Vedeau; ay, Vedeau, now I have it; let me see, do you name him in yours? Yes, Mr. John Vedeau is the brother; but where does this brother live? I'll inquire. This was a fast-day for the public; so I dined late with Sir Matthew Dudley, whom I have not been with a great while. He is one of those that must lose his employment whenever the great shake comes; and I can't contribute to keep him in, though I have dropped words in his favour to the Ministry; but he is too violent a Whig, and friend to the Lord Treasurer, to stay in. 'Tis odd to think how long they let those people keep their places; but the reason is, they have not enough to satisfy all expecters, and so they keep them all in hopes, that they may be good boys in the meantime; and thus the old ones hold in still. The Comptroller told me that there are eight people expect his staff. I walked after dinner to-day round the Park. What, do I write politics to little young women? Hold your tongue, and go to your Dean's.

29. Morning. If this be a fine day, I will walk into the City, and see Charles Barnard's library. What care I for your letter, saucy N. 12? I will say nothing to it yet: faith, I believe this will be full before its time, and then go it must. I will always write once a fortnight; and if it goes sooner by filling sooner, why, then there is so much clear gain. Morrow, morrow, rogues and lasses both, I can't lie scribbling here in bed for your play; I must rise, and so morrow again.—At night. Your friend Montgomery and his sister are here, as I am told by Patrick. I have seen him often, but take no notice of him: he is grown very ugly and pimpled. They tell me he is a gamester, and wins money.—How could I help it, pray? Patrick snuffed the candle too short, and the grease ran down upon the paper. It an't my fault, 'tis Patrick's fault; pray now don't blame Presto. I walked to-day in the City, and dined at a private house, and went to see the auction of poor Charles Barnard's books; they were in the middle of the physic books, so I bought none; and they are so dear, I believe I shall buy none, and there is an end; and go to Stoyte's, and I'll go sleep.

30. Morning. This is Good Friday, you must know; and I must rise and go to Mr. Secretary about some business, and Mrs. Vanhomrigh desires me to breakfast with her, because she is to intercede for Patrick, who is so often drunk and quarrelsome in the house, that I was resolved to send him over; but he knows all the places where I send, and is so used to my ways, that it would be inconvenient to me; but when I come to Ireland, I will discharge him. Sir Thomas Mansel, one of the Lords of the Treasury, setting me down at my door to-day, saw Patrick, and swore he was a Teague-lander. I am so used to his face, I never observed it, but thought him a pretty fellow. Sir Andrew Fountaine and I supped this fast-day with Mrs. Vanhomrigh. We were afraid Mr. Harley's wound would turn to a fistula; but we think the danger is now past. He rises every day, and walks about his room, and we hope he will be out in a fortnight. Prior showed me a handsome paper of verses he has writ on Mr. Harley's accident: they are not out; I will send them to you, if he will give me a copy.

31. Morning. What shall we do to make April fools this year, now it happens on Sunday? Patrick brings word that Mr. Harley still mends, and is up every day. I design to see him in a few days: and he brings me word too that he has found out Vedeau's brother's shop: I shall call there in a day or two. It seems the wife lodges next door to the brother. I doubt the scoundrel was broke, and got a commission, or perhaps is a volunteer gentleman, and expects to get one by his valour. Morrow, sirrahs, let me rise.—At night. I dined to-day with Sir Thomas Mansel. We were walking in the Park, and Mr. Lewis came to us. Mansel asked where we dined. We said, "Together." He said, we should dine with him, only his wife desired him to bring nobody, because she had only a leg of mutton. I said I would dine with him to choose; but he would send a servant to order a plate or two: yet this man has ten thousand pounds a year in land, and is a Lord of the Treasury, and is not covetous neither, but runs out merely by slattering and negligence. The worst dinner I ever saw at the Dean's was better: but so it is with abundance of people here. I called at night at Mr. Harley's, who begins to walk in his room with a stick, but is mighty weak.—See how much I have lost with that ugly grease. 'Tis your fault, pray; and I'll go to bed.

April 1. The Duke of Buckingham's house fell down last night with an earthquake, and is half swallowed up; won't you go and see it?—An

April fool, an April fool, oh ho, young women. Well, don't be angry. I will make you an April fool no more till the next time; we had no sport here, because it is Sunday, and Easter Sunday. I dined with the Secretary, who seemed terribly down and melancholy, which Mr. Prior and Lewis observed as well as I: perhaps something is gone wrong; perhaps there is nothing in it. God bless my own dearest MD, and all is well.

2. We have such windy weather, 'tis troublesome walking, yet all the rabble have got into our Park these Easter holidays. I am plagued with one Richardson, an Irish parson, and his project of printing Irish Bibles, etc., to make you Christians in that country: I befriend him what I can, on account of the Archbishop and Bishop of Clogher.— But what business have I to meddle, etc. Do not you remember that, sirrah Stella? what was that about, when you thought I was meddling with something that was not my business? O, faith, you are an impudent slut, I remember your doings, I'll never forget you as long as I live. Lewis and I dined together at his lodgings. But where's the answer to this letter of MD's? O, faith, Presto, you must think of that. Time enough, says saucy Presto.

3. I was this morning to see Mrs. Barton: I love her better than anybody here, and see her seldomer. Why, really now, so it often happens in the world, that where one loves a body best—pshah, pshah, you are so silly with your moral observations. Well, but she told me a very good story. An old gentlewoman died here two months ago, and left in her will, to have eight men and eight maids bearers, who should have two guineas apiece, ten guineas to the parson for a sermon, and two guineas to the clerk. But bearers, parson, and clerk must be all true virgins; and not to be admitted till they took their oaths of virginity: so the poor woman still lies unburied, and so must do till the general resurrection.—I called at Mr. Secretary's, to see what the D— ailed him on Sunday. I made him a very proper speech; told him I observed he was much out of temper; that I did not expect he would tell me the cause, but would be glad to see he was in better; and one thing I warned him of, never to appear cold to me, for I would not be treated like a schoolboy; that I had felt too much of that in my life already (meaning from Sir William Temple); that I expected every great Minister who honoured me with his acquaintance, if he heard or saw anything to my disadvantage, would

let me know it in plain words, and not put me in pain to guess by the change or coldness of his countenance or behaviour; for it was what I would hardly bear from a crowned head, and I thought no subject's favour was worth it; and that I designed to let my Lord Keeper and Mr. Harley know the same thing, that they might use me accordingly. He took all right; said I had reason; vowed nothing ailed him but sitting up whole nights at business, and one night at drinking; would have had me dine with him and Mrs. Masham's brother, to make up matters; but I would not. I don't know, but I would not. But indeed I was engaged with my old friend Rollinson; you never heard of him before.

4. I sometimes look a line or two back, and see plaguy mistakes of the pen; how do you get over them? You are puzzled sometimes. Why, I think what I said to Mr. Secretary was right. Don't you remember how I used to be in pain when Sir William Temple would look cold and out of humour for three or four days, and I used to suspect a hundred reasons? I have plucked up my spirit since then, faith; he spoilt a fine gentleman. I dined with my neighbour Vanhomrigh, and MD, poor MD, at home on a loin of mutton and half a pint of wine, and the mutton was raw, poor Stella could not eat, poor dear rogue, and Dingley was so vexed; but we will dine at Stoyte's to-morrow. Mr. Harley promised to see me in a day or two, so I called this evening; but his son and others were abroad, and he asleep, so I came away, and found out Mrs. Vedeau. She drew out a letter from Dingley, and said she would get a friend to receive the money. I told her I would employ Mr. Tooke in it henceforward. Her husband bought a lieutenancy of foot, and is gone to Portugal. He sold his share of the shop to his brother, and put out the money to maintain her, all but what bought the commission. She lodges within two doors of her brother. She told me it made her very melancholy to change her manner of life thus, but trade was dead, etc. She says she will write to you soon. I design to engage Ben Tooke, and then receive the parchment from her.—I gave Mr. Dopping a copy of Prior's verses on Mr. Harley; he sent them yesterday to Ireland, so go look for them, for I won't be at the trouble to transcribe them here. They will be printed in a day or two. Give my hearty service to Stoyte and Catherine: upon my word I love them dearly, and desire you will tell them so: pray desire Goody Stoyte not to let Mrs. Walls and Mrs. Johnson cheat her of her money at ombre, but assure her from me that she is a bungler.

Dine with her to-day, and tell her so, and drink my health, and good voyage, and speedy return, and so you're a rogue.

5. Morning. Now let us proceed to examine a saucy letter from one Madam MD.—God Almighty bless poor dear Stella, and send her a great many birthdays, all happy, and healthy, and wealthy, and with me ever together, and never asunder again, unless by chance. When I find you are happy or merry there, it makes me so here, and I can hardly imagine you absent when I am reading your letter, or writing to you. No, faith, you are just here upon this little paper, and therefore I see and talk with you every evening constantly, and sometimes in the morning, but not always in the morning, because that is not so modest to young ladies.—What, you would fain palm a letter on me more than you sent: and I, like a fool, must look over all yours, to see whether this was really N. 12, or more. (Patrick has this moment brought me letters from the Bishop of Clogher and Parvisol; my heart was at my mouth for fear of one from MD; what a disgrace would it be to have two of yours to answer together! But, faith, this shall go to-night, for fear; and then come when it will, I defy it.) No, you are not naughty at all, write when you are disposed. And so the Dean told you the story of Mr. Harley from the Archbishop; I warrant it never spoiled your supper, or broke off your game. Nor yet, have not you the box? I wish Mrs. Edgworth had the—. But you have it now, I suppose; and is the chocolate good, or has the tobacco spoilt it? Leigh stays till Sterne has done his business, no longer; and when that will be, God knows: I befriend him as much as I can, but Harley's accident stops that as well as all things else. You guess, Madam Dingley, that I shall stay a round twelvemonth; as hope saved, I would come over, if I could, this minute; but we will talk of that by and by. Your affair of Vedeau I have told you of already; now to the next, turn over the leaf. Mrs. Dobbins lies, I have no more provision here or in Ireland than I had. I am pleased that Stella the conjurer approves what I did with Mr. Harley; but your generosity makes me mad; I know you repine inwardly at Presto's absence; you think he has broken his word of coming in three months, and that this is always his trick; and now Stella says she does not see possibly how I can come away in haste, and that MD is satisfied, etc. An't you a rogue to overpower me thus? I did not expect to find such friends as I have done. They may indeed deceive me too. But there are important reasons (Pox on this grease, this candle tallow!) why they

should not. I have been used barbarously by the late Ministry; I am a little piqued in honour to let people see I am not to be despised. The assurances they give me, without any scruple or provocation, are such as are usually believed in the world; they may come to nothing, but the first opportunity that offers, and is neglected, I shall depend no more, but come away. I could say a thousand things on this head, if I were with you. I am thinking why Stella should not go to the Bath, if she be told it will do her good. I will make Parvisol get up fifty pounds, and pay it you; and you may be good housewives, and live cheap there some months, and return in autumn, or visit London, as you please: pray think of it. I writ to Bernage, directed to Curry's; I wish he had the letter. I will send the bohea tea, if I can. The Bishop of Kilmore, I don't keep such company; an old dying fool whom I never was with in my life. So I am no godfather; all the better. Pray, Stella, explain those two words of yours to me, what you mean by *villian* and *dainger*; and you, Madam Dingley, what is *christianing*?—Lay your letter *this way*, *this way*, and the devil a bit of difference between this way and the other way. No; I will show you, lay them *this way*, *this way*, and not *that way*, *that way*.—You shall have your aprons; and I will put all your commissions as they come, in a paper together, and do not think I will forget MD's orders, because they are friends; I will be as careful as if they were strangers. I knew not what to do about this Clements. Walls will not let me say anything as if Mr. Pratt was against him; and now the Bishop of Clogher has written to me in his behalf. This thing does not rightly fall in my way, and that people never consider: I always give my good offices where they are proper, and that I am judge of; however, I will do what I can. But, if he has the name of a Whig, it will be hard, considering my Lord Anglesea and Hyde are very much otherwise, and you know they have the employment of Deputy Treasurer. If the frolic should take you of going to the Bath, I here send you a note on Parvisol; if not, you may tear it, and there's an end. Farewell.

If you have an imagination that the Bath will do you good, I say again, I would have you go; if not, or it be inconvenient, burn this note. Or, if you would go, and not take so much money, take thirty pounds, and I will return you twenty from hence. Do as you please, sirrahs. I suppose it will not be too late for the first season; if it be, I would have you resolve however to go the second season, if the doctors say it will do you good, and you fancy so.

LETTER XX

LONDON, *April* 5, 1711

I put my nineteenth in the post-office just now myself, as I came out
of the City, where I dined. This rain ruins me in coach-hire; I walked
away sixpennyworth, and came within a shilling length, and then took
a coach, and got a lift back for nothing; and am now busy.

6. Mr. Secretary desired I would see him this morning; said he had
several things to say to me, and said not one; and the Duke of Ormond
sent to desire I would meet him at Mr. Southwell's by ten this morning
too, which I did, thinking it was some particular matter. All the Irish in
town were there, to consult upon preventing a Bill for laying a duty on
Irish yarn; so we talked a while, and then all went to the lobby of the
House of Commons, to solicit our friends, and the Duke came among
the rest; and Lord Anglesea solicited admirably, and I did wonders. But,
after all, the matter was put off till Monday, and then we are to be at it
again. I dined with Lord Mountjoy, and looked over him at chess, which
put me in mind of Stella and Griffyth. I came home, and that dog Patrick
was not within; so I fretted, and fretted, and what good did that do me?

> *And so get you gone to your deans,*
> *You couple of queans.*

I cannot find rhyme to Walls and Stoyte.—Yes, yes,

> *You expect Mrs. Walls,*
> *Be dressed when she calls,*
> *To carry you to Stoyte,*
> *Or else* honi soit.

Henley told me that the Tories were insup-port-able people, because
they are for bringing in French claret, and will not *sup-port*. Mr. Harley
will hardly get abroad this week or ten days yet. I reckon, when I send
away this letter, he will be just got into the House of Commons. My last
letter went in twelve days, and so perhaps may this. No it won't, for those
letters that go under a fortnight are answers to one of yours, otherwise
you must take the days as they happen, some dry, some wet, some barren,

some fruitful, some merry, some insipid; some, etc.—I will write you word exactly the first day I see young gooseberries, and pray observe how much later you are. We have not had five fine days this five weeks, but rain or wind. 'Tis a late spring they say here.—Go to bed, you two dear saucy brats, and don't keep me up all night.

7. Ford has been at Epsom, to avoid Good Friday and Easter Sunday. He forced me to-day to dine with him; and tells me there are letters from Ireland, giving an account of a great indiscretion in the Archbishop of Dublin, who applied a story out of Tacitus very reflectingly on Mr. Harley, and that twenty people have written of it; I do not believe it yet. I called this evening to see Mr. Secretary, who has been very ill with the gravel and pain in his back, by burgundy and champagne, added to the sitting up all night at business; I found him drinking tea while the rest were at champagne, and was very glad of it. I have chid him so severely that I hardly knew whether he would take it well: then I went and sat an hour with Mrs. St. John, who is growing a great favourite of mine; she goes to the Bath on Wednesday, for she is much out of health, and has begged me to take care of the Secretary.

8. I dined to-day with Mr. Secretary St. John; he gave me a letter to read, which was from the publisher of the newspaper called the *Postboy*; in it there was a long copy of a letter from Dublin, giving an account of what the Whigs said upon Mr. Harley's being stabbed, and how much they abuse him and Mr. Secretary St. John; and at the end there were half a dozen lines, telling the story of the Archbishop of Dublin, and abusing him horribly; this was to be printed on Tuesday. I told the Secretary I would not suffer that about the Archbishop to be printed, and so I crossed it out; and afterwards, to prevent all danger, I made him give me the letter, and, upon further thought, would let none of it be published: and I sent for the printer, and told him so, and ordered him, in the Secretary's name, to print nothing reflecting on anybody in Ireland till he had showed it me. Thus I have prevented a terrible scandal to the Archbishop, by a piece of perfect good fortune. I will let him know it by next post; and pray, if you pick it out, let me know, and whether he is thankful for it; but say nothing.

9. I was to-day at the House of Commons again about their yarn, at Lord Anglesea's desire; but the business is again put off till Monday.

I dined with Sir John Stanley, by an assignation I had made with Mr. St. John, and George Granville, the Secretary at War; but they let in other company, some ladies, and so we were not so easy as I intended. My head is pretty tolerable, but every day I feel some little disorders; I have left off snuff since Sunday, finding myself much worse after taking a good deal at the Secretary's. I would not let him drink one drop of champagne or burgundy without water, and in compliment I did so myself. He is much better; but when he is well, he is like Stella, and will not be governed. So go to your Stoyte's, and I'll go sleep.

10. I have been visiting Lady Worsley and Mrs. Barton to-day, and dined soberly with my friend Lewis. The Dauphin is dead of an apoplexy; I wish he had lived till the finishing of this letter, that it might be news to you. Duncombe, the rich alderman, died to-day, and I hear has left the Duke of Argyle, who married his niece, two hundred thousand pounds; I hope it is true, for I love that Duke mightily. I writ this evening to the Archbishop of Dublin, about what I told you; and then went to take leave of poor Mrs. St. John, who gave me strict charge to take care of the Secretary in her absence; said she had none to trust but me; and the poor creature's tears came fresh in her eyes. Before we took leave, I was drawn in by the other ladies and Sir John Stanley to raffle for a fan, with a pox; it was four guineas, and we put in seven shillings apiece, several raffling for absent people; but I lost, and so missed an opportunity of showing my gallantry to Mrs. St. John, whom I designed to have presented it to if I had won. Is Dilly gone to the Bath? His face will whizz in the water; I suppose he will write to us from thence, and will take London in his way back.—The rabble will say, "There goes a drunken parson"; and, which is worse, they will say true. Oh, but you must know I carried Ford to dine with Mr. St. John last Sunday, that he may brag, when he goes back, of dining with a Secretary of State. The Secretary and I went away early, and left him drinking with the rest, and he told me that two or three of them were drunk. They talk of great promotions to be made; that Mr. Harley is to be Lord Treasurer, and Lord Poulett Master of the Horse, etc., but they are only conjecture. The Speaker is to make Mr. Harley a compliment the first time he comes into the House, which I hope will be in a week. He has had an ill surgeon, by the caprice of that puppy Dr. Radcliffe, which has kept him back so long; and yesterday he got a cold, but is better to-day.—What! I think I am stark mad, to write so much in one

day to little saucy MD; here is a deal of stuff, indeed! can't you bid those little dear rogues good-night, and let them go sleep, Mr. Presto? When your tongue runs there's no ho with you, pray.

11. Again at the lobby (like a lobcock) of the House of Commons, about your Irish yarn, and again put off till Friday; and I and Patrick went into the City by water, where I dined, and then I went to the auction of Charles Barnard's books; but the good ones were so monstrous dear, I could not reach them, so I laid out one pound seven shillings but very indifferently, and came away, and will go there no more. Henley would fain engage me to go with Steele and Rowe, etc., to an invitation at Sir William Read's. Surely you have heard of him. He has been a mountebank, and is the Queen's oculist; he makes admirable punch, and treats you in gold vessels. But I am engaged, and will not go, neither indeed am I fond of the jaunt. So good-night, and go sleep.

12. I went about noon to the Secretary, who is very ill with a cold, and sometimes of the gravel, with his champagne, etc. I scolded him like a dog, and he promises faithfully more care for the future. To-day my Lord Anglesea, and Sir Thomas Hammer, and Prior, and I dined, by appointment, with Lieutenant-General Webb. My lord and I stayed till ten o'clock; but we drank soberly, and I always with water. There was with us one Mr. Campain, one of the October Club, if you know what that is; a Club of country members, who think the Ministers are too backward in punishing and turning out the Whigs. I found my lord and the rest thought I had more credit with the Ministry than I pretend to have, and would have engaged me to put them upon something that would satisfy their desires, and indeed I think they have some reason to complain; however, I will not burn my fingers. I will remember Stella's chiding, "What had you to do with what did not belong to you?" etc. However, you will give me leave to tell the Ministry my thoughts when they ask them, and other people's thoughts sometimes when they do not ask; so thinks Dingley.

13. I called this morning at Mrs. Vedeau's again, who has employed a friend to get the money; it will be done in a fortnight, and then she will deliver me up the parchment. I went then to see Mr. Harley, who I hope will be out in a few days; he was in excellent good humour, only complained to me of the neglect of Guiscard's cure, how glad he would

have been to have had him live. Mr. Secretary came in to us, and we were very merry till Lord Chamberlain (Duke of Shrewsbury) came up; then Colonel Masham and I went off, after I had been presented to the Duke, and that we made two or three silly compliments suitable to the occasion. Then I attended at the House of Commons about your yarn, and it is again put off. Then Ford drew me to dine at a tavern; it happened to be the day and the house where the October Club dine. After we had dined, coming down we called to inquire whether our yarn business had been over that day, and I sent into the room for Sir George Beaumont. But I had like to be drawn into a difficulty; for in two minutes out comes Mr. Finch, Lord Guernsey's son, to let me know that my Lord Compton, the steward of this feast, desired, in the name of the Club, that I would do them the honour to dine with them. I sent my excuses, adorned with about thirty compliments, and got off as fast as I could. It would have been a most improper thing for me to dine there, considering my friendship with the Ministry. The Club is about a hundred and fifty, and near eighty of them were then going to dinner at two long tables in a great ground-room. At evening I went to the auction of Barnard's books, and laid out three pounds three shillings, but I'll go there no more; and so I said once before, but now I'll keep to it. I forgot to tell that when I dined at Webb's with Lord Anglesea, I spoke to him of Clements, as one recommended for a very honest gentleman and good officer, and hoped he would keep him. He said he had not thought otherwise, and that he should certainly hold his place while he continued to deserve it; and I could not find there had been any intentions from his lordship against him. But I tell you, hunny, the impropriety of this. A great man will do a favour for me, or for my friend; but why should he do it for my friend's friend? Recommendations should stop before they come to that. Let any friend of mine recommend one of his to me for a thing in my power, I will do it for his sake; but to speak to another for my friend's friend is against all reason; and I desire you will understand this, and discourage any such troubles given me.—I hope this may do some good to Clements, it can do him no hurt; and I find by Mrs. Pratt, that her husband is his friend; and the Bishop of Clogher says Clements's danger is not from Pratt, but from some other enemies, that think him a Whig.

14. I was so busy this morning that I did not go out till late. I writ to-day to the Duke of Argyle, but said nothing of Bernage, who, I believe,

will not see him till Spain is conquered, and that is, not at all. I was to-day at Lord Shelburne's, and spoke to Mrs. Pratt again about Clements; her husband himself wants some good offices, and I have done him very good ones lately, and told Mrs. Pratt I expected her husband should stand by Clements in return. Sir Andrew Fountaine and I dined with neighbour Vanhomrigh; he is mighty ill of an asthma, and apprehends himself in much danger; 'tis his own fault, that will rake and drink, when he is but just crawled out of his grave. I will send this letter just now, because I think my half-year is out for my lodging; and, if you please, I would be glad it were paid off, and some deal boxes made for my books, and kept in some safe place. I would give something for their keeping: but I doubt that lodging will not serve me when I come back; I would have a larger place for books, and a stable, if possible. So pray be so kind to pay the lodging, and all accounts about it; and get Mrs. Brent to put up my things. I would have no books put in that trunk where my papers are. If you do not think of going to the Bath, I here send you a bill on Parvisol for twenty pounds Irish, out of which you will pay for the lodging, and score the rest to me. Do as you please, and love poor Presto, that loves MD better than his life a thousand millions of times. Farewell, MD, etc. etc.

Letter XXI

Remember, sirrahs, that there are but nine days between the dates of my two former letters. I sent away my twentieth this moment, and now am writing on like a fish, as if nothing was done. But there was a cause for my hasting away the last, for fear it should not come time enough before a new quarter began. I told you where I dined to-day; but forgot to tell you what I believe, that Mr. Harley will be Lord Treasurer in a short time, and other great removes and promotions made. This is my thought, etc.

15. I was this morning with Mr. Secretary, and he is grown pretty well. I dined with him to-day, and drank some of that wine which the Duke of Tuscany used to send to Sir William Temple: he always sends some to the chief Ministers. I liked it mightily, but he does not; and he ordered his butler to send me a chest of it to-morrow. Would to God MD had it! The Queen is well again, and was at chapel to-day, etc.

16. I went with Ford into the City to-day, and dined with Stratford, and drank Tokay, and then we went to the auction; but I did not lay out above twelve shillings. My head is a little out of order to-night, though no formal fit. My Lord Keeper has sent to invite me to dinner to-morrow, and you'll dine better with the Dean; and God bless you. I forgot to tell you that yesterday was sent me a *Narrative* printed, with all the circumstances of Mr. Harley's stabbing. I had not time to do it myself; so I sent my hints to the author of the *Atalantis*, and she has cooked it into a sixpenny pamphlet, in her own style, only the first page is left as I was beginning it. But I was afraid of disobliging Mr. Harley or Mr. St. John in one critical point about it, and so would not do it myself. It is worth your reading, for the circumstances are all true. My chest of Florence was sent me this morning, and cost me seven and sixpence to two servants. I would give two guineas you had it, etc.

17. I was so out of order with my head this morning, that I was going to send my excuses to my Lord Keeper; but however I got up at eleven,

and walked there after two, and stayed till eight. There was Sir Thomas Mansel, Prior, George Granville, and Mr. Cæsar, and we were very merry. My head is still wrong, but I have had no formal fit, only I totter a little. I have left off snuff altogether. I have a noble roll of tobacco for grating, very good. Shall I send it to MD, if she likes that sort? My Lord Keeper and our this day's company are to dine on Saturday with George Granville, and to-morrow I dine with Lord Anglesea.

18. Did you ever see such a blundering goosecap as Presto? I saw the number 21 at top, and so I went on as if it were the day of the month, whereas this is but Wednesday the 18th. How shall I do to blot and alter them? I have made a shift to do it behind, but it is a great botch. I dined with Lord Anglesea to-day, but did not go to the House of Commons about the yarn; my head was not well enough. I know not what is the matter; it has never been thus before: two days together giddy from morning till night, but not with any violence or pain; and I totter a little, but can make shift to walk. I doubt I must fall to my pills again: I think of going into the country a little way. I tell you what you must do henceforward: you must enclose your letter in a fair half-sheet of paper, and direct the outside "To Erasmus Lewis, Esquire, at my Lord Dartmouth's office at Whitehall": for I never go to the Coffee-house, and they will grudge to take in my letters. I forgot to tell you that your mother was to see me this morning, and brought me a flask of sweet-water for a present, admirable for my head; but I shall not smell to it. She is going to Sheen, with Lady Giffard: she would fain send your papers over to you, or give them to me. Say what you would have done, and it shall be done; because I love Stella, and she is a good daughter, they say, and so is Dingley.

19. This morning General Webb was to give me a visit: he goes with a crutch and stick, yet was forced to come up two pair of stairs. I promised to dine with him, but afterwards sent my excuses, and dined privately in my friend Lewis's lodgings at Whitehall, with whom I had much business to talk of, relating to the public and myself. Little Harrison the Tatler goes to-morrow to the secretaryship I got him at the Hague, and Mr. St. John has made him a present of fifty guineas to bear his charges. An't I a good friend? Why are not you a young fellow, that I might prefer you? I had a letter from Bernage from Kinsale: he tells me his commission for captain-lieutenant was ready for him at his arrival:

so there are two jackanapeses I have done with. My head is something better this evening, though not well.

20. I was this morning with Mr. Secretary, whose packets were just come in, and among them a letter from Lord Peterborow to me: he writes so well, I have no mind to answer him, and so kind, that I must answer him. The Emperor's death must, I think, cause great alterations in Europe, and, I believe, will hasten a peace. We reckon our King Charles will be chosen Emperor, and the Duke of Savoy set up for Spain; but I believe he will make nothing of it. Dr. Freind and I dined in the City at a printer's, and it has cost me two shillings in coach-hire, and a great deal more this week and month, which has been almost all rain, with now and then sunshine, and is the truest April that I have known these many years. The lime-trees in the Park are all out in leaves, though not large leaves yet. Wise people are going into the country; but many think the Parliament can hardly be up these six weeks. Mr. Harley was with the Queen on Tuesday. I believe certainly he will be Lord Treasurer: I have not seen him this week.

21. Morning. Lord Keeper, and I, and Prior, and Sir Thomas Mansel, have appointed to dine this day with George Granville. My head, I thank God, is better; but to be giddyish three or four days together mortified me. I take no snuff, and I will be very regular in eating little and the gentlest meats. How does poor Stella just now, with her deans and her Stoytes? Do they give you health for the money you lose at ombre, sirrah? What say you to that? Poor Dingley frets to see Stella lose that four and elevenpence, the other night. Let us rise. Morrow, sirrahs. I will rise, spite of your little teeth; good-morrow.—At night. O, faith, you are little dear saucyboxes. I was just going in the morning to tell you that I began to want a letter from MD, and in four minutes after Mr. Ford sends me one that he had picked up at St. James's Coffee-house; for I go to no coffee-house at all. And, faith, I was glad at heart to see it, and to see Stella so brisk. O Lord, what pretending? Well, but I will not answer it yet; I'll keep it for t'other side. Well, we dined to-day according to appointment: Lord Keeper went away at near eight, I at eight, and I believe the rest will be fairly fuddled; for young Harcourt, Lord Keeper's son, began to prattle before I came away. It will not do with Prior's lean carcass. I drink little, miss my glass often, put water in my wine, and go away before the rest, which

I take to be a good receipt for sobriety. Let us put it into rhyme, and so make a proverb—

> *Drink little at a time;*
> *Put water with your wine;*
> *Miss your glass when you can;*
> *And go off the first man.*

God be thanked, I am much better than I was, though something of a totterer. I ate but little to-day, and of the gentlest meat. I refused ham and pigeons, pease-soup, stewed beef, cold salmon, because they were too strong. I take no snuff at all, but some herb snuff prescribed by Dr. Radcliffe.

> *Go to your deans,*
> *You couple of queans.*

I believe I said that already. What care I? what cares Presto?

22. Morning. I must rise and go to the Secretary's. Mr. Harley has been out of town this week to refresh himself before he comes into Parliament. Oh, but I must rise, so there is no more to be said; and so morrow, sirrahs both.—Night. I dined to-day with the Secretary, who has engaged me for every Sunday; and I was an hour with him this morning deep in politics, where I told him the objections of the October Club, and he answered all except one, that no inquiries are made into past mismanagement. But indeed I believe they are not yet able to make any: the late Ministry were too cunning in their rogueries, and fenced themselves with an Act of general pardon. I believe Mr. Harley must be Lord Treasurer; yet he makes one difficulty which is hard to answer: he must be made a lord, and his estate is not large enough, and he is too generous to make it larger; and if the Ministry should change soon by any accident, he will be left in the suds. Another difficulty is, that if he be made a peer, they will want him prodigiously in the House of Commons, of which he is the great mover, and after him the Secretary, and hardly any else of weight. Two shillings more to-day for coach and chair. I shall be ruined.

23. So you expect an answer to your letter, do you so? Yes, yes, you shall have an answer, you shall, young women. I made a good pun on Saturday

to my Lord Keeper. After dinner we had coarse Doiley napkins, fringed at each end, upon the table, to drink with: my Lord Keeper spread one of them between him and Mr. Prior; I told him I was glad to see there was such a fringeship (friendship) between Mr. Prior and his lordship. Prior swore it was the worst he ever heard: I said I thought so too; but at the same time I thought it was most like one of Stella's that ever I heard. I dined to-day with Lord Mountjoy, and this evening saw the Venetian Ambassador coming from his first public audience. His coach was the most monstrous, huge, fine, rich gilt thing that ever I saw. I loitered this evening, and came home late.

24. I was this morning to visit the Duchess of Ormond, who has long desired it, or threatened she would not let me visit her daughters. I sat an hour with her, and we were good company, when in came the Countess of Bellamont, with a pox. I went out, and we did not know one another; yet hearing me named, she asked, "What, is that Dr. Swift?" said she and I were very well acquainted, and fell a railing at me without mercy, as a lady told me that was there; yet I never was but once in the company of that drab of a Countess. Sir Andrew Fountaine and I dined with my neighbour Van. I design in two days, if possible, to go lodge at Chelsea for the air, and put myself under a necessity of walking to and from London every day. I writ this post to the Bishop of Clogher a long politic letter, to entertain him. I am to buy statues and harnese for them, with a vengeance. I have packed and sealed up MD's twelve letters against I go to Chelsea. I have put the last commissions of MD in my account-book; but if there be any former ones, I have forgot them. I have Dingley's pocket-book down, and Stella's green silk apron, and the pound of tea; pray send me word if you have any other, and down they shall go. I will not answer your letter yet, saucy boxes. You are with the Dean just now, Madam Stella, losing your money. Why do not you name what number you have received? You say you have received my letters, but do not tell the number.

25. I was this day dining in the City with very insignificant, low, and scurvy company. I had a letter from the Archbishop of Dublin, with a long denial of the report raised on him, which yet has been since assured to me from those who say they have it from the first hand; but I cannot believe them. I will show it to the Secretary to-morrow. I will not answer yours till I get to Chelsea.

26. Chelsea. I have sent two boxes of lumber to my friend Darteneuf's house, and my chest of Florence and other things to Mrs. Vanhomrigh, where I dined to-day. I was this morning with the Secretary, and showed him the Archbishop's letter, and convinced him of his Grace's innocence, and I will do the same to Mr. Harley. I got here in the stage-coach with Patrick and my portmanteau for sixpence, and pay six shillings a week for one silly room with confounded coarse sheets. We have had such a horrible deal of rain, that there is no walking to London, and I must go as I came until it mends; and besides the whelp has taken my lodging as far from London as this town could afford, at least half a mile farther than he need; but I must be content. The best is, I lodge just over against Dr. Atterbury's house, and yet perhaps I shall not like the place the better for that. Well, I will stay till to-morrow before I answer your letter; and you must suppose me always writing at Chelsea from henceforward, till I alter, and say London. This letter goes on Saturday, which will be just a fortnight; so go and cheat Goody Stoyte, etc.

27. Do you know that I fear my whole chest of Florence is turned sour, at least the two first flasks were so, and hardly drinkable. How plaguy unfortunate am I! and the Secretary's own is the best I ever tasted; and I must not tell him, but be as thankful as if it were the best in Christendom. I went to town in the sixpenny stage to-day; and hearing Mr. Harley was not at home, I went to see him, because I knew by the message of his lying porter that he was at home. He was very well, and just going out, but made me promise to dine with him; and betwixt that and indeed strolling about, I lost four pound seven shillings at play— with a—a—a—bookseller, and got but about half a dozen books. I will buy no more books now, that's certain. Well, I dined at Mr. Harley's, came away at six, shifted my gown, cassock, and periwig, and walked hither to Chelsea, as I always design to do when it is fair. I am heartily sorry to find my friend the Secretary stand a little ticklish with the rest of the Ministry; there have been one or two disobliging things that have happened, too long to tell: and t'other day in Parliament, upon a debate of about thirty-five millions that have not been duly accounted for, Mr. Secretary, in his warmth of speech, and zeal for his friend Mr. Brydges, on whom part of the blame was falling, said he did not know that either Mr. Brydges or the late Ministry were at all to blame in this matter; which was very desperately spoken, and giving up the whole cause: for the chief quarrel against the late Ministry was the ill

management of the treasure, and was more than all the rest together. I had heard of this matter: but Mr. Foley beginning to discourse to-day at table, without naming Mr. St. John, I turned to Mr. Harley, and said if the late Ministry were not to blame in that article, he (Mr. Harley) ought to lose his head for putting the Queen upon changing them. He made it a jest; but by some words dropped, I easily saw that they take things ill of Mr. St. John; and by some hints given me from another hand that I deal with, I am afraid the Secretary will not stand long. This is the fate of Courts. I will, if I meet Mr. St. John alone on Sunday, tell him my opinion, and beg him to set himself right, else the consequences may be very bad; for I see not how they can well want him neither, and he would make a troublesome enemy. But enough of politics.

28. Morning. I forgot to tell you that Mr. Harley asked me yesterday how he came to disoblige the Archbishop of Dublin. Upon which (having not his letter about me) I told him what the Bishop had written to me on that subject, and desired I might read him the letter some other time. But after all, from what I have heard from other hands, I am afraid the Archbishop is a little guilty. Here is one Brent Spencer, a brother of Mr. Proby's, who affirms it, and says he has leave to do so from Charles Dering, who heard the words; and that Ingoldsby, abused the Archbishop, etc. Well, but now for your saucy letter: I have no room to answer it; O yes, enough on t'other side. Are you no sicker? Stella jeers Presto for not coming over by Christmas; but indeed Stella does not jeer, but reproach, poor poor Presto. And how can I come away and the First-Fruits not finished? I am of opinion the Duke of Ormond will do nothing in them before he goes, which will be in a fortnight, they say; and then they must fall to me to be done in his absence. No, indeed, I have nothing to print: you know they have printed the *Miscellanies* already. Are they on your side yet? If you have my snuff box, I will have your strong box. Hi, does Stella take snuff again? or is it only because it is a fine box? Not the *Meddle*, but the *Medley*, you fool. Yes, yes, a wretched thing, because it is against you Tories: now I think it very fine, and the *Examiner* a wretched thing.—Twist your mouth, sirrah. Guiscard, and what you will read in the *Narrative*, I ordered to be written, and nothing else. The *Spectator* is written by Steele, with Addison's help: it is often very pretty. Yesterday it was made of a noble hint I gave him long ago for his *Tatlers*, about an Indian supposed to write his Travels into England. I repent he ever had it. I intended to have written a book on that subject. I believe he has

spent it all in one paper, and all the under-hints there are mine too; but I never see him or Addison. The Queen is well, but I fear will be no long liver; for I am told she has sometimes the gout in her bowels (I hate the word *bowels*). My ears have been, these three months past, much better than any time these two years; but now they begin to be a little out of order again. My head is better, though not right; but I trust to air and walking. You have got my letter, but what number? I suppose 18. Well, my shin has been well this month. No, Mrs. Westley came away without her husband's knowledge, while she was in the country: she has written to me for some tea. They lie; Mr. Harley's wound was very terrible: he had convulsions, and very narrowly escaped. The bruise was nine times worse than the wound: he is weak still. Well, Brooks married; I know all that. I am sorry for Mrs. Walls's eye: I hope 'tis better. O yes, you are great walkers: but I have heard them say, "Much talkers, little walkers": and I believe I may apply the old proverb to you—

> *If you talked no more than you walked,*
> *Those that think you wits would be baulked.*

Yes, Stella shall have a large printed Bible: I have put it down among my commissions for MD. I am glad to hear you have taken the fancy of intending to read the Bible. Pox take the box; is not it come yet? This is trusting to your young fellows, young women; 'tis your fault: I thought you had such power with Sterne that he would fly over Mount Atlas to serve you. You say you are not splenetic; but if you be, faith, you will break poor Presto's—I will not say the rest; but I vow to God, if I could decently come over now, I would, and leave all schemes of politics and ambition for ever. I have not the opportunities here of preserving my health by riding, etc., that I have in Ireland; and the want of health is a great cooler of making one's court. You guess right about my being bit with a direction from Walls, and the letter from MD: I believe I described it in one of my last. This goes to-night; and I must now rise and walk to town, and walk back in the evening. God Almighty bless and preserve poor MD. Farewell.

O, faith, don't think, saucy noses, that I'll fill this third side: I can't stay a letter above a fortnight: it must go then; and you would rather see a short one like this, than want it a week longer.

My humble service to the Dean, and Mrs. Walls, and good, kind, hearty Mrs. Stoyte, and honest Catherine.

Letter XXII

At night. I say at night, because I finished my twenty-first this morning here, and put it into the post-office my own self, like a good boy. I think I am a little before you now, young women: I am writing my twenty-second, and have received your thirteenth. I got to town between twelve and one, and put on my new gown and periwig, and dined with Lord Abercorn, where I had not been since the marriage of his son Lord Peasley, who has got ten thousand pounds with a wife. I am now a country gentleman. I walked home as I went, and am a little weary, and am got into bed: I hope in God the air and exercise will do me a little good. I have been inquiring about statues for Mrs. Ashe: I made Lady Abercorn go with me; and will send them word next post to Clogher. I hate to buy for her: I am sure she will maunder. I am going to study.

29. I had a charming walk to and from town to-day: I washed, shaved and all, and changed gown and periwig, by half an hour after nine, and went to the Secretary, who told me how he had differed with his friends in Parliament: I apprehended this division, and told him a great deal of it. I went to Court, and there several mentioned it to me as what they much disliked. I dined with the Secretary; and we proposed doing some business of importance in the afternoon, which he broke to me first, and said how he and Mr. Harley were convinced of the necessity of it; yet he suffered one of his under-secretaries to come upon us after dinner, who stayed till six, and so nothing was done: and what care I? he shall send to me the next time, and ask twice. To-morrow I go to the election at Westminster School, where lads are chosen for the University: they say it is a sight, and a great trial of wits. Our Expedition Fleet is but just sailed: I believe it will come to nothing. Mr. Secretary frets at their tediousness, but hopes great things from it, though he owns four or five princes are in the secret; and, for that reason, I fear it is no secret to France. There are eight regiments; and the Admiral is your Walker's brother the midwife.

30. Morn. I am here in a pretty pickle: it rains hard; and the cunning natives of Chelsea have outwitted me, and taken up all the three stage coaches. What shall I do? I must go to town: this is your fault. I cannot

walk: I will borrow a coat. This is the blind side of my lodging out of town; I must expect such inconveniences as these. Faith, I'll walk in the rain. Morrow.—At night. I got a gentleman's chaise by chance, and so went to town for a shilling, and lie this night in town. I was at the election of lads at Westminster to-day, and a very silly thing it is; but they say there will be fine doings to-morrow. I dined with Dr. Freind, the second master of the school, with a dozen parsons and others: Prior would make me stay. Mr. Harley is to hear the election to-morrow; and we are all to dine with tickets, and hear fine speeches. 'Tis terrible rainy weather again: I lie at a friend's in the City.

May 1. I wish you a merry May Day, and a thousand more. I was baulked at Westminster; I came too late: I heard no speeches nor verses. They would not let me in to their dining-place for want of a ticket; and I would not send in for one, because Mr. Harley excused his coming, and Atterbury was not there; and I cared not for the rest: and so my friend Lewis and I dined with Kitt Musgrave, if you know such a man: and, the weather mending, I walked gravely home this evening; and so I design to walk and walk till I am well: I fancy myself a little better already. How does poor Stella? Dingley is well enough. Go, get you gone, naughty girl, you are well enough. O dear MD, contrive to have some share of the country this spring: go to Finglas, or Donnybrook, or Clogher, or Killala, or Lowth. Have you got your box yet? Yes, yes. Do not write to me again till this letter goes: I must make haste, that I may write two for one. Go to the Bath: I hope you are now at the Bath, if you had a mind to go; or go to Wexford: do something for your living. Have you given up my lodging, according to order? I have had just now a compliment from Dean Atterbury's lady, to command the garden and library, and whatever the house affords. I lodge just over against them; but the Dean is in town with his Convocation: so I have my Dean and Prolocutor as well as you, young women, though he has not so good wine, nor so much meat.

2. A fine day, but begins to grow a little warm; and that makes your little fat Presto sweat in the forehead. Pray, are not the fine buns sold here in our town; was it not *Rrrrrrrrrare Chelsea buns*? I bought one to-day in my walk; it cost me a penny; it was stale, and I did not like it, as the man said, etc. Sir Andrew Fountaine and I dined at Mrs. Vanhomrigh's, and had a flask of my Florence, which lies in their cellar; and so I came

home gravely, and saw nobody of consequence to-day. I am very easy here, nobody plaguing me in a morning; and Patrick saves many a score lies. I sent over to Mrs. Atterbury to know whether I might wait on her; but she is gone a visiting: we have exchanged some compliments, but I have not seen her yet. We have no news in our town.

3. I did not go to town to-day, it was so terrible rainy; nor have I stirred out of my room till eight this evening, when I crossed the way to see Mrs. Atterbury, and thank her for her civilities. She would needs send me some veal, and small beer, and ale, to-day at dinner; and I have lived a scurvy, dull, splenetic day, for want of MD: I often thought how happy I could have been, had it rained eight thousand times more, if MD had been with a body. My Lord Rochester is dead this morning; they say at one o'clock; and I hear he died suddenly. To-morrow I shall know more. He is a great loss to us: I cannot think who will succeed him as Lord President. I have been writing a long letter to Lord Peterborow, and am dull.

4. I dined to-day at Lord Shelburne's, where Lady Kerry made me a present of four India handkerchiefs, which I have a mind to keep for little MD, only that I had rather, etc. I have been a mighty handkerchief-monger, and have bought abundance of snuff ones since I have left off taking snuff. And I am resolved, when I come over, MD shall be acquainted with Lady Kerry: we have struck up a mighty friendship; and she has much better sense than any other lady of your country. We are almost in love with one another: but she is most egregiously ugly; but perfectly well-bred, and governable as I please. I am resolved, when I come, to keep no company but MD: you know I kept my resolution last time; and, except Mr. Addison, conversed with none but you and your club of deans and Stoytes. 'Tis three weeks, young women, since I had a letter from you; and yet, methinks, I would not have another for five pounds till this is gone; and yet I send every day to the Coffee-house, and I would fain have a letter, and not have a letter: and I do not know what, nor I do not know how, and this goes on very slow; it is a week to-morrow since I began it. I am a poor country gentleman, and do not know how the world passes. Do you know that every syllable I write I hold my lips just for all the world as if I were talking in our own little language to MD? Faith, I am very silly; but I cannot help it for my life. I got home early to-night. My solicitors, that used to ply me

every morning, knew not where to find me; and I am so happy not to hear "Patrick, Patrick," called a hundred times every morning. But I looked backward, and find I have said this before. What care I? Go to the Dean, and roast the oranges.

5. I dined to-day with my friend Lewis, and we were deep in politics how to save the present Ministry; for I am afraid of Mr. Secretary, as I believe I told you. I went in the evening to see Mr. Harley; and, upon my word, I was in perfect joy. Mr. Secretary was just going out of the door; but I made him come back, and there was the old Saturday Club, Lord Keeper, Lord Rivers, Mr. Secretary, Mr. Harley, and I; the first time since his stabbing. Mr. Secretary went away; but I stayed till nine, and made Mr. Harley show me his breast, and tell all the story; and I showed him the Archbishop of Dublin's letter, and defended him effectually. We were all in mighty good humour. Lord Keeper and I left them together, and I walked here after nine two miles, and I found a parson drunk fighting with a seaman, and Patrick and I were so wise to part them, but the seaman followed him to Chelsea, cursing at him, and the parson slipped into a house, and I know no more. It mortified me to see a man in my coat so overtaken. A pretty scene for one that just came from sitting with the Prime Ministers! I had no money in my pocket, and so could not be robbed. However, nothing but Mr. Harley shall make me take such a journey again. We don't yet know who will be President in Lord Rochester's room. I measured, and found that the penknife would have killed Mr. Harley if it had gone but half the breadth of my thumb-nail lower, so near was he to death. I was so curious as to ask him what were his thoughts while they were carrying him home in the chair. He said he concluded himself a dead man. He will not allow that Guiscard gave him the second stab; though my Lord Keeper, who is blind, and I that was not there, are positive in it. He wears a plaster still as broad as half a crown. Smoke how wide the lines are, but, faith, I don't do it on purpose: but I have changed my side in this new Chelsea bed, and I do not know how, methinks, but it is so unfit, and so awkward, never saw the like.

6. You must remember to enclose your letters in a fair paper, and direct the outside thus: "To Erasmus Lewis, Esq.; at my Lord Dartmouth's office at Whitehall." I said so before, but it may miscarry, you know, yet I think none of my letters did ever miscarry; faith, I think never

one; among all the privateers and the storms. O, faith, my letters are too good to be lost. MD's letters may tarry, but never miscarry, as the old woman used to say. And indeed, how should they miscarry, when they never come before their time? It was a terrible rainy day; yet I made a shift to steal fair weather overhead enough to go and come in. I was early with the Secretary, and dined with him afterwards. In the morning I began to chide him, and tell him my fears of his proceedings. But Arthur Moore came up and relieved him. But I forgot, for you never heard of Arthur Moore. But when I get Mr. Harley alone, I will know the bottom. You will have Dr. Raymond over before this letter, and what care you?

7. I hope and believe my walks every day do me good. I was busy at home, and set out late this morning, and dined with Mrs. Vanhomrigh, at whose lodgings I always change my gown and periwig. I visited this afternoon, and among others, poor Biddy Floyd, who is very red, but I believe won't be much marked. As I was coming home, I met Sir George Beaumont in the Pall Mall, who would needs walk with me as far as Buckingham House. I was telling him of my head; he said he had been ill of the same disorder, and by all means forbid me bohea tea, which, he said, always gave it him; and that Dr. Radcliffe said it was very bad. Now I had observed the same thing, and have left it off this month, having found myself ill after it several times; and I mention it that Stella may consider it for her own poor little head: a pound lies ready packed up and directed for Mrs. Walls, to be sent by the first convenience. Mr. Secretary told me yesterday that Mr. Harley would this week be Lord Treasurer and a peer; so I expect it every day; yet perhaps it may not be till Parliament is up, which will be in a fortnight.

8. I was to-day with the Duke of Ormond, and recommended to him the care of poor Joe Beaumont, who promises me to do him all justice and favour, and give him encouragement; and desired I would give a memorial to Ned Southwell about it, which I will, and so tell Joe when you see him, though he knows it already by a letter I writ to Mr. Warburton. It was bloody hot walking to-day. I dined in the City, and went and came by water; and it rained so this evening again, that I thought I should hardly be able to get a dry hour to walk home in. I will send to-morrow to the Coffee-house for a letter from MD; but I would not have one methinks till this is gone, as it shall on Saturday.

JONATHAN SWIFT

I visited the Duchess of Ormond this morning; she does not go over with the Duke. I spoke to her to get a lad touched for the evil, the son of a grocer in Capel Street, one Bell; the ladies have bought sugar and plums of him. Mrs. Mary used to go there often. This is Patrick's account; and the poor fellow has been here some months with his boy. But the Queen has not been able to touch, and it now grows so warm, I fear she will not at all. Go, go, go to the Dean's, and let him carry you to Donnybrook, and cut asparagus. Has Parvisol sent you any this year? I cannot sleep in the beginnings of the nights, the heat or something hinders me, and I am drowsy in the mornings.

9. Dr. Freind came this morning to visit Atterbury's lady and children as physician, and persuaded me to go with him to town in his chariot. He told me he had been an hour before with Sir Cholmley Dering, Charles Dering's nephew, and head of that family in Kent, for which he is Knight of the shire. He said he left him dying of a pistol-shot quite through the body, by one Mr. Thornhill. They fought at sword and pistol this morning in Tuttle Fields, their pistols so near that the muzzles touched. Thornhill discharged first; and Dering, having received the shot, discharged his pistol as he was falling, so it went into the air. The story of this quarrel is long. Thornhill had lost seven teeth by a kick in the mouth from Dering, who had first knocked him down; this was above a fortnight ago. Dering was next week to be married to a fine young lady. This makes a noise here, but you will not value it. Well, Mr. Harley, Lord Keeper, and one or two more, are to be made lords immediately; their patents are now passing, and I read the preamble to Mr. Harley's, full of his praises. Lewis and I dined with Ford: I found the wine; two flasks of my Florence, and two bottles of six that Dr. Raymond sent me of French wine; he sent it to me to drink with Sir Robert Raymond and Mr. Harley's brother, whom I had introduced him to; but they never could find time to come; and now I have left the town, and it is too late. Raymond will think it a cheat. What care I, sirrah?

10. Pshaw, pshaw. Patrick brought me four letters to-day: from Dilly at Bath; Joe; Parvisol; and what was the fourth, who can tell? Stand away, who'll guess? Who can it be? You old man with a stick, can you tell who the fourth is from? Iss, an please your honour, it is from one Madam MD, Number Fourteen. Well; but I can't send this away now,

because it was here, and I was in town; but it shall go on Saturday, and this is Thursday night, and it will be time enough for Wexford. Take my method: I write here to Parvisol to lend Stella twenty pounds, and to take her note promissory to pay it in half a year, etc. You shall see, and if you want more, let me know afterwards; and be sure my money shall be always paid constantly too. Have you been good or ill housewives, pray?

11. Joe has written me to get him a collector's place, nothing less; he says all the world knows of my great intimacy with Mr. Harley, and that the smallest word to him will do. This is the constant cant of puppies who are at a distance, and strangers to Courts and Ministers. My answer is this, which pray send: that I am ready to serve Joe as far as I can; that I have spoken to the Duke of Ormond about his money, as I writ to Warburton; that for the particular he mentions, it is a work of time, which I cannot think of at present; but, if accidents and opportunities should happen hereafter, I would not be wanting; that I know best how far my credit goes; that he is at a distance, and cannot judge; that I would be glad to do him good, and if fortune throws an opportunity in my way I shall not be wanting. This is my answer, which you may send or read to him. Pray contrive that Parvisol may not run away with my two hundred pounds; but get Burton's note, and let the money be returned me by bill. Don't laugh, for I will be suspicious. Teach Parvisol to enclose, and direct the outside to Mr. Lewis. I will answer your letter in my next, only what I take notice of here excepted. I forgot to tell you that at the Court of Requests to-day I could not find a dinner I liked, and it grew late, and I dined with Mrs. Vanhomrigh, etc.

12. Morning. I will finish this letter before I go to town, because I shall be busy, and have neither time nor place there. Farewell, etc. etc.

Letter XXIII

I sent you my twenty-second this afternoon in town. I dined with Mr. Harley and the old Club, Lord Rivers, Lord Keeper, and Mr. Secretary. They rallied me last week, and said I must have Mr. St. John's leave; so I writ to him yesterday, that foreseeing I should never dine again with Sir Simon Harcourt, Knight, and Robert Harley, Esq., I was resolved to do it to-day. The jest is, that before Saturday next we expect they will be lords; for Mr. Harley's patent is drawing, to be Earl of Oxford. Mr. Secretary and I came away at seven, and he brought me to our town's end in his coach; so I lost my walk. St. John read my letter to the company, which was all raillery, and passed purely.

13. It rained all last night and this morning as heavy as lead; but I just got fair weather to walk to town before church. The roads are all over in deep puddle. The hay of our town is almost fit to be mowed. I went to Court after church (as I always do on Sundays), and then dined with Mr. Secretary, who has engaged me for every Sunday; and poor MD dined at home upon a bit of veal and a pint of wine. Is it not plaguy insipid to tell you every day where I dine? yet now I have got into the way of it, I cannot forbear it neither. Indeed, Mr. Presto, you had better go answer MD's letter, N. 14. I will answer it when I please, Mr. Doctor. What is that you say? The Court was very full this morning, expecting Mr. Harley would be declared Earl of Oxford and have the Treasurer's staff. Mr. Harley never comes to Court at all; somebody there asked me the reason. "Why," said I, "the Lord of Oxford knows." He always goes to the Queen by the back stairs. I was told for certain, you jackanapes, Lord Santry was dead, Captain Cammock assured me so; and now he's alive again, they say; but that shan't do: he shall be dead to me as long as he lives. Dick Tighe and I meet, and never stir our hats. I am resolved to mistake him for Witherington, the little nasty lawyer that came up to me so sternly at the Castle the day I left Ireland. I'll ask the gentleman I saw walking with him how long Witherington has been in town.

14. I went to town to-day by water. The hail quite discouraged me from walking, and there is no shade in the greatest part of the way. I took the

first boat, and had a footman my companion; then I went again by water, and dined in the City with a printer, to whom I carried a pamphlet in manuscript, that Mr. Secretary gave me. The printer sent it to the Secretary for his approbation, and he desired me to look it over, which I did, and found it a very scurvy piece. The reason I tell you so, is because it was done by your parson Slap, Scrap, Flap (what d'ye call him), Trapp, your Chancellor's chaplain. 'Tis called *A Character of the Present Set of Whigs*, and is going to be printed, and no doubt the author will take care to produce it in Ireland. Dr. Freind was with me, and pulled out a twopenny pamphlet just published, called *The State of Wit*, giving a character of all the papers that have come out of late. The author seems to be a Whig, yet he speaks very highly of a paper called the *Examiner*, and says the supposed author of it is Dr. Swift. But above all things he praises the *Tatlers* and *Spectators*; and I believe Steele and Addison were privy to the printing of it. Thus is one treated by these impudent dogs. And that villain Curll has scraped up some trash, and calls it Dr. Swift's *Miscellanies*, with the name at large: and I can get no satisfaction of him. Nay, Mr. Harley told me he had read it, and only laughed at me before Lord Keeper and the rest. Since I came home, I have been sitting with the Prolocutor, Dean Atterbury, who is my neighbour over the way, but generally keeps in town with his Convocation. 'Tis late, etc.

15. My walk to town to-day was after ten, and prodigiously hot. I dined with Lord Shelburne, and have desired Mrs. Pratt, who lodges there, to carry over Mrs. Walls's tea; I hope she will do it, and they talk of going in a fortnight. My way is this: I leave my best gown and periwig at Mrs. Vanhomrigh's, then walk up the Pall Mall, through the Park, out at Buckingham House, and so to Chelsea a little beyond the church: I set out about sunset, and get here in something less than an hour; it is two good miles, and just five thousand seven hundred and forty-eight steps; so there is four miles a day walking, without reckoning what I walk while I stay in town. When I pass the Mall in the evening, it is prodigious to see the number of ladies walking there; and I always cry shame at the ladies of Ireland, who never walk at all, as if their legs were of no use, but to be laid aside. I have been now almost three weeks here, and I thank God, am much better in my head, if it does but continue. I tell you what, if I was with you, when we went to Stoyte at Donnybrook, we would only take a coach to the hither end of Stephen's Green, and from thence go every step on foot, yes, faith, every step; it would do

DD good as well as Presto. Everybody tells me I look better already; for, faith, I looked sadly, that is certain. My breakfast is milk porridge: I do not love it; faith, I hate it, but it is cheap and wholesome; and I hate to be obliged to either of those qualities for anything.

16. I wonder why Presto will be so tedious in answering MD's letters; because he would keep the best to the last, I suppose. Well, Presto must be humoured, it must be as he will have it, or there will be an old to do. Dead with heat; are not you very hot? My walks make my forehead sweat rarely; sometimes my morning journey is by water, as it was to-day with one Parson Richardson, who came to see me, on his going to Ireland; and with him I send Mrs. Walls's tea, and three books I got from the Lords of the Treasury for the College. I dined with Lord Shelburne to-day; Lady Kerry and Mrs. Pratt are going likewise for Ireland.—Lord! I forgot, I dined with Mr. Prior to-day, at his house, with Dean Atterbury and others; and came home pretty late, and I think I'm in a fuzz, and don't know what I say, never saw the like.

17. Sterne came here by water to see me this morning, and I went back with him to his boat. He tells me that Mrs. Edgworth married a fellow in her journey to Chester; so I believe she little thought of anybody's box but her own. I desired Sterne to give me directions where to get the box in Chester, which he says he will to-morrow; and I will write to Richardson to get it up there as he goes by, and whip it over. It is directed to Mrs. Curry: you must caution her of it, and desire her to send it you when it comes. Sterne says Jemmy Leigh loves London mightily; that makes him stay so long, I believe, and not Sterne's business, which Mr. Harley's accident has put much backward. We expect now every day that he will be Earl of Oxford and Lord Treasurer. His patent is passing; but, they say, Lord Keeper's not yet; at least his son, young Harcourt, told me so t'other day. I dined to-day privately with my friend Lewis at his lodgings at Whitehall. T'other day at Whitehall I met a lady of my acquaintance, whom I had not seen before since I came to England; we were mighty glad to see each other, and she has engaged me to visit her, as I design to do. It is one Mrs. Colledge: she has lodgings at Whitehall, having been seamstress to King William, worth three hundred a year. Her father was a fanatic joiner, hanged for treason in Shaftesbury's plot. This noble person and I were brought

acquainted, some years ago, by Lady Berkeley. I love good creditable acquaintance: I love to be the worst of the company: I am not of those that say, "For want of company, welcome trumpery." I was this evening with Lady Kerry and Mrs. Pratt at Vauxhall, to hear the nightingales; but they are almost past singing.

18. I was hunting the Secretary to-day in vain about some business, and dined with Colonel Crowe, late Governor of Barbados, and your friend Sterne was the third: he is very kind to Sterne, and helps him in his business, which lies asleep till Mr. Harley is Lord Treasurer, because nothing of moment is now done in the Treasury, the change being expected every day. I sat with Dean Atterbury till one o'clock after I came home; so 'tis late, etc.

19. Do you know that about our town we are mowing already and making hay, and it smells so sweet as we walk through the flowery meads; but the hay-making nymphs are perfect drabs, nothing so clean and pretty as farther in the country. There is a mighty increase of dirty wenches in straw hats since I knew London. I stayed at home till five o'clock, and dined with Dean Atterbury; then went by water to Mr. Harley's, where the Saturday Club was met, with the addition of the Duke of Shrewsbury. I whispered Lord Rivers that I did not like to see a stranger among us; and the rogue told it aloud: but Mr. Secretary said the Duke writ to have leave; so I appeared satisfied, and so we laughed. Mr. Secretary told me the Duke of Buckingham had been talking to him much about me, and desired my acquaintance. I answered it could not be, for he had not made sufficient advances. Then the Duke of Shrewsbury said he thought that Duke was not used to make advances. I said I could not help that; for I always expected advances in proportion to men's quality, and more from a duke than any other man. The Duke replied that he did not mean anything of his quality; which was handsomely said enough; for he meant his pride: and I have invented a notion to believe that nobody is proud. At ten all the company went away; and from ten to twelve Mr. Harley and I sat together, where we talked through a great deal of matters I had a mind to settle with him; and then walked in a fine moonshine night to Chelsea, where I got by one. Lord Rivers conjured me not to walk so late; but I would, because I had no other way; but I had no money to lose.

20. By what the Lord Keeper told me last night, I find he will not be made a peer so soon; but Mr. Harley's patent for Earl of Oxford is now drawing, and will be done in three days. We made him own it, which he did scurvily, and then talked of it like the rest. Mr. Secretary had too much company with him to-day; so I came away soon after dinner. I give no man liberty to swear or talk b—dy, and I found some of them were in constraint, so I left them to themselves. I wish you a merry Whitsuntide, and pray tell me how you pass away your time; but, faith, you are going to Wexford, and I fear this letter is too late; it shall go on Thursday, and sooner it cannot, I have so much business to hinder me answering yours. Where must I direct in your absence? Do you quit your lodgings?

21. Going to town this morning, I met in the Pall Mall a clergyman of Ireland, whom I love very well and was glad to see, and with him a little jackanapes, of Ireland too, who married Nanny Swift, Uncle Adam's daughter, one Perry; perhaps you may have heard of him. His wife has sent him here, to get a place from Lowndes; because my uncle and Lowndes married two sisters, and Lowndes is a great man here in the Treasury; but by good luck I have no acquaintance with him: however, he expected I should be his friend to Lowndes, and one word of mine, etc., the old cant. But I will not go two yards to help him. I dined with Mrs. Vanhomrigh, where I keep my best gown and periwig, to put on when I come to town and be a spark.

22. I dined to-day in the City, and coming home this evening, I met Sir Thomas Mansel and Mr. Lewis in the Park. Lewis whispered me that Mr. Harley's patent for the Earl of Oxford was passed in Mr. Secretary St. John's office; so to-morrow or next day, I suppose, he will be declared Earl of Oxford, and have the staff. This man has grown by persecutions, turnings out, and stabbing. What waiting, and crowding, and bowing will be at his levee! yet, if human nature be capable of so much constancy, I should believe he will be the same man still, bating the necessary forms of grandeur he must keep up. 'Tis late, sirrahs, and I'll go sleep.

23. Morning. I sat up late last night, and waked late to-day; but will now answer your letter in bed before I go to town, and I will send it to-morrow; for perhaps you mayn't go so soon to Wexford.—No, you are not out in your number; the last was Number 14, and so I told you

twice or thrice; will you never be satisfied? What shall we do for poor Stella? Go to Wexford, for God's sake: I wish you were to walk there by three miles a day, with a good lodging at every mile's end. Walking has done me so much good, that I cannot but prescribe it often to poor Stella. Parvisol has sent me a bill for fifty pounds, which I am sorry for, having not written to him for it, only mentioned it two months ago; but I hope he will be able to pay you what I have drawn upon him for: he never sent me any sum before, but one bill of twenty pounds half a year ago. You are welcome as my blood to every farthing I have in the world; and all that grieves me is, I am not richer, for MD's sake, as hope saved. I suppose you give up your lodgings when you go to Wexford; yet that will be inconvenient too: yet I wish again you were under a necessity of rambling the country until Michaelmas, faith. No, let them keep the shelves, with a pox; yet they are exacting people about those four weeks; or Mrs. Brent may have the shelves, if she please. I am obliged to your Dean for his kind offer of lending me money. Will that be enough to say? A hundred people would lend me money, or to any man who has not the reputation of a squanderer. O, faith, I should be glad to be in the same kingdom with MD, however, although you are at Wexford. But I am kept here by a most capricious fate, which I would break through, if I could do it with decency or honour.—To return without some mark of distinction would look extremely little; and I would likewise gladly be somewhat richer than I am. I will say no more, but beg you to be easy till Fortune take her course, and to believe that MD's felicity is the great end I aim at in all my pursuits. And so let us talk no more on this subject, which makes me melancholy, and that I would fain divert. Believe me, no man breathing at present has less share of happiness in life than I: I do not say I am unhappy at all, but that everything here is tasteless to me for want of being as I would be. And so, a short sigh, and no more of this. Well, come and let's see what's next, young women. Pox take Mrs. Edgworth and Sterne! I will take some methods about that box. What orders would you have me give about the picture? Can't you do with it as if it were your own? No, I hope Manley will keep his place; for I hear nothing of Sir Thomas Frankland's losing his. Send nothing under cover to Mr. Addison, but "To Erasmus Lewis, Esq.; at my Lord Dartmouth's office at Whitehall." Direct your outside so.—Poor dear Stella, don't write in the dark, nor in the light neither, but dictate to Dingley; she is a naughty, healthy girl, and may drudge for both. Are you good company together? and don't you quarrel too often? Pray love one another, and kiss one another just now, as Dingley is reading this; for you quarrelled this morning just after Mrs. Marget had poured water on Stella's head: I heard the little bird say so. Well, I have answered everything in your letter that required it, and yet the second side is not full. I'll come home at night, and say more; and to-morrow this goes for certain. Go, get you gone to your own chambers, and let Presto rise like a modest gentleman, and walk to town. I fancy I begin to sweat less in the forehead by constant walking than I used to do; but then I shall be so sunburnt, the ladies will not like me. Come, let me rise, sirrahs. Morrow.—At night. I dined with Ford to-day at his lodgings, and I found wine out of my own cellar, some of my own chest of the great Duke's wine: it begins to turn. They say wine with you in Ireland is half a crown a bottle. 'Tis as Stella says; nothing that once grows dear in Ireland ever grows cheap again, except corn, with a pox, to ruin the parson. I had a letter to-day from the Archbishop of Dublin, giving me further thanks about vindicating him to Mr. Harley and Mr. St. John, and telling me a long story about your Mayor's election, wherein I find he has had a finger, and given way to further talk about him; but we know nothing of it here yet. This walking to and fro, and dressing myself, takes up so much of my time that I cannot go among company so much as formerly; yet what must a body do? I thank God I yet continue much better since I left the town; I know not how long it may last. I am sure it has done me some good for the present. I do not totter as I did, but walk firm as a cock, only once or twice for a minute, I do not know how; but it went off, and I never followed it. Does Dingley read my hand as well as ever? do you, sirrah? Poor Stella must not read Presto's ugly small hand.

Preserve your eyes,
If you be wise.

Your friend Walls's tea will go in a day or two towards Chester by one Parson Richardson. My humble service to her, and to good Mrs. Stoyte, and Catherine; and pray walk while you continue in Dublin. I expect your next but one will be from Wexford. God bless dearest MD.

24. Morning. Mr. Secretary has sent his groom hither, to invite me to dinner to-day, etc. God Almighty for ever bless and preserve you both, and give you health, etc. Amen. Farewell, etc.

Do not I often say the same thing two or three times in the same letter, sirrah?

Great wits, they say, have but short memories; that's good vile conversation.

LETTER XXIV

Morning. Once in my life the number of my letters and of the day of the month is the same; that's lucky, boys; that's a sign that things will meet, and that we shall make a figure together. What, will you still have the impudence to say London, England, because I say Dublin, Ireland? Is there no difference between London and Dublin, saucyboxes? I have sealed up my letter, and am going to town. Morrow, sirrahs.—At night. I dined with the Secretary to-day; we sat down between five and six. Mr. Harley's patent passed this morning: he is now Earl of Oxford, Earl Mortimer, and Lord Harley of Wigmore Castle. My letter was sealed, or I would have told you this yesterday; but the public news may tell it you. The Queen, for all her favour, has kept a rod for him in her closet this week; I suppose he will take it from her, though, in a day or two. At eight o'clock this evening it rained prodigiously, as it did from five; however, I set out, and in half-way the rain lessened, and I got home, but tolerably wet; and this is the first wet walk I have had in a month's time that I am here but, however, I got to bed, after a short visit to Atterbury.

25. It rained this morning, and I went to town by water; and Ford and I dined with Mr. Lewis by appointment. I ordered Patrick to bring my gown and periwig to Mr. Lewis, because I designed to go to see Lord Oxford, and so I told the dog; but he never came, though I stayed an hour longer than I appointed; so I went in my old gown, and sat with him two hours, but could not talk over some business I had with him; so he has desired me to dine with him on Sunday, and I must disappoint the Secretary. My lord set me down at a coffee-house, where I waited for the Dean of Carlisle's chariot to bring me to Chelsea; for it has rained prodigiously all this afternoon. The Dean did not come himself, but sent me his chariot, which has cost me two shillings to the coachman; and so I am got home, and Lord knows what is become of Patrick. I think I must send him over to you; for he is an intolerable rascal. If I had come without a gown, he would have served me so, though my life and preferment should have lain upon it: and I am making a livery for him will cost me four pounds; but I will order the tailor to-morrow to stop till further orders. My Lord Oxford can't yet

abide to be called "my lord"; and when I called him "my lord," he called me "Dr. Thomas Swift," which he always does when he has a mind to tease me. By a second hand, he proposed my being his chaplain, which I by a second hand excused; but we had no talk of it to-day: but I will be no man's chaplain alive. But I must go and be busy.

26. I never saw Patrick till this morning, and that only once, for I dressed myself without him; and when I went to town he was out of the way. I immediately sent for the tailor, and ordered him to stop his hand in Patrick's clothes till further orders. Oh, if it were in Ireland, I should have turned him off ten times ago; and it is no regard to him, but myself, that has made me keep him so long. Now I am afraid to give the rogue his clothes. What shall I do? I wish MD were here to entreat for him, just here at the bed's side. Lady Ashburnham has been engaging me this long time to dine with her, and I set to-day apart for it; and whatever was the mistake, she sent me word she was at dinner and undressed, but would be glad to see me in the afternoon: so I dined with Mrs. Vanhomrigh, and would not go to see her at all, in a huff. My fine Florence is turning sour with a vengeance, and I have not drunk half of it. As I was coming home to-night, Sir Thomas Mansel and Tom Harley met me in the Park, and made me walk with them till nine, like unreasonable whelps; so I got not here till ten: but it was a fine evening, and the foot-path clean enough already after this hard rain.

27. Going this morning to town, I saw two old lame fellows, walking to a brandy-shop, and when they got to the door, stood a long time complimenting who should go in first. Though this be no jest to tell, it was an admirable one to see. I dined to-day with my Lord Oxford and the ladies, the new Countess, and Lady Betty, who has been these three days a lady born. My lord left us at seven, and I had no time to speak to him about some affairs; but he promises in a day or two we shall dine alone; which is mighty likely, considering we expect every moment that the Queen will give him the staff, and then he will be so crowded he will be good for nothing: for aught I know he may have it to-night at Council.

28. I had a petition sent me t'other day from one Stephen Gernon, setting forth that he formerly lived with Harry Tenison, who gave him

an employment of gauger, and that he was turned out after Harry's death, and came for England, and is now starving, or, as he expresses it, *that the staff of life has been of late a stranger to his appetite*. To-day the poor fellow called, and I knew him very well, a young slender fellow with freckles in his face: you must remember him; he waited at table as a better sort of servant. I gave him a crown, and promised to do what I could to help him to a service, which I did for Harry Tenison's memory. It was bloody hot walking to-day, and I was so lazy I dined where my new gown was, at Mrs. Vanhomrigh's, and came back like a fool, and the Dean of Carlisle has sat with me till eleven. Lord Oxford has not the staff yet.

29. I was this morning in town by ten, though it was shaving-day, and went to the Secretary about some affairs, then visited the Duke and Duchess of Ormond; but the latter was dressing to go out, and I could not see her. My Lord Oxford had the staff given him this morning; so now I must call him Lord Oxford no more, but Lord Treasurer: I hope he will stick there: this is twice he has changed his name this week; and I heard to-day in the City (where I dined) that he will very soon have the Garter.—Pr'ythee, do not you observe how strangely I have changed my company and manner of living? I never go to a coffee-house; you hear no more of Addison, Steele, Henley, Lady Lucy, Mrs. Finch, Lord Somers, Lord Halifax, etc. I think I have altered for the better. Did I tell you the Archbishop of Dublin has writ me a long letter of a squabble in your town about choosing a Mayor, and that he apprehended some censure for the share he had in it? I have not heard anything of it here; but I shall not be always able to defend him. We hear your Bishop Hickman is dead; but nobody here will do anything for me in Ireland; so they may die as fast or slow as they please.—Well, you are constant to your deans, and your Stoyte, and your Walls. Walls will have her tea soon; Parson Richardson is either going or gone to Ireland, and has it with him. I hear Mr. Lewis has two letters for me: I could not call for them to-day, but will to-morrow; and perhaps one of them may be from our little MD, who knows, man? who can tell? Many a more unlikely thing has happened.—Pshaw, I write so plaguy little, I can hardly see it myself. *Write bigger, sirrah* Presto. No, but I won't. Oh, you are a saucy rogue, Mr. Presto, you are so impudent. Come, dear rogues, let Presto go to sleep; I have been with the Dean, and 'tis near twelve.

30. I am so hot and lazy after my morning's walk, that I loitered at Mrs. Vanhomrigh's, where my best gown and periwig are, and out of mere listlessness dine there very often; so I did to-day; but I got little MD's letter, N. 15 (you see, sirrahs, I remember to tell the number), from Mr. Lewis, and I read it in a closet they lend me at Mrs. Van's; and I find Stella is a saucy rogue and a great writer, and can write finely still when her hand is in, and her pen good. When I came here to-night, I had a mighty mind to go swim after I was cool, for my lodging is just by the river; and I went down with only my nightgown and slippers on at eleven, but came up again; however, one of these nights I will venture.

31. I was so hot this morning with my walk, that I resolve to do so no more during this violent burning weather. It is comical that now we happen to have such heat to ripen the fruit there has been the greatest blast that was ever known, and almost all the fruit is despaired of. I dined with Lord Shelburne: Lady Kerry and Mrs. Pratt are going to Ireland. I went this evening to Lord Treasurer, and sat about two hours with him in mixed company; he left us, and went to Court, and carried two staves with him, so I suppose we shall have a new Lord Steward or Comptroller to-morrow; I smoked that State secret out by that accident. I will not answer your letter yet, sirrahs; no I won't, madam.

June 1. I wish you a merry month of June. I dined again with the Vans and Sir Andrew Fountaine. I always give them a flask of my Florence, which now begins to spoil, but it is near an end. I went this afternoon to Mrs. Vedeau's, and brought away Madam Dingley's parchment and letter of attorney. Mrs. Vedeau tells me she has sent the bill a fortnight ago. I will give the parchment to Ben Tooke, and you shall send him a letter of attorney at your leisure, enclosed to Mr. Presto. Yes, I now think your mackerel is full as good as ours, which I did not think formerly. I was bit about two staves, for there is no new officer made to-day. This letter will find you still in Dublin, I suppose, or at Donnybrook, or losing your money at Walls' (how does she do?).

2. I missed this day by a blunder and dining in the City.

3. No boats on Sunday, never: so I was forced to walk, and so hot by the time I got to Ford's lodging that I was quite spent; I think the weather is mad. I could not go to church. I dined with the Secretary as usual,

and old Colonel Graham that lived at Bagshot Heath, and they said it was Colonel Graham's house. Pshaw, I remember it very well, when I used to go for a walk to London from Moor Park. What, I warrant you do not remember the Golden Farmer neither, figgarkick soley?

4. When must we answer this letter, this N. 15 of our little MD? Heat and laziness, and Sir Andrew Fountaine, made me dine to-day again at Mrs. Van's; and, in short, this weather is unsupportable: how is it with you? Lady Betty Butler and Lady Ashburnham sat with me two or three hours this evening in my closet at Mrs. Van's. They are very good girls; and if Lady Betty went to Ireland, you should let her be acquainted with you. How does Dingley do this hot weather? Stella, I think, never complains of it; she loves hot weather. There has not been a drop of rain since Friday se'ennight. Yes, you do love hot weather, naughty Stella, you do so; and Presto can't abide it. Be a good girl then, and I will love you; and love one another, and don't be quarrelling girls.

5. I dined in the City to-day, and went from hence early to town, and visited the Duke of Ormond and Mr. Secretary. They say my Lord Treasurer has a dead warrant in his pocket; they mean a list of those who are to be turned out of employment; and we every day now expect those changes. I passed by the Treasury to-day, and saw vast crowds waiting to give Lord Treasurer petitions as he passes by. He is now at the top of power and favour: he keeps no levees yet. I am cruel thirsty this hot weather.—I am just this minute going to swim. I take Patrick down with me, to hold my nightgown, shirt, and slippers, and borrow a napkin of my landlady for a cap. So farewell till I come up; but there is no danger, don't be frighted.—I have been swimming this half-hour and more; and when I was coming out I dived, to make my head and all through wet, like a cold bath; but, as I dived, the napkin fell off and is lost, and I have that to pay for. O, faith, the great stones were so sharp, I could hardly set my feet on them as I came out. It was pure and warm. I got to bed, and will now go sleep.

6. Morning. This letter shall go to-morrow; so I will answer yours when I come home to-night. I feel no hurt from last night's swimming. I lie with nothing but the sheet over me, and my feet quite bare. I must rise and go to town before the tide is against me. Morrow, sirrahs; dear sirrahs, morrow.—At night. I never felt so hot a day as this since I was

born. I dined with Lady Betty Germaine, and there was the young Earl of Berkeley and his fine lady. I never saw her before, nor think her near so handsome as she passes for.—After dinner, Mr. Bertue would not let me put ice in my wine, but said my Lord Dorchester got the bloody flux with it, and that it was the worst thing in the world. Thus are we plagued, thus are we plagued; yet I have done it five or six times this summer, and was but the drier and the hotter for it. Nothing makes me so excessively peevish as hot weather. Lady Berkeley after dinner clapped my hat on another lady's head, and she in roguery put it upon the rails. I minded them not; but in two minutes they called me to the window, and Lady Carteret showed me my hat out of her window five doors off, where I was forced to walk to it, and pay her and old Lady Weymouth a visit, with some more beldames. Then I went and drank coffee, and made one or two puns, with Lord Pembroke, and designed to go to Lord Treasurer; but it was too late, and beside I was half broiled, and broiled without butter; for I never sweat after dinner, if I drink any wine. Then I sat an hour with Lady Betty Butler at tea, and everything made me hotter and drier. Then I walked home, and was here by ten, so miserably hot, that I was in as perfect a passion as ever I was in my life at the greatest affront or provocation. Then I sat an hour, till I was quite dry and cool enough to go swim; which I did, but with so much vexation that I think I have given it over: for I was every moment disturbed by boats, rot them; and that puppy Patrick, standing ashore, would let them come within a yard or two, and then call sneakingly to them. The only comfort I proposed here in hot weather is gone; for there is no jesting with those boats after it is dark: I had none last night. I dived to dip my head, and held my cap on with both my hands, for fear of losing it. Pox take the boats! Amen. 'Tis near twelve, and so I'll answer your letter (it strikes twelve now) to-morrow morning.

7. Morning. Well, now let us answer MD's letter, N. 15, 15, 15, 15. Now have I told you the number? 15, 15; there, impudence, to call names in the beginning of your letter, before you say, How do you do, Mr. Presto? There is your breeding! Where is your manners, sirrah, to a gentleman? Get you gone, you couple of jades.—No, I never sit up late now; but this abominable hot weather will force me to eat or drink something that will do me hurt. I do venture to eat a few strawberries.— Why then, do you know in Ireland that Mr. St. John talked so in Parliament? Your Whigs are plaguily bit; for he is entirely for their

being all out.—And are you as vicious in snuff as ever? I believe, as you say, it does neither hurt nor good; but I have left it off, and when anybody offers me their box, I take about a tenth part of what I used to do, and then just smell to it, and privately fling the rest away. I keep to my tobacco still, as you say; but even much less of that than formerly, only mornings and evenings, and very seldom in the day.—As for Joe, I have recommended his case heartily to my Lord Lieutenant; and, by his direction, given a memorial of it to Mr. Southwell, to whom I have recommended it likewise. I can do no more, if he were my brother. His business will be to apply himself to Southwell. And you must desire Raymond, if Price of Galway comes to town, to desire him to wait on Mr. Southwell, as recommended by me for one of the Duke's chaplains, which was all I could do for him; and he must be presented to the Duke, and make his court, and ply about, and find out some vacancy, and solicit early for it. The bustle about your Mayor I had before, as I told you, from the Archbishop of Dublin. Was Raymond not come till May 18? So he says fine things of me? Certainly he lies. I am sure I used him indifferently enough; and we never once dined together, or walked, or were in any third place; only he came sometimes to my lodgings, and even there was oftener denied than admitted.—What an odd bill is that you sent of Raymond's! A bill upon one Murry in Chester, which depends entirely not only upon Raymond's honesty, but his discretion; and in money matters he is the last man I would depend on. Why should Sir Alexander Cairnes in London pay me a bill, drawn by God knows who, upon Murry in Chester? I was at Cairnes's, and they can do no such thing. I went among some friends, who are merchants, and I find the bill must be sent to Murry, accepted by him, and then returned back, and then Cairnes may accept or refuse it as he pleases. Accordingly I gave Sir Thomas Frankland the bill, who has sent it to Chester, and ordered the postmaster there to get it accepted, and then send it back, and in a day or two I shall have an answer; and therefore this letter must stay a day or two longer than I intended, and see what answer I get. Raymond should have written to Murry at the same time, to desire Sir Alexander Cairnes to have answered such a bill, if it come. But Cairnes's clerks (himself was not at home) said they had received no notice of it, and could do nothing; and advised me to send to Murry.—I have been six weeks to-day at Chelsea, and you know it but just now. And so Dean—thinks I write the *Medley*. Pox of his judgment! It is equal to his honesty. Then you han't seen the *Miscellany* yet? Why, 'tis a four-shilling book: has nobody carried it over?—No, I believe Manley will not lose his place; for his friend in England is so far from being out that he has taken a new patent since the Post Office Act; and his brother Jack Manley here takes his part firmly; and I have often spoken to Southwell in his behalf, and he seems very well inclined to him. But the Irish folks here in general are horribly violent against him. Besides, he must consider he could not send Stella wine if he were put out. And so he is very kind, and sends you a dozen bottles of wine *at a time*, and you win eight shillings *at a time*; and how much do you lose? No, no, never one syllable about that, I warrant you.—Why, this same Stella is so unmerciful a writer, she has hardly left any room for Dingley. If you have such summer there as here, sure the Wexford waters are good by this time. I forgot what weather we had May 6th; go look in my journal. We had terrible rain the 24th and 25th, and never a drop since. Yes, yes, I remember Berested's bridge; the coach sosses up and down as one goes that way, just as at Hockley-in-the-Hole. I never impute any illness or health I have to good or ill weather, but to want of exercise, or ill air, or something I have eaten, or hard study, or sitting up; and so I fence against those as well as I can: but who a deuce can help the weather? Will Seymour, the General, was excessively hot with the sun shining full upon him; so he turns to the sun, and says, "Harkee, friend, you had better go and ripen cucumbers than plague me at this rate," etc. Another time, fretting at the heat, a gentleman by said it was such weather as pleased God: Seymour said, "Perhaps it may; but I am sure it pleases nobody else." Why, Madam Dingley, the First-Fruits are done. Southwell told me they went to inquire about them, and Lord Treasurer said they were done, and had been done long ago. And I'll tell you a secret you must not mention, that the Duke of Ormond is ordered to take notice of them in his speech in your Parliament: and I desire you will take care to say on occasion that my Lord Treasurer Harley did it many months ago, before the Duke was Lord Lieutenant. And yet I cannot possibly come over yet: so get you gone to Wexford, and make Stella well. Yes, yes, I take care not to walk late; I never did but once, and there are five hundred people on the way as I walk. Tisdall is a puppy, and I will excuse him the half-hour he would talk with me. As for the *Examiner*, I have heard a whisper that after that of this day, which tells us what this Parliament has done, you will hardly find them so good. I prophesy they will be trash for the future; and methinks in this day's *Examiner* the author talks doubtfully, as if he would write no more. Observe whether the change be discovered in Dublin, only for your own curiosity, that's all. Make a mouth there. Mrs. Vedeau's business I have answered, and I hope the bill is not lost. Morrow. 'Tis stewing hot, but I must rise and go to town between fire and water. Morrow, sirrahs both, morrow.—At night. I dined to-day with Colonel Crowe, Governor of Jamaica, and your friend Sterne. I presented Sterne to my Lord Treasurer's brother, and gave him his case, and engaged him in his favour. At dinner there fell the swingingest long shower, and the most grateful to me, that ever I saw: it thundered fifty times at least, and the air is so cool that a body is able to live; and I walked home to-night with comfort, and without dirt. I went this evening to Lord Treasurer, and sat with him two hours, and we were in very good humour, and he abused me, and called me Dr. Thomas Swift fifty times: I have told you he does that when he has mind to make me mad. Sir Thomas Frankland gave me to-day a letter from Murry, accepting my bill; so all is well: only, by a letter from Parvisol, I find there are some perplexities.—Joe has likewise written to me, to thank me for what I have done for him; and desires I would write to the Bishop of Clogher, that Tom Ashe may not hinder his father from being portreve. I have written and sent to Joe several times, that I will not trouble myself at all about Trim. I wish them their liberty, but they do not deserve it: so tell Joe, and send to him. I am mighty happy with this rain: I was at the end of my patience, but now I live again. This cannot go till Saturday; and perhaps I may go out of town with Lord Shelburne and Lady Kerry to-morrow for two or three days. Lady Kerry has written to desire it; but to-morrow I shall know farther.—O this dear rain, I cannot forbear praising it: I never felt myself to be revived so in my life. It lasted from three till five, hard as a horn, and mixed with hail.

8. Morning. I am going to town, and will just finish this there, if I go into the country with Lady Kerry and Lord Shelburne: so morrow, till an hour or two hence.—In town. I met Cairnes, who, I suppose, will pay me the money; though he says I must send him the bill first, and I will get it done in absence. Farewell, etc. etc.

Letter XXV

I have been all this time at Wycombe, between Oxford and London, with Lord Shelburne, who has the squire's house at the town's end, and an estate there in a delicious country. Lady Kerry and Mrs. Pratt were with us, and we passed our time well enough; and there I wholly disengaged myself from all public thoughts, and everything but MD, who had the impudence to send me a letter there; but I'll be revenged: I will answer it. This day, the 20th, I came from Wycombe with Lady Kerry after dinner, lighted at Hyde Park Corner, and walked: it was twenty-seven miles, and we came it in about five hours.

21. I went at noon to see Mr. Secretary at his office, and there was Lord Treasurer: so I killed two birds, etc., and we were glad to see one another, and so forth. And the Secretary and I dined at Sir William Wyndham's, who married Lady Catharine Seymour, your acquaintance, I suppose. There were ten of us at dinner. It seems, in my absence, they had erected a Club, and made me one; and we made some laws to-day, which I am to digest and add to, against next meeting. Our meetings are to be every Thursday. We are yet but twelve: Lord Keeper and Lord Treasurer were proposed; but I was against them, and so was Mr. Secretary, though their sons are of it, and so they are excluded; but we design to admit the Duke of Shrewsbury. The end of our Club is, to advance conversation and friendship, and to reward deserving persons with our interest and recommendation. We take in none but men of wit or men of interest; and if we go on as we begin, no other Club in this town will be worth talking of. The Solicitor-General, Sir Robert Raymond, is one of our Club; and I ordered him immediately to write to your Lord Chancellor in favour of Dr. Raymond: so tell Raymond, if you see him; but I believe this will find you at Wexford. This letter will come three weeks after the last, so there is a week lost; but that is owing to my being out of town; yet I think it is right, because it goes enclosed to Mr. Reading: and why should he know how often Presto writes to MD, pray?—I sat this evening with Lady Betty Butler and Lady Ashburnham, and then came home by eleven, and had a good cool walk; for we have had no extreme hot weather this fortnight, but

a great deal of rain at times, and a body can live and breathe. I hope it will hold so. We had peaches to-day.

22. I went late to-day to town, and dined with my friend Lewis. I saw Will Congreve attending at the Treasury, by order, with his brethren, the Commissioners of the Wine Licences. I had often mentioned him with kindness to Lord Treasurer; and Congreve told me that, after they had answered to what they were sent for, my lord called him privately, and spoke to him with great kindness, promising his protection, etc. The poor man said he had been used so ill of late years that he was quite astonished at my lord's goodness, etc., and desired me to tell my lord so; which I did this evening, and recommended him heartily. My lord assured me he esteemed him very much, and would be always kind to him; that what he said was to make Congreve easy, because he knew people talked as if his lordship designed to turn everybody out, and particularly Congreve: which indeed was true, for the poor man told me he apprehended it. As I left my Lord Treasurer, I called on Congreve (knowing where he dined), and told him what had passed between my lord and me; so I have made a worthy man easy, and that is a good day's work. I am proposing to my lord to erect a society or academy for correcting and settling our language, that we may not perpetually be changing as we do. He enters mightily into it, so does the Dean of Carlisle; and I design to write a letter to Lord Treasurer with the proposals of it, and publish it; and so I told my lord, and he approves it. Yesterday's was a sad *Examiner*, and last week was very indifferent, though some little scraps of the old spirit, as if he had given some hints; but yesterday's is all trash. It is plain the hand is changed.

23. I have not been in London to-day: for Dr. Gastrell and I dined, by invitation, with the Dean of Carlisle, my neighbour; so I know not what they are doing in the world, a mere country gentleman. And are not you ashamed both to go into the country just when I did, and stay ten days, just as I did, saucy monkeys? But I never rode; I had no horses, and our coach was out of order, and we went and came in a hired one. Do you keep your lodgings when you go to Wexford? I suppose you do; for you will hardly stay above two months. I have been walking about our town to-night, and it is a very scurvy place for walking. I am thinking to leave it, and return to town, now the Irish folks are gone. Ford goes in three days. How does Dingley divert herself while Stella is

riding? work, or read, or walk? Does Dingley ever read to you? Had you ever a book with you in the country? Is all that left off? Confess. Well, I'll go sleep; 'tis past eleven, and I go early to sleep: I write nothing at night but to MD.

24. Stratford and I, and Pastoral Philips (just come from Denmark) dined at Ford's to-day, who paid his way, and goes for Ireland on Tuesday. The Earl of Peterborow is returned from Vienna without one servant: he left them scattered in several towns of Germany. I had a letter from him, four days ago, from Hanover, where he desires I would immediately send him an answer to his house at Parson's Green, about five miles off. I wondered what he meant, till I heard he was come. He sent expresses, and got here before them. He is above fifty, and as active as one of five-and-twenty. I have not seen him yet, nor know when I shall, or where to find him.

25. Poor Duke of Shrewsbury has been very ill of a fever: we were all in a fright about him: I thank God, he is better. I dined to-day at Lord Ashburnham's, with his lady, for he was not at home: she is a very good girl, and always a great favourite of mine. Sterne tells me he has desired a friend to receive your box in Chester, and carry it over. I fear he will miscarry in his business, which was sent to the Treasury before he was recommended; for I was positive only to second his recommendations, and all his other friends failed him. However, on your account I will do what I can for him to-morrow with the secretary of the Treasury.

26. We had much company to-day at dinner at Lord Treasurer's. Prior never fails: he is a much better courtier than I; and we expect every day that he will be a Commissioner of the Customs, and that in a short time a great many more will be turned out. They blame Lord Treasurer for his slowness in turning people out; but I suppose he has his reasons. They still keep my neighbour Atterbury in suspense about the deanery of Christ Church, which has been above six months vacant, and he is heartily angry. I reckon you are now preparing for your Wexford expedition; and poor Dingley is full of carking and caring, scolding. How long will you stay? Shall I be in Dublin before you return? Don't fall and hurt yourselves, nor overturn the coach. Love one another, and be good girls; and drink Presto's health in water, Madam Stella; and in good ale, Madam Dingley.

27. The Secretary appointed me to dine with him to-day, and we were to do a world of business: he came at four, and brought Prior with him, and had forgot the appointment, and no business was done. I left him at eight, and went to change my gown at Mrs. Vanhomrigh's; and there was Sir Andrew Fountaine at ombre with Lady Ashburnham and Lady Frederic Schomberg, and Lady Mary Schomberg, and Lady Betty Butler, and others, talking; and it put me in mind of the Dean and Stoyte, and Walls, and Stella at play, and Dingley and I looking on. I stayed with them till ten, like a fool. Lady Ashburnham is something like Stella; so I helped her, and wished her good cards. It is late, etc.

28. Well, but I must answer this letter of our MD's. Saturday approaches, and I han't written down this side. O, faith, Presto has been a sort of a lazy fellow: but Presto will remove to town this day se'ennight; the Secretary has commanded me to do so; and I believe he and I shall go for some days to Windsor, where he will have leisure to mind some business we have together. To-day, our Society (it must not be called a Club) dined at Mr. Secretary's: we were but eight; the rest sent excuses, or were out of town. We sat till eight, and made some laws and settlements; and then I went to take leave of Lady Ashburnham, who goes out of town to-morrow, as a great many of my acquaintance are already, and left the town very thin. I shall make but short journeys this summer, and not be long out of London. The days are grown sensibly short already, all our fruit blasted. Your Duke of Ormond is still at Chester; and perhaps this letter will be with you as soon as he. Sterne's business is quite blown up: they stand to it to send him back to the Commissioners of the Revenue in Ireland for a reference, and all my credit could not alter it, though I almost fell out with the secretary of the Treasury, who is my Lord Treasurer's cousin-germain, and my very good friend. It seems every step he has hitherto taken hath been wrong; at least they say so, and that is the same thing. I am heartily sorry for it; and I really think they are in the wrong, and use him hardly; but I can do no more.

29. Steele has had the assurance to write to me that I would engage my Lord Treasurer to keep a friend of his in an employment: I believe I told you how he and Addison served me for my good offices in Steele's behalf; and I promised Lord Treasurer never to speak for either of them again. Sir Andrew Fountaine and I dined to-day at Mrs. Vanhomrigh's.

Dilly Ashe has been in town this fortnight: I saw him twice; he was four days at Lord Pembroke's in the country, punning with him; his face is very well. I was this evening two or three hours at Lord Treasurer's, who called me Dr. Thomas Swift twenty times; that's his way of teasing. I left him at nine, and got home here by ten, like a gentleman; and tomorrow morning I'll answer your little letter, sirrahs.

30. Morning. I am terribly sleepy always in a morning; I believe it is my walk over-night that disposes me to sleep: faith, 'tis now striking eight, and I am but just awake. Patrick comes early, and wakes me five or six times; but I have excuses, though I am three parts asleep. I tell him I sat up late, or slept ill in the night, and often it is a lie. I have now got little MD's letter before me, N. 16, no more, nor no less, no mistake. Dingley says, "This letter won't be above six lines"; and I was afraid it was true, though I saw it filled on both sides. The Bishop of Clogher writ me word you were in the country, and that he heard you were well: I am glad at heart MD rides, and rides, and rides. Our hot weather ended in May, and all this month has been moderate: it was then so hot I was not able to endure it; I was miserable every moment, and found myself disposed to be peevish and quarrelsome: I believe a very hot country would make me stark mad.—Yes, my head continues pretty tolerable, and I impute it all to walking. Does Stella eat fruit? I eat a little; but I always repent, and resolve against it. No, in very hot weather I always go to town by water; but I constantly walk back, for then the sun is down. And so Mrs. Proby goes with you to Wexford: she's admirable company; you'll grow plaguy wise with those you frequent. Mrs. Taylor and Mrs. Proby! take care of infection. I believe my two hundred pounds will be paid, but that Sir Alexander Cairnes is a scrupulous puppy: I left the bill with Mr. Stratford, who is to have the money. Now, Madam Stella, what say you? you ride every day; I know that already, sirrah; and, if you rid every day for a twelvemonth, you would be still better and better. No, I hope Parvisol will not have the impudence to make you stay an hour for the money; if he does, I'll *un-parvisol* him; pray let me know. O Lord, how hasty we are! Stella can't stay writing and writing; she must write and go a cock-horse, pray now. Well, but the horses are not come to the door; the fellow can't find the bridle; your stirrup is broken; where did you put the whips, Dingley? Marget, where have you laid Mrs. Johnson's ribbon to tie about her? reach me my mask: sup up this before you go. So, so, a gallop, a gallop: sit fast, sirrah, and don't ride hard upon the

stones.—Well, now Stella is gone, tell me, Dingley, is she a good girl? and what news is that you are to tell me?—No, I believe the box is not lost: Sterne says it is not.—No, faith, you must go to Wexford without seeing your Duke of Ormond, unless you stay on purpose; perhaps you may be so wise.—I tell you this is your sixteenth letter; will you never be satisfied? No, no, I will walk late no more; I ought less to venture it than other people, and so I was told: but I will return to lodge in town next Thursday. When you come from Wexford, I would have you send a letter of attorney to Mr. Benjamin Tooke, bookseller, in London, directed to me; and he shall manage your affair. I have your parchment safely locked up in London.—O, Madam Stella, welcome home; was it pleasant riding? did your horse stumble? how often did the man light to settle your stirrup? ride nine miles! faith, you have galloped indeed. Well, but where is the fine thing you promised me? I have been a good boy, ask Dingley else. I believe you did not meet the fine-thing-man: faith, you are a cheat. So you will see Raymond and his wife in town. Faith, that riding to Laracor gives me short sighs, as well as you. All the days I have passed here have been dirt to those. I have been gaining enemies by the scores, and friends by the couples; which is against the rules of wisdom, because they say one enemy can do more hurt than ten friends can do good. But I have had my revenge at least, if I get nothing else. And so let Fate govern.—Now I think your letter is answered; and mine will be shorter than ordinary, because it must go to-day. We have had a great deal of scattering rain for some days past, yet it hardly keeps down the dust.—We have plays acted in our town; and Patrick was at one of them, oh oh. He was damnably mauled one day when he was drunk; he was at cuffs with a brother-footman, who dragged him along the floor upon his face, which looked for a week after as if he had the leprosy; and I was glad enough to see it. I have been ten times sending him over to you; yet now he has new clothes, and a laced hat, which the hatter brought by his orders, and he offered to pay for the lace out of his wages.—I am to dine to-day with Dilly at Sir Andrew Fountaine's, who has bought a new house, and will be weary of it in half a year. I must rise and shave, and walk to town, unless I go with the Dean in his chariot at twelve, which is too late: and I have not seen that Lord Peterborow yet. The Duke of Shrewsbury is almost well again, and will be abroad in a day or two: what care you? There it is now: you do not care for my friends. Farewell, my dearest lives and delights; I love you better than ever, if possible, as hope saved, I do, and ever will. God Almighty bless you ever, and make us happy together! I pray for this twice every day; and I hope God will hear my poor hearty prayers.—Remember, if I am used ill and ungratefully, as I have formerly been, 'tis what I am prepared for, and shall not wonder at it. Yet I am now envied, and thought in high favour, and have every day numbers of considerable men teasing me to solicit for them. And the Ministry all use me perfectly well; and all that know them say they love me. Yet I can count upon nothing, nor will, but upon MD's love and kindness.—They think me useful; they pretended they were afraid of none but me, and that they resolved to have me; they have often confessed this: yet all makes little impression on me.—Pox of these speculations! they give me the spleen; and that is a disease I was not born to. Let me alone, sirrahs, and be satisfied: I am, as long as MD and Presto are well.

Little wealth,
And much health,
And a life by stealth:

that is all we want; and so farewell, dearest MD; Stella, Dingley, Presto, all together, now and for ever all together. Farewell again and again.

LETTER XXVI

See what large paper I am forced to take, to write to MD; Patrick
has brought me none clipped; but, faith, the next shall be smaller. I
dined to-day, as I told you, with Dilly at Sir Andrew Fountaine's: there
were we wretchedly punning, and writing together to Lord Pembroke.
Dilly is just such a puppy as ever; and it is so uncouth, after so long an
intermission. My twenty-fifth is gone this evening to the post. I think
I will direct my next (which is this) to Mr. Curry's, and let them send it
to Wexford; and then the next enclosed to Reading. Instruct me how I
shall do. I long to hear from you from Wexford, and what sort of place it
is. The town grows very empty and dull. This evening I have had a letter
from Mr. Philips, the pastoral poet, to get him a certain employment from
Lord Treasurer. I have now had almost all the Whig poets my solicitors;
and I have been useful to Congreve, Steele, and Harrison: but I will do
nothing for Philips; I find he is more a puppy than ever, so don't solicit
for him. Besides, I will not trouble Lord Treasurer, unless upon some
very extraordinary occasion.

July 1. Dilly lies conveniently for me when I come to town from Chelsea
of a Sunday, and go to the Secretary's; so I called at his lodgings this
morning, and sent for my gown, and dressed myself there. He had
a letter from the Bishop, with an account that you were set out for
Wexford the morning he writ, which was June 26, and he had the letter
the 30th; that was very quick: the Bishop says you design to stay there
two months or more. Dilly had also a letter from Tom Ashe, full of Irish
news; that your Lady Lyndon is dead, and I know not what besides of
Dr. Coghill losing his drab, etc. The Secretary was gone to Windsor,
and I dined with Mrs. Vanhomrigh. Lord Treasurer is at Windsor too;
they will be going and coming all summer, while the Queen is there,
and the town is empty, and I fear I shall be sometimes forced to stoop
beneath my dignity, and send to the ale-house for a dinner. Well, sirrahs,
had you a good journey to Wexford? did you drink ale by the way? were
you never overturned? how many things did you forget? do you lie on
straw in your new town where you are? Cudshoe, the next letter to
Presto will be dated from Wexford. What fine company have you there?
what new acquaintance have you got? You are to write constantly to

Mrs. Walls and Mrs. Stoyte: and the Dean said, "Shall we never hear from you?" "Yes, Mr. Dean, we'll make bold to trouble you with a letter." Then at Wexford; when you meet a lady, "Did your waters pass well this morning, madam?" Will Dingley drink them too? Yes, I warrant; to get her a stomach. I suppose you are all gamesters at Wexford. Do not lose your money, sirrah, far from home. I believe I shall go to Windsor in a few days; at least, the Secretary tells me so. He has a small house there, with just room enough for him and me; and I would be satisfied to pass a few days there sometimes. Sirrahs, let me go to sleep, it is past twelve in our town.

2. Sterne came to me this morning, and tells me he has yet some hopes of compassing his business: he was with Tom Harley, the secretary of the Treasury, and made him doubt a little he was in the wrong; the poor man tells me it will almost undo him if he fails. I called this morning to see Will Congreve, who lives much by himself, is forced to read for amusement, and cannot do it without a magnifying-glass. I have set him very well with the Ministry, and I hope he is in no danger of losing his place. I dined in the City with Dr. Freind, not among my merchants, but with a scrub instrument of mischief of mine, whom I never mentioned to you, nor am like to do. You two little saucy Wexfordians, you are now drinking waters. You drink waters! you go fiddlestick. Pray God send them to do you good; if not, faith, next summer you shall come to the Bath.

3. Lord Peterborow desired to see me this morning at nine; I had not seen him before since he came home. I met Mrs. Manley there, who was soliciting him to get some pension or reward for her service in the cause, by writing her *Atalantis*, and prosecution, etc., upon it. I seconded her, and hope they will do something for the poor woman. My lord kept me two hours upon politics: he comes home very sanguine; he has certainly done great things at Savoy and Vienna, by his negotiations: he is violent against a peace, and finds true what I writ to him, that the Ministry seems for it. He reasons well; yet I am for a peace. I took leave of Lady Kerry, who goes to-morrow for Ireland; she picks up Lord Shelburne and Mrs. Pratt at Lord Shelburne's house. I was this evening with Lord Treasurer: Tom Harley was there, and whispered me that he began to doubt about Sterne's business; I told him he would find he was in the wrong. I sat two or three hours at Lord Treasurer's; he rallied

me sufficiently upon my refusing to take him into our Club, and told a judge who was with us that my name was Thomas Swift. I had a mind to prevent Sir H. Belasyse going to Spain, who is a most covetous cur, and I fell a railing against avarice, and turned it so that he smoked me, and named Belasyse. I went on, and said it was a shame to send him; to which he agreed, but desired I would name some who understood business, and do not love money, for he could not find them. I said there was something in a Treasurer different from other men; that we ought not to make a man a Bishop who does not love divinity, or a General who does not love war; and I wondered why the Queen would make a man Lord Treasurer who does not love money. He was mightily pleased with what I said. He was talking of the First-Fruits of England, and I took occasion to tell him that I would not for a thousand pounds anybody but he had got them for Ireland, who got them for England too. He bid me consider what a thousand pounds was; I said I would have him to know I valued a thousand pounds as little as he valued a million.—Is it not silly to write all this? but it gives you an idea what our conversation is with mixed company. I have taken a lodging in Suffolk Street, and go to it on Thursday; and design to walk the Park and the town, to supply my walking here: yet I will walk here sometimes too, in a visit now and then to the Dean. When I was almost at home, Patrick told me he had two letters for me, and gave them to me in the dark, yet I could see one of them was from saucy MD. I went to visit the Dean for half an hour; and then came home, and first read the other letter, which was from the Bishop of Clogher, who tells me the Archbishop of Dublin mentioned in a full assembly of the clergy the Queen's granting the First-Fruits, said it was done by the Lord Treasurer, and talked much of my merit in it: but reading yours I find nothing of that: perhaps the Bishop lies, out of a desire to please me. I dined with Mrs. Vanhomrigh. Well, sirrahs, you are gone to Wexford; but I'll follow you.

4. Sterne came to me again this morning, to advise about reasons and memorials he is drawing up; and we went to town by water together; and having nothing to do, I stole into the City to an instrument of mine, and then went to see poor Patty Rolt, who has been in town these two months with a cousin of hers. Her life passes with boarding in some country town as cheap as she can, and, when she runs out, shifting to some cheaper place, or coming to town for a month. If I were rich, I would ease her, which a little thing would do. Some months ago I sent

her a guinea, and it patched up twenty circumstances. She is now going to Berkhamstead in Hertfordshire. It has rained and hailed prodigiously to-day, with some thunder. This is the last night I lie at Chelsea; and I got home early, and sat two hours with the Dean, and ate victuals, having had a very scurvy dinner. I'll answer your letter when I come to live in town. You shall have a fine London answer: but first I will go sleep, and dream of MD.

London, July 5. This day I left Chelsea for good (that's a genteel phrase), and am got into Suffolk Street. I dined to-day at our Society, and we are adjourned for a month, because most of us go into the country: we dined at Lord Keeper's with young Harcourt, and Lord Keeper was forced to sneak off, and dine with Lord Treasurer, who had invited the Secretary and me to dine with him; but we scorned to leave our company, as George Granville did, whom we have threatened to expel: however, in the evening I went to Lord Treasurer, and, among other company, found a couple of judges with him; one of them, Judge Powell, an old fellow with grey hairs, was the merriest old gentleman I ever saw, spoke pleasant things, and laughed and chuckled till he cried again. I stayed till eleven, because I was not now to walk to Chelsea.

6. An ugly rainy day. I was to visit Mrs. Barton, then called at Mrs. Vanhomrigh's, where Sir Andrew Fountaine and the rain kept me to dinner; and there did I loiter all the afternoon, like a fool, out of perfect laziness, and the weather not permitting me to walk: but I'll do so no more. Are your waters at Wexford good in this rain? I long to hear how you are established there, how and whom you visit, what is your lodging, what are your entertainments. You are got far southwards; but I think you must eat no fruit while you drink the waters. I ate some Kentish cherries t'other day, and I repent it already; I have felt my head a little disordered. We had not a hot day all June, or since, which I reckon a mighty happiness. Have you left a direction with Reading for Wexford? I will, as I said, direct this to Curry's, and the next to Reading; or suppose I send this at a venture straight to Wexford? It would vex me to have it miscarry. I had a letter to-night from Parvisol, that White has paid me most of my remaining money; and another from Joe, that they have had their election at Trim, but not a word of who is chosen portreeve. Poor Joe is full of complaints, says he has enemies, and fears he will never get his two hundred pounds; and I fear so too, although I

have done what I could.—I'll answer your letter when I think fit, when saucy Presto thinks fit, sirrahs. I am not at leisure yet; when I have nothing to do, perhaps I may vouchsafe.—O Lord, the two Wexford ladies; I'll go dream of you both.

7. It was the dismallest rainy day I ever saw: I went to the Secretary in the morning, and he was gone to Windsor. Then it began raining, and I struck in to Mrs. Vanhomrigh's, and dined, and stayed till night very dull and insipid. I hate this town in summer; I'll leave it for a while, if I can have time.

8. I have a fellow of your town, one Tisdall, lodges in the same house with me. Patrick told me Squire Tisdall and his lady lodged here. I pretended I never heard of him; but I knew his ugly face, and saw him at church in the next pew to me, and he often looked for a bow, but it would not do. I think he lives in Capel Street, and has an ugly fine wife in a fine coach. Dr. Freind and I dined in the City by invitation, and I drank punch, very good, but it makes me hot. People here are troubled with agues by this continuance of wet, cold weather; but I am glad to find the season so temperate. I was this evening to see Will Congreve, who is a very agreeable companion.

9. I was to-day in the City, and dined with Mr. Stratford, who tells me Sir Alexander Cairnes makes difficulties about paying my bill; so that I cannot give order yet to Parvisol to deliver up the bond to Dr. Raymond. To-morrow I shall have a positive answer: that Cairnes is a shuffling scoundrel; and several merchants have told me so: what can one expect from a Scot and a fanatic? I was at Bateman's the bookseller's, to see a fine old library he has bought; and my fingers itched, as yours would do at a china-shop; but I resisted, and found everything too dear, and I have fooled away too much money that way already. So go and drink your waters, saucy rogue, and make yourself well; and pray walk while you are there: I have a notion there is never a good walk in Ireland. Do you find all places without trees? Pray observe the inhabitants about Wexford; they are old English; see what they have particular in their manners, names, and language: magpies have been always there, and nowhere else in Ireland, till of late years. They say the cocks and dogs go to sleep at noon, and so do the people. Write your travels, and bring home good eyes and health.

10. I dined to-day with Lord Treasurer: we did not sit down till four. I despatched three businesses with him, and forgot a fourth. I think I have got a friend an employment; and besides I made him consent to let me bring Congreve to dine with him. You must understand I have a mind to do a small thing, only turn out all the Queen's physicians; for in my conscience they will soon kill her among them. And I must talk over that matter with some people. My Lord Treasurer told me the Queen and he between them have lost the paper about the First-Fruits, but desires I will let the bishops know it shall be done with the first opportunity.

11. I dined to-day with neighbour Van, and walked pretty well in the Park this evening. Stella, hussy, don't you remember, sirrah, you used to reproach me about meddling in other folk's affairs? I have enough of it now: two people came to me to-night in the Park to engage to speak to Lord Treasurer in their behalf, and I believe they make up fifty who have asked me the same favour. I am hardened, and resolve to trouble him, or any other Minister, less than ever. And I observe those who have ten times more credit than I will not speak a word for anybody. I met yesterday the poor lad I told you of, who lived with Mr. Tenison, who has been ill of an ague ever since I saw him. He looked wretchedly, and was exceeding thankful for half a crown I gave him. He had a crown from me before.

12. I dined to-day with young Manley in the City, who is to get me out a box of books and a hamper of wine from Hamburg. I inquired of Mr. Stratford, who tells me that Cairnes has not yet paid my two hundred pounds, but shams and delays from day to day. Young Manley's wife is a very indifferent person of a young woman, goggle-eyed, and looks like a fool: yet he is a handsome fellow, and married her for love after long courtship, and she refused him until he got his last employment.—I believe I shall not be so good a boy for writing as I was during your stay at Wexford, unless I may send my letters every second time to Curry's; pray let me know. This, I think, shall go there: or why not to Wexford itself? That is right, and so it shall this next Tuesday, although it costs you tenpence. What care I?

13. This toad of a Secretary is come from Windsor, and I cannot find him; and he goes back on Sunday, and I can't see him to-morrow. I dined scurvily to-day with Mr. Lewis and a parson; and then went to

see Lord Treasurer, and met him coming from his house in his coach: he smiled, and I shrugged, and we smoked each other; and so my visit is paid. I now confine myself to see him only twice a week: he has invited me to Windsor, and betwixt two stools, etc. I will go live at Windsor, if possible, that's pozzz. I have always the luck to pass my summer in London. I called this evening to see poor Sir Matthew Dudley, a Commissioner of the Customs; I know he is to be out for certain: he is in hopes of continuing: I would not tell him bad news, but advised him to prepare for the worst. Dilly was with me this morning, to invite me to dine at Kensington on Sunday with Lord Mountjoy, who goes soon for Ireland. Your late Chief-Justice Broderick is here, and they say violent as a tiger. How is party among you at Wexford? Are the majority of ladies for the late or present Ministry? Write me Wexford news, and love Presto, because he is a good boy.

14. Although it was shaving-day, I walked to Chelsea, and was there by nine this morning; and the Dean of Carlisle and I crossed the water to Battersea, and went in his chariot to Greenwich, where we dined at Dr. Gastrell's, and passed the afternoon at Lewisham, at the Dean of Canterbury's; and there I saw Moll Stanhope, who is grown monstrously tall, but not so handsome as formerly. It is the first little rambling journey I have had this summer about London, and they are the agreeablest pastimes one can have, in a friend's coach, and to good company. Bank Stock is fallen three or four per cent. by the whispers about the town of the Queen's being ill, who is however very well.

15. How many books have you carried with you to Wexford? What, not one single book? Oh, but your time will be so taken up; and you can borrow of the parson. I dined to-day with Sir Andrew Fountaine and Dilly at Kensington with Lord Mountjoy; and in the afternoon Stratford came there, and told me my two hundred pounds were paid at last; so that business is over, and I am at ease about it; and I wish all your money was in the Bank too. I will have my other hundred pounds there, that is in Hawkshaw's hands. Have you had the interest of it paid yet? I ordered Parvisol to do it. What makes Presto write so crooked? I will answer your letter to-morrow, and send it on Tuesday. Here's hot weather come again, yesterday and to-day: fine drinking waters now. We had a sad pert dull parson at Kensington to-day. I almost repent my coming to town; I want the walks I had.

16. I dined in the City to-day with a hedge acquaintance, and the day passed without any consequence. I will answer your letter to-morrow.

17. Morning. I have put your letter before me, and am going to answer it. Hold your tongue: stand by. Your weather and ours were not alike; we had not a bit of hot weather in June, yet you complain of it on the 19th day. What, you used to love hot weather then? I could never endure it: I detest and abominate it. I would not live in a hot country, to be king of it. What a splutter you keep about my bonds with Raymond, and all to affront Presto! Presto will be suspicious of everything but MD, in spite of your little nose. Soft and fair, Madam Stella, how you gallop away, in your spleen and your rage, about repenting my journey, and preferment here, and sixpence a dozen, and nasty England, and Laracor all my life. Hey-dazy, will you never have done? I had no offers of any living. Lord Keeper told me some months ago he would give me one when I pleased; but I told him I would not take any from him; and the Secretary told me t'other day he had refused a very good one for me, but it was in a place he did not like; and I know nothing of getting anything here, and, if they would give me leave, I would come over just now. Addison, I hear, has changed his mind about going over; but I have not seen him these four months.—Oh ay, that's true, Dingley; that's like herself: millions of businesses to do before she goes. Yes, my head has been pretty well, but threatening within these two or three days, which I impute to some fruit I ate; but I will eat no more: not a bit of any sort. I suppose you had a journey without dust, and that was happy. I long for a Wexford letter, but must not think of it yet: your last was finished but three weeks ago. It is d—d news you tell me of Mrs. F—; it makes me love England less a great deal. I know nothing of the trunk being left or taken; so 'tis odd enough, if the things in it were mine; and I think I was told that there are some things for me that my mother left particularly to me. I am really sorry for—; that scoundrel—will have his estate after his mother's death. Let me know if Mrs. Walls has got her tea: I hope Richardson stayed in Dublin till it came. Mrs. Walls needed not have that blemish in her eye; for I am not in love with her at all. No, I do not like anything in the *Examiner* after the 45th, except the first part of the 46th; all the rest is trash; and if you like them, especially the 47th, your judgment is spoiled by ill company and want of reading, which I am more sorry for than you think: and I have spent fourteen years in improving you to little purpose.

(Mr. Tooke is come here, and I must stop.)—At night. I dined with Lord Treasurer to-day, and he kept me till nine; so I cannot send this to-night, as I intended, nor write some other letters. Green, his surgeon, was there, and dressed his breast; that is, put on a plaster, which is still requisite: and I took an opportunity to speak to him of the Queen; but he cut me short with this saying, "*Laissez faire à Don Antoine*," which is a French proverb, expressing, "Leave that to me." I find he is against her taking much physic; and I doubt he cannot persuade her to take Dr. Radcliffe. However, she is very well now, and all the story of her illness, except the first day or two, was a lie. We had some business, that company hindered us from doing, though he is earnest for it, yet would not appoint me a certain day, but bids me come at all times till we can have leisure. This takes up a great deal of my time, and I can do nothing I would do for them. I was with the Secretary this morning, and we both think to go to Windsor for some days, to despatch an affair, if we can have leisure. Sterne met me just now in the street by his lodgings, and I went in for an hour to Jemmy Leigh, who loves London dearly: he asked after you with great respect and friendship.—To return to your letter. Your Bishop Mills hates me mortally: I wonder he should speak well of me, having abused me in all places where he went. So you pay your way. Cudsho: you had a fine supper, I warrant; two pullets, and a bottle of wine, and some currants.—It is just three weeks to-day since you set out to Wexford; you were three days going, and I do not expect a letter these ten days yet, or rather this fortnight. I got a grant of the *Gazette* for Ben Tooke this morning from Mr. Secretary: it will be worth to him a hundred pounds a year.

18. To-day I took leave of Mrs. Barton, who is going into the country; and I dined with Sir John Stanley, where I have not been this great while. There dined with us Lord Rochester, and his fine daughter, Lady Jane, just growing a top-toast. I have been endeavouring to save Sir Matthew Dudley, but fear I cannot. I walked the Mall six times to-night for exercise, and would have done more; but, as empty as the town is, a fool got hold of me, and so I came home, to tell you this shall go to-morrow, without fail, and follow you to Wexford, like a dog.

19. Dean Atterbury sent to me to dine with him at Chelsea. I refused his coach, and walked, and am come back by seven, because I would finish this letter, and some others I am writing. Patrick tells me the

maid says one Mr. Walls, a clergyman, a tall man, was here to visit me. Is it your Irish Archdeacon? I shall be sorry for it; but I shall make shift to see him seldom enough, as I do Dilly. What can he do here? or is it somebody else? The Duke of Newcastle is dead by the fall he had from his horse. God send poor Stella her health, and keep MD happy! Farewell, and love Presto, who loves MD above all things ten million of times. God bless the dear Wexford girls. Farewell again, etc. etc.

Letter XXVII

I have just sent my 26th, and have nothing to say, because I have other letters to write (pshaw, I began too high); but I must lay the beginning like a nest-egg: to-morrow I will say more, and fetch up this line to be straight. This is enough at present for two dear saucy naughty girls.

20. Have I told you that Walls has been with me, and leaves the town in three days? He has brought no gown with him. Dilly carried him to a play. He has come upon a foolish errand, and goes back as he comes. I was this day with Lord Peterborow, who is going another ramble: I believe I told you so. I dined with Lord Treasurer, but cannot get him to do his own business with me; he has put me off till to-morrow.

21, 22. I dined yesterday with Lord Treasurer, who would needs take me along with him to Windsor, although I refused him several times, having no linen, etc. I had just time to desire Lord Forbes to call at my lodging and order my man to send my things to-day to Windsor by his servant. I lay last night at the Secretary's lodgings at Windsor, and borrowed one of his shirts to go to Court in. The Queen is very well. I dined with Mr. Masham; and not hearing anything of my things, I got Lord Winchelsea to bring me to town. Here I found that Patrick had broke open the closet to get my linen and nightgown, and sent them to Windsor, and there they are; and he, not thinking I would return so soon, is gone upon his rambles: so here I am left destitute, and forced to borrow a nightgown of my landlady, and have not a rag to put on to-morrow: faith, it gives me the spleen.

23. Morning. It is a terrible rainy day, and rained prodigiously on Saturday night. Patrick lay out last night, and is not yet returned: faith, poor Presto is a desolate creature; neither servant, nor linen, nor anything.— Night. Lord Forbes's man has brought back my portmantua, and Patrick is come; so I am in Christian circumstances: I shall hardly commit such a frolic again. I just crept out to Mrs. Van's, and dined, and stayed there the afternoon: it has rained all this day. Windsor is a delicious place: I never saw it before, except for an hour about seventeen years ago. Walls has been here in my absence, I suppose, to take his leave; for

he designed not to stay above five days in London. He says he and his wife will come here for some months next year; and, in short, he dares not stay now for fear of her.

24. I dined to-day with a hedge friend in the City; and Walls overtook me in the street, and told me he was just getting on horseback for Chester. He has as much curiosity as a cow: he lodged with his horse in Aldersgate Street: he has bought his wife a silk gown, and himself a hat. And what are you doing? what is poor MD doing now? how do you pass your time at Wexford? how do the waters agree with you? Let Presto know soon; for Presto longs to know, and must know. Is not Madam Proby curious company? I am afraid this rainy weather will spoil your waters. We have had a great deal of wet these three days. Tell me all the particulars of Wexford: the place, the company, the diversions, the victuals, the wants, the vexations. Poor Dingley never saw such a place in her life; sent all over the town for a little parsley to a boiled chicken, and it was not to be had; the butter is stark naught, except an old English woman's; and it is such a favour to get a pound from her now and then! I am glad you carried down your sheets with you, else you must have lain in sackcloth. O Lord!

25. I was this forenoon with Mr. Secretary at his office, and helped to hinder a man of his pardon, who is condemned for a rape. The Under Secretary was willing to save him, upon an old notion that a woman cannot be ravished; but I told the Secretary he could not pardon him without a favourable report from the judge; besides, he was a fiddler, and consequently a rogue, and deserved hanging for some thing else; and so he shall swing. What, I must stand up for the honour of the fair sex! 'Tis true the fellow had lain with her a hundred times before, but what care I for that! What, must a woman be ravished because she is a whore?—The Secretary and I go on Saturday to Windsor for a week. I dined with Lord Treasurer, and stayed with him till past ten. I was to-day at his levee, where I went against my custom, because I had a mind to do a good office for a gentleman: so I talked with him before my lord, that he might see me, and then found occasion to recommend him this afternoon. I was forced to excuse my coming to the levee, that I did it to see the sight; for he was going to chide me away: I had never been there but once, and that was long before he was Treasurer. The rooms were all full, and as many Whigs as Tories. He whispered me

a jest or two, and bid me come to dinner. I left him but just now; and 'tis late.

26. Mr. Addison and I have at last met again. I dined with him and Steele to-day at young Jacob Tonson's. The two Jacobs think it is I who have made the Secretary take from them the printing of the *Gazette*, which they are going to lose, and Ben Tooke and another are to have it. Jacob came to me the other day, to make his court; but I told him it was too late, and that it was not my doing. I reckon they will lose it in a week or two. Mr. Addison and I talked as usual, and as if we had seen one another yesterday; and Steele and I were very easy, though I writ him lately a biting letter, in answer to one of his, where he desired me to recommend a friend of his to Lord Treasurer. Go, get you gone to your waters, sirrah. Do they give you a stomach? Do you eat heartily?—We have had much rain to-day and yesterday.

27. I dined to-day in the City, and saw poor Patty Rolt, and gave her a pistole to help her a little forward against she goes to board in the country. She has but eighteen pounds a year to live on, and is forced to seek out for cheap places. Sometimes they raise their price, and sometimes they starve her, and then she is forced to shift. Patrick the puppy put too much ink in my standish, and, carrying too many things together, I spilled it on my paper and floor. The town is dull, wet, and empty; Wexford is worth two of it; I hope so at least, and that poor little MD finds it so. I reckon upon going to Windsor to-morrow with Mr. Secretary, unless he changes his mind, or some other business prevents him. I shall stay there a week, I hope.

28. Morning. Mr. Secretary sent me word he will call at my lodgings by two this afternoon, to take me to Windsor; so I must dine nowhere; and I promised Lord Treasurer to dine with him to-day; but I suppose we shall dine at Windsor at five, for we make but three hours there. I am going abroad, but have left Patrick to put up my things, and to be sure to be at home half an hour before two.—Windsor, at night. We did not leave London till three, and dined here between six and seven; at nine I left the company, and went to see Lord Treasurer, who is just come. I chid him for coming so late; he chid me for not dining with him; said he stayed an hour for me. Then I went and sat with Mr. Lewis till just now, and it is past eleven. I lie in the same house with the Secretary,

one of the Prebendary's houses. The Secretary is not come from his apartment in the Castle. Do you think that abominable dog Patrick was out after two to-day, and I in a fright every moment, for fear the chariot should come; and when he came in, he had not put up one rag of my things! I never was in a greater passion, and would certainly have cropped one of his ears, if I had not looked every moment for the Secretary, who sent his equipage to my lodging before, and came in a chair from Whitehall to me, and happened to stay half an hour later than he intended. One of Lord Treasurer's servants gave me a letter to-night: I found it was from—, with an offer of fifty pounds, to be paid me in what manner I pleased; because, he said, he desired to be well with me. I was in a rage; but my friend Lewis cooled me, and said it is what the best men sometimes meet with; and I have been not seldom served in the like manner, although not so grossly. In these cases I never demur a moment, nor ever found the least inclination to take anything. Well, I will go try to sleep in my new bed, and to dream of poor Wexford MD, and Stella that drinks water, and Dingley that drinks ale.

29. I was at Court and church to-day, as I was this day se'ennight: I generally am acquainted with about thirty in the drawing-room, and I am so proud I make all the lords come up to me: one passes half an hour pleasant enough. We had a dunce to preach before the Queen to-day, which often happens. Windsor is a delicious situation, but the town is scoundrel. I have this morning got the *Gazette* for Ben Tooke and one Barber a printer; it will be about three hundred pounds a year between them. The other fellow was printer of the *Examiner*, which is now laid down. I dined with the Secretary: we were a dozen in all, three Scotch lords, and Lord Peterborow. The Duke of Hamilton would needs be witty, and hold up my train as I walked upstairs. It is an ill circumstance that on Sundays much company always meet at the great tables. Lord Treasurer told at Court what I said to Mr. Secretary on this occasion. The Secretary showed me his bill of fare, to encourage me to dine with him. "Poh," said I, "show me a bill of company, for I value not your dinner." See how this is all blotted, I can write no more here, but to tell you I love MD dearly, and God bless them.

30. In my conscience, I fear I shall have the gout. I sometimes feel pains about my feet and toes: I never drank till within these two years,

and I did it to cure my head. I often sit evenings with some of these people, and drink in my turn; but I am now resolved to drink ten times less than before; but they advise me to let what I drink be all wine, and not to put water to it. Tooke and the printer stayed to-day to finish their affair, and treated me and two of the Under Secretaries upon their getting the *Gazette*. Then I went to see Lord Treasurer, and chid him for not taking notice of me at Windsor. He said he kept a place for me yesterday at dinner, and expected me there; but I was glad I did not go, because the Duke of Buckingham was there, and that would have made us acquainted; which I have no mind to. However, we appointed to sup at Mr. Masham's, and there stayed till past one o'clock; and that is late, sirrahs: and I have much business.

31. I have sent a noble haunch of venison this afternoon to Mrs. Vanhomrigh: I wish you had it, sirrahs. I dined gravely with my landlord the Secretary. The Queen was abroad to-day in order to hunt; but, finding it disposed to rain, she kept in her coach; she hunts in a chaise with one horse, which she drives herself, and drives furiously, like Jehu, and is a mighty hunter, like Nimrod. Dingley has heard of Nimrod, but not Stella, for it is in the Bible. I was to-day at Eton, which is but just cross the bridge, to see my Lord Kerry's son, who is at school there. Mr. Secretary has given me a warrant for a buck; I can't send it to MD. It is a sad thing, faith, considering how Presto loves MD, and how MD would love Presto's venison for Presto's sake. God bless the two dear Wexford girls!

Aug. 1. We had for dinner the fellow of that haunch of venison I sent to London; 'twas mighty fat and good, and eight people at dinner; that was bad. The Queen and I were going to take the air this afternoon, but not together; and were both hindered by a sudden rain. Her coaches and chaises all went back, and the guards too; and I scoured into the market-place for shelter. I intended to have walked up the finest avenue I ever saw, two miles long, with two rows of elms on each side. I walked in the evening a little upon the terrace, and came home at eight: Mr. Secretary came soon after, and we were engaging in deep discourse, and I was endeavouring to settle some points of the greatest consequence, and had wormed myself pretty well into him, when his Under Secretary came in (who lodges in the same house with us) and interrupted all my scheme. I have just left him: it is late, etc.

2. I have been now five days at Windsor, and Patrick has been drunk three times that I have seen, and oftener I believe. He has lately had clothes that have cost me five pounds, and the dog thinks he has the whip-hand of me: he begins to master me; so now I am resolved to part with him, and will use him without the least pity. The Secretary and I have been walking three or four hours to-day. The Duchess of Shrewsbury asked him, was not that Dr.— Dr.— and she could not say my name in English, but said Dr. Presto, which is Italian for Swift. Whimsical enough, as Billy Swift says. I go to-morrow with the Secretary to his house at Bucklebury, twenty-five miles from hence, and return early on Sunday morning. I will leave this letter behind me locked up, and give you an account of my journey when I return. I had a letter yesterday from the Bishop of Clogher, who is coming up to his Parliament. Have you any correspondence with him to Wexford? Methinks, I now long for a letter from you, dated Wexford, July 24, etc. O Lord, that would be so pretending; and then, says you, Stella can't write much, because it is bad to write when one drinks the waters; and I think, says you, I find myself better already, but I cannot tell yet whether it be the journey or the waters. Presto is so silly to-night; yes he be; but Presto loves MD dearly, as hope saved.

3. Morning. I am to go this day at noon, as I told you, to Bucklebury: we dine at twelve, and expect to be there in four hours. I cannot bid you good-night now, because I shall be twenty-five miles from this paper to-night, and so my journal must have a break; so good-morrow, etc.

4, 5. I dined yesterday at Bucklebury, where we lay two nights, and set out this morning at eight, and were here at twelve; in four hours we went twenty-six miles. Mr. Secretary was a perfect country gentleman at Bucklebury: he smoked tobacco with one or two neighbours; he inquired after the wheat in such a field; he went to visit his hounds, and knew all their names; he and his lady saw me to my chamber just in the country fashion. His house is in the midst of near three thousand pounds a year he had by his lady, who is descended from Jack Newbury, of whom books and ballads are written; and there is an old picture of him in the house. She is a great favourite of mine. I lost church to-day; but I dressed and shaved, and went to Court, and would not dine with the Secretary, but engaged myself to a private dinner with Mr. Lewis, and one friend more. We go to London to-morrow; for

Lord Dartmouth, the other Secretary, is come, and they are here their weeks by turns.

6. Lord Treasurer comes every Saturday to Windsor, and goes away on Monday or Tuesday. I was with him this morning at his levee, for one cannot see him otherwise here, he is so hurried: we had some talk; and I told him I would stay this week at Windsor by myself, where I can have more leisure to do some business that concerns them. Lord Treasurer and the Secretary thought to mortify me; for they told me they had been talking a great deal of me to-day to the Queen, and she said she had never heard of me. I told them that was their fault, and not hers, etc., and so we laughed. I dined with the Secretary, and let him go to London at five without me; and here am I alone in the Prebendary's house, which Mr. Secretary has taken; only Mr. Lewis is in my neighbourhood, and we shall be good company. The Vice-Chamberlain, and Mr. Masham, and the Green Cloth, have promised me dinners. I shall want but four till Mr. Secretary returns. We have a music-meeting in our town to-night. I went to the rehearsal of it, and there was Margarita, and her sister, and another drab, and a parcel of fiddlers: I was weary, and would not go to the meeting, which I am sorry for, because I heard it was a great assembly. Mr. Lewis came from it, and sat with me till just now; and 'tis late.

7. I can do no business, I fear, because Mr. Lewis, who has nothing or little to do here, sticks close to me. I dined to-day with the gentlemen ushers, among scurvy company; but the Queen was hunting the stag till four this afternoon, and she drove in her chaise above forty miles, and it was five before we went to dinner. Here are fine walks about this town. I sometimes walk up the avenue.

8. There was a Drawing-room to-day at Court; but so few company, that the Queen sent for us into her bed-chamber, where we made our bows, and stood about twenty of us round the room, while she looked at us round with her fan in her mouth, and once a minute said about three words to some that were nearest her, and then she was told dinner was ready, and went out. I dined at the Green Cloth, by Mr. Scarborow's invitation, who is in waiting. It is much the best table in England, and costs the Queen a thousand pounds a month while she is at Windsor or Hampton Court, and is the only mark of magnificence or hospitality I can

see in the Queen's family: it is designed to entertain foreign Ministers, and people of quality, who come to see the Queen, and have no place to dine at.

9. Mr. Coke, the Vice-Chamberlain, made me a long visit this morning, and invited me to dinner; but the toast, his lady, was unfortunately engaged to Lady Sunderland. Lord Treasurer stole here last night, but did not lie at his lodgings in the Castle; and, after seeing the Queen, went back again. I just drank a dish of chocolate with him. I fancy I shall have reason to be angry with him very soon; but what care I? I believe I shall die with Ministries in my debt.—This night I received a certain letter from a place called Wexford, from two dear naughty girls of my acquaintance; but, faith, I will not answer it here, no in troth. I will send this to Mr. Reading, supposing it will find you returned; and I hope better for the waters.

10. Mr. Vice-Chamberlain lent me his horses to ride about and see the country this morning. Dr. Arbuthnot, the Queen's physician and favourite, went out with me to show me the places: we went a little after the Queen, and overtook Miss Forester, a maid of honour, on her palfrey, taking the air; we made her go along with us. We saw a place they have made for a famous horse-race to-morrow, where the Queen will come. We met the Queen coming back, and Miss Forester stood, like us, with her hat off while the Queen went by. The Doctor and I left the lady where we found her, but under other conductors; and we dined at a little place he has taken, about a mile off.—When I came back I found Mr. Scarborow had sent all about to invite me to the Green Cloth, and lessened his company on purpose to make me easy. It is very obliging, and will cost me thanks. Much company is come to town this evening, to see to-morrow's race. I was tired with riding a trotting mettlesome horse a dozen miles, having not been on horseback this twelvemonth. And Miss Forester did not make it easier; she is a silly true maid of honour, and I did not like her, although she be a toast, and was dressed like a man.

11. I will send this letter to-day. I expect the Secretary by noon. I will not go to the race unless I can get room in some coach. It is now morning. I must rise, and fold up and seal my letter. Farewell, and God preserve dearest MD.

I believe I shall leave this town on Monday.

Letter XXVIII

WINDSOR, *Aug.* 11, 1711

I sent away my twenty-seventh this morning in an express to London, and directed to Mr. Reading: this shall go to your lodgings, where I reckon you will be returned before it reaches you. I intended to go to the race to-day, but was hindered by a visit: I believe I told you so in my last. I dined to-day at the Green Cloth, where everybody had been at the race but myself, and we were twenty in all, and very noisy company; but I made the Vice-Chamberlain and two friends more sit at a side table, to be a little quiet. At six I went to see the Secretary, who is returned; but Lord Keeper sent to desire I would sup with him, where I stayed till just now: Lord Treasurer and Secretary were to come to us, but both failed. 'Tis late, etc.

12. I was this morning to visit Lord Keeper, who made me reproaches that I had never visited him at Windsor. He had a present sent him of delicious peaches, and he was champing and champing, but I durst not eat one; I wished Dingley had some of them, for poor Stella can no more eat fruit than Presto. Dilly Ashe is come to Windsor; and after church I carried him up to the drawing-room, and talked to the Keeper and Treasurer, on purpose to show them to him; and he saw the Queen and several great lords, and the Duchess of Montagu; he was mighty happy, and resolves to fill a letter to the Bishop. My friend Lewis and I dined soberly with Dr. Adams, the only neighbour prebendary. One of the prebendaries here is lately a peer, by the death of his father. He is now Lord Willoughby of Broke, and will sit in the House of Lords with his gown. I supped to-night at Masham's with Lord Treasurer, Mr. Secretary, and Prior. The Treasurer made us stay till twelve, before he came from the Queen, and 'tis now past two.

13. I reckoned upon going to London to-day; but by an accident the Cabinet Council did not sit last night, and sat to-day, so we go to-morrow at six in the morning. I missed the race to-day by coming out too late, when everybody's coach was gone, and ride I would not: I felt my last riding three days after. We had a dinner to-day at the Secretary's lodgings without him: Mr. Hare, his Under Secretary, Mr. Lewis, Brigadier Sutton, and I, dined together; and I made the

Vice-Chamberlain take a snap with us, rather than stay till five for his lady, who was gone to the race. The reason why the Cabinet Council was not held last night was because Mr. Secretary St. John would not sit with your Duke of Somerset. So to-day the Duke was forced to go to the race while the Cabinet was held. We have music-meetings in our town, and I was at the rehearsal t'other day; but I did not value it, nor would go to the meeting. Did I tell you this before?

London, 14. We came to town this day in two hours and forty minutes: twenty miles are nothing here. I found a letter from the Archbishop of Dublin, sent me the Lord knows how. He says some of the bishops will hardly believe that Lord Treasurer got the Queen to remit the First-Fruits before the Duke of Ormond was declared Lord Lieutenant, and that the bishops have written a letter to Lord Treasurer to thank him. He has sent me the address of the Convocation, ascribing, in good part, that affair to the Duke, who had less share in it than MD; for if it had not been for MD, I should not have been so good a solicitor. I dined to-day in the City, about a little bit of mischief, with a printer.—I found Mrs. Vanhomrigh all in combustion, squabbling with her rogue of a landlord; she has left her house, and gone out of our neighbourhood a good way. Her eldest daughter is come of age, and going to Ireland to look after her fortune, and get it in her own hands.

15. I dined to-day with Mrs. Van, who goes to-night to her new lodgings. I went at six to see Lord Treasurer; but his company was gone, contrary to custom, and he was busy, and I was forced to stay some time before I could see him. We were together hardly an hour, and he went away, being in haste. He desired me to dine with him on Friday, because there would be a friend of his that I must see: my Lord Harley told me, when he was gone, that it was Mrs. Masham his father meant, who is come to town to lie-in, and whom I never saw, though her husband is one of our Society. God send her a good time! her death would be a terrible thing.—Do you know that I have ventured all my credit with these great Ministers, to clear some misunderstandings betwixt them; and if there be no breach, I ought to have the merit of it. 'Tis a plaguy ticklish piece of work, and a man hazards losing both sides. It is a pity the world does not know my virtue.—I thought the clergy in Convocation in Ireland would have given me thanks for being their solicitor; but I hear of no such thing. Pray talk occasionally on that subject, and let me know what

you hear. Do you know the greatness of my spirit, that I value their thanks not a rush, but at my return shall freely let all people know that it was my Lord Treasurer's action, wherein the Duke of Ormond had no more share than a cat? And so they may go whistle, and I'll go sleep.

16. I was this day in the City, and dined at Pontack's with Stratford, and two other merchants. Pontack told us, although his wine was so good, he sold it cheaper than others; he took but seven shillings a flask. Are not these pretty rates? The books he sent for from Hamburg are come, but not yet got out of the custom-house. My library will be at least double when I come back. I shall go to Windsor again on Saturday, to meet our Society, who are to sup at Mr. Secretary's; but I believe I shall return on Monday, and then I will answer your letter, that lies here safe underneath;—I see it; lie still: I will answer you when the ducks have eaten up the dirt.

17. I dined to-day at Lord Treasurer's with Mrs. Masham, and she is extremely like one Mrs. Malolly, that was once my landlady in Trim. She was used with mighty kindness and respect, like a favourite. It signifies nothing going to this Lord Treasurer about business, although it be his own. He was in haste, and desires I will come again, and dine with him to-morrow. His famous lying porter is fallen sick, and they think he will die: I wish I had all my half-crowns again. I believe I have told you he is an old Scotch fanatic, and the damn'dest liar in his office alive. I have a mind to recommend Patrick to succeed him: I have trained him up pretty well. I reckon for certain you are now in town. The weather now begins to alter to rain.

Windsor, 18. I dined to-day with Lord Treasurer, and he would make me go with him to Windsor, although I was engaged to the Secretary, to whom I made my excuses: we had in the coach besides, his son and son-in-law, Lord Harley and Lord Dupplin, who are two of our Society, and seven of us met by appointment, and supped this night with the Secretary. It was past nine before we got here, but a fine moonshiny night. I shall go back, I believe, on Monday. 'Tis very late.

19. The Queen did not stir out to-day, she is in a little fit of the gout. I dined at Mr. Masham's; we had none but our Society members, six in all, and I supped with Lord Treasurer. The Queen has ordered twenty

thousand pounds to go on with the building at Blenheim, which has been starved till now, since the change of the Ministry. I suppose it is to reward his last action of getting into the French lines. Lord Treasurer kept me till past twelve.

London, 20. It rained terribly every step of our journey to-day: I returned with the Secretary after a dinner of cold meat, and went to Mrs. Van's, where I sat the evening. I grow very idle, because I have a great deal of business. Tell me how you passed your time at Wexford; and are not you glad at heart you have got home safe to your lodgings at St. Mary's, pray? And so your friends come to visit you; and Mrs. Walls is much better of her eye; and the Dean is just as he used to be: and what does Walls say of London? 'tis a reasoning coxcomb. And Goody Stoyte, and Hannah what d'ye call her; no, her name an't Hannah, Catherine I mean; they were so glad to see the ladies again! and Mrs. Manley wanted a companion at ombre.

21. I writ to-day to the Archbishop of Dublin, and enclosed a long politic paper by itself. You know the bishops are all angry (smoke the wax-candle drop at the bottom of this paper) I have let the world know the First-Fruits were got by Lord Treasurer before the Duke of Ormond was Governor. I told Lord Treasurer all this, and he is very angry; but I pacified him again by telling him they were fools, and knew nothing of what passed here; but thought all was well enough if they complimented the Duke of Ormond. Lord Treasurer gave me t'other day a letter of thanks he received from the bishops of Ireland, signed by seventeen; and says he will write them an answer. The Dean of Carlisle sat with me to-day till three; and I went to dine with Lord Treasurer, who dined abroad, so did the Secretary, and I was left in the suds. 'Twas almost four, and I got to Sir Matthew Dudley, who had half dined. Thornhill, who killed Sir Cholmley Dering, was murdered by two men, on Turnham Green, last Monday night: as they stabbed him, they bid him remember Sir Cholmley Dering. They had quarrelled at Hampton Court, and followed and stabbed him on horseback. We have only a Grub Street paper of it, but I believe it is true. I went myself through Turnham Green the same night, which was yesterday.

22. We have had terrible rains these two or three days. I intended to dine at Lord Treasurer's, but went to see Lady Abercorn, who is

come to town, and my lord; and I dined with them, and visited Lord Treasurer this evening. His porter is mending. I sat with my lord about three hours, and am come home early to be busy. Passing by White's Chocolate-house, my brother Masham called me, and told me his wife was brought to bed of a boy, and both very well. (Our Society, you must know, are all brothers.) Dr. Garth told us that Mr. Henley is dead of an apoplexy. His brother-in-law, Earl Poulett, is gone down to the Grange, to take care of his funeral. The Earl of Danby, the Duke of Leeds's eldest grandson, a very hopeful young man of about twenty, is dead at Utrecht of the smallpox.—I long to know whether you begin to have any good effect by your waters.—Methinks this letter goes on slowly; 'twill be a fortnight next Saturday since it was begun, and one side not filled. O fie for shame, Presto! Faith, I'm so tosticated to and from Windsor, that I know not what to say; but, faith, I'll go to Windsor again on Saturday, if they ask me, not else. So lose your money again, now you are come home; do, sirrah.

Take your magnifying-glass, Madam Dingley.

You shan't read this, sirrah Stella; don't read it for your life, for fear of your dearest eyes.

There's enough for this side; these Ministers hinder me.

Pretty, dear, little, naughty, saucy MD.

Silly, impudent, loggerhead Presto.

23. Dilly and I dined to-day with Lord Abercorn, and had a fine fat haunch of venison, that smelt rarely on one side: and after dinner Dilly won half a crown of me at backgammon at his lodgings, to his great content. It is a scurvy empty town this melancholy season of the year; but I think our weather begins to mend. The roads are as deep as in winter. The grapes are sad things; but the peaches are pretty good, and there are some figs. I sometimes venture to eat one, but always repent it. You say nothing of the box sent half a year ago. I wish you would pay me for Mrs. Walls's tea. Your mother is in the country, I suppose. Pray send me the account of MD, Madam Dingley, as it stands since November, that is to say, for this year (excluding the twenty pounds lent Stella for Wexford), for I cannot look in your letters. I think I ordered that Hawkshaw's interest should be paid to you. When you think proper, I will let Parvisol know you have paid that twenty pounds, or part of it; and so go play with the Dean, and I will answer your letter to-morrow. Good-night, sirrahs, and love Presto, and be good girls.

24. I dined to-day with Lord Treasurer, who chid me for not dining with him yesterday, for it seems I did not understand his invitation; and their Club of the Ministry dined together, and expected me. Lord Radnor and I were walking the Mall this evening; and Mr. Secretary met us, and took a turn or two, and then stole away, and we both believed it was to pick up some wench; and to-morrow he will be at the Cabinet with the Queen: so goes the world! Prior has been out of town these two months, nobody knows where, and is lately returned. People confidently affirm he has been in France, and I half believe it. It is said he was sent by the Ministry, and for some overtures towards a peace. The Secretary pretends he knows nothing of it. I believe your Parliament will be dissolved. I have been talking about the quarrel between your Lords and Commons with Lord Treasurer, and did, at the request of some people, desire that the Queen's answer to the Commons' address might express a dislike of some principles, etc.; but was answered dubiously.—And so now to your letter, fair ladies. I know drinking is bad; I mean writing is bad in drinking the waters; and was angry to see so much in Stella's hand. But why Dingley drinks them, I cannot imagine; but truly she'll drink waters as well as Stella: why not? I hope you now find the benefit of them since you are returned; pray let me know particularly. I am glad you are forced upon exercise, which, I believe, is as good as the waters for the heart of them. 'Tis now past the middle of August; so by your reckoning you are in Dublin. It would vex me to the dogs that letters should miscarry between Dublin and Wexford, after 'scaping the salt seas. I will write no more to that nasty town in haste again, I warrant you. I have been four Sundays together at Windsor, of which a fortnight together; but I believe I shall not go to-morrow, for I will not, unless the Secretary asks me. I know all your news about the Mayor: it makes no noise here at all, but the quarrel of your Parliament does; it is so very extraordinary, and the language of the Commons so very pretty. The *Examiner* has been down this month, and was very silly the five or six last papers; but there is a pamphlet come out, in answer to a letter to the seven Lords who examined Gregg. The Answer is by the real author of the *Examiner*, as I believe; for it is very well written. We had Trapp's poem on the Duke of Ormond printed here, and the printer sold just eleven of them. 'Tis a dull piece, not half so good as Stella's; and she is very modest to compare herself with such a poetaster. I am heartily sorry for poor Mrs. Parnell's death; she seemed to be an excellent good-

natured young woman, and I believe the poor lad is much afflicted; they appeared to live perfectly well together. Dilly is not tired at all with England, but intends to continue here a good while: he is mighty easy to be at distance from his two sisters-in-law. He finds some sort of scrub acquaintance; goes now and then in disguise to a play; smokes his pipe; reads now and then a little trash, and what else the Lord knows. I see him now and then; for he calls here, and the town being thin, I am less pestered with company than usual. I have got rid of many of my solicitors, by doing nothing for them: I have not above eight or nine left, and I'll be as kind to them. Did I tell you of a knight who desired me to speak to Lord Treasurer to give him two thousand pounds, or five hundred pounds a year, until he could get something better? I honestly delivered my message to the Treasurer, adding, the knight was a puppy, whom I would not give a groat to save from the gallows. Cole Reading's father-in-law has been two or three times at me, to recommend his lights to the Ministry, assuring me that a word of mine would, etc. Did not that dog use to speak ill of me, and profess to hate me? He knows not where I lodge, for I told him I lived in the country; and I have ordered Patrick to deny me constantly to him.— Did the Bishop of London die in Wexford? poor gentleman! Did he drink the waters? were you at his burial? was it a great funeral? so far from his friends! But he was very old: we shall all follow. And yet it was a pity, if God pleased. He was a good man; not very learned: I believe he died but poor. Did he leave any charity legacies? who held up his pall? was there a great sight of clergy? do they design a tomb for him?—Are you sure it was the Bishop of London? because there is an elderly gentleman here that we give the same title to: or did you fancy all this in your water, as others do strange things in their wine? They say these waters trouble the head, and make people imagine what never came to pass. Do you make no more of killing a Bishop? are these your Whiggish tricks?—Yes, yes, I see you are in a fret. O, faith, says you, saucy Presto, I'll break your head; what, can't one report what one hears, without being made a jest and a laughing-stock? Are these your English tricks, with a murrain? And Sacheverell will be the next Bishop? He would be glad of an addition of two hundred pounds a year to what he has, and that is more than they will give him, for aught I see. He hates the new Ministry mortally, and they hate him, and pretend to despise him too. They will not allow him to have been the occasion of the late change; at least some of them will not: but my Lord Keeper owned it to me the other day. No, Mr. Addison does not go to Ireland this year: he pretended he would; but he is gone to Bath with Pastoral Philips, for his eyes.—So now I have run over your letter; and I think this shall go to-morrow, which will be just a fortnight from the last, and bring things to the old form again, after your rambles to Wexford, and mine to Windsor. Are there not many literal faults in my letters? I never read them over, and I fancy there are. What do you do then? do you guess my meaning, or are you acquainted with my manner of mistaking? I lost my handkerchief in the Mall to-night with Lord Radnor; but I made him walk with me to find it, and find it I did not. Tisdall (that lodges with me) and I have had no conversation, nor do we pull off our hats in the streets. There is a cousin of his (I suppose,) a young parson, that lodges in the house too; a handsome, genteel fellow. Dick Tighe and his wife lodged over against us; and he has been seen, out of our upper windows, beating her two or three times: they are both gone to Ireland, but not together; and he solemnly vows never to live with her. Neighbours do not stick to say that she has a tongue: in short, I am told she is the most urging, provoking devil that ever was born; and he a hot, whiffling puppy, very apt to resent. I'll keep this bottom till to-morrow: I'm sleepy.

25. I was with the Secretary this morning, who was in a mighty hurry, and went to Windsor in a chariot with Lord Keeper; so I was not invited, and am forced to stay at home, but not at all against my will; for I could have gone, and would not. I dined in the City with one of my printers, for whom I got the *Gazette*, and am come home early; and have nothing to say to you more, but finish this letter, and not send it by the bellman. Days grow short, and the weather grows bad, and the town is splenetic, and things are so oddly contrived that I cannot be absent; otherwise I would go for a few days to Oxford, as I promised.— They say it is certain that Prior has been in France, nobody doubts it: I had not time to ask the Secretary, he was in such haste. Well, I will take my leave of dearest MD for a while; for I must begin my next letter to-night: consider that, young women; and pray be merry, and good girls, and love Presto. There is now but one business the Ministry want me for, and when that is done, I will take my leave of them. I never got a penny from them, nor expect it. In my opinion, some things stand very ticklish; I dare say nothing at this distance. Farewell, dear sirrahs, dearest lives: there is peace and quiet with MD, and nowhere else. They

JONATHAN SWIFT

have not leisure here to think of small things, which may ruin them; and I have been forward enough. Farewell again, dearest rogues; I am never happy but when I write or think of MD. I have enough of Courts and Ministries, and wish I were at Laracor; and if I could with honour come away this moment, I would. Bernage came to see me to-day; he is just landed from Portugal, and come to raise recruits; he looks very well, and seems pleased with his station and manner of life. He never saw London nor England before; he is ravished with Kent, which was his first prospect when he landed. Farewell again, etc. etc.

Letter XXIX

I have got a pretty small gilt sheet of paper, to write to MD. I have this moment sent my 28th by Patrick, who tells me he has put it in the post-office; 'tis directed to your lodgings: if it wants more particular direction, you must set me right. It is now a solar month and two days since the date of your last, N. 18; and I reckon you are now quiet at home, and thinking to begin your 19th, which will be full of your quarrel between the two Houses, all which I know already. Where shall I dine to-morrow? can you tell? Mrs. Vanhomrigh boards now, and cannot invite one; and there I used to dine when I was at a loss: and all my friends are gone out of town, and your town is now at the fullest, with your Parliament and Convocation. But let me alone, sirrahs; for Presto is going to be very busy; not Presto, but the other I.

26. People have so left the town that I am at a loss for a dinner. It is a long time since I have been at London upon a Sunday; and the Ministers are all at Windsor. It cost me eighteenpence in coach-hire before I could find a place to dine in. I went to Frankland's, and he was abroad, and the drab his wife looked out at window, and bowed to me without inviting me up: so I dined with Mr. Coote, my Lord Mountrath's brother; my lord is with you in Ireland. This morning at five my Lord Jersey died of the gout in his stomach, or apoplexy, or both: he was abroad yesterday, and his death was sudden. He was Chamberlain to King William, and a great favourite, turned out by the Queen as a Tory, and stood now fair to be Privy Seal; and by his death will, I suppose, make that matter easier, which has been a very stubborn business at Court, as I have been informed. I never remember so many people of quality to have died in so short a time.

27. I went to-day into the City, to thank Stratford for my books, and dine with him, and settle my affairs of my money in the Bank, and receive a bill for Mrs. Wesley for some things I am to buy for her; and the d—a one of all these could I do. The merchants were all out of town, and I was forced to go to a little hedge place for my dinner. May my enemies live here in summer! and yet I am so unlucky that I cannot possibly be out of the way at this juncture. People leave the town so late in

summer, and return so late in winter, that they have almost inverted the seasons. It is autumn this good while in St. James's Park; the limes have been losing their leaves, and those remaining on the trees are all parched: I hate this season, where everything grows worse and worse. The only good thing of it is the fruit, and that I dare not eat. Had you any fruit at Wexford? A few cherries, and durst not eat them. I do not hear we have yet got a new Privy Seal. The Whigs whisper that our new Ministry differ among themselves, and they begin to talk out Mr. Secretary: they have some reasons for their whispers, although I thought it was a greater secret. I do not much like the posture of things; I always apprehended that any falling out would ruin them, and so I have told them several times. The Whigs are mighty full of hopes at present; and whatever is the matter, all kind of stocks fall. I have not yet talked with the Secretary about Prior's journey. I should be apt to think it may foretell a peace, and that is all we have to preserve us. The Secretary is not come from Windsor, but I expect him to-morrow. Burn all politics!

28. We begin to have fine weather, and I walked to-day to Chelsea, and dined with the Dean of Carlisle, who is laid up with the gout. It is now fixed that he is to be Dean of Christ Church in Oxford. I was advising him to use his interest to prevent any misunderstanding between our Ministers; but he is too wise to meddle, though he fears the thing and the consequences as much as I. He will get into his own warm, quiet deanery, and leave them to themselves; and he is in the right.—When I came home to-night, I found a letter from Mr. Lewis, who is now at Windsor; and in it, forsooth, another which looked like Presto's hand; and what should it be but a 19th from MD? O, faith, I 'scaped narrowly, for I sent my 28th but on Saturday; and what should I have done if I had two letters to answer at once? I did not expect another from Wexford, that is certain. Well, I must be contented; but you are dear saucy girls, for all that, to write so soon again, faith; an't you?

29. I dined to-day with Lord Abercorn, and took my leave of them: they set out to-morrow for Chester, and, I believe, will now fix in Ireland. They have made a pretty good journey of it: his eldest son is married to a lady with ten thousand pounds; and his second son has, t'other day, got a prize in the lottery of four thousand pounds, beside two small ones of two hundred pounds each: nay, the family was so fortunate,

that my lord bestowing one ticket, which is a hundred pounds, to one of his servants, who had been his page, the young fellow got a prize, which has made it another hundred. I went in the evening to Lord Treasurer, who desires I will dine with him to-morrow, when he will show me the answer he designs to return to the letter of thanks from your bishops in Ireland. The Archbishop of Dublin desired me to get myself mentioned in the answer which my lord would send; but I sent him word I would not open my lips to my lord upon it. He says it would convince the bishops of what I have affirmed, that the First-Fruits were granted before the Duke of Ormond was declared Governor; and I writ to him that I would not give a farthing to convince them. My Lord Treasurer began a health to my Lord Privy Seal: Prior punned, and said it was so privy, he knew not who it was; but I fancy they have fixed it all, and we shall know to-morrow. But what care you who is Privy Seal, saucy sluttikins?

30. When I went out this morning, I was surprised with the news that the Bishop of Bristol is made Lord Privy Seal. You know his name is Robinson, and that he was many years Envoy in Sweden. All the friends of the present Ministry are extremely glad, and the clergy above the rest. The Whigs will fret to death to see a civil employment given to a clergyman. It was a very handsome thing in my Lord Treasurer, and will bind the Church to him for ever. I dined with him to-day, but he had not written his letter; but told me he would not offer to send it without showing it to me: he thought that would not be just, since I was so deeply concerned in the affair. We had much company: Lord Rivers, Mar, and Kinnoull, Mr. Secretary, George Granville, and Masham: the last has invited me to the christening of his son to-morrow se'ennight; and on Saturday I go to Windsor with Mr. Secretary.

31. Dilly and I walked to-day to Kensington to Lady Mountjoy, who invited us to dinner. He returned soon, to go to a play, it being the last that will be acted for some time: he dresses himself like a beau, and no doubt makes a fine figure. I went to visit some people at Kensington: Ophy Butler's wife there lies very ill of an ague, which is a very common disease here, and little known in Ireland. I am apt to think we shall soon have a peace, by the little words I hear thrown out by the Ministry. I have just thought of a project to bite the town. I have told you that it

is now known that Mr. Prior has been lately in France. I will make a printer of my own sit by me one day, and I will dictate to him a formal relation of Prior's journey, with several particulars, all pure invention; and I doubt not but it will take.

Sept. 1. Morning. I go to-day to Windsor with Mr. Secretary; and Lord Treasurer has promised to bring me back. The weather has been fine for some time, and I believe we shall have a great deal of dust.—At night. Windsor. The Secretary and I dined to-day at Parson's Green, at my Lord Peterborow's house, who has left it and his gardens to the Secretary during his absence. It is the finest garden I have ever seen about this town; and abundance of hot walls for grapes, where they are in great plenty, and ripening fast. I durst not eat any fruit but one fig; but I brought a basket full to my friend Lewis here at Windsor. Does Stella never eat any? what, no apricots at Donnybrook! nothing but claret and ombre! I envy people maunching and maunching peaches and grapes, and I not daring to eat a bit. My head is pretty well, only a sudden turn any time makes me giddy for a moment, and sometimes it feels very stuffed; but if it grows no worse, I can bear it very well. I take all opportunities of walking; and we have a delicious park here just joining to the Castle, and an avenue in the great park very wide and two miles long, set with a double row of elms on each side. Were you ever at Windsor? I was once, a great while ago; but had quite forgotten it.

2. The Queen has the gout, and did not come to chapel, nor stir out from her chamber, but received the sacrament there, as she always does the first Sunday in the month. Yet we had a great Court; and, among others, I saw your Ingoldsby, who, seeing me talk very familiarly with the Keeper, Treasurer, etc., came up and saluted me, and began a very impertinent discourse about the siege of Bouchain. I told him I could not answer his questions, but I would bring him one that should; so I went and fetched Sutton (who brought over the express about a month ago), and delivered him to the General, and bid him answer his questions; and so I left them together. Sutton after some time comes back in a rage, finds me with Lord Rivers and Masham, and there complains of the trick I had played him, and swore he had been plagued to death with Ingoldsby's talk. But he told me Ingoldsby asked him what I meant by bringing him; so, I suppose, he smoked me a little. So we laughed, etc. My Lord Willoughby, who is one of the chaplains,

and Prebendary of Windsor, read prayers last night to the family; and the Bishop of Bristol, who is Dean of Windsor, officiated last night at the Cathedral. This they do to be popular; and it pleases mightily. I dined with Mr. Masham, because he lets me have a select company: for the Court here have got by the end a good thing I said to the Secretary some weeks ago. He showed me his bill of fare, to tempt me to dine with him. "Poh," said I, "I value not your bill of fare; give me your bill of company." Lord Treasurer was mightily pleased, and told it everybody as a notable thing. I reckon upon returning to-morrow: they say the Bishop will then have the Privy Seal delivered him at a great Council.

3. Windsor still. The Council was held so late to-day that I do not go back to town till to-morrow. The Bishop was sworn Privy Councillor, and had the Privy Seal given him: and now the patents are passed for those who were this long time to be made lords or earls. Lord Raby, who is Earl of Strafford, is on Thursday to marry a namesake of Stella's; the daughter of Sir H. Johnson in the City; he has three-score thousand pounds with her, ready money; besides the rest at the father's death. I have got my friend Stratford to be one of the directors of the South Sea Company, who were named to-day. My Lord Treasurer did it for me a month ago; and one of those whom I got to be printer of the *Gazette* I am recommending to be printer to the same company. He treated Mr. Lewis and me to-day at dinner. I supped last night and this with Lord Treasurer, Keeper, etc., and took occasion to mention the printer. I said it was the same printer whom my Lord Treasurer has appointed to print for the South Sea Company. He denied, and I insisted on it; and I got the laugh on my side.

London, 4. I came as far as Brentford in Lord Rivers's chariot, who had business with Lord Treasurer; then I went into Lord Treasurer's. We stopped at Kensington, where Lord Treasurer went to see Mrs. Masham, who is now what they call in the straw. We got to town by three, and I lighted at Lord Treasurer's, who commanded me not to stir: but I was not well; and when he went up, I begged the young lord to excuse me, and so went into the City by water, where I could be easier, and dined with the printer, and dictated to him some part of Prior's *Journey to France*. I walked from the City, for I take all occasions of exercise. Our journey was horridly dusty.

5. When I went out to-day, I found it had rained mightily in the night, and the streets were as dirty as winter: it is very refreshing after ten days dry.—I went into the City, and dined with Stratford, thanked him for his books, gave him joy of his being director, of which he had the first notice by a letter from me. I ate sturgeon, and it lies on my stomach. I almost finished Prior's *Journey* at the printer's; and came home pretty late, with Patrick at my heels.

7. Morning. But what shall we do about this letter of MD's, N. 19? Not a word answered yet, and so much paper spent! I cannot do anything in it, sweethearts, till night.—At night. O Lord, O Lord! the greatest disgrace that ever was has happened to Presto. What do you think? but, when I was going out this forenoon a letter came from MD, N. 20, dated Dublin. O dear, O dear! O sad, O sad!—Now I have two letters together to answer: here they are, lying together. But I will only answer the first; for I came in late. I dined with my friend Lewis at his lodgings, and walked at six to Kensington to Mrs. Masham's son's christening. It was very private; nobody there but my Lord Treasurer, his son and son-in-law, that is to say, Lord Harley and Lord Dupplin, and Lord Rivers and I. The Dean of Rochester christened the child, but soon went away. Lord Treasurer and Lord Rivers were godfathers; and Mrs. Hill, Mrs. Masham's sister, godmother. The child roared like a bull, and I gave Mrs. Masham joy of it; and she charged me to take care of my nephew, because, Mr. Masham being a brother of our Society, his son, you know, is consequently a nephew. Mrs. Masham sat up dressed in bed, but not, as they do in Ireland, with all smooth about her, as if she was cut off in the middle; for you might see the counterpane (what d'ye call it?) rise about her hips and body. There is another name of the counterpane; and you will laugh now, sirrahs. George Granville came in at supper, and we stayed till eleven; and Lord Treasurer set me down at my lodging in Suffolk Street. Did I ever tell you that Lord Treasurer hears ill with the left ear, just as I do? He always turns the right, and his servants whisper him at that only. I dare not tell him that I am so too, for fear he should think I counterfeited, to make my court.

6. You must read this before the other; for I mistook, and forgot to write yesterday's journal, it was so insignificant. I dined with Dr. Cockburn, and sat the evening with Lord Treasurer till ten o'clock. On Thursdays

he has always a large select company, and expects me. So good-night for last night, etc.

8. Morning. I go to Windsor with Lord Treasurer to-day, and will leave this behind me, to be sent to the post. And now let us hear what says the first letter, N. 19. You are still at Wexford, as you say, Madam Dingley. I think no letter from me ever yet miscarried. And so Inish-Corthy, and the river Slainy; fine words those in a lady's mouth. Your hand like Dingley's, you scambling, scattering sluttikin! *Yes, mighty like indeed, is not it?* Pisshh, do not talk of writing or reading till your eyes are well, and long well; only I would have Dingley read sometimes to you, that you may not lose the desire of it. God be thanked, that the ugly numbing is gone! Pray use exercise when you go to town. What game is that ombra which Dr. Elwood and you play at? is it the Spanish game ombre? Your card-purse? you a card-purse! you a fiddlestick. You have luck indeed; and luck in a bag. What a devil! is that eight-shilling tea-kettle copper, or tin japanned? It is like your Irish politeness, raffling for tea-kettles. What a splutter you keep, to convince me that Walls has no taste! My head continues pretty well. Why do you write, dear sirrah Stella, when you find your eyes so weak that you cannot see? what comfort is there in reading what you write, when one knows that? So Dingley cannot write, because of the clutter of new company come to Wexford! I suppose the noise of their hundred horses disturbs you; or do you lie in one gallery, as in an hospital? What! you are afraid of losing in Dublin the acquaintance you have got in Wexford, and chiefly the Bishop of Raphoe, an old, doting, perverse coxcomb? Twenty at a time at breakfast. That is like five pounds at a time, when it was never but once. I doubt, Madam Dingley, you are apt to lie in your travels, though not so bad as Stella; she tells thumpers, as I shall prove in my next, if I find this receives encouragement.—So Dr. Elwood says there are a world of pretty things in my works. A pox on his praises! an enemy here would say more. The Duke of Buckingham would say as much, though he and I are terribly fallen out; and the great men are perpetually inflaming me against him: they bring me all he says of me, and, I believe, make it worse out of roguery.—No, 'tis not your pen is bewitched, Madam Stella, but your old *scrawling, splay-foot pot-hooks*, *s, s*, ay that's it: there the s, s, s, there, there, that's exact. Farewell, etc.

Our fine weather is gone; and I doubt we shall have a rainy journey to-day. Faith, 'tis shaving-day, and I have much to do. When Stella says her pen was bewitched, it was only because there was a hair in it. You know, the fellow they call God-help-it had the same thoughts of his wife, and for the same reason. I think this is very well observed, and I unfolded the letter to tell you it.

Cut off those two notes above; and see the nine pounds indorsed, and receive the other; and send me word how my accounts stand, that they may be adjusted by Nov. 1. Pray be very particular; but the twenty pounds I lend you is not to be included: so make no blunder. I won't wrong you, nor you shan't wrong me; that is the short. O Lord, how stout Presto is of late! But he loves MD more than his life a thousand times, for all his stoutness; tell them that; and that I'll swear it, as hope saved, ten millions of times, etc. etc.

I open my letter once more, to tell Stella that if she does not use exercise after her waters, it will lose all the effects of them: I should not live if I did not take all opportunities of walking. Pray, pray, do this, to oblige poor Presto.

LETTER XXX

WINDSOR, *Sept.* 8, 1711

I made the coachman stop, and put in my twenty-ninth at the post-office at two o'clock to-day, as I was going to Lord Treasurer, with whom I dined, and came here by a quarter-past eight; but the moon shone, and so we were not in much danger of overturning; which, however, he values not a straw, and only laughs when I chide at him for it. There was nobody but he and I, and we supped together, with Mr. Masham, and Dr. Arbuthnot, the Queen's favourite physician, a Scotchman. I could not keep myself awake after supper, but did all I was able to disguise it, and thought I came off clear; but, at parting, he told me I had got my nap already. It is now one o'clock; but he loves sitting up late.

9. The Queen is still in the gout, but recovering: she saw company in her bed-chamber after church; but the crowd was so great, I could not see her. I dined with my brother Sir William Wyndham, and some others of our Society, to avoid the great tables on Sunday at Windsor, which I hate. The usual company supped to-night at Lord Treasurer's, which was Lord Keeper, Mr. Secretary, George Granville, Masham, Arbuthnot, and I. But showers have hindered me from walking to-day, and that I do not love.—Noble fruit, and I dare not eat a bit. I ate one fig to-day, and sometimes a few mulberries, because it is said they are wholesome, and you know a good name does much. I shall return to town to-morrow, though I thought to have stayed a week, to be at leisure for something I am doing. But I have put it off till next; for I shall come here again on Saturday, when our Society are to meet at supper at Mr. Secretary's. My life is very regular here: on Sunday morning I constantly visit Lord Keeper, and sup at Lord Treasurer's with the same set of company. I was not sleepy to-night; I resolved I would not; yet it is past midnight at this present writing.

London, 10. Lord Treasurer and Masham and I left Windsor at three this afternoon: we dropped Masham at Kensington with his lady, and got home by six. It was seven before we sat down to dinner, and I stayed till past eleven. Patrick came home with the Secretary: I am more plagued with Patrick and my portmantua than with myself. I forgot to tell you that when I went to Windsor on Saturday I overtook Lady Giffard

240   JONATHAN SWIFT

and Mrs. Fenton in a chariot, going, I suppose, to Sheen. I was then in a chariot too, of Lord Treasurer's brother, who had business with the Treasurer; and my lord came after, and overtook me at Turnham Green, four miles from London; and then the brother went back, and I went in the coach with Lord Treasurer: so it happened that those people saw me, and not with Lord Treasurer. Mrs. F. was to see me about a week ago; and desired I would get her son into the Charter-house.

11. This morning the printer sent me an account of Prior's *Journey*; it makes a twopenny pamphlet. I suppose you will see it, for I dare engage it will run; 'tis a formal, grave lie, from the beginning to the end. I writ all but about the last page; that I dictated, and the printer writ. Mr. Secretary sent to me to dine where he did; it was at Prior's: when I came in, Prior showed me the pamphlet, seemed to be angry, and said, "Here is our English liberty!" I read some of it, and said I liked it mightily, and envied the rogue the thought; for, had it come into my head, I should have certainly done it myself. We stayed at Prior's till past ten; and then the Secretary received a packet with the news of Bouchain being taken, for which the guns will go off to-morrow. Prior owned his having been in France, for it was past denying: it seems he was discovered by a rascal at Dover, who had positive orders to let him pass. I believe we shall have a peace.

12. It is terrible rainy weather, and has cost me three shillings in coaches and chairs to-day, yet I was dirty into the bargain. I was three hours this morning with the Secretary about some business of moment, and then went into the City to dine. The printer tells me he sold yesterday a thousand of Prior's *Journey*, and had printed five hundred more. It will do rarely, I believe, and is a pure bite. And what is MD doing all this while? got again to their cards, their Walls, their deans, their Stoytes, and their claret? Pray present my service to Mr. Stoyte and Catherine. Tell Goody Stoyte she owes me a world of dinners, and I will shortly come over and demand them.—Did I tell you of the Archbishop of Dublin's last letter? He had been saying, in several of his former, that he would shortly write to me something about myself; and it looked as if he intended something for me: at last out it comes, and consists of two parts. First, he advises me to strike in for some preferment now I have friends; and secondly, he advises me, since I have parts, and learning, and a happy pen, to think of some new subject in divinity not handled

by others, which I should manage better than anybody. A rare spark this, with a pox! but I shall answer him as rarely. Methinks he should have invited me over, and given me some hopes or promises. But hang him! and so good-night, etc.

13. It rained most furiously all this morning till about twelve, and sometimes thundered; I trembled for my shillings, but it cleared up, and I made a shift to get a walk in the Park, and then went with the Secretary to dine with Lord Treasurer. Upon Thursdays there is always a select company: we had the Duke of Shrewsbury, Lord Rivers, the two Secretaries, Mr. Granville, and Mr. Prior. Half of them went to Council at six; but Rivers, Granville, Prior, and I, stayed till eight. Prior was often affecting to be angry at the account of his journey to Paris; and indeed the two last pages, which the printer got somebody to add, are so romantic, they spoil all the rest. Dilly Ashe pretended to me that he was only going to Oxford and Cambridge for a fortnight, and then would come back. I could not see him as I appointed t'other day; but some of his friends tell me he took leave of them as going to Ireland; and so they say at his lodging. I believe the rogue was ashamed to tell me so, because I advised him to stay the winter, and he said he would. I find he had got into a good set of scrub acquaintance, and I thought passed his time very merrily; but I suppose he languished after Balderig, and the claret of Dublin; and, after all, I think he is in the right; for he can eat, drink, and converse better there than here. Bernage was with me this morning: he calls now and then; he is in terrible fear of a peace. He said he never had his health so well as in Portugal. He is a favourite of his Colonel.

14. I was mortified enough to-day, not knowing where in the world to dine, the town is so empty. I met H. Coote, and thought he would invite me, but he did not: Sir John Stanley did not come into my head; so I took up with Mrs. Van, and dined with her and her damned landlady, who, I believe, by her eyebrows, is a bawd. This evening I met Addison and Pastoral Philips in the Park, and supped with them at Addison's lodgings: we were very good company, and I yet know no man half so agreeable to me as he is. I sat with them till twelve, so you may think it is late, young women; however, I would have some little conversation with MD before your Presto goes to bed, because it makes me sleep, and dream, and so forth. Faith, this letter goes on slowly enough, sirrahs;

but I cannot write much at a time till you are quite settled after your journey, you know, and have gone all your visits, and lost your money at ombre. You never play at chess now, Stella. That puts me in mind of Dick Tighe; I fancy I told you he used to beat his wife here; and she deserved it; and he resolves to part with her; and they went to Ireland in different coaches. O Lord, I said all this before, I am sure. Go to bed, sirrahs.

Windsor, 15. I made the Secretary stop at Brentford, because we set out at two this afternoon, and fasting would not agree with me. I only designed to eat a bit of bread-and-butter; but he would light, and we ate roast beef like dragons. And he made me treat him and two more gentlemen; faith, it cost me a guinea. I do not like such jesting, yet I was mightily pleased with it too. To-night our Society met at the Secretary's: there were nine of us; and we have chosen a new member, the Earl of Jersey, whose father died lately. 'Tis past one, and I have stolen away.

16. I design to stay here this week by myself, about some business that lies on my hands, and will take up a great deal of time. Dr. Adams, one of the canons, invited me to-day to dinner. The tables are so full here on Sunday that it is hard to dine with a few, and Dr. Adams knows I love to do so; which is very obliging. The Queen saw company in her bed-chamber; she looks very well, but she sat down. I supped with Lord Treasurer as usual, and stayed till past one as usual, and with our usual company, except Lord Keeper, who did not come this time to Windsor. I hate these suppers mortally, but I seldom eat anything.

17. Lord Treasurer and Mr. Secretary stay here till to-morrow; some business keeps them, and I am sorry for it, for they hinder me a day. Mr. Lewis and I were going to dine soberly with a little Court friend at one. But Lord Harley and Lord Dupplin kept me by force, and said we should dine at Lord Treasurer's, who intended to go at four to London. I stayed like a fool, and went with the two young lords to Lord Treasurer, who very fairly turned us all three out of doors. They both were invited to the Duke of Somerset, but he was gone to a horse-race, and would not come till five; so we were forced to go to a tavern, and sent for wine from Lord Treasurer's, who at last, we were told, did not go to town till the morrow, and at Lord Treasurer's we supped again; and I desired him

to let me add four shillings to the bill I gave him. We sat up till two, yet I must write to little MD.

18. They are all gone early this morning, and I am alone to seek my fortune; but Dr. Arbuthnot engages me for my dinners; and he yesterday gave me my choice of place, person, and victuals for to-day. So I chose to dine with Mrs. Hill, who is one of the dressers, and Mrs. Masham's sister, no company but us three, and to have a shoulder of mutton, a small one; which was exactly, only there was too much victuals besides; and the Doctor's wife was of the company. And to-morrow Mrs. Hill and I are to dine with the Doctor. I have seen a fellow often about Court whom I thought I knew. I asked who he was, and they told me it was the gentleman porter; then I called him to mind; he was Killy's acquaintance (I won't say yours); I think his name is Lovet, or Lovel, or something like it. I believe he does not know me, and in my present posture I shall not be fond of renewing old acquaintance; I believe I used to see him with the Bradleys; and, by the way, I have not seen Mrs. Bradley since I came to England. I left your letter in London, like a fool; and cannot answer it till I go back, which will not be until Monday next; so this will be above a fortnight from my last; but I will fetch it up in my next; so go and walk to the Dean's for your health this fine weather.

19. The Queen designs to have cards and dancing here next week, which makes us think she will stay here longer than we believed. Mrs. Masham is not well after her lying-in: I doubt she got some cold; she is lame in one of her legs with a rheumatic pain. Dr. Arbuthnot and Mrs. Hill go to-morrow to Kensington to see her, and return the same night. Mrs. Hill and I dined with the Doctor to-day. I rode out this morning with the Doctor to see Cranburn, a house of Lord Ranelagh's, and the Duchess of Marlborough's lodge, and the Park; the finest places they are, for nature and plantations, that ever I saw; and the finest riding upon artificial roads, made on purpose for the Queen. Arbuthnot made me draw up a sham subscription for a book, called *A History of the Maids of Honour since Harry the Eighth*, showing they make the best wives, with a list of all the maids of honour since, etc.; to pay a crown in hand, and the other crown upon delivery of the book; and all in common forms of those things. We got a gentleman to write it fair, because my hand is known; and we sent it to the maids of honour, when they came to

supper. If they bite at it, it will be a very good Court jest; and the Queen will certainly have it: we did not tell Mrs. Hill.

20. To-day I was invited to the Green Cloth by Colonel Godfrey, who married the Duke of Marlborough's sister, mother to the Duke of Berwick by King James: I must tell you those things that happened before you were born. But I made my excuses, and young Harcourt (Lord Keeper's son) and I dined with my next neighbour, Dr. Adams. Mrs. Masham is better, and will be here in three or four days. She had need; for the Duchess of Somerset is thought to gain ground daily.— We have not sent you over all your bills; and I think we have altered your money-bill. The Duke of Ormond is censured here, by those in power, for very wrong management in the affair of the mayoralty. He is governed by fools, and has usually much more sense than his advisers, but never proceeds by it. I must know how your health continues after Wexford. Walk and use exercise, sirrahs both; and get somebody to play at shuttlecock with you, Madam Stella, and walk to the Dean's and Donnybrook.

21. Colonel Godfrey sent to me again to-day; so I dined at the Green Cloth, and we had but eleven at dinner, which is a small number there, the Court being always thin of company till Saturday night.—This new ink and pen make a strange figure; *I must write larger, yes I must, or Stella will not be able to read this*. S. S. S., there is your S's for you, Stella. The maids of honour are bit, and have all contributed their crowns, and are teasing others to subscribe for the book. I will tell Lord Keeper and Lord Treasurer to-morrow; and I believe the Queen will have it. After a little walk this evening, I squandered away the rest of it in sitting at Lewis's lodging, while he and Dr. Arbuthnot played at picquet. I have that foolish pleasure, which I believe nobody has beside me, except old Lady Berkeley. But I fretted when I came away: I will loiter so no more, for I have a plaguy deal of business upon my hands, and very little time to do it. The pamphleteers begin to be very busy against the Ministry: I have begged Mr. Secretary to make examples of one or two of them, and he assures me he will. They are very bold and abusive.

22. This being the day the Ministry come to Windsor, I ate a bit or two at Mr. Lewis's lodgings, because I must sup with Lord Treasurer;

and at half an hour after one, I led Mr. Lewis a walk up the avenue, which is two miles long. We walked in all about five miles; but I was so tired with his slow walking, that I left him here, and walked two miles towards London, hoping to meet Lord Treasurer, and return with him; but it grew darkish, and I was forced to walk back, so I walked nine miles in all; and Lord Treasurer did not come till after eight; which is very wrong, for there was no moon, and I often tell him how ill he does to expose himself so; but he only makes a jest of it. I supped with him, and stayed till now, when it is half an hour after two. He is as merry and careless and disengaged as a young heir at one-and-twenty. 'Tis late indeed.

23. The Secretary did not come last night, but at three this afternoon. I have not seen him yet, but I verily think they are contriving a peace as fast as they can, without which it will be impossible to subsist. The Queen was at church to-day, but was carried in a chair. I and Mr. Lewis dined privately with Mr. Lowman, Clerk of the Kitchen. I was to see Lord Keeper this morning, and told him the jest of the maids of honour; and Lord Treasurer had it last night. That rogue Arbuthnot puts it all upon me. The Court was very full to-day. I expected Lord Treasurer would have invited me to supper; but he only bowed to me; and we had no discourse in the drawing-room. It is now seven at night, and I am at home; and I hope Lord Treasurer will not send for me to supper: if he does not, I will reproach him; and he will pretend to chide me for not coming.—So farewell till I go to bed, for I am going to be busy.—It is now past ten, and I went down to ask the servants about Mr. Secretary: they tell me the Queen is yet at Council, and that she went to supper, and came out to the Council afterwards. It is certain they are managing a peace. I will go to bed, and there is an end.—It is now eleven, and a messenger is come from Lord Treasurer to sup with them; but I have excused myself, and am glad I am in bed; for else I should sit up till two, and drink till I was hot. Now I'll go sleep.

London, 24. I came to town by six with Lord Treasurer, and have stayed till ten. That of the Queen's going out to sup, and coming in again, is a lie, as the Secretary told me this morning; but I find the Ministry are very busy with Mr. Prior, and I believe he will go again to France. I am told so much, that we shall certainly have a peace very soon. I had charming weather all last week at Windsor; but we have had a little rain to-day, and yesterday was windy. Prior's *Journey* sells still; they have sold two thousand, although the town is empty. I found a letter from Mrs. Fenton here, desiring me, in Lady Giffard's name, to come and pass a week at Sheen, while she is at Moor Park. I will answer it with a vengeance: and now you talk of answering, there is MD's N. 20 is yet to be answered: I had put it up so safe, I could hardly find it; but here it is, faith, and I am afraid I cannot send this till Thursday; for I must see the Secretary to-morrow morning, and be in some other place in the evening.

25. Stella writes like an emperor, and gives such an account of her journey, never saw the like. Let me see; stand away, let us compute; you stayed four days at Inish-Corthy, two nights at Mrs. Proby's mother's, and yet was but six days in journey; for your words are, "We left Wexford this day se'ennight, and came here last night." I have heard them say that "travellers may lie by authority." Make up this, if you can. How far is it from Wexford to Dublin? how many miles did you travel in a day? Let me see—thirty pounds in two months is nine score pounds a year; a matter of nothing in Stella's purse! I dreamed Billy Swift was alive, and that I told him you writ me word he was dead, and that you had been at his funeral; and I admired at your impudence, and was in mighty haste to run and let you know what lying rogues you were. Poor lad! he is dead of his mother's former folly and fondness; and yet now I believe, as you say, that her grief will soon wear off.—O yes, Madam Dingley, mightily tired of the company, no doubt of it, at Wexford! And your description of it is excellent; clean sheets, but bare walls; I suppose then you lay upon the walls.— Mrs. Walls has got her tea; but who pays me the money? Come, I shall never get it; so I make a present of it, to stop some gaps, etc. Where's the thanks of the house? So, that's well; why, it cost four-and-thirty shillings English—you must adjust that with Mrs. Walls; I think that is so many pence more with you.—No, Leigh and Sterne, I suppose, were not at the water-side: I fear Sterne's business will not be done; I have not seen him this good while. I hate him, for the management of that box; and I was the greatest fool in nature for trusting to such a young jackanapes; I will speak to him once more about it, when I see him. Mr. Addison and I met once more since, and I supped with him; I believe I told you so somewhere in this letter. The Archbishop chose an admirable messenger in Walls, to send to me; yet I think

him fitter for a messenger than anything.—The D—she has! I did not observe her looks. Will she rot out of modesty with Lady Giffard? I pity poor Jenny—but her husband is a dunce, and with respect to him she loses little by her deafness. I believe, Madam Stella, in your accounts you mistook one liquor for another, and it was an hundred and forty quarts of wine, and thirty-two of water.—This is all written in the morning before I go to the Secretary, as I am now doing. I have answered your letter a little shorter than ordinary; but I have a mind it should go to-day, and I will give you my journal at night in my next; for I'm so afraid of another letter before this goes: I will never have two together again unanswered.—What care I for Dr. Tisdall and Dr. Raymond, or how many children they have! I wish they had a hundred apiece.—Lord Treasurer promises me to answer the bishops' letter to-morrow, and show it me; and I believe it will confirm all I said, and mortify those that threw the merit on the Duke of Ormond; for I have made him jealous of it; and t'other day, talking of the matter, he said, "I am your witness, you got it for them before the Duke was Lord Lieutenant." My humble service to Mrs. Walls, Mrs. Stoyte, and Catherine. Farewell, etc.

What do you do when you see any literal mistakes in my letters? how do you set them right? for I never read them over to correct them. Farewell, again.

Pray send this note to Mrs. Brent, to get the money when Parvisol comes to town, or she can send to him.

Letter XXXI

I dined in the City to-day, and at my return I put my 30th into the post-office; and when I got home I found for me one of the noblest letters I ever read: it was from—, three sides and a half in folio, on a large sheet of paper; the two first pages made up of satire upon London, and crowds and hurry, stolen from some of his own schoolboy's exercises: the side and a half remaining is spent in desiring me to recommend Mrs. South, your Commissioner's widow, to my Lord Treasurer for a pension. He is the prettiest, discreetest fellow that ever my eyes beheld, or that ever dipped pen into ink. I know not what to say to him. A pox on him, I have too many such customers on this side already. I think I will send him word that I never saw my Lord Treasurer in my life: I am sure I industriously avoided the name of any great person when I saw him, for fear of his reporting it in Ireland. And this recommendation must be a secret too, for fear the Duke of Bolton should know it, and think it was too mean. I never read so d—d a letter in my life: a little would make me send it over to you.—I must send you a pattern, the first place I cast my eyes on, I will not pick and choose. *In this place* (meaning the Exchange in London), *which is the compendium of old Troynovant, as that is of the whole busy world, I got such a surfeit, that I grew sick of mankind, and resolved for ever after to bury myself in the shady retreat of*—. You must know that London has been called by some Troynovant, or New Troy. Will you have any more? Yes, one little bit for Stella, because she'll be fond of it. This wondrous theatre (meaning London) was no more to me than a desert, and I should less complain of solitude in a Connaught shipwreck, or even the great bog of Allen. A little scrap for Mrs. Marget, and then I have done. *Their royal fanum, wherein the idol Pecunia is daily worshipped, seemed to me to be just like a hive of bees working and labouring under huge weights of cares.* Fanum is a temple, but he means the Exchange; and Pecunia is money: so now Mrs. Marget will understand her part. One more paragraph, and I— Well, come, don't be in such a rage, you shall have no more. Pray, Stella, be satisfied; 'tis very pretty: and that I must be acquainted with such a dog as this!—Our peace goes on fast. Prior was with the Secretary two hours this morning: I was there a little after he went away, and was told it. I believe he will soon be despatched again to France; and I will put somebody to write an account of his second journey: I hope you have seen the other. This latter has taken up my time with storming at it.

26. Bernage has been with me these two days; yesterday I sent for him to let him know that Dr. Arbuthnot is putting in strongly to have his brother made a captain over Bernage's head. Arbuthnot's brother is but an ensign, but the Doctor has great power with the Queen: yet he told me he would not do anything hard to a gentleman who is my friend; and I have engaged the Secretary and his Colonel for him. To-day he told me very melancholy, that the other had written from Windsor (where he went to solicit) that he has got the company; and Bernage is full of the spleen. I made the Secretary write yesterday a letter to the Colonel in Bernage's behalf. I hope it will do yet; and I have written to Dr. Arbuthnot to Windsor, not to insist on doing such a hardship. I dined in the City at Pontack's, with Stratford; it cost me seven shillings: he would have treated, but I did not let him. I have removed my money from the Bank to another fund. I desire Parvisol may speak to Hawkshaw to pay in my money when he can, for I will put it in the funds; and, in the meantime, borrow so much of Mr. Secretary, who offers to lend it me. Go to the Dean's, sirrahs.

27. Bernage was with me again to-day, and is in great fear, and so was I; but this afternoon, at Lord Treasurer's, where I dined, my brother, George Granville, Secretary at War, after keeping me a while in suspense, told me that Dr. Arbuthnot had waived the business, because he would not wrong a friend of mine; that his brother is to be a lieutenant, and Bernage is made a captain. I called at his lodging, and the soldier's coffee-house, to put him out of pain, but cannot find him; so I have left word, and shall see him to-morrow morning, I suppose. Bernage is now easy; he has ten shillings a day, beside lawful cheating. However, he gives a private sum to his Colonel, but it is very cheap: his Colonel loves him well, but is surprised to see him have so many friends. So he is now quite off my hands. I left the company early to-night, at Lord Treasurer's; but the Secretary followed me, to desire I would go with him to W—. Mr. Lewis's man came in before I could finish that word beginning with a W, which ought to be Windsor, and brought me a very handsome rallying letter from Dr. Arbuthnot, to tell me he had, in compliance to me, given up his brother's pretensions in favour of Bernage, this very morning;

that the Queen had spoken to Mr. Granville to make the company easy in the other's having the captainship. Whether they have done it to oblige me or no, I must own it so. He says he this very morning begged Her Majesty to give Mr. Bernage the company. I am mighty well pleased to have succeeded so well; but you will think me tedious, although you like the man, as I think.

Windsor, 28. I came here a day sooner than ordinary, at Mr. Secretary's desire, and supped with him and Prior, and two private Ministers from France, and a French priest. I know not the two Ministers' names; but they are come about the peace. The names the Secretary called them, I suppose, were feigned; they were good rational men. We have already settled all things with France, and very much to the honour and advantage of England; and the Queen is in mighty good humour. All this news is a mighty secret; the people in general know that a peace is forwarding. The Earl of Strafford is to go soon to Holland, and let them know what we have been doing: and then there will be the devil and all to pay; but we'll make them swallow it with a pox. The French Ministers stayed with us till one, and the Secretary and I sat up talking till two; so you will own 'tis late, sirrahs, and time for your little saucy Presto to go to bed and sleep adazy; and God bless poor little MD: I hope they are now fast asleep, and dreaming of Presto.

29. Lord Treasurer came to-night, as usual, at half an hour after eight, as dark as pitch. I am weary of chiding him; so I commended him for observing his friend's advice, and coming so early, etc. I was two hours with Lady Oglethorpe to-night, and then supped with Lord Treasurer, after dining at the Green Cloth: I stayed till two; this is the effect of Lord Treasurer's being here; I must sup with him; and he keeps cursed hours. Lord Keeper and the Secretary were absent; they cannot sit up with him. This long sitting up makes the periods in my letters so short. I design to stay here all the next week, to be at leisure by myself, to finish something of weight I have upon my hands, and which must soon be done. I shall then think of returning to Ireland, if these people will let me; and I know nothing else they have for me to do. I gave Dr. Arbuthnot my thanks for his kindness to Bernage, whose commission is now signed. Methinks I long to know something of Stella's health, how it continues after Wexford waters.

30. The Queen was not at chapel to-day, and all for the better, for we had a dunce to preach: she has a little of the gout. I dined with my brother Masham, and a moderate company, and would not go to Lord Treasurer's till after supper at eleven o'clock, and pretended I had mistaken the hour; so I ate nothing: and a little after twelve the company broke up, the Keeper and Secretary refusing to stay; so I saved this night's debauch. Prior went away yesterday with his Frenchmen, and a thousand reports are raised in this town. Some said they knew one to be the Abbé de Polignac: others swore it was the Abbé du Bois. The Whigs are in a rage about the peace; but we'll wherret them, I warrant, boys. Go, go, go to the Dean's and don't mind politics, young women, they are not good after the waters; they are stark naught: they strike up into the head. Go, get two black aces, and fish for a manilio.

Oct. 1. Sir John Walter, an honest drunken fellow, is now in waiting, and invited me to the Green Cloth to-day, that he might not be behindhand with Colonel Godfrey, who is a Whig. I was engaged to the Mayor's feast with Mr. Masham; but waiting to take leave of Lord Treasurer, I came too late, and so returned sneaking to the Green Cloth, and did not see my Lord Treasurer neither; but was resolved not to lose two dinners for him. I took leave to-day of my friend and solicitor Lord Rivers, who is commanded by the Queen to set out for Hanover on Thursday. The Secretary does not go to town till to-morrow; he and I, and two friends more, drank a sober bottle of wine here at home, and parted at twelve; he goes by seven to-morrow morning, so I shall not see him. I have power over his cellar in his absence, and make little use of it. Lord Dartmouth and my friend Lewis stay here this week; but I can never work out a dinner from Dartmouth. Masham has promised to provide for me: I squired his lady out of her chaise to-day, and must visit her in a day or two. So you have had a long fit of the finest weather in the world; but I am every day in pain that it will go off. I have done no business to-day; I am very idle.

2. My friend Lewis and I, to avoid over much eating and great tables, dined with honest Jemmy Eckershall, Clerk of the Kitchen, now in waiting, and I bespoke my dinner: but the cur had your acquaintance Lovet, the gentleman porter, to be our company. Lovet, towards the end of dinner, after twenty wrigglings, said he had the honour to see me formerly at Moor Park, and thought he remembered my face. I said I

thought I remembered him, and was glad to see him, etc., and I escaped for that much, for he was very pert. It has rained all this day, and I doubt our good weather is gone. I have been very idle this afternoon, playing at twelvepenny picquet with Lewis: I won seven shillings, which is the only money I won this year: I have not played above four times, and I think always at Windsor. Cards are very dear: there is a duty on them of sixpence a pack, which spoils small gamesters.

3. Mr. Masham sent this morning to desire I would ride out with him, the weather growing again very fine. I was very busy, and sent my excuses; but desired he would provide me a dinner. I dined with him, his lady, and her sister, Mrs. Hill, who invites us to-morrow to dine with her, and we are to ride out in the morning. I sat with Lady Oglethorpe till eight this evening, then was going home to write; looked about for the woman that keeps the key of the house: she told me Patrick had it. I cooled my heels in the cloisters till nine, then went in to the music-meeting, where I had been often desired to go; but was weary in half an hour of their fine stuff, and stole out so privately that everybody saw me; and cooled my heels in the cloisters again till after ten: then came in Patrick. I went up, shut the chamber door, and gave him two or three swinging cuffs on the ear, and I have strained the thumb of my left hand with pulling him, which I did not feel until he was gone. He was plaguily afraid and humbled.

4. It was the finest day in the world, and we got out before eleven, a noble caravan of us. The Duchess of Shrewsbury in her own chaise with one horse, and Miss Touchet with her, Mrs. Masham and Mrs. Scarborow, one of the dressers, in one of the Queen's chaises; Miss Forester and Miss Scarborow, two maids of honour, and Mrs. Hill on horseback. The Duke of Shrewsbury, Mr. Masham, George Fielding, Arbuthnot, and I, on horseback too. Mrs. Hill's horse was hired for Miss Scarborow, but she took it in civility; her own horse was galled and could not be rid, but kicked and winced: the hired horse was not worth eighteenpence. I borrowed coat, boots, and horse, and in short we had all the difficulties, and more than we used to have in making a party from Trim to Longfield's. My coat was light camlet, faced with red velvet, and silver buttons. We rode in the great park and the forest about a dozen miles, and the Duchess and I had much conversation: we got home by two, and Mr. Masham, his lady, Arbuthnot and I, dined

with Mrs. Hill. Arbuthnot made us all melancholy, by some symptoms of bloody u—e: he expects a cruel fit of the stone in twelve hours; he says he is never mistaken, and he appears like a man that was to be racked to-morrow. I cannot but hope it will not be so bad; he is a perfectly honest man, and one I have much obligation to. It rained a little this afternoon, and grew fair again. Lady Oglethorpe sent to speak to me, and it was to let me know that Lady Rochester desires she and I may be better acquainted. 'Tis a little too late; for I am not now in love with Lady Rochester: they shame me out of her, because she is old. Arbuthnot says he hopes my strained thumb is not the gout; for he has often found people so mistaken. I do not remember the particular thing that gave it me, only I had it just after beating Patrick, and now it is better; so I believe he is mistaken.

5. The Duchess of Shrewsbury sent to invite me to dinner; but I was abroad last night when her servant came, and this morning I sent my excuses, because I was engaged, which I was sorry for. Mrs. Forester taxed me yesterday about the *History of the Maids of Honour*; but I told her fairly it was no jest of mine; for I found they did not relish it altogether well; and I have enough already of a quarrel with that brute Sir John Walter, who has been railing at me in all companies ever since I dined with him; that I abused the Queen's meat and drink, and said nothing at the table was good, and all a d—d lie; for after dinner, commending the wine, I said I thought it was something small. You would wonder how all my friends laugh at this quarrel. It will be such a jest for the Keeper, Treasurer, and Secretary.—I dined with honest Colonel Godfrey, took a good walk of an hour on the terrace, and then came up to study; but it grows bloody cold, and I have no waistcoat here.

6. I never dined with the chaplains till to-day; but my friend Gastrell and the Dean of Rochester had often invited me, and I happened to be disengaged: it is the worst provided table at Court. We ate on pewter: every chaplain, when he is made a dean, gives a piece of plate, and so they have got a little, some of it very old. One who was made Dean of Peterborough (a small deanery) said he would give no plate; he was only Dean of Pewterborough. The news of Mr. Hill's miscarriage in his expedition came to-day, and I went to visit Mrs. Masham and Mrs. Hill, his two sisters, to condole with them. I advised them by all means to go

to the music-meeting to-night, to show they were not cast down, etc., and they thought my advice was right, and went. I doubt Mr. Hill and his admiral made wrong steps; however, we lay it all to a storm, etc. I sat with the Secretary at supper; then we both went to Lord Treasurer's supper, and sat till twelve. The Secretary is much mortified about Hill, because this expedition was of his contriving, and he counted much upon it; but Lord Treasurer was just as merry as usual, and old laughing at Sir John Walter and me falling out. I said nothing grieved me but that they would take example, and perhaps presume upon it, and get out of my government; but that I thought I was not obliged to govern bears, though I governed men. They promise to be as obedient as ever, and so we laughed; and so I go to bed; for it is colder still, and you have a fire now, and are at cards at home.

7. Lord Harley and I dined privately to-day with Mrs. Masham and Mrs. Hill, and my brother Masham. I saw Lord Halifax at Court, and we joined and talked; and the Duchess of Shrewsbury came up and reproached me for not dining with her. I said that was not so soon done, for I expected more advances from ladies, especially duchesses: she promised to comply with any demands I pleased; and I agreed to dine with her to-morrow, if I did not go to London too soon, as I believe I shall before dinner. Lady Oglethorpe brought me and the Duchess of Hamilton together to-day in the drawing-room, and I have given her some encouragement, but not much. Everybody has been teasing Walter. He told Lord Treasurer that he took his company from him that were to dine with him: my lord said, "I will send you Dr. Swift:" Lord Keeper bid him take care what he did; "for," said he, "Dr. Swift is not only all our favourite, but our governor." The old company supped with Lord Treasurer, and got away by twelve.

London, 8. I believe I shall go no more to Windsor, for we expect the Queen will come in ten days to Hampton Court. It was frost last night, and cruel cold to-day. I could not dine with the Duchess, for I left Windsor half an hour after one with Lord Treasurer, and we called at Kensington, where Mrs. Masham was got to see her children for two days. I dined, or rather supped, with Lord Treasurer, and stayed till after ten. Tisdall and his family are gone from hence, upon some wrangle with the family. Yesterday I had two letters brought me to Mr. Masham's; one from Ford, and t'other from our little MD, N. 21. I would not tell you till to-day, because I would not. I won't answer it till the next, because I have slipped two days by being at Windsor, which I must recover here. Well, sirrahs, I must go to sleep. The roads were as dry as at midsummer to-day. This letter shall go to-morrow.

9. Morning. It rains hard this morning. I suppose our fair weather is now at an end. I think I'll put on my waistcoat to-day: shall I? Well, I will then, to please MD. I think of dining at home to-day upon a chop and a pot. The town continues yet very thin. Lord Strafford is gone to Holland, to tell them what we have done here toward a peace. We shall soon hear what the Dutch say, and how they take it. My humble service to Mrs. Walls, Mrs. Stoyte, and Catherine.—Morrow, dearest sirrahs, and farewell; and God Almighty bless MD, poor little dear MD, for so I mean, and Presto too. I'll write to you again to-night, that is, I'll begin my next letter. Farewell, etc.

This little bit belongs to MD; we must always write on the margin: you are saucy rogues.

LETTER XXXII

LONDON, *Oct.* 9, 1711

I was forced to lie down at twelve to-day, and mend my night's sleep: I slept till after two, and then sent for a bit of mutton and pot of ale from the next cook's shop, and had no stomach. I went out at four, and called to see Biddy Floyd, which I had not done these three months: she is something marked, but has recovered her complexion quite, and looks very well. Then I sat the evening with Mrs. Vanhomrigh, and drank coffee, and ate an egg. I likewise took a new lodging to-day, not liking a ground-floor, nor the ill smell, and other circumstances. I lodge, or shall lodge, by Leicester Fields, and pay ten shillings a week; that won't hold out long, faith. I shall lie here but one night more. It rained terribly till one o'clock to-day. I lie, for I shall lie here two nights, till Thursday, and then remove. Did I tell you that my friend Mrs. Barton has a brother drowned, that went on the expedition with Jack Hill? He was a lieutenant-colonel, and a coxcomb; and she keeps her chamber in form, and the servants say she receives no messages.—Answer MD's letter, Presto, d'ye hear? No, says Presto, I won't yet, I'm busy; you're a saucy rogue. Who talks?

10. It cost me two shillings in coach-hire to dine in the City with a printer. I have sent, and caused to be sent, three pamphlets out in a fortnight. I will ply the rogues warm; and whenever anything of theirs makes a noise, it shall have an answer. I have instructed an under spur-leather to write so, that it is taken for mine. A rogue that writes a newspaper, called *The Protestant Postboy*, has reflected on me in one of his papers; but the Secretary has taken him up, and he shall have a squeeze extraordinary. He says that an ambitious tantivy, missing of his towering hopes of preferment in Ireland, is come over to vent his spleen on the late Ministry, etc. I'll tantivy him with a vengeance. I sat the evening at home, and am very busy, and can hardly find time to write, unless it were to MD. I am in furious haste.

11. I dined to-day with Lord Treasurer. Thursdays are now his days when his choice company comes, but we are too much multiplied. George Granville sent his excuses upon being ill; I hear he apprehends the apoplexy, which would grieve me much. Lord Treasurer calls Prior

nothing but Monsieur Baudrier, which was the feigned name of the Frenchman that writ his *Journey to Paris*. They pretend to suspect me, so I talk freely of it, and put them out of their play. Lord Treasurer calls me now Dr. Martin, because martin is a sort of a swallow, and so is a swift. When he and I came last Monday from Windsor, we were reading all the signs on the road. He is a pure trifler; tell the Bishop of Clogher so. I made him make two lines in verse for the Bell and Dragon, and they were rare bad ones. I suppose Dilly is with you by this time: what could his reason be of leaving London, and not owning it? 'Twas plaguy silly. I believe his natural inconstancy made him weary. I think he is the king of inconstancy. I stayed with Lord Treasurer till ten; we had five lords and three commoners. Go to ombre, sirrahs.

12. Mrs. Vanhomrigh has changed her lodging as well as I. She found she had got with a bawd, and removed. I dined with her to-day; for though she boards, her landlady does not dine with her. I am grown a mighty lover of herrings; but they are much smaller here than with you. In the afternoon I visited an old major-general, and ate six oysters; then sat an hour with Mrs. Colledge, the joiner's daughter that was hanged; it was the joiner was hanged, and not his daughter; with Thompson's wife, a magistrate. There was the famous Mrs. Floyd of Chester, who, I think, is the handsomest woman (except MD) that ever I saw. She told me that twenty people had sent her the verses upon Biddy, as meant to her: and, indeed, in point of handsomeness, she deserves them much better. I will not go to Windsor to-morrow, and so I told the Secretary to-day. I hate the thoughts of Saturday and Sunday suppers with Lord Treasurer. Jack Hill is come home from his unfortunate expedition, and is, I think, now at Windsor: I have not yet seen him. He is privately blamed by his own friends for want of conduct. He called a council of war, and therein it was determined to come back. But they say a general should not do that, because the officers will always give their opinion for returning, since the blame will not lie upon them, but the general. I pity him heartily. Bernage received his commission to-day.

13. I dined to-day with Colonel Crowe, late Governor of Barbadoes; he is a great acquaintance of your friend Sterne, to whom I trusted the box. Lord Treasurer has refused Sterne's business, and I doubt he is a rake; Jemmy Leigh stays for him, and nobody knows where to find him.

I am so busy now I have hardly time to spare to write to our little MD, but in a fortnight I hope it will be over. I am going now to be busy, etc.

14. I was going to dine with Dr. Cockburn, but Sir Andrew Fountaine met me, and carried me to Mrs. Van's, where I drank the last bottle of Raymond's wine, admirable good, better than any I get among the Ministry. I must pick up time to answer this letter of MD's; I'll do it in a day or two for certain.—I am glad I am not at Windsor, for it is very cold, and I won't have a fire till November. I am contriving how to stop up my grate with bricks. Patrick was drunk last night; but did not come to me, else I should have given him t'other cuff. I sat this evening with Mrs. Barton; it is the first day of her seeing company; but I made her merry enough, and we were three hours disputing upon Whig and Tory. She grieved for her brother only for form, and he was a sad dog. Is Stella well enough to go to church, pray? no numbings left? no darkness in your eyes? do you walk and exercise? Your exercise is ombre.—People are coming up to town: the Queen will be at Hampton Court in a week. Lady Betty Germaine, I hear, is come; and Lord Pembroke is coming: his wife is as big with child as she can tumble.

15. I sat at home till four this afternoon to-day writing, and ate a roll and butter; then visited Will Congreve an hour or two, and supped with Lord Treasurer, who came from Windsor to-day, and brought Prior with him. The Queen has thanked Prior for his good service in France, and promised to make him a Commissioner of the Customs. Several of that Commission are to be out; among the rest, my friend Sir Matthew Dudley. I can do nothing for him, he is so hated by the Ministry. Lord Treasurer kept me till twelve, so I need not tell you it is now late.

16. I dined to-day with Mr. Secretary at Dr. Coatesworth's, where he now lodges till his house be got ready in Golden Square. One Boyer, a French dog, has abused me in a pamphlet, and I have got him up in a messenger's hands: the Secretary promises me to swinge him. Lord Treasurer told me last night that he had the honour to be abused with me in a pamphlet. I must make that rogue an example, for warning to others. I was to see Jack Hill this morning, who made that unfortunate expedition; and there is still more misfortune; for that ship, which was admiral of his fleet, is blown up in the Thames, by an accident

and carelessness of some rogue, who was going, as they think, to steal some gunpowder: five hundred men are lost. We don't yet know the particulars. I am got home by seven, and am going to be busy, and you are going to play and supper; you live ten times happier than I; but I should live ten times happier than you if I were with MD. I saw Jemmy Leigh to-day in the street, who tells me that Sterne has not lain above once these three weeks in his lodgings, and he doubts he takes ill courses; he stays only till he can find Sterne to go along with him, and he cannot hear of him. I begged him to inquire about the box when he comes to Chester, which he promises.

17. The Secretary and I dined to-day with Brigadier Britton, a great friend of his. The lady of the house is very gallant, about thirty-five; she is said to have a great deal of wit; but I see nothing among any of them that equals MD by a bar's length, as hope saved. My Lord Treasurer is much out of order; he has a sore throat, and the gravel, and a pain in his breast where the wound was: pray God preserve him. The Queen comes to Hampton Court on Tuesday next; people are coming fast to town, and I must answer MD's letter, which I can hardly find time to do, though I am at home the greatest part of the day. Lady Betty Germaine and I were disputing Whig and Tory to death this morning. She is grown very fat, and looks mighty well. Biddy Floyd was there, and she is, I think, very much spoiled with the smallpox.

18. Lord Treasurer is still out of order, and that breaks our method of dining there to-day. He is often subject to a sore throat, and some time or other it will kill him, unless he takes more care than he is apt to do. It was said about the town that poor Lord Peterborow was dead at Frankfort; but he is something better, and the Queen is sending him to Italy, where I hope the warm climate will recover him: he has abundance of excellent qualities, and we love one another mightily. I was this afternoon in the City, ate a bit of meat, and settled some things with a printer. I will answer your letter on Saturday, if possible, and then send away this; so to fetch up the odd days I lost at Windsor, and keep constant to my fortnight. Ombre time is now coming on, and we shall have nothing but Manley, and Walls, and Stoytes, and the Dean. Have you got no new acquaintance? Poor girls; nobody knows MD's good qualities.—'Tis very cold; but I will not have a fire till November, that's pozz.—Well, but coming home to-night, I found on my table a letter

from MD; faith, I was angry, that is, with myself; and I was afraid too to see MD's hand so soon, for fear of something, I don't know what: at last I opened it, and it was over well, and a bill for the two hundred guineas. However, 'tis a sad thing that this letter is not gone, nor your twenty-first answered yet.

19. I was invited to-day to dine with Mrs. Van, with some company who did not come; but I ate nothing but herrings; you must know I hardly ever eat of above one thing, and that the plainest ordinary meat at table; I love it best, and believe it wholesomest. You love rarities; yes you do; I wish you had all that I ever see where I go. I was coming home early, and met the Secretary in his chair, who persuaded me to go with him to Britton's; for he said he had been all day at business, and had eaten nothing. So I went, and the time passed so, that we stayed till two, so you may believe 'tis late enough.

20. This day has gone all wrong, by sitting up so late last night. Lord Treasurer is not yet well, and can't go to Windsor. I dined with Sir Matthew Dudley, and took occasion to hint to him that he would lose his employment, for which I am very sorry. Lord Pembroke and his family are all come to town. I was kept so long at a friend's this evening that I cannot send this to-night. When I knocked at my lodgings, a fellow asked me where lodged Dr. Swift? I told him I was the person: he gave me a letter he brought from the Secretary's office, and I gave him a shilling: when I came up, I saw Dingley's hand: faith, I was afraid, I do not know what. At last it was a formal letter, from Dingley about her exchequer business. Well, I'll do it on Monday, and settle it with Tooke. And now, boys, for your letter, I mean the first, N. 21. Let's see; come out, little letter. I never had the letter from the Bishop that Raymond mentions; but I have written to Ned Southwell, to desire the Duke of Ormond to speak to his reverence, that he may leave off his impertinence. What a pox can they think I am doing for the Archbishop here? You have a pretty notion of me in Ireland, to make me an agent for the Archbishop of Dublin.—Why! do you think I value your people's ingratitude about my part in serving them? I remit them their first-fruits of ingratitude, as freely as I got the other remitted to them. The Lord Treasurer defers writing his letter to them, or else they would be plaguily confounded by this time. For he designs to give the merit of it wholly to the Queen and me, and to let them know it was done before

the Duke of Ormond was Lord Lieutenant. You visit, you dine abroad, you see friends; you pilgarlick; you walk from Finglas, you a cat's foot. O Lord—Lady Gore hung her child by the *waist*; what is that waist? I don't understand that word; he must hang on till you explain or spell it.—I don't believe he was pretty, that's a liiii.—Pish! burn your First-Fruits; again at it. Stella has made twenty false spellings in her writing; I'll send them to you all back again on the other side of this letter, to mend them; I won't miss one. Why, I think there were seventeen bishops' names to the letter Lord Oxford received.—I will send you some pamphlets by Leigh; put me in mind of it on Monday, for I shall go then to the printer; yes, and the *Miscellany*. I am mightily obliged to Walls, but I don't deserve it by any usage of him here, having seen him but twice, and once en passant. Mrs. Manley forsworn ombre! What! and no blazing star appear? no monsters born? no whale thrown up? have you not found out some evasion for her? She had no such regard to oaths in her younger days. I got the books for nothing, Madam Dingley; but the wine I got not; it was but a promise.—Yes, my head is pretty well in the main, only now and then a little threatening or so.—You talk of my reconciling some great folks. I tell you what. The Secretary told me last night that he had found the reason why the Queen was cold to him for some months past; that a friend had told it him yesterday; and it was, that they suspected he was at the bottom with the Duke of Marlborough. Then he said he had reflected upon all I had spoken to him long ago, but he thought it had only been my suspicion, and my zeal and kindness for him. I said I had reason to take that very ill, to imagine I knew so little of the world as to talk at a venture to a great Minister; that I had gone between him and Lord Treasurer often, and told each of them what I had said to the other, and that I had informed him so before. He said all that you may imagine to excuse himself, and approve my conduct. I told him I knew all along that this proceeding of mine was the surest way to send me back to my willows in Ireland, but that I regarded it not, provided I could do the kingdom service in keeping them well together. I minded him how often I had told Lord Treasurer, Lord Keeper, and him together, that all things depended on their union, and that my comfort was to see them love one another; and I had told them all singly that I had not said this by chance, etc. He was in a rage to be thus suspected; swears he will be upon a better foot, or none at all; and I do not see how they can well want him in this juncture. I hope to find a way of settling this matter. I act an honest part, that will bring me neither honour nor praise. MD must think the better of me for it: nobody else shall ever know of it. Here's politics enough for once; but Madam DD gave me occasion for it. I think I told you I have got into lodgings that don't smell ill—O Lord! the spectacles: well, I'll do that on Monday too; although it goes against me to be employed for folks that neither you nor I care a groat for. Is the eight pounds from Hawkshaw included in the thirty-nine pounds five shillings and twopence? How do I know by this how my account stands? Can't you write five or six lines to cast it up? Mine is forty-four pounds per annum, and eight pounds from Hawkshaw makes fifty-two pounds. Pray set it right, and let me know; you had best.—And so now I have answered N. 21, and 'tis late, and I will answer N. 22 in my next: this cannot go to-night, but shall on Tuesday: and so go to your play, and lose your money, with your two eggs a penny; silly jade; you witty? very pretty.

21. Mrs. Van would have me dine with her again to-day, and so I did, though Lady Mountjoy has sent two or three times to have me see and dine with her, and she is a little body I love very well. My head has ached a little in the evenings these three or four days, but it is not of the giddy sort, so I do not much value it. I was to see Lord Harley to-day, but Lord Treasurer took physic; and I could not see him. He has voided much gravel, and is better, but not well: he talks of going on Tuesday to see the Queen at Hampton Court; I wish he may be able. I never saw so fine a summer day as this was: how is it with you, pray? and can't you remember, naughty packs? I han't seen Lord Pembroke yet. He will be sorry to miss Dilly: I wonder you say nothing of Dilly's being got to Ireland; if he be not there soon, I shall have some certain odd thoughts: guess them if you can.

22. I dined in the City to-day with Dr. Freind, at one of my printers: I inquired for Leigh, but could not find him: I have forgot what sort of apron you want. I must rout among your letters, a needle in a bottle of hay. I gave Sterne directions, but where to find him Lord knows. I have bespoken the spectacles; got a set of *Examiners*, and five pamphlets, which I have either written or contributed to, except the best, which is the *Vindication of the Duke of Marlborough*, and is entirely of the author of the *Atalantis*. I have settled Dingley's affair with Tooke, who has undertaken it, and understands it. I have bespoken a *Miscellany*: what would you have me do more? It cost me a shilling coming home; it

rains terribly, and did so in the morning. Lord Treasurer has had an ill day, in much pain. He writes and does business in his chamber now he is ill: the man is bewitched: he desires to see me, and I'll maul him, but he will not value it a rush. I am half weary of them all. I often burst out into these thoughts, and will certainly steal away as soon as I decently can. I have many friends, and many enemies; and the last are more constant in their nature. I have no shuddering at all to think of retiring to my old circumstances, if you can be easy; but I will always live in Ireland as I did the last time; I will not hunt for dinners there, nor converse with more than a very few.

23. Morning. This goes to-day, and shall be sealed by and by. Lord Treasurer takes physic again to-day: I believe I shall dine with Lord Dupplin. Mr. Tooke brought me a letter directed for me at Morphew's the bookseller. I suppose, by the postage, it came from Ireland. It is a woman's hand, and seems false spelt on purpose: it is in such sort of verse as Harris's petition; rallies me for writing merry things, and not upon divinity; and is like the subject of the Archbishop's last letter, as I told you. Can you guess whom it came from? It is not ill written; pray find it out. There is a Latin verse at the end of it all rightly spelt; yet the English, as I think, affectedly wrong in many places. My plaguing time is coming. A young fellow brought me a letter from Judge Coote, with recommendation to be lieutenant of a man-of-war. He is the son of one Echlin, who was minister of Belfast before Tisdall, and I have got some other new customers; but I shall trouble my friends as little as possible. Saucy Stella used to jeer me for meddling with other folks' affairs; but now I am punished for it.—Patrick has brought the candle, and I have no more room. Farewell, etc. etc.

Here is a full and true account of Stella's new spelling:—

Plaguely,	Plaguily.
Dineing,	Dining.
Straingers,	Strangers.
Chais,	Chase.
Waist,	Wast.
Houer,	Hour.
Immagin,	Imagine.
A bout,	About.
Intellegence,	Intelligence.

Merrit,	Merit.
Aboundance,	Abundance.
Secreet,	Secret.
Phamphlets,	Pamphlets.
Bussiness,	Business.

Tell me truly, sirrah, how many of these are mistakes of the pen, and how many are you to answer for as real ill spelling? There are but fourteen; I said twenty by guess. You must not be angry, for I will have you spell right, let the world go how it will. Though, after all, there is but a mistake of one letter in any of these words. I allow you henceforth but six false spellings in every letter you send me.

Letter XXXIII

I dined with Lord Dupplin as I told you I would, and put my thirty-second into the post-office my own self; and I believe there has not been one moment since we parted wherein a letter was not upon the road going or coming to or from PMD. If the Queen knew it, she would give us a pension; for it is we bring good luck to their post-boys and their packets; else they would break their necks and sink. But, an old saying and a true one:

> *Be it snow, or storm, or hail,*
> *PMD's letters never fail;*
> *Cross winds may sometimes make them tarry,*
> *But PMD's letters can't miscarry.*

Terrible rain to-day, but it cleared up at night enough to save my twelvepence coming home. Lord Treasurer is much better this evening. I hate to have him ill, he is so confoundedly careless. I won't answer your letter yet, so be satisfied.

24. I called at Lord Treasurer's to-day at noon: he was eating some broth in his bed-chamber, undressed, with a thousand papers about him. He has a little fever upon him, and his eye terribly bloodshot; yet he dressed himself and went out to the Treasury. He told me he had a letter from a lady with a complaint against me; it was from Mrs. Cutts, a sister of Lord Cutts, who writ to him that I had abused her brother: you remember the "Salamander," it is printed in the *Miscellany*. I told my lord that I would never regard complaints, and that I expected, whenever he received any against me, he would immediately put them into the fire, and forget them, else I should have no quiet. I had a little turn in my head this morning; which, though it did not last above a moment, yet being of the true sort, has made me as weak as a dog all this day. 'Tis the first I have had this half-year. I shall take my pills if I hear of it again. I dined at Lady Mountjoy's with Harry Coote, and went to see Lord Pembroke upon his coming to town.—The Whig party are furious against a peace, and every day some ballad comes out reflecting on the Ministry on that

account. The Secretary St. John has seized on a dozen booksellers and publishers into his messengers' hands. Some of the foreign Ministers have published the preliminaries agreed on here between France and England; and people rail at them as insufficient to treat a peace upon; but the secret is, that the French have agreed to articles much more important, which our Ministers have not communicated, and the people, who think they know all, are discontented that there is no more. This was an inconvenience I foretold to the Secretary, but we could contrive no way to fence against it. So there's politics for you.

25. The Queen is at Hampton Court: she went on Tuesday in that terrible rain. I dined with Lewis at his lodgings, to despatch some business we had. I sent this morning and evening to Lord Treasurer, and he is much worse by going out; I am in pain about evening. He has sent for Dr. Radcliffe; pray God preserve him. The Chancellor of the Exchequer showed me to-day a ballad in manuscript against Lord Treasurer and his South Sea project; it is very sharply written: if it be not printed, I will send it you. If it be, it shall go in your packet of pamphlets.—I found out your letter about directions for the apron, and have ordered to be bought a cheap green silk work apron; I have it by heart. I sat this evening with Mrs. Barton, who is my near neighbour. It was a delicious day, and I got my walk, and was thinking whether MD was walking too just at that time that Presto was. This paper does not cost me a farthing, I have it from the Secretary's office. I long till to-morrow to know how my Lord Treasurer sleeps this night, and to hear he mends: we are all undone without him; so pray for him, sirrahs, and don't stay too late at the Dean's.

26. I dined with Mrs. Van; for the weather is so bad, and I am so busy, that I can't dine with great folks: and besides I dare eat but little, to keep my head in order, which is better. Lord Treasurer is very ill, but I hope in no danger. We have no quiet with the Whigs, they are so violent against a peace; but I'll cool them, with a vengeance, very soon. I have not heard from the Bishop of Clogher, whether he has got his statues. I writ to him six weeks ago; he's so busy with his Parliament. I won't answer your letter yet, say what you will, saucy girls.

27. I forgot to go about some business this morning, which cost me double the time; and I was forced to be at the Secretary's office till four,

and lose my dinner; so I went to Mrs. Van's, and made them get me three herrings, which I am very fond of, and they are a light victuals: besides, I was to have supped at Lady Ashburnham's; but the drab did not call for us in her coach, as she promised, but sent for us, and so I sent my excuses. It has been a terrible rainy day, but so flattering in the morning, that I would needs go out in my new hat. I met Leigh and Sterne as I was going into the Park. Leigh says he will go to Ireland in ten days, if he can get Sterne to go with him; so I will send him the things for MD, and I have desired him to inquire about the box. I hate that Sterne for his carelessness about it; but it was my fault.

29. I was all this terrible rainy day with my friend Lewis upon business of importance; and I dined with him, and came home about seven, and thought I would amuse myself a little, after the pains I had taken. I saw a volume of Congreve's plays in my room, that Patrick had taken to read; and I looked into it, and in mere loitering read in it till twelve, like an owl and a fool: if ever I do so again; never saw the like. Count Gallas, the Emperor's Envoy, you will hear, is in disgrace with us: the Queen has ordered her Ministers to have no more commerce with him; the reason is, the fool writ a rude letter to Lord Dartmouth, Secretary of State, complaining of our proceedings about a peace; and he is always in close confidence with Lord Wharton and Sunderland, and others of the late Ministry. I believe you begin to think there will be no peace; the Whigs here are sure it cannot be, and stocks are fallen again. But I am confident there will, unless France plays us tricks; and you may venture a wager with any of your Whig acquaintance that we shall not have another campaign. You will get more by it than by ombre, sirrah.—I let slip telling you yesterday's journal, which I thought to have done this morning, but blundered. I dined yesterday at Harry Coote's, with Lord Hatton, Mr. Finch, a son of Lord Nottingham, and Sir Andrew Fountaine. I left them soon, but hear they stayed till two in the morning, and were all drunk: and so good-night for last night, and good-night for to-night. You blundering goosecap, an't you ashamed to blunder to young ladies? I shall have a fire in three or four days now, oh ho.

30. I was to-day in the City concerting some things with a printer, and am to be to-morrow all day busy with Mr. Secretary about the same. I won't tell you now; but the Ministers reckon it will do abundance of good, and open the eyes of the nation, who are half bewitched against

a peace. Few of this generation can remember anything but war and taxes, and they think it is as it should be; whereas 'tis certain we are the most undone people in Europe, as I am afraid I shall make appear beyond all contradiction. But I forgot; I won't tell you what I will do, nor what I will not do: so let me alone, and go to Stoyte, and give Goody Stoyte and Catherine my humble service; I love Goody Stoyte better than Goody Walls. Who'll pay me for this green apron? I will have the money; it cost ten shillings and sixpence. I think it plaguy dear for a cheap thing; but they said that English silk would cockle, and I know not what. You have the making into the bargain. 'Tis right Italian: I have sent it and the pamphlets to Leigh, and will send the *Miscellanies* and spectacles in a day or two. I would send more; but, faith, I'm plaguy poor at present.

31. The devil's in this Secretary: when I went this morning he had people with him; but says he, "we are to dine with Prior to-day, and then will do all our business in the afternoon": at two, Prior sends word he is otherwise engaged; then the Secretary and I go and dine with Brigadier Britton, sit till eight, grow merry, no business done; he is in haste to see Lady Jersey; we part, and appoint no time to meet again. This is the fault of all the present Ministers, teasing me to death for my assistance, laying the whole weight of their affairs upon it, yet slipping opportunities. Lord Treasurer mends every day, though slowly: I hope he will take care of himself. Pray, will you send to Parvisol to send me a bill of twenty pounds as soon as he can, for I want money. I must have money; I will have money, sirrahs.

Nov. 1. I went to-day into the City to settle some business with Stratford, and to dine with him; but he was engaged, and I was so angry I would not dine with any other merchant, but went to my printer, and ate a bit, and did business of mischief with him, and I shall have the spectacles and *Miscellany* to-morrow, and leave them with Leigh. A fine day always makes me go into the City, if I can spare time, because it is exercise; and that does me more good than anything. I have heard nothing since of my head, but a little, I don't know how, sometimes: but I am very temperate, especially now the Treasurer is ill, and the Ministers often at Hampton Court, and the Secretary not yet fixed in his house, and I hate dining with many of my old acquaintance. Here has been a fellow discovered going out of the East India House with sixteen thousand pounds in money and bills; he would have escaped, if he had not been so uneasy with thirst, that he stole out before his time, and was caught. But what is that to MD? I wish we had the money, provided the East India Company was never the worse; you know we must not covet, etc. Our weather, for this fortnight past, is chequered, a fair and a rainy day: this was very fine, and I have walked four miles; wish MD would do so, lazy sluttikins.

2. It has rained all day with a continuendo, and I went in a chair to dine with Mrs. Van; always there in a very rainy day. But I made a shift to come back afoot. I live a very retired life, pay very few visits, and keep but very little company; I read no newspapers. I am sorry I sent you the *Examiner*, for the printer is going to print them in a small volume: it seems the author is too proud to have them printed by subscription, though his friends offered, they say, to make it worth five hundred pounds to him. The *Spectators* are likewise printing in a larger and a smaller volume, so I believe they are going to leave them off, and indeed people grow weary of them, though they are often prettily written. We have had no news for me to send you now towards the end of my letter. The Queen has the gout a little: I hoped the Lord Treasurer would have had it too, but Radcliffe told me yesterday it was the rheumatism in his knee and foot; however, he mends, and I hope will be abroad in a short time. I am told they design giving away several employments before the Parliament sits, which will be the thirteenth instant. I either do not like, or not understand this policy; and if Lord Treasurer does not mend soon, they must give them just before the session. But he is the greatest procrastinator in the world.

3. A fine day this, and I walked a pretty deal. I stuffed the Secretary's pockets with papers, which he must read and settle at Hampton Court, where he went to-day, and stays some time. They have no lodgings for me there, so I can't go, for the town is small, chargeable, and inconvenient. Lord Treasurer had a very ill night last night, with much pain in his knee and foot, but is easier to-day.—And so I went to visit Prior about some business, and so he was not within, and so Sir Andrew Fountaine made me dine to-day again with Mrs. Van, and I came home soon, remembering this must go to-night, and that I had a letter of MD's to answer. O Lord, where is it? let me see; so, so, here it is. You grudge writing so soon. Pox on that bill! the woman would have me

manage that money for her. I do not know what to do with it now I have it: I am like the unprofitable steward in the Gospel: I laid it up in a napkin; there thou hast what is thine own, etc. Well, well, I know of your new Mayor. (I'll tell you a pun: a fishmonger owed a man two crowns; so he sent him a piece of bad ling and a tench, and then said he was paid: how is that now? find it out; for I won't tell it you: which of you finds it out?) Well, but as I was saying, what care I for your Mayor? I fancy Ford may tell Forbes right about my returning to Ireland before Christmas, or soon after. I'm sorry you did not go on with your story about Pray God you be John; I never heard it in my life, and wonder what it can be.—Ah, Stella, faith, you leaned upon your Bible to think what to say when you writ that. Yes, that story of the Secretary's making me an example is true; "never heard it before;" why, how could you hear it? is it possible to tell you the hundredth part of what passes in our companies here? The Secretary is as easy with me as Mr. Addison was. I have often thought what a splutter Sir William Temple makes about being Secretary of State: I think Mr. St. John the greatest young man I ever knew; wit, capacity, beauty, quickness of apprehension, good learning, and an excellent taste; the best orator in the House of Commons, admirable conversation, good nature, and good manners; generous, and a despiser of money. His only fault is talking to his friends in way of complaint of too great a load of business, which looks a little like affectation; and he endeavours too much to mix the fine gentleman and man of pleasure with the man of business. What truth and sincerity he may have I know not: he is now but thirty-two, and has been Secretary above a year. Is not all this extraordinary? how he stands with the Queen and Lord Treasurer I have told you before. This is his character; and I believe you will be diverted by knowing it. I writ to the Archbishop of Dublin, Bishop of Cloyne and of Clogher together, five weeks ago from Windsor: I hope they had my letters; pray know if Clogher had his.—Fig for your physician and his advice, Madam Dingley: if I grow worse, I will; otherwise I will trust to temperance and exercise: your fall of the leaf; what care I when the leaves fall? I am sorry to see them fall with all my heart; but why should I take physic because leaves fall off from trees? that won't hinder them from falling. If a man falls from a horse, must I take physic for that?—This arguing makes you mad; but it is true right reason, not to be disproved.—I am glad at heart to hear poor Stella is better; use exercise and walk, spend pattens and spare potions, wear out clogs and waste claret. Have you found out my pun of the fishmonger? don't read a word more till you have got it. And Stella is handsome again, you say? and is she fat? I have sent to Leigh the set of *Examiners*: the first thirteen were written by several hands, some good, some bad; the next three-and-thirty were all by one hand, that makes forty-six: then that author, whoever he was, laid it down on purpose to confound guessers; and the last six were written by a woman. Then there is an account of Guiscard by the same woman, but the facts sent by Presto. Then an answer to the letter to the Lords about Gregg by Presto; Prior's *Journey* by Presto; *Vindication of the Duke of Marlborough*, entirely by the same woman; Comment on Hare's Sermon by the same woman, only hints sent to the printer from Presto to give her. Then there's the *Miscellany*, an apron for Stella, a pound of chocolate, without sugar, for Stella, a fine snuff-rasp of ivory, given me by Mrs. St. John for Dingley, and a large roll of tobacco, which she must hide or cut shorter out of modesty, and four pair of spectacles for the Lord knows who. There's the cargo, I hope it will come safe. Oh, Mrs. Masham and I are very well; we write to one another, but it is upon business; I believe I told you so before: pray pardon my forgetfulness in these cases; poor Presto can't help it. MD shall have the money as soon as Tooke gets it. And so I think I have answered all, and the paper is out, and now I have fetched up my week, and will send you another this day fortnight.—Why, you rogues, two crowns make *tench-ill-ling*: you are so dull you could never have found it out. Farewell, etc. etc.

LETTER XXXIV

LONDON, *Nov.* 3, 1711

My thirty-third lies now before me just finished, and I am going to seal
and send it, so let me know whether you would have me add anything:
I gave you my journal of this day; and it is now nine at night, and I am
going to be busy for an hour or two.

4. I left a friend's house to-day where I was invited, just when dinner
was setting on, and pretended I was engaged, because I saw some
fellows I did not know; and went to Sir Matthew Dudley's, where I
had the same inconvenience, but he would not let me go; otherwise
I would have gone home, and sent for a slice of mutton and a pot of
ale, rather than dine with persons unknown, as bad, for aught I know,
as your deans, parsons, and curates. Bad slabby weather to-day.—Now
methinks I write at ease, when I have no letter of MD's to answer. But
I mistook, and have got the large paper. The Queen is laid up with the
gout at Hampton Court: she is now seldom without it any long time
together; I fear it will wear her out in a very few years. I plainly find I
have less twitchings about my toes since these Ministers are sick and
out of town, and that I don't dine with them. I would compound for a
light easy gout to be perfectly well in my head.—Pray walk when the
frost comes, young ladies go a frost-biting. It comes into my head, that,
from the very time you first went to Ireland, I have been always plying
you to walk and read. The young fellows here have begun a kind of
fashion to walk, and many of them have got swingeing strong shoes on
purpose; it has got as far as several young lords; if it hold, it would be a
very good thing. Lady Lucy and I are fallen out; she rails at me, and I
have left visiting her.

5. MD was very troublesome to me last night in my sleep; I was a
dreamed, methought, that Stella was here. I asked her after Dingley,
and she said she had left her in Ireland, because she designed her stay
to be short, and such stuff.—Monsieur Pontchartain, the Secretary of
State in France, and Monsieur Fontenelle, the Secretary of the Royal
Academy there (who writ the *Dialogues des Morts*, etc.), have sent letters
to Lord Pembroke that the Academy have, with the King's consent,
chosen him one of their members in the room of one who is lately dead.

But the cautious gentleman has given me the letters to show my Lord Dartmouth and Mr. St. John, our two Secretaries, and let them see there is no treason in them; which I will do on Wednesday, when they come from Hampton Court. The letters are very handsome, and it is a very great mark of honour and distinction to Lord Pembroke. I hear the two French Ministers are come over again about the peace; but I have seen nobody of consequence to know the truth. I dined to-day with a lady of my acquaintance, who was sick, in her bed-chamber, upon three herrings and a chicken: the dinner was my bespeaking. We begin now to have chestnuts and Seville oranges; have you the latter yet? 'Twas a terrible windy day, and we had processions in carts of the Pope and the Devil, and the butchers rang their cleavers. You know this is the Fifth of November, Popery and gunpowder.

6. Since I am used to this way of writing, I fancy I could hardly make out a long letter to MD without it. I think I ought to allow for every line taken up by telling you where I dined; but that will not be above seven lines in all, half a line to a dinner. Your Ingoldsby is going over, and they say here he is to be made a lord.—Here was I staying in my room till two this afternoon for that puppy Sir Andrew Fountaine, who was to go with me into the City, and never came; and if I had not shot a dinner flying, with one Mr. Murray, I might have fasted, or gone to an alehouse.—You never said one word of Goody Stoyte in your letter; but I suppose these winter nights we shall hear more of her. Does the Provost laugh as much as he used to do? We reckon him here a good-for-nothing fellow.—I design to write to your Dean one of these days, but I can never find time, nor what to say.—I will think of something: but if DD were not in Ireland I believe seriously I should not think of the place twice a year. Nothing there ever makes the subject of talk in any company where I am.

7. I went to-day to the City on business; but stopped at a printer's, and stayed there: it was a most delicious day. I hear the Parliament is to be prorogued for a fortnight longer; I suppose, either because the Queen has the gout, or that Lord Treasurer is not well, or that they would do something more towards a peace. I called at Lord Treasurer's at noon, and sat a while with Lord Harley, but his father was asleep. A bookseller has reprinted or new-titled a sermon of Tom Swift's, printed last year, and publishes an advertisement calling it *Dr. Swift's Sermon.*

Some friend of Lord Galway has, by his directions, published a four-shilling book about his conduct in Spain, to defend him; I have but just seen it. But what care you for books, except Presto's *Miscellanies*? Leigh promised to call and see me, but has not yet; I hope he will take care of his cargo, and get your Chester box. A murrain take that box! everything is spoiled that is in it. How does the strong box do? You say nothing of Raymond: is his wife brought to bed again; or how? has he finished his house; paid his debts; and put out the rest of the money to use? I am glad to hear poor Joe is like to get his two hundred pounds. I suppose Trim is now reduced to slavery again. I am glad of it; the people were as great rascals as the gentlemen. But I must go to bed, sirrahs: the Secretary is still at Hampton Court with my papers, or is come only to-night. They plague me with attending them.

8. I was with the Secretary this morning, and we dined with Prior, and did business this afternoon till about eight; and I must alter and undo, and a clutter. I am glad the Parliament is prorogued. I stayed with Prior till eleven; the Secretary left us at eight. Prior, I believe, will be one of those employed to make the peace, when a Congress is opened. Lord Ashburnham told to-day at the Coffee-house that Lord Harley was yesterday morning married to the Duke of Newcastle's daughter, the great heiress, and it got about all the town. But I saw Lord Harley yesterday at noon in his nightgown, and he dined in the City with Prior and others; so it is not true; but I hope it will be so; for I know it has been privately managing this long time: the lady will not have half her father's estate; for the Duke left Lord Pelham's son his heir. The widow Duchess will not stand to the will, and she is now at law with Pelham. However, at worst, the girl will have about ten thousand pounds a year to support the honour; for Lord Treasurer will never save a groat for himself. Lord Harley is a very valuable young gentleman; and they say the girl is handsome, and has good sense, but red hair.

9. I designed a jaunt into the City to-day to be merry, but was disappointed; so one always is in this life; and I could not see Lord Dartmouth to-day, with whom I had some business. Business and pleasure both disappointed. You can go to your Dean, and for want of him, Goody Stoyte, or Walls, or Manley, and meet everywhere with cards and claret. I dined privately with a friend on a herring and chicken, and half a flask of bad Florence. I begin to have fires now, when the

mornings are cold. I have got some loose bricks at the back of my grate for good husbandry. Fine weather. Patrick tells me my caps are wearing out. I know not how to get others. I want a necessary woman strangely. I am as helpless as an elephant.—I had three packets from the Archbishop of Dublin, cost me four shillings, all about Higgins, printed stuff, and two long letters. His people forgot to enclose them to Lewis; and they were only directed to Doctor Swift, without naming London or anything else. I wonder how they reached me, unless the postmaster directed them. I have read all the trash, and am weary.

10. Why, if you must have it out, something is to be published of great moment, and three or four great people are to see there are no mistakes in point of fact: and 'tis so troublesome to send it among them, and get their corrections, that I am weary as a dog. I dined to-day with the printer, and was there all the afternoon; and it plagues me, and there's an end, and what would you have? Lady Dupplin, Lord Treasurer's daughter, is brought to bed of a son. Lord Treasurer has had an ugly return of his gravel. 'Tis good for us to live in gravel pits, but not for gravel pits to live in us; a man in this case should leave no stone unturned. Lord Treasurer's sickness, the Queen's gout, the forwarding the peace, occasion putting off the Parliament a fortnight longer. My head has had no ill returns. I had good walking to-day in the City, and take all opportunities of it on purpose for my health; but I can't walk in the Park, because that is only for walking's sake, and loses time, so I mix it with business. I wish MD walked half as much as Presto. If I was with you, I'd make you walk; I would walk behind or before you, and you should have masks on, and be tucked up like anything; and Stella is naturally a stout walker, and carries herself firm; methinks I see her strut, and step clever over a kennel; and Dingley would do well enough if her petticoats were pinned up; but she is so embroiled, and so fearful, and then Stella scolds, and Dingley stumbles, and is so daggled. Have you got the whalebone petticoats among you yet? I hate them; a woman here may hide a moderate gallant under them. Pshaw, what's all this I'm saying? Methinks I am talking to MD face to face.

11. Did I tell you that old Frowde, the old fool, is selling his estate at Pepperhara, and is skulking about the town nobody knows where? and who do you think manages all this for him, but that rogue Child, the double squire of Farnham? I have put Mrs. Masham, the Queen's

favourite, upon buying it, but that is yet a great secret; and I have employed Lady Oglethorpe to inquire about it. I was with Lady Oglethorpe to-day, who is come to town for a week or two, and to-morrow I will see to hunt out the old fool: he is utterly ruined, and at this present in some blind alley with some dirty wench. He has two sons that must starve, and he never gives them a farthing. If Mrs. Masham buys the land, I will desire her to get the Queen to give some pension to the old fool, to keep him from absolutely starving. What do you meddle with other people's affairs for? says Stella. Oh, but Mr. Masham and his wife are very urgent with me, since I first put them in the head of it. I dined with Sir Matthew Dudley, who, I doubt, will soon lose his employment.

12. Morning. I am going to hunt out old Frowde, and to do some business in the City. I have not yet called to Patrick to know whether it be fair.—It has been past dropping these two days. Rainy weather hurts my pate and my purse. He tells me 'tis very windy, and begins to look dark; woe be to my shillings! an old saying and a true,

> *Few fillings,*
> *Many shillings.*

If the day be dark, my purse will be light.

> *To my enemies be this curse,*
> *A dark day and a light purse.*

And so I'll rise, and go to my fire, for Patrick tells me I have a fire; yet it is not shaving-day, nor is the weather cold; this is too extravagant. What is become of Dilly? I suppose you have him with you. Stella is just now showing a white leg, and putting it into the slipper. Present my service to her, and tell her I am engaged to the Dean, and desire she will come too: or, Dingley, can't you write a note? This is Stella's morning dialogue, no, morning speech I mean.—Morrow, sirrahs, and let me rise as well as you; but I promise you Walls can't dine with the Dean to-day, for she is to be at Mrs. Proby's just after dinner, and to go with Gracy Spencer to the shops to buy a yard of muslin, and a silver lace for an under petticoat. Morrow again, sirrahs.—At night. I dined with Stratford in the City, but could not finish my affairs with him; but now I am resolved to buy five hundred pounds South Sea Stock, which will cost me three hundred and eighty ready money; and I will make use of the bill of a hundred pounds you sent me, and transfer Mrs. Walls over to Hawkshaw; or if she dislikes it, I will borrow a hundred pounds of the Secretary, and repay her. Three shillings coach-hire to-day. I have spoken to Frowde's brother to get me the lowest price of the estate, to tell Mrs. Masham.

13. I dined privately with a friend to-day in the neighbourhood. Last Saturday night I came home, and the drab had just washed my room, and my bed-chamber was all wet, and I was forced to go to bed in my own defence, and no fire: I was sick on Sunday, and now have got a swingeing cold. I scolded like a dog at Patrick, although he was out with me: I detest washing of rooms; can't they wash them in a morning, and make a fire, and leave open the windows? I slept not a wink last night for hawking and spitting: and now everybody has colds. Here's a clutter: I'll go to bed and sleep if I can.

14. Lady Mountjoy sent to me two days ago, so I dined with her to-day, and in the evening went to see Lord Treasurer. I found Patrick had been just there with a how d'ye, and my lord had returned answer that he desired to see me. Mrs. Masham was with him when I came, and they are never disturbed: 'tis well she is not very handsome; they sit alone together settling the nation. I sat with Lady Oxford, and stopped Mrs. Masham as she came out, and told her what progress I had made, etc., and then went to Lord Treasurer: he is very well, only uneasy at rising or sitting, with some rheumatic pain in his thigh, and a foot weak. He showed me a small paper, sent by an unknown hand to one Mr. Cook, who sent it to my lord: it was written in plain large letters thus

"Though G——d's knife did not succeed,
A F——n's yet may do the deed."

And a little below: *"Burn this, you dog."* My lord has frequently such letters as these: once he showed me one, which was a vision describing a certain man, his dress, his sword, and his countenance, who was to murder my lord. And he told me he saw a fellow in the chapel at Windsor with a dress very like it. They often send him letters signed,

"Your humble servant, The Devil," and such stuff. I sat with him till after ten, and have business to do.

15. The Secretary came yesterday to town from Hampton Court, so I went to him early this morning; but he went back last night again: and coming home to-night I found a letter from him to tell me that he was just come from Hampton Court, and just returning, and will not be here till Saturday night. A pox take him! he stops all my business. I'll beg leave to come back when I have got over this, and hope to see MD in Ireland soon after Christmas.—I'm weary of Courts, and want my journeys to Laracor; they did me more good than all the Ministries these twenty years. I dined to-day in the City, but did no business as I designed. Lady Mountjoy tells me that Dilly is got to Ireland, and that the Archbishop of Dublin was the cause of his returning so soon. The Parliament was prorogued two days ago for a fortnight, which, with the Queen's absence, makes the town very dull and empty. They tell me the Duke of Ormond brings all the world away with him from Ireland. London has nothing so bad in it in winter as your knots of Irish folks; but I go to no coffee-house, and so I seldom see them. This letter shall go on Saturday; and then I am even with the world again. I have lent money, and cannot get it, and am forced to borrow for myself.

16. My man made a blunder this morning, and let up a visitor, when I had ordered to see nobody; so I was forced to hurry a hang-dog instrument of mine into my bed-chamber, and keep him cooling his heels there above an hour.—I am going on fairly in the common forms of a great cold; I believe it will last me about ten days in all.—I should have told you, that in those two verses sent to Lord Treasurer, G—d stands for Guiscard; that is easy; but we differed about F—n; I thought it was for Frenchman, because he hates them, and they him: and so it would be, That although Guiscard's knife missed its design, the knife of a Frenchman might yet do it. My lord thinks it stands for Felton, the name of him that stabbed the first Duke of Buckingham. Sir Andrew Fountaine and I dined with the Vans to-day, and my cold made me loiter all the evening. Stay, young women, don't you begin to owe me a letter? just a month to-day since I had your N. 22. I'll stay a week longer, and then, I'll expect like agog; till then you may play at ombre, and so forth, as you please. The Whigs are still crying down our peace, but we will have it, I hope, in spite of them: the Emperor comes now with his

two eggs a penny, and promises wonders to continue the war; but it is too late; only I hope the fear of it will serve to spur on the French to be easy and sincere: Night, sirrahs; I'll go early to bed.

17. Morning. This goes to-night; I will put it myself in the post-office. I had just now a long letter from the Archbishop of Dublin, giving me an account of the ending your session, how it ended in a storm; which storm, by the time it arrives here, will be only half nature. I can't help it, I won't hide. I often advised the dissolution of that Parliament, although I did not think the scoundrels had so much courage; but they have it only in the wrong, like a bully that will fight for a whore, and run away in an army. I believe, by several things the Archbishop says, he is not very well either with the Government or clergy.—See how luckily my paper ends with a fortnight.—God Almighty bless and preserve dearest little MD.—I suppose your Lord Lieutenant is now setting out for England. I wonder the Bishop of Clogher does not write to me, or let me know of his statues, and how he likes them: I will write to him again, as soon as I have leisure. Farewell, dearest MD, and love Presto, who loves MD infinitely above all earthly things, and who will.—My service to Mrs. Stoyte and Catherine. I'm sitting in my bed, but will rise to seal this. Morrow, dear rogues: Farewell again, dearest MD, etc.

LETTER XXXV

LONDON, *Nov.* 17, 1711

I put my last this evening in the post-office. I dined with Dr. Cockburn. This being Queen Elizabeth's birthday, we have the D—and all to do among us. I just heard of the stir as my letter was sealed this morning, and was so cross I would not open it to tell you. I have been visiting Lady Oglethorpe and Lady Worsley; the latter is lately come to town for the winter, and with child, and what care you? This is Queen Elizabeth's birthday, usually kept in this town by apprentices, etc.; but the Whigs designed a mighty procession by midnight, and had laid out a thousand pounds to dress up the Pope, Devil, cardinals, Sacheverell, etc., and carry them with torches about, and burn them. They did it by contribution. Garth gave five guineas; Dr. Garth I mean, if ever you heard of him. But they were seized last night, by order from the Secretary: you will have an account of it, for they bawl it about the streets already. They had some very foolish and mischievous designs; and it was thought they would have put the rabble upon assaulting my Lord Treasurer's house and the Secretary's, and other violences. The militia was raised to prevent it, and now, I suppose, all will be quiet. The figures are now at the Secretary's office at Whitehall. I design to see them if I can.

18. I was this morning with Mr. Secretary, who just came from Hampton Court. He was telling me more particulars about this business of burning the Pope. It cost a great deal of money, and had it gone on, would have cost three times as much; but the town is full of it, and half a dozen Grub Street papers already. The Secretary and I dined at Brigadier Britton's, but I left them at six, upon an appointment with some sober company of men and ladies, to drink punch at Sir Andrew Fountaine's. We were not very merry; and I don't love rack punch, I love it better with brandy; are you of my opinion? Why then, twelvepenny weather; sirrahs, why don't you play at shuttlecock? I have thought of it a hundred times; faith, Presto will come over after Christmas, and will play with Stella before the cold weather is gone. Do you read the *Spectators*? I never do; they never come in my way; I go to no coffee-houses. They say abundance of them are very pretty; they are going to be printed in small volumes; I'll bring them over with me. I shall be out

of my hurry in a week, and if Leigh be not gone over, I will send you by him what I am now finishing. I don't know where Leigh is; I have not seen him this good while, though he promised to call: I shall send to him. The Queen comes to town on Thursday for good and all.

19. I was this morning at Lord Dartmouth's office, and sent out for him from the Committee of Council, about some business. I was asking him more concerning this bustle about the figures in wax-work of the Pope, and Devil, etc. He was not at leisure, or he would have seen them. I hear the owners are so impudent, that they design to replevin them by law. I am assured that the figure of the Devil is made as like Lord Treasurer as they could. Why, I dined with a friend in St. James's Street. Lord Treasurer, I am told, was abroad to-day; I will know to-morrow how he does after it. The Duke of Marlborough is come, and was yesterday at Hampton Court with the Queen; no, it was t'other day; no, it was yesterday; for to-day I remember Mr. Secretary was going to see him, when I was there, not at the Duke of Marlborough's, but at the Secretary's; the Duke is not so fond of me. What care I? I won seven shillings to-night at picquet: I play twice a year or so.

20. I have been so teased with Whiggish discourse by Mrs. Barton and Lady Betty Germaine, never saw the like. They turn all this affair of the Pope-burning into ridicule; and, indeed, they have made too great a clutter about it, if they had no real reason to apprehend some tumults. I dined with Lady Betty. I hear Prior's commission is passed to be Ambassador Extraordinary and Plenipotentiary for the peace; my Lord Privy Seal, who you know is Bishop of Bristol, is the other; and Lord Strafford, already Ambassador at The Hague, the third: I am forced to tell you, ignorant sluts, who is who. I was punning scurvily with Sir Andrew Fountaine and Lord Pembroke this evening: do you ever pun now? Sometimes with the Dean, or Tom Leigh. Prior puns very well. Odso, I must go see His Excellency, 'tis a noble advancement: but they could do no less, after sending him to France. Lord Strafford is as proud as Hell, and how he will bear one of Prior's mean birth on an equal character with him, I know not. And so I go to my business, and bid you good-night.

21. I was this morning busy with my printer: I gave him the fifth sheet, and then I went and dined with him in the City, to correct something,

and alter, etc., and I walked home in the dusk, and the rain overtook me: and I found a letter here from Mr. Lewis; well, and so I opened it; and he says the peace is past danger, etc. Well, and so there was another letter enclosed in his: well, and so I looked on the outside of this t'other letter. Well, and so who do you think this t'other letter was from? Well, and so I'll tell you; it was from little MD, N. 23, 23, 23, 23. I tell you it is no more, I have told you so before: but I just looked again to satisfy you. Hie, Stella, you write like an emperor, a great deal together; a very good hand, and but four false spellings in all. Shall I send them to you? I am glad you did not take my correction ill. Well, but I won't answer your letter now, sirrah saucyboxes, no, no; not yet; just a month and three days from the last, which is just five weeks: you see it comes just when I begin to grumble.

22. Morning. Tooke has just brought me Dingley's money. I will give you a note for it at the end of this letter. There was half a crown for entering the letter of attorney; but I swore to stop that. I'll spend your money bravely here. Morrow, dear sirrahs.—At night. I dined to-day with Sir Thomas Hanmer; his wife, the Duchess of Grafton, dined with us: she wears a great high head-dress, such as was in fashion fifteen years ago, and looks like a mad woman in it; yet she has great remains of beauty. I was this evening to see Lord Harley, and thought to have sat with Lord Treasurer, but he was taken up with the Dutch Envoy and such folks; and I would not stay. One particular in life here, different from what I have in Dublin, is, that whenever I come home I expect to find some letter for me, and seldom miss; and never any worth a farthing, but often to vex me. The Queen does not come to town till Saturday. Prior is not yet declared; but these Ministers being at Hampton Court, I know nothing; and if I write news from common hands, it is always lies. You will think it affectation; but nothing has vexed me more for some months past, than people I never saw pretending to be acquainted with me, and yet speak ill of me too; at least some of them. An old crooked Scotch countess, whom I never heard of in my life, told the Duchess of Hamilton t'other day that I often visited her. People of worth never do that; so that a man only gets the scandal of having scurvy acquaintance. Three ladies were railing against me some time ago, and said they were very well acquainted with me; two of which I had never heard of, and the third I had only seen twice where I happened to visit. A man who has once seen me in a coffee-house will ask me how I do, when he sees

me talking at Court with a Minister of State; who is sure to ask me how I came acquainted with that scoundrel. But come, sirrahs, this is all stuff to you, so I'll say no more on this side the paper, but turn over.

23. My printer invited Mr. Lewis and me to dine at a tavern to-day, which I have not done five times since I came to England; I never will call it Britain, pray don't call it Britain. My week is not out, and one side of this paper is out, and I have a letter to answer of MD's into the bargain: must I write on the third side? faith, that will give you an ill habit. I saw Leigh last night: he gives a terrible account of Sterne; he reckons he is seduced by some wench; he is over head and ears in debt, and has pawned several things. Leigh says he goes on Monday next for Ireland, but believes Sterne will not go with him; Sterne has kept him these three months. Leigh has got the apron and things, and promises to call for the box at Chester; but I despair of it. Good-night, sirrahs; I have been late abroad.

24. I have finished my pamphlet to-day, which has cost me so much time and trouble: it will be published in three or four days, when the Parliament begins sitting. I suppose the Queen is come to town, but know nothing, having been in the City finishing and correcting with the printer. When I came home, I found letters on my table as usual, and one from your mother, to tell me that you desire your writings and a picture should be sent to me, to be sent over to you. I have just answered her letter, and promised to take care of them if they be sent to me. She is at Farnham: it is too late to send them by Leigh; besides, I will wait your orders, Madam Stella. I am going to finish a letter to Lord Treasurer about reforming our language; but first I must put an end to a ballad; and go you to your cards, sirrahs, this is card season.

25. I was early with the Secretary to-day, but he was gone to his devotions, and to receive the sacrament: several rakes did the same; it was not for piety, but employments; according to Act of Parliament. I dined with Lady Mary Dudley; and passed my time since insipidly, only I was at Court at noon, and saw fifty acquaintance I had not met this long time: that is the advantage of a Court, and I fancy I am better known than any man that goes there. Sir John Walter's quarrel with me has entertained the town ever since; and yet we never had a word, only he railed at me behind my back. The Parliament is again to be

prorogued for eight or nine days, for the Whigs are too strong in the House of Lords: other reasons are pretended, but that is the truth. The prorogation is not yet known, but will be to-morrow.

26. Mr. Lewis and I dined with a friend of his, and unexpectedly there dined with us an Irish knight, one Sir John St. Leger, who follows the law here, but at a great distance: he was so pert, I was forced to take him down more than once. I saw to-day the Pope, and Devil, and the other figures of cardinals, etc., fifteen in all, which have made such a noise. I have put an under-strapper upon writing a twopenny pamphlet to give an account of the whole design. My large pamphlet will be published to-morrow; copies are sent to the great men this night. Domville is come home from his travels; I am vexed at it: I have not seen him yet; I design to present him to all the great men.

27. Domville came to me this morning, and we dined at Pontack's, and were all day together, till six this evening: he is perfectly as fine a gentleman as I know; he set me down at Lord Treasurer's, with whom I stayed about an hour, till Monsieur Buys, the Dutch Envoy, came to him about business. My Lord Treasurer is pretty well, but stiff in the hips with the remains of the rheumatism. I am to bring Domville to my Lord Harley in a day or two. It was the dirtiest rainy day that ever I saw. The pamphlet is published; Lord Treasurer had it by him on the table, and was asking me about the mottoes in the title-page; he gave me one of them himself. I must send you the pamphlet, if I can.

28. Mrs. Van sent to me to dine with her to-day, because some ladies of my acquaintance were to be there; and there I dined. I was this morning to return Domville his visit, and went to visit Mrs. Masham, who was not within. I am turned out of my lodging by my landlady: it seems her husband and her son are coming home; but I have taken another lodging hard by, in Leicester Fields. I presented Mr. Domville to Mr. Lewis and Mr. Prior this morning. Prior and I are called the two Sosias, in a Whig newspaper. Sosias, can you read it? The pamphlet begins to make a noise: I was asked by several whether I had seen it, and they advised me to read it, for it was something very extraordinary. I shall be suspected; and it will have several paltry answers. It must take its fate, as Savage said of his sermon that he preached at Farnham on Sir William Temple's death. Domville saw Savage in Italy, and says he

is a coxcomb, and half mad: he goes in red, and with yellow waistcoats, and was at ceremony kneeling to the Pope on a Palm Sunday, which is much more than kissing his toe; and I believe it will ruin him here when 'tis told. I'll answer your letter in my new lodgings: I have hardly room; I must borrow from the other side.

29. New lodgings. My printer came this morning to tell me he must immediately print a second edition, and Lord Treasurer made one or two small additions: they must work day and night to have it out on Saturday; they sold a thousand in two days. Our Society met to-day; nine of us were present: we dined at our brother Bathurst's. We made several regulations, and have chosen three new members, Lord Orrery, Jack Hill, who is Mrs. Masham's brother, he that lately miscarried in the expedition to Quebec, and one Colonel Disney.—We have taken a room in a house near St. James's to meet in. I left them early about correcting the pamphlet, etc., and am now got home, etc.

30. This morning I carried Domville to see my Lord Harley, and I did some business with Lord Treasurer, and have been all this afternoon with the printer, adding something to the second edition. I dined with the printer: the pamphlet makes a world of noise, and will do a great deal of good; it tells abundance of most important facts which were not at all known. I'll answer your letter to-morrow morning; or suppose I answer it just now, though it is pretty late. Come then.—You say you are busy with Parliaments, etc.; that's more than ever I will be when I come back; but you will have none these two years. Lord Santry, etc., yes, I have had enough on't. I am glad Dilly is mended; does not he thank me for showing him the Court and the great people's faces? He had his glass out at the Queen and the rest. 'Tis right what Dilly says: I depend upon nothing from my friends, but to go back as I came. Never fear Laracor, 'twill mend with a peace, or surely they'll give me the Dublin parish. Stella is in the right: the Bishop of Ossory is the silliest, best-natured wretch breathing, of as little consequence as an egg-shell. Well, the spelling I have mentioned before; only the next time say *at least*, and not *at lest*. Pox on your Newbury! what can I do for him? I'll give his case (I am glad it is not a woman's) to what members I know; that's all I can do. Lord Treasurer's lameness goes off daily. Pray God preserve poor good Mrs. Stoyte; she would be a great loss to us all: pray give her my service, and tell her she has my heartiest prayers. I pity

poor Mrs. Manley; but I think the child is happy to die, considering how little provision it would have had.—Poh, every pamphlet abuses me, and for things that I never writ. Joe should have written me thanks for his two hundred pounds: I reckon he got it by my means; and I must thank the Duke of Ormond, who I dare swear will say he did it on my account. Are they golden pippins, those seven apples? We have had much rain every day as well as you. £7, 17s., 8d., old blunderer, not 18s.: I have reckoned it eighteen times. Hawkshaw's eight pounds is not reckoned and if it be secure, it may lie where it is, unless they desire to pay it: so Parvisol may let it drop till further orders; for I have put Mrs. Wesley's money into the Bank, and will pay her with Hawkshaw's.—I mean that Hawkshaw's money goes for an addition to MD, you know; but be good housewives. Bernage never comes now to see me; he has no more to ask; but I hear he has been ill.—A pox on Mrs. South's affair; I can do nothing in it, but by way of assisting anybody else that solicits it, by dropping a favourable word, if it comes in my way. Tell Walls I do no more for anybody with my Lord Treasurer, especially a thing of this kind. Tell him I have spent all my discretion, and have no more to use.—And so I have answered your letter fully and plainly.—And so I have got to the third side of my paper, which is more than belongs to you, young women.

It goes to-morrow,
To nobody's sorrow.

You are silly, not I; I'm a poet, if I had but, etc.—Who's silly now? rogues and lasses, tinderboxes and buzzards. O Lord, I am in a high vein of silliness; methought I was speaking to dearest little MD face to face. There; so, lads, enough for to-night; to cards with the blackguards. Good-night, my delight, etc.

Dec. 1. Pish, sirrahs, put a date always at the bottom of your letter, as well as the top, that I may know when you send it; your last is of November 3, yet I had others at the same time, written a fortnight after. Whenever you would have any money, send me word three weeks before, and in that time you will certainly have an answer, with a bill on Parvisol: pray do this; for my head is full, and it will ease my memory. Why, I think I quoted to you some of—'s letter, so you may imagine how witty the rest was; for it was all of a bunch, as Goodman Peesley says. Pray let us have no more *bussiness*, but *busyness*: the deuce take me if I know how to spell it; your wrong spelling, Madam Stella, has put me out: it does not look right; let me see, *bussiness*, *busyness*, *business*, *bisyness*, *bisness*, *bysness*; faith, I know not which is right, I think the second; I believe I never writ the word in my life before; yes, sure I must, though; *business*, *busyness*, *bisyness*.—I have perplexed myself, and can't do it. Prithee ask Walls. *Business*, I fancy that's right. Yes it is; I looked in my own pamphlet, and found it twice in ten lines, to convince you that I never writ it before. Oh, now I see it as plain as can be; so yours is only an *s* too much. The Parliament will certainly meet on Friday next: the Whigs will have a great majority in the House of Lords, no care is taken to prevent it; there is too much neglect; they are warned of it, and that signifies nothing: it was feared there would be some peevish address from the Lords against a peace. 'Tis said about the town that several of the Allies begin now to be content that a peace should be treated. This is all the news I have. The Queen is pretty well: and so now I bid poor dearest MD farewell till to-night; then I will talk with them again.

The fifteen images that I saw were not worth forty pounds, so I stretched a little when I said a thousand. The Grub Street account of that tumult is published. The Devil is not like Lord Treasurer: they were all in your odd antic masks, bought in common shops. I fear Prior will not be one of the plenipotentiaries.

I was looking over this letter, and find I make many mistakes of leaving out words; so 'tis impossible to find my meaning, unless you be conjurers. I will take more care for the future, and read over every day just what I have written that day, which will take up no time to speak of.

Letter XXXVI

My last was put in this evening. I intended to dine with Mr. Masham to-day, and called at White's chocolate house to see if he was there. Lord Wharton saw me at the door, and I saw him, but took no notice, and was going away, but he came through the crowd, called after me, and asked me how I did, etc. This was pretty; and I believe he wished every word he spoke was a halter to hang me. Masham did not dine at home, so I ate with a friend in the neighbourhood. The printer has not sent me the second edition; I know not the reason, for it certainly came out to-day; perhaps they are glutted with it already. I found a letter from Lord Harley on my table, to tell me that his father desires I would make two small alterations. I am going to be busy, etc.

2. Morning. See the blunder; I was making it the 37th day of the month, from the number above. Well, but I am staying here for old Frowde, who appointed to call this morning: I am ready dressed to go to church: I suppose he dare not stir out but on Sundays. The printer called early this morning, told me the second edition went off yesterday in five hours, and he must have a third ready to-morrow, for they might have sold half another: his men are all at work with it, though it be Sunday. This old fool will not come, and I shall miss church. Morrow, sirrahs.—At night. I was at Court to-day: the Queen is well, and walked through part of the rooms. I dined with the Secretary, and despatched some business. He tells me the Dutch Envoy designs to complain of that pamphlet. The noise it makes is extraordinary. It is fit it should answer the pains I have been at about it. I suppose it will be printed in Ireland. Some lay it to Prior, others to Mr. Secretary St. John, but I am always the first they lay everything to. I'll go sleep, etc.

3. I have ordered Patrick not to let any odd fellow come up to me; and a fellow would needs speak with me from Sir George Pretyman. I had never heard of him, and would not see the messenger: but at last it proved that this Sir George has sold his estate, and is a beggar. Smithers, the Farnham carrier, brought me this morning a letter from your mother, with three papers enclosed of Lady Giffard's writing; one owning some exchequer business of £100 to be Stella's; another for

£100 that she has of yours, which I made over to you for Mariston; and a third for £300; the last is on stamped paper. I think they had better lie in England in some good hand till Lady Giffard dies; and I will think of some such hand before I come over. I was asking Smithers about all the people of Farnham. Mrs. White has left off dressing, is troubled with lameness and swelled legs, and seldom stirs out; but her old hang-dog husband as hearty as ever. I was this morning with Lord Treasurer, about something he would have altered in the pamphlet; but it can't be till the fourth edition, which I believe will be soon; for I dined with the printer, and he tells me they have sold off half the third. Mrs. Perceval and her daughter have been in town these three weeks, which I never heard till to-day; and Mrs. Wesley is come to town too, to consult Dr. Radcliffe. The Whigs are resolved to bring that pamphlet into the House of Lords to have it condemned, so I hear. But the printer will stand to it, and not own the author; he must say he had it from the penny-post. Some people talk as if the House of Lords would do some peevish thing, for the Whigs are now a great majority in it; our Ministers are too negligent of such things: I have never slipped giving them warning; some of them are sensible of it; but Lord Treasurer stands too much upon his own legs. I fancy his good fortune will bear him out in everything; but in reason I should think this Ministry to stand very unsteady; if they can carry a peace, they may hold; I believe not else.

4. Mr. Secretary sent to me to-day to dine with him alone; but we had two more with us, which hindered me doing some business. I was this morning with young Harcourt, secretary to our Society, to take a room for our weekly meetings; and the fellow asked us five guineas a week only to have leave to dine once a week; was not that pretty? so we broke off with him, and are to dine next Thursday at Harcourt's (he is Lord Keeper's son). They have sold off above half the third edition, and answers are coming out: the Dutch Envoy refused dining with Dr. Davenant, because he was suspected to write it: I have made some alterations in every edition, and it has cost me more trouble, for the time, since the printing, than before. 'Tis sent over to Ireland, and I suppose you will have it reprinted.

5. They are now printing the fourth edition, which is reckoned very extraordinary, considering 'tis a dear twelvepenny book, and not bought

up in numbers by the party to give away, as the Whigs do, but purely upon its own strength. I have got an under spur-leather to write an *Examiner* again, and the Secretary and I will now and then send hints; but we would have it a little upon the Grub Street, to be a match for their writers. I dined with Lord Treasurer to-day at five: he dined by himself after his family, and drinks no claret yet, for fear of his rheumatism, of which he is almost well. He was very pleasant, as he is always: yet I fancied he was a little touched with the present posture of affairs. The Elector of Hanover's Minister here has given in a violent memorial against the peace, and caused it to be printed. The Whig lords are doing their utmost for a majority against Friday, and design, if they can, to address the Queen against the peace. Lord Nottingham, a famous Tory and speech-maker, is gone over to the Whig side: they toast him daily, and Lord Wharton says, It is Dismal (so they call him from his looks) will save England at last. Lord Treasurer was hinting as if he wished a ballad was made on him, and I will get up one against to-morrow. He gave me a scurrilous printed paper of bad verses on himself, under the name of the English Catiline, and made me read them to the company. It was his birthday, which he would not tell us, but Lord Harley whispered it to me.

6. I was this morning making the ballad, two degrees above Grub Street: at noon I paid a visit to Mrs. Masham, and then went to dine with our Society. Poor Lord Keeper dined below stairs, I suppose, on a bit of mutton. We chose two members: we were eleven met, the greatest meeting we ever had: I am next week to introduce Lord Orrery. The printer came before we parted, and brought the ballad, which made them laugh very heartily a dozen times. He is going to print the pamphlet in small, a fifth edition, to be taken off by friends, and sent into the country. A sixpenny answer is come out, good for nothing, but guessing me, among others, for the author. To-morrow is the fatal day for the Parliament meeting, and we are full of hopes and fears. We reckon we have a majority of ten on our side in the House of Lords; yet I observed Mrs. Masham a little uneasy: she assures me the Queen is stout. The Duke of Marlborough has not seen the Queen for some days past; Mrs. Masham is glad of it, because she says he tells a hundred lies to his friends of what she says to him: he is one day humble, and the next day on the high ropes. The Duke of Ormond, they say, will be in town to-night by twelve.

7. This being the day the Parliament was to meet, and the great question to be determined, I went with Dr. Freind to dine in the City, on purpose to be out of the way, and we sent our printer to see what was our fate; but he gave us a most melancholy account of things. The Earl of Nottingham began, and spoke against a peace, and desired that in their address they might put in a clause to advise the Queen not to make a peace without Spain; which was debated, and carried by the Whigs by about six voices: and this has happened entirely by my Lord Treasurer's neglect, who did not take timely care to make up all his strength, although every one of us gave him caution enough. Nottingham has certainly been bribed. The question is yet only carried in the Committee of the whole House, and we hope when it is reported to the House to-morrow, we shall have a majority, by some Scotch lords coming to town. However, it is a mighty blow and loss of reputation to Lord Treasurer, and may end in his ruin. I hear the thing only as the printer brought it, who was at the debate; but how the Ministry take it, or what their hopes and fears are, I cannot tell until I see them. I shall be early with the Secretary to-morrow, and then I will tell you more, and shall write a full account to the Bishop of Clogher to-morrow, and to the Archbishop of Dublin, if I have time. I am horribly down at present. I long to know how Lord Treasurer bears this, and what remedy he has. The Duke of Ormond came this day to town, and was there.

8. I was early this morning with the Secretary, and talked over this matter. He hoped that when it was reported this day in the House of Lords, they would disagree with their Committee, and so the matter would go off, only with a little loss of reputation to the Lord Treasurer. I dined with Mr. Cockburn, and after, a Scotch member came in, and told us that the clause was carried against the Court in the House of Lords almost two to one. I went immediately to Mrs. Masham, and meeting Dr. Arbuthnot (the Queen's favourite physician), we went together. She was just come from waiting at the Queen's dinner, and going to her own. She had heard nothing of the thing being gone against us. It seems Lord Treasurer had been so negligent that he was with the Queen while the question was put in the House: I immediately told Mrs. Masham that either she and Lord Treasurer had joined with the Queen to betray us, or that they two were betrayed by the Queen: she protested solemnly it was not the former, and I believed her; but she gave me some lights to suspect the Queen is changed. For yesterday, when the

Queen was going from the House, where she sat to hear the debate, the Duke of Shrewsbury, Lord Chamberlain, asked her whether he or the Great Chamberlain Lindsey ought to lead her out; she answered short, "Neither of you," and gave her hand to the Duke of Somerset, who was louder than any in the House for the clause against peace. She gave me one or two more instances of this sort, which convince me that the Queen is false, or at least very much wavering. Mr. Masham begged us to stay, because Lord Treasurer would call, and we were resolved to fall on him about his negligence in securing a majority. He came, and appeared in good humour as usual, but I thought his countenance was much cast down. I rallied him, and desired him to give me his staff, which he did: I told him, if he would secure it me a week, I would set all right: he asked how; I said I would immediately turn Lord Marlborough, his two daughters, the Duke and Duchess of Somerset, and Lord Cholmondeley, out of all their employments; and I believe he had not a friend but was of my opinion. Arbuthnot asked how he came not to secure a majority. He could answer nothing but that he could not help it, if people would lie and forswear. A poor answer for a great Minister. There fell from him a Scripture expression, that "the hearts of kings are unsearchable." I told him it was what I feared, and was from him the worst news he could tell me. I begged him to know what he had to trust to: he stuck a little; but at last bid me not fear, for all would be well yet. We would fain have had him eat a bit where he was, but he would go home, it was past six: he made me go home with him. There we found his brother and Mr. Secretary. He made his son take a list of all in the House of Commons who had places, and yet voted against the Court, in such a manner as if they should lose their places: I doubt he is not able to compass it. Lord Keeper came in an hour, and they were going upon business. So I left him, and returned to Mrs. Masham; but she had company with her, and I would not stay.—This is a long journal, and of a day that may produce great alterations, and hazard the ruin of England. The Whigs are all in triumph; they foretold how all this would be, but we thought it boasting. Nay, they said the Parliament should be dissolved before Christmas, and perhaps it may: this is all your d—d Duchess of Somerset's doings. I warned them of it nine months ago, and a hundred times since: the Secretary always dreaded it. I told Lord Treasurer I should have the advantage of him; for he would lose his head, and I should only be hanged, and so carry my body entire to the grave.

9. I was this morning with Mr. Secretary: we are both of opinion that the Queen is false. I told him what I heard, and he confirmed it by other circumstances. I then went to my friend Lewis, who had sent to see me. He talks of nothing but retiring to his estate in Wales. He gave me reasons to believe the whole matter is settled between the Queen and the Whigs; he hears that Lord Somers is to be Treasurer, and believes that, sooner than turn out the Duchess of Somerset, she will dissolve the Parliament, and get a Whiggish one, which may be done by managing elections. Things are now in the crisis, and a day or two will determine. I have desired him to engage Lord Treasurer that as soon as he finds the change is resolved on, he will send me abroad as Queen's Secretary somewhere or other, where I may remain till the new Ministers recall me; and then I will be sick for five or six months, till the storm has spent itself. I hope he will grant me this; for I should hardly trust myself to the mercy of my enemies while their anger is fresh. I dined to-day with the Secretary, who affects mirth, and seems to hope all will yet be well. I took him aside after dinner, told him how I had served them, and had asked no reward, but thought I might ask security; and then desired the same thing of him, to send me abroad before a change. He embraced me, and swore he would take the same care of me as himself, etc., but bid me have courage, for that in two days my Lord Treasurer's wisdom would appear greater than ever; that he suffered all that had happened on purpose, and had taken measures to turn it to advantage. I said, "God send it"; but I do not believe a syllable; and, as far as I can judge, the game is lost. I shall know more soon, and my letters will at least be a good history to show you the steps of this change.

10. I was this morning with Lewis, who thinks they will let the Parliament sit till they have given the money, and then dissolve them in spring, and break the Ministry. He spoke to Lord Treasurer about what I desired him. My lord desired him with great earnestness to assure me that all would be well, and that I should fear nothing. I dined in the City with a friend. This day the Commons went to the Queen with their address, and all the Lords who were for the peace went with them, to show their zeal. I have now some further conviction that the Queen is false, and it begins to be known.

11. I went between two and three to see Mrs. Masham; while I was there she went to her bed-chamber to try a petticoat. Lord Treasurer came

in to see her, and seeing me in the outer room, fell a rallying me: says he, "You had better keep company with me, than with such a fellow as Lewis, who has not the soul of a chicken, nor the heart of a mite." Then he went in to Mrs. Masham, and as he came back desired her leave to let me go home with him to dinner. He asked whether I was not afraid to be seen with him. I said I never valued my Lord Treasurer in my life, and therefore should have always the same esteem for Mr. Harley and Lord Oxford. He seemed to talk confidently, as if he reckoned that all this would turn to advantage. I could not forbear hinting that he was not sure of the Queen, and that those scoundrel, starving lords would never have dared to vote against the Court, if Somerset had not assured them that it would please the Queen. He said that was true, and Somerset did so. I stayed till six; then De Buys, the Dutch Envoy, came to him, and I left him. Prior was with us a while after dinner. I see him and all of them cast down, though they make the best of it.

12. Ford is come to town; I saw him last night: he is in no fear, but sanguine, although I have told him the state of things. This change so resembles the last, that I wonder they do not observe it. The Secretary sent for me yesterday to dine with him, but I was abroad; I hope he had something to say to me. This is morning, and I write in bed. I am going to the Duke of Ormond, whom I have not yet seen. Morrow, sirrahs.— At night. I was to see the Duke of Ormond this morning: he asked me two or three questions after his civil way, and they related to Ireland: at last I told him that, from the time I had seen him, I never once thought of Irish affairs. He whispered me that he hoped I had done some good things here: I said, if everybody else had done half as much, we should not be as we are: then we went aside, and talked over affairs. I told him how all things stood, and advised him what was to be done. I then went and sat an hour with the Duchess; then as long with Lady Oglethorpe, who is so cunning a devil that I believe she could yet find a remedy, if they would take her advice. I dined with a friend at Court.

13. I was this morning with the Secretary: he will needs pretend to talk as if things would be well: "Will you believe it," said he, "if you see these people turned out?" I said, yes, if I saw the Duke and Duchess of Somerset out: he swore if they were not, he would give up his place. Our Society dined to-day at Sir William Wyndham's; we were thirteen present. Lord Orrery and two other members were introduced: I left

them at seven. I forgot to tell you that the printer told me yesterday that Morphew, the publisher, was sent for by that Lord Chief-Justice, who was a manager against Sacheverell; he showed him two or three papers and pamphlets; among the rest mine of the *Conduct of the Allies*, threatened him, asked who was the author, and has bound him over to appear next term. He would not have the impudence to do this, if he did not foresee what was coming at Court.

14. Lord Shelburne was with me this morning, to be informed of the state of affairs, and desired I would answer all his objections against a peace, which was soon done, for he would not give me room to put in a word. He is a man of good sense enough; but argues so violently, that he will some day or other put himself into a consumption. He desires that he may not be denied when he comes to see me, which I promised, but will not perform. Leigh and Sterne set out for Ireland on Monday se'nnight: I suppose they will be with you long before this.—I was to-night drinking very good wine in scurvy company, at least some of them; I was drawn in, but will be more cautious for the future; 'tis late, etc.

15. Morning. They say the Occasional Bill is brought to-day into the House of Lords; but I know not. I will now put an end to my letter, and give it into the post-house myself. This will be a memorable letter, and I shall sigh to see it some years hence. Here are the first steps toward the ruin of an excellent Ministry; for I look upon them as certainly ruined; and God knows what may be the consequences.—I now bid my dearest MD farewell; for company is coming, and I must be at Lord Dartmouth's office by noon. Farewell, dearest MD; I wish you a merry Christmas; I believe you will have this about that time. Love Presto, who loves MD above all things a thousand times. Farewell again, dearest MD, etc.

Letter XXXVII

I put in my letter this evening myself. I was to-day inquiring at the Secretary's office of Mr. Lewis how things went: I there met Prior, who told me he gave all for gone, etc., and was of opinion the whole Ministry would give up their places next week: Lewis thinks they will not till spring, when the session is over; both of them entirely despair. I went to see Mrs. Masham, who invited me to dinner; but I was engaged to Lewis. At four I went to Masham's. He came and whispered me that he had it from a very good hand that all would be well, and I found them both very cheerful. The company was going to the opera, but desired I would come and sup with them. I did so at ten, and Lord Treasurer was there, and sat with us till past twelve, and was more cheerful than I have seen him these ten days. Mrs. Masham told me he was mightily cast down some days ago, and he could not indeed hide it from me. Arbuthnot is in good hopes that the Queen has not betrayed us, but only has been frightened, and flattered, etc. But I cannot yet be of his opinion, whether my reasons are better, or that my fears are greater. I do resolve, if they give up, or are turned out soon, to retire for some months, and I have pitched upon the place already: but I will take methods for hearing from MD, and writing to them. But I would be out of the way upon the first of the ferment; for they lay all things on me, even some I have never read.

16. I took courage to-day, and went to Court with a very cheerful countenance. It was mightily crowded; both parties coming to observe each other's faces. I have avoided Lord Halifax's bow till he forced it on me; but we did not talk together. I could not make less than fourscore bows, of which about twenty might be to Whigs. The Duke of Somerset is gone to Petworth, and, I hear, the Duchess too, of which I shall be very glad. Prince Eugene, who was expected here some days ago, we are now told, will not come at all. The Whigs designed to have met him with forty thousand horse. Lord Treasurer told me some days ago of his discourse with the Emperor's Resident, that puppy Hoffman, about Prince Eugene's coming; by which I found my lord would hinder it, if he could; and we shall be all glad if he does not come, and think it a good point gained. Sir Andrew Fountaine, Ford, and I dined to-day with Mrs. Van, by invitation.

17. I have mistaken the day of the month, and been forced to mend it thrice. I dined to-day with Mr. Masham and his lady, by invitation. Lord Treasurer was to be there, but came not. It was to entertain Buys, the Dutch Envoy, who speaks English well enough: he was plaguily politic, telling a thousand lies, of which none passed upon any of us. We are still in the condition of suspense, and I think have little hopes. The Duchess of Somerset is not gone to Petworth; only the Duke, and that is a poor sacrifice. I believe the Queen certainly designs to change the Ministry, but perhaps may put it off till the session is over: and I think they had better give up now, if she will not deal openly; and then they need not answer for the consequences of a peace, when it is in other hands, and may yet be broken. They say my Lord Privy Seal sets out for Holland this week: so the peace goes on.

18. It has rained hard from morning till night, and cost me three shillings in coach-hire. We have had abundance of wet weather. I dined in the City, and was with the printer, who has now a fifth edition of the *Conduct*, etc.: it is in small, and sold for sixpence; they have printed as many as three editions, because they are to be sent in numbers into the country by great men, etc., who subscribe for hundreds. It has been sent a fortnight ago to Ireland: I suppose you will print it there. The Tory Lords and Commons in Parliament argue all from it; and all agree that never anything of that kind was of so great consequence, or made so many converts. By the time I have sent this letter, I expect to hear from little MD: it will be a month, two days hence, since I had your last, and I will allow ten days for accidents. I cannot get rid of the leavings of a cold I got a month ago, or else it is a new one. I have been writing letters all this evening till I am weary, and I am sending out another little thing, which I hope to finish this week, and design to send to the printer in an unknown hand. There was printed a Grub Street speech of Lord Nottingham; and he was such an owl to complain of it in the House of Lords, who have taken up the printer for it. I heard at Court that Walpole (a great Whig member) said that I and my whimsical Club writ it at one of our meetings, and that I should pay for it. He will find he lies: and I shall let him know by a third hand my thoughts of him. He is to be Secretary of State, if the Ministry changes; but he has lately had a bribe proved against him in Parliament, while he was Secretary at War. He is one of the Whigs' chief speakers.

19. Sad dismal weather. I went to the Secretary's office, and Lewis made me dine with him. I intended to have dined with Lord Treasurer. I have not seen the Secretary this week. Things do not mend at all. Lord Dartmouth despairs, and is for giving up; Lewis is of the same mind; but Lord Treasurer only says, "Poh, poh, all will be well." I am come home early to finish something I am doing; but I find I want heart and humour, and would read any idle book that came in my way. I have just sent away a penny paper to make a little mischief. Patrick is gone to the burial of an Irish footman, who was Dr. King's servant; he died of a consumption, a fit death for a poor starving wit's footman. The Irish servants always club to bury a countryman.

20. I was with the Secretary this morning, and, for aught I can see, we shall have a languishing death: I can know nothing, nor themselves neither. I dined, you know, with our Society, and that odious Secretary would make me President next week; so I must entertain them this day se'nnight at the Thatched House Tavern, where we dined to-day: it will cost me five or six pounds; yet the Secretary says he will give me wine. I found a letter when I came home from the Bishop of Clogher.

21. This is the first time I ever got a new cold before the old one was going: it came yesterday, and appeared in all due forms, eyes and nose running, etc., and is now very bad; and I cannot tell how I got it. Sir Andrew Fountaine and I were invited to dine with Mrs. Van. I was this morning with the Duke of Ormond; and neither he nor I can think of anything to comfort us in present affairs. We must certainly fall, if the Duchess of Somerset be not turned out; and nobody believes the Queen will ever part with her. The Duke and I were settling when Mr. Secretary and I should dine with him, and he fixes upon Tuesday; and when I came away I remembered it was Christmas Day. I was to see Lady—, who is just up after lying-in; and the ugliest sight I have seen, pale, dead, old and yellow, for want of her paint. She has turned my stomach. But she will soon be painted, and a beauty again.

22. I find myself disordered with a pain all round the small of my back, which I imputed to champagne I had drunk; but find it to have been only my new cold. It was a fine frosty day, and I resolved to walk into the City. I called at Lord Treasurer's at eleven, and stayed some time with him.—He showed me a letter from a great Presbyterian parson to

him, complaining how their friends had betrayed them by passing this Conformity Bill; and he showed me the answer he had written, which his friends would not let him send; but was a very good one. He is very cheerful; but gives one no hopes, nor has any to give. I went into the City, and there I dined.

23. Morning. As I was dressing to go to church, a friend that was to see me advised me not to stir out; so I shall keep at home to-day, and only eat some broth, if I can get it. It is a terrible cold frost, and snow fell yesterday, which still remains: look there, you may see it from the penthouses. The Lords made yesterday two or three votes about peace, and Hanover, of a very angry kind to vex the Ministry, and they will meet sooner by a fortnight than the Commons; and they say, are preparing some knocking addresses. Morrow, sirrahs. I'll sit at home, and when I go to bed I will tell you how I am.—I have sat at home all day, and eaten only a mess of broth and a roll. I have written a *Prophecy*, which I design to print; I did it to-day, and some other verses.

24. I went into the City to-day in a coach, and dined there. My cold is going. It is now bitter hard frost, and has been so these three or four days. My *Prophecy* is printed, and will be published after Christmas Day; I like it mightily: I don't know how it will pass. You will never understand it at your distance, without help. I believe everybody will guess it to be mine, because it is somewhat in the same manner with that of "Merlin" in the *Miscellanies*. My Lord Privy Seal set out this day for Holland: he'll have a cold journey. I gave Patrick half a crown for his Christmas box, on condition he would be good, and he came home drunk at midnight. I have taken a memorandum of it, because I never design to give him a groat more. 'Tis cruel cold.

25. I wish MD a merry Christmas, and many a one; but mine is melancholy: I durst not go to church to-day, finding myself a little out of order, and it snowing prodigiously, and freezing. At noon I went to Mrs. Van, who had this week engaged me to dine there to-day: and there I received the news that poor Mrs. Long died at Lynn in Norfolk on Saturday last, at four in the morning: she was sick but four hours. We suppose it was the asthma, which she was subject to as well as the dropsy, as she sent me word in her last letter, written about five weeks ago; but then said she was recovered. I never was more afflicted at any

death. The poor creature had retired to Lynn two years ago, to live cheap, and pay her debts. In her last letter she told me she hoped to be easy by Christmas; and she kept her word, although she meant it otherwise. She had all sorts of amiable qualities, and no ill ones, but the indiscretion of too much neglecting her own affairs. She had two thousand pounds left her by an old grandmother, with which she intended to pay her debts, and live on an annuity she had of one hundred pounds a year, and Newburg House, which would be about sixty pounds more. That odious grandmother living so long, forced her to retire; for the two thousand pounds was settled on her after the old woman's death, yet her brute of a brother, Sir James Long, would not advance it for her; else she might have paid her debts, and continued here, and lived still: I believe melancholy helped her on to her grave. I have ordered a paragraph to be put in the *Postboy*, giving an account of her death, and making honourable mention of her; which is all I can do to serve her memory: but one reason was spite; for her brother would fain have her death a secret, to save the charge of bringing her up here to bury her, or going into mourning. Pardon all this, for the sake of a poor creature I had so much friendship for.

26. I went to Mr. Secretary this morning, and he would have me dine with him. I called at noon at Mrs. Masham's, who desired me not to let the *Prophecy* be published, for fear of angering the Queen about the Duchess of Somerset; so I writ to the printer to stop them. They have been printed and given about, but not sold. I saw Lord Treasurer there, who had been two hours with the Queen; and Mrs. Masham is in hopes things will do well again. I went at night again, and supped at Mr. Masham's, and Lord Treasurer sat with us till one o'clock. So 'tis late, etc.

27. I entertained our Society at the Thatched House Tavern to-day at dinner; but brother Bathurst sent for wine, the house affording none. The printer had not received my letter, and so he brought up dozens apiece of the *Prophecy*; but I ordered him to part with no more. 'Tis an admirable good one, and people are mad for it. The frost still continues violently cold. Mrs. Masham invited me to come to-night and play at cards; but our Society did not part till nine. But I supped with Mrs. Hill, her sister, and there was Mrs. Masham and Lord Treasurer, and we stayed till twelve. He is endeavouring to get a majority against

next Wednesday, when the House of Lords is to meet, and the Whigs intend to make some violent addresses against a peace, if not prevented. God knows what will become of us.—It is still prodigiously cold; but so I told you already. We have eggs on the spit, I wish they may not be addled. When I came home to-night I found, forsooth, a letter from MD, N. 24, 24, 24, 24; there, do you know the numbers now? and at the same time one from Joe, full of thanks: let him know I have received it, and am glad of his success, but won't put him to the charge of a letter. I had a letter some time ago from Mr. Warburton, and I beg one of you will copy out what I shall tell you, and send it by some opportunity to Warburton. 'Tis as follows: The Doctor has received Mr. Warburton's letter, and desires he will let the Doctor know where that accident he mentions is like soon to happen, and he will do what he can in it.—And pray, madam, let them know that I do this to save myself the trouble, and them the expense of a letter. And I think that this is enough for one that comes home at twelve from a Lord Treasurer and Mrs. Masham. Oh, I could tell you ten thousand things of our mad politics, upon what small circumstances great affairs have turned. But I will go rest my busy head.

28. I was this morning with brother Bathurst to see the Duke of Ormond. We have given his Grace some hopes to be one of our Society. The Secretary and I and Bathurst are to dine with him on Sunday next. The Duke is not in much hopes, but has been very busy in endeavouring to bring over some lords against next Wednesday. The Duchess caught me as I was going out; she is sadly in fear about things, and blames me for not mending them by my credit with Lord Treasurer; and I blame her. She met me in the street at noon, and engaged me to dine with her, which I did; and we talked an hour after dinner in her closet. If we miscarry on Wednesday, I believe it will be by some strange sort of neglect. They talk of making eight new lords by calling up some peers' eldest sons; but they delay strangely. I saw Judge Coote to-day at the Duke of Ormond's: he desires to come and see me, to justify his principles.

29. Morning. This goes to-day. I will not answer yours, your 24th, till next, which shall begin to-night, as usual. Lord Shelburne has sent to invite me to dinner, but I am engaged with Lewis at Ned Southwell's. Lord Northampton and Lord Aylesbury's sons are both made peers; but we shall want more. I write this post to your Dean. I owe the Archbishop

a letter this long time. All people that come from Ireland complain of him, and scold me for protecting him. Pray, Madam Dingley, let me know what Presto has received for this year, or whether anything is due to him for last: I cannot look over your former letters now. As for Dingley's own account of her exchequer money, I will give it on t'other side. Farewell, my own dearest MD, and love Presto; and God ever bless dearest MD, etc. etc. I wish you many happy Christmases and new years.

I have owned to the Dean a letter I just had from you, but that I had not one this great while before.

Dingley's Account

Received of Mr. Tooke	£6	17	6
Deducted for entering the letter of attorney	0	2	6
For the three half-crowns it used to cost you, I don't know why nor wherefore	0	7	6
For exchange to Ireland	0	10	0
For coach-hire	0	2	6
In all, just	8	0	0

So there's your money, and we are both even: for I'll pay you no more than that eight pounds Irish, and pray be satisfied.

Churchwarden's accounts, boys.

Saturday night. I have broke open my letter, and tore it into the bargain, to let you know that we are all safe: the Queen has made no less than twelve lords, to have a majority; nine new ones, the other three peers' sons; and has turned out the Duke of Somerset. She is awaked at last, and so is Lord Treasurer: I want nothing now but to see the Duchess out. But we shall do without her. We are all extremely happy. Give me joy, sirrahs. This is written in a coffee-house. Three of the new lords are of our Society.

Letter XXXVIII

LONDON, *Dec.* 29, 1711

I put my letter in this evening, after coming from dinner at Ned Southwell's, where I drank very good Irish wine, and we are in great joy at this happy turn of affairs. The Queen has been at last persuaded to her own interest and security, and I freely think she must have made both herself and kingdom very unhappy, if she had done otherwise. It is still a mighty secret that Masham is to be one of the new lords; they say he does not yet know it himself; but the Queen is to surprise him with it. Mr. Secretary will be a lord at the end of the session; but they want him still in Parliament. After all, it is a strange unhappy necessity of making so many peers together; but the Queen has drawn it upon herself, by her confounded trimming and moderation. Three, as I told you, are of our Society.

30. I writ the Dean and you a lie yesterday; for the Duke of Somerset is not yet turned out. I was to-day at Court, and resolved to be very civil to the Whigs; but saw few there. When I was in the bed-chamber talking to Lord Rochester, he went up to Lady Burlington, who asked him who I was; and Lady Sunderland and she whispered about me: I desired Lord Rochester to tell Lady Sunderland I doubted she was not as much in love with me as I was with her; but he would not deliver my message. The Duchess of Shrewsbury came running up to me, and clapped her fan up to hide us from the company, and we gave one another joy of this change; but sighed when we reflected on the Somerset family not being out. The Secretary and I, and brother Bathurst, and Lord Windsor, dined with the Duke of Ormond. Bathurst and Windsor are to be two of the new lords. I desired my Lord Radnor's brother, at Court to-day, to let my lord know I would call on him at six, which I did, and was arguing with him three hours to bring him over to us, and I spoke so closely that I believe he will be tractable; but he is a scoundrel, and though I said I only talked for my love to him, I told a lie; for I did not care if he were hanged: but everyone gained over is of consequence. The Duke of Marlborough was at Court to-day, and nobody hardly took notice of him. Masham's being a lord begins to take wind: nothing at Court can be kept a secret. Wednesday will be a great day: you shall know more.

304

31. Our frost is broken since yesterday, and it is very slabbery; yet I walked to the City and dined, and ordered some things with the printer. I have settled Dr. King in the Gazette; it will be worth two hundred pounds a year to him. Our new lords' patents are passed: I don't like the expedient, if we could have found any other. I see I have said this before. I hear the Duke of Marlborough is turned out of all his employments: I shall know to-morrow when I am to carry Dr. King to dine with the Secretary.—These are strong remedies; pray God the patient is able to bear them. The last Ministry people are utterly desperate.

Jan. 1. Now I wish my dearest little MD many happy new years; yes, both Dingley and Stella, ay and Presto too, many happy new years. I dined with the Secretary, and it is true that the Duke of Marlborough is turned out of all. The Duke of Ormond has got his regiment of foot-guards, I know not who has the rest. If the Ministry be not sure of a peace, I shall wonder at this step, and do not approve it at best. The Queen and Lord Treasurer mortally hate the Duke of Marlborough, and to that he owes his fall, more than to his other faults: unless he has been tampering too far with his party, of which I have not heard any particulars; however it be, the world abroad will blame us. I confess my belief that he has not one good quality in the world beside that of a general, and even that I have heard denied by several great soldiers. But we have had constant success in arms while he commanded. Opinion is a mighty matter in war, and I doubt the French think it impossible to conquer an army that he leads, and our soldiers think the same; and how far even this step may encourage the French to play tricks with us, no man knows. I do not love to see personal resentment mix with public affairs.

2. This being the day the Lords meet, and the new peers to be introduced, I went to Westminster to see the sight; but the crowd was too great in the house. So I only went into the robing-room, to give my four brothers joy, and Sir Thomas Mansel, and Lord Windsor; the other six I am not acquainted with. It was apprehended the Whigs would have raised some difficulties, but nothing happened. I went to see Lady Masham at noon, and wish her joy of her new honour, and a happy new year. I found her very well pleased; for peerage will be some sort of protection to her upon any turn of affairs. She engaged me to come at night, and sup with her and Lord Treasurer: I went at nine, and she

was not at home, so I would not stay.—No, no, I won't answer your letter yet, young women. I dined with a friend in the neighbourhood. I see nothing here like Christmas, except brawn or mince-pies in places where I dine, and giving away my half-crowns like farthings to great men's porters and butlers. Yesterday I paid seven good guineas to the fellow at the tavern where I treated the Society. I have a great mind to send you the bill. I think I told you some articles. I have not heard whether anything was done in the House of Lords after introducing the new ones. Ford has been sitting with me till peeast tweeleve a clock.

3. This was our Society day: Lord Dupplin was President; we choose every week; the last President treats and chooses his successor. I believe our dinner cost fifteen pounds beside wine. The Secretary grew brisk, and would not let me go, nor Lord Lansdowne, who would fain have gone home to his lady, being newly married to Lady Mary Thynne. It was near one when we parted, so you must think I cannot write much to-night. The adjourning of the House of Lords yesterday, as the Queen desired, was just carried by the twelve new lords, and one more. Lord Radnor was not there: I hope I have cured him. Did I tell you that I have brought Dr. King in to be Gazetteer? It will be worth above two hundred pounds a year to him: I believe I told you so before, but I am forgetful. Go, get you gone to ombre, and claret, and toasted oranges. I'll go sleep.

4. I cannot get rid of the leavings of my cold. I was in the City to-day, and dined with my printer, and gave him a ballad made by several hands, I know not whom. I believe Lord Treasurer had a finger in it; I added three stanzas; I suppose Dr. Arbuthnot had the greatest share. I had been overseeing some other little prints, and a pamphlet made by one of my under-strappers. Somerset is not out yet. I doubt not but you will have the *Prophecy* in Ireland, although it is not published here, only printed copies given to friends. Tell me, do you understand it? No, faith, not without help. Tell me what you stick at, and I'll explain. We turned out a member of our Society yesterday for gross neglect and non-attendance. I writ to him by order to give him notice of it. It is Tom Harley, secretary to the Treasurer, and cousin-german to Lord Treasurer. He is going to Hanover from the Queen. I am to give the Duke of Ormond notice of his election as soon as I can see him.

5. I went this morning with a parishioner of mine, one Nuttal, who came over here for a legacy of one hundred pounds, and a roguish lawyer had refused to pay him, and would not believe he was the man. I writ to the lawyer a sharp letter, that I had taken Nuttal into my protection, and was resolved to stand by him, and the next news was, that the lawyer desired I would meet him, and attest he was the man, which I did, and his money was paid upon the spot. I then visited Lord Treasurer, who is now right again, and all well, only that the Somerset family is not out yet. I hate that; I don't like it, as the man said, by, etc. Then I went and visited poor Will Congreve, who had a French fellow tampering with one of his eyes; he is almost blind of both. I dined with some merchants in the City, but could not see Stratford, with whom I had business. Presto, leave off your impertinence, and answer our letter, saith MD. Yes, yes, one of these days, when I have nothing else to do. O, faith, this letter is a week written, and not one side done yet. These ugly spots are not tobacco, but this is the last gilt sheet I have of large paper, therefore hold your tongue. Nuttal was surprised when they gave him bits of paper instead of money, but I made Ben Tooke put him in his geers: he could not reckon ten pounds, but was puzzled with the Irish way. Ben Tooke and my printer have desired me to make them stationers to the Ordnance, of which Lord Rivers is Master, instead of the Duke of Marlborough. It will be a hundred pounds a year apiece to them, if I can get it. I will try to-morrow.

6. I went this morning to Earl Rivers, gave him joy of his new employment, and desired him to prefer my printer and bookseller to be stationers to his office. He immediately granted it me; but, like an old courtier, told me it was wholly on my account, but that he heard I had intended to engage Mr. Secretary to speak to him, and desired I would engage him to do so, but that, however, he did it only for my sake. This is a Court trick, to oblige as many as you can at once. I read prayers to poor Mrs. Wesley, who is very much out of order, instead of going to church; and then I went to Court, which I found very full, in expectation of seeing Prince Eugene, who landed last night, and lies at Leicester House; he was not to see the Queen till six this evening. I hope and believe he comes too late to do the Whigs any good. I refused dining with the Secretary, and was like to lose my dinner, which was at a private acquaintance's. I went at six to see the Prince at Court, but he was gone in to the Queen; and when he came out, Mr. Secretary,

who introduced him, walked so near him that he quite screened me from him with his great periwig. I'll tell you a good passage: as Prince Eugene was going with Mr. Secretary to Court, he told the Secretary that Hoffman, the Emperor's Resident, said to His Highness that it was not proper to go to Court without a long wig, and his was a tied-up one: "Now," says the Prince, "I knew not what to do, for I never had a long periwig in my life; and I have sent to all my valets and footmen, to see whether any of them have one, that I might borrow it, but none of them has any."—Was not this spoken very greatly with some sort of contempt? But the Secretary said it was a thing of no consequence, and only observed by gentlemen ushers. I supped with Lord Masham, where Lord Treasurer and Mr. Secretary supped with us: the first left us at twelve, but the rest did not part till two, yet I have written all this, because it is fresh: and now I'll go sleep if I can; that is, I believe I shall, because I have drank a little.

7. I was this morning to give the Duke of Ormond notice of the honour done him to make him one of our Society, and to invite him on Thursday next to the Thatched House: he has accepted it with the gratitude and humility such a preferment deserves, but cannot come till the next meeting, because Prince Eugene is to dine with him that day, which I allowed for: a good excuse, and will report accordingly. I dined with Lord Masham, and sat there till eight this evening, and came home, because I was not very well, but a little griped; but now I am well again, I will not go, at least but very seldom, to Lord Masham's suppers. Lord Treasurer is generally there, and that tempts me, but late sitting up does not agree with me: there's the short and the long, and I won't do it; so take your answer, dear little young women; and I have no more to say to you to-night, because of the Archbishop, for I am going to write a long letter to him, but not so politely as formerly: I won't trust him.

8. Well, then, come, let us see this letter; if I must answer it, I must. What's here now? yes, faith, I lamented my birthday two days after, and that's all: and you rhyme, Madam Stella; were those verses made upon my birthday? faith, when I read them, I had them running in my head all the day, and said them over a thousand times; they drank your health in all their glasses, and wished, etc. I could not get them out of my head. What? no, I believe it was not; what do I say upon the eighth of December? Compare, and see whether I say so. I am glad of

Mrs. Stoyte's recovery, heartily glad; your Dolly Manley's and Bishop of Cloyne's child I have no concern about: I am sorry in a civil way, that's all. Yes, yes, Sir George St. George dead.—Go, cry, Madam Dingley; I have written to the Dean. Raymond will be rich, for he has the building itch. I wish all he has got may put him out of debt. Poh, I have fires like lightning; they cost me twelvepence a week, beside small coal. I have got four new caps, madam, very fine and convenient, with striped cambric, instead of muslin; so Patrick need not mend them, but take the old ones. Stella snatched Dingley's word out of her pen; Presto a cold? Why, all the world here is dead with them: I never had anything like it in my life; 'tis not gone in five weeks. I hope Leigh is with you before this, and has brought your box. How do you like the ivory rasp? Stella is angry; but I'll have a finer thing for her. Is not the apron as good? I'm sure I shall never be paid it; so all's well again.—What? the quarrel with Sir John Walter? Why, we had not one word of quarrel; only he railed at me when I was gone: and Lord Keeper and Treasurer teased me for a week. It was nuts to them; a serious thing with a vengeance.—The Whigs may sell their estates then, or hang themselves, as they are disposed; for a peace there will be. Lord Treasurer told me that Connolly was going to Hanover. Your Provost is a coxcomb. Stella is a good girl for not being angry when I tell her of spelling; I see none wrong in this. God Almighty be praised that your disorder lessens; it increases my hopes mightily that they will go off. And have you been plagued with the fear of the plague? never mind those reports; I have heard them five hundred times. Replevi? Replevin, simpleton, 'tis Dingley I mean; but it is a hard word, and so I'll excuse it. I stated Dingley's accounts in my last. I forgot Catherine's sevenpenny dinner. I hope it was the beef-steaks; I'll call and eat them in spring; but Goody Stoyte must give me coffee, or green tea, for I drink no bohea. Well, ay, the pamphlet; but there are some additions to the fourth edition; the fifth edition was of four thousand, in a smaller print, sold for sixpence. Yes, I had the twenty-pound bill from Parvisol: and what then? Pray now eat the Laracor apples; I beg you not to keep them, but tell me what they are. You have had Tooke's bill in my last. And so there now, your whole letter is answered. I tell you what I do; I lay your letter before me, and take it in order, and answer what is necessary; and so and so. Well, when I expected we were all undone, I designed to retire for six months, and then steal over to Laracor; and I had in my mouth a thousand times two lines of Shakespeare, where Cardinal Wolsey says,

"A weak old man, battered with storms of state,
Is come to lay his weary bones among you."

I beg your pardon; I have cheated you all this margin, I did not perceive it; and I went on wider and wider like Stella; awkward sluts; *she writes so so, there*: that's as like as two eggs a penny.—"A weak old man," now I am saying it, and shall till to-morrow.—The Duke of Marlborough says there is nothing he now desires so much as to contrive some way how to soften Dr. Swift. He is mistaken; for those things that have been hardest against him were not written by me. Mr. Secretary told me this from a friend of the Duke's; and I'm sure now he is down, I shall not trample on him; although I love him not, I dislike his being out.— Bernage was to see me this morning, and gave some very indifferent excuses for not calling here so long. I care not twopence. Prince Eugene did not dine with the Duke of Marlborough on Sunday, but was last night at Lady Betty Germaine's assemblee, and a vast number of ladies to see him. Mr. Lewis and I dined with a private friend. I was this morning to see the Duke of Ormond, who appointed me to meet him at the Cockpit at one, but never came. I sat too some time with the Duchess. We don't like things very well yet. I am come home early, and going to be busy. I'll go write.

9. I could not go sleep last night till past two, and was waked before three by a noise of people endeavouring to break open my window. For a while I would not stir, thinking it might be my imagination; but hearing the noise continued, I rose and went to the window, and then it ceased. I went to bed again, and heard it repeated more violently; then I rose and called up the house, and got a candle: the rogues had lifted up the sash a yard; there are great sheds before my windows, although my lodgings be a storey high; and if they get upon the sheds they are almost even with my window. We observed their track, and panes of glass fresh broken. The watchmen told us to-day they saw them, but could not catch them. They attacked others in the neighbourhood about the same time, and actually robbed a house in Suffolk Street, which is the next street but one to us. It is said they are seamen discharged from service. I went up to call my man, and found his bed empty; it seems he often lies abroad. I challenged him this morning as one of the robbers. He is a sad dog; and the minute I come to Ireland I will discard him. I have this day got double iron bars to every window in my dining-room

and bed-chamber; and I hide my purse in my thread stocking between the bed's head and the wainscot. Lewis and I dined with an old Scotch friend, who brought the Duke of Douglas and three or four more Scots upon us.

10. This was our Society day, you know; but the Duke of Ormond could not be with us, because he dined with Prince Eugene. It cost me a guinea contribution to a poet, who had made a copy of verses upon monkeys, applying the story to the Duke of Marlborough; the rest gave two guineas, except the two physicians, who followed my example. I don't like this custom: the next time I will give nothing. I sat this evening at Lord Masham's with Lord Treasurer: I don't like his countenance; nor I don't like the posture of things well.

> *We cannot be stout,*
> *Till Somerset's out:*

as the old saying is.

11. Mr. Lewis and I dined with the Chancellor of the Exchequer, who eats the most elegantly of any man I know in town. I walked lustily in the Park by moonshine till eight, to shake off my dinner and wine; and then went to sup at Mr. Domville's with Ford, and stayed till twelve. It is told me to-day as a great secret that the Duke of Somerset will be out soon, that the thing is fixed; but what shall we do with the Duchess? They say the Duke will make her leave the Queen out of spite, if he be out. It has stuck upon that fear a good while already. Well, but Lewis gave me a letter from MD, N. 25. O Lord, I did not expect one this fortnight, faith. You are mighty good, that's certain: but I won't answer it, because this goes to-morrow, only what you say of the printer being taken up; I value it not; all's safe there; nor do I fear anything, unless the Ministry be changed: I hope that danger is over. However, I shall be in Ireland before such a change; which could not be, I think, till the end of the session, if the Whigs' designs had gone on.—Have not you an apron by Leigh, Madam Stella? have you all I mentioned in a former letter?

12. Morning. This goes to-day as usual. I think of going into the City; but of that at night. 'Tis fine moderate weather these two or three days last. Farewell, etc. etc.

Letter XXXIX

When I sealed up my letter this morning, I looked upon myself to be not worth a groat in the world. Last night, after Mr. Ford and I left Domville, Ford desired me to go with him for a minute upon earnest business, and then told me that both he and I were ruined; for he had trusted Stratford with five hundred pounds for tickets for the lottery, and he had been with Stratford, who confessed he had lost fifteen thousand pounds by Sir Stephen Evans, who broke last week; that he concluded Stratford must break too; that he could not get his tickets, but Stratford made him several excuses, which seemed very blind ones, etc. And Stratford had near four hundred pounds of mine, to buy me five hundred pounds in the South Sea Company. I came home reflecting a little; nothing concerned me but MD. I called all my philosophy and religion up; and, I thank God, it did not keep me awake beyond my usual time above a quarter of an hour. This morning I sent for Tooke, whom I had employed to buy the stock of Stratford, and settle things with him. He told me I was secure; for Stratford had transferred it to me in form in the South Sea House, and he had accepted it for me, and all was done on stamped parchment. However, he would be further informed; and at night sent me a note to confirm me. However, I am not yet secure; and, besides, am in pain for Ford, whom I first brought acquainted with Stratford. I dined in the City.

13. Domville and I dined with Ford to-day by appointment: the Lord Mansel told me at Court to-day that I was engaged to him; but Stratford had promised Ford to meet him and me to-night at Ford's lodgings. He did so; said he had hopes to save himself in his affair with Evans. Ford asked him for his tickets: he said he would send them to-morrow; but looking in his pocket-book, said he believed he had some of them about him, and gave him as many as came to two hundred pounds, which rejoiced us much; besides, he talked so frankly, that we might think there is no danger. I asked him, Was there any more to be settled between us in my affair? He said, No; and answered my questions just as Tooke had got them from others; so I hope I am safe. This has been a scurvy affair. I believe Stella would have half laughed at me, to see a suspicious fellow like me overreached. I saw Prince Eugene to-day at

Court: I don't think him an ugly-faced fellow, but well enough, and a good shape.

14. The Parliament was to sit to-day, and met; but were adjourned by the Queen's directions till Thursday. She designs to make some important speech then. She pretended illness; but I believe they were not ready, and they expect some opposition: and the Scotch lords are angry, and must be pacified. I was this morning to invite the Duke of Ormond to our Society on Thursday, where he is then to be introduced. He has appointed me at twelve to-morrow about some business: I would fain have his help to impeach a certain lord; but I doubt we shall make nothing of it. I intended to have dined with Lord Treasurer, but I was told he would be busy: so I dined with Mrs. Van; and at night I sat with Lord Masham till one. Lord Treasurer was there, and chid me for not dining with him: he was in very good humour. I brought home two flasks of burgundy in my chair: I wish MD had them. You see it is very late; so I'll go to bed, and bid MD good night.

15. This morning I presented my printer and bookseller to Lord Rivers, to be stationers to the Ordnance; stationers, that's the word; I did not write it plain at first. I believe it will be worth three hundred pounds a year between them. This is the third employment I have got for them. Rivers told them the Doctor commanded him, and he durst not refuse it. I would have dined with Lord Treasurer to-day again, but Lord Mansel would not let me, and forced me home with him. I was very deep with the Duke of Ormond to-day at the Cockpit, where we met to be private; but I doubt I cannot do the mischief I intended. My friend Penn came there, Will Penn the Quaker, at the head of his brethren, to thank the Duke for his kindness to their people in Ireland. To see a dozen scoundrels with their hats on, and the Duke complimenting with his off, was a good sight enough. I sat this evening with Sir William Robinson, who has mighty often invited me to a bottle of wine: and it is past twelve.

16. This being fast-day, Dr. Freind and I went into the City to dine late, like good fasters. My printer and bookseller want me to hook in another employment for them in the Tower, because it was enjoyed before by a stationer, although it be to serve the Ordnance with oil, tallow, etc., and is worth four hundred pounds per annum more: I will

try what I can do. They are resolved to ask several other employments of the same nature to other offices; and I will then grease fat sows, and see whether it be possible to satisfy them. Why am not I a stationer? The Parliament sits to-morrow, and Walpole, late Secretary at War, is to be swinged for bribery, and the Queen is to communicate something of great importance to the two Houses, at least they say so. But I must think of answering your letter in a day or two.

17. I went this morning to the Duke of Ormond about some business, and he told me he could not dine with us to-day, being to dine with Prince Eugene. Those of our Society of the House of Commons could not be with us, the House sitting late on Walpole. I left them at nine, and they were not come. We kept some dinner for them. I hope Walpole will be sent to the Tower, and expelled the House; but this afternoon the members I spoke with in the Court of Requests talked dubiously of it. It will be a leading card to maul the Duke of Marlborough for the same crime, or at least to censure him. The Queen's message was only to give them notice of the peace she is treating, and to desire they will make some law to prevent libels against the Government; so farewell to Grub Street.

18. I heard to-day that the commoners of our Society did not leave the Parliament till eleven at night, then went to those I left, and stayed till three in the morning. Walpole is expelled, and sent to the Tower. I was this morning again with Lord Rivers, and have made him give the other employment to my printer and bookseller; 'tis worth a great deal. I dined with my friend Lewis privately, to talk over affairs. We want to have this Duke of Somerset out, and he apprehends it will not be, but I hope better. They are going now at last to change the Commissioners of the Customs; my friend Sir Matthew Dudley will be out, and three more, and Prior will be in. I have made Ford copy out a small pamphlet, and sent it to the press, that I might not be known for author; 'tis *A Letter to the October Club*, if ever you heard of such a thing.—Methinks this letter goes on but slowly for almost a week: I want some little conversation with MD, and to know what they are doing just now. I am sick of politics. I have not dined with Lord Treasurer these three weeks: he chides me, but I don't care: I don't.

19. I dined to-day with Lord Treasurer: this is his day of choice company, where they sometimes admit me, but pretend to grumble. And to-day

they met on some extraordinary business; the Keeper, Steward, both Secretaries, Lord Rivers, and Lord Anglesea: I left them at seven, and came away, and have been writing to the Bishop of Clogher. I forgot to know where to direct to him since Sir George St. George's death, but I have directed to the same house: you must tell me better, for the letter is sent by the bellman. Don't write to me again till this is gone, I charge you, for I won't answer two letters together. The Duke of Somerset is out, and was with his yellow liveries at Parliament to-day. You know he had the same with the Queen, when he was Master of the Horse: we hope the Duchess will follow, or that he will take her away in spite. Lord Treasurer, I hope, has now saved his head. Has the Dean received my letter? ask him at cards to-night.

20. There was a world of people to-day at Court to see Prince Eugene, but all bit, for he did not come. I saw the Duchess of Somerset talking with the Duke of Buckingham; she looked a little down, but was extremely courteous. The Queen has the gout, but is not in much pain. Must I fill this line too? well then, so let it be. The Duke of Beaufort has a mighty mind to come into our Society; shall we let him? I spoke to the Duke of Ormond about it, and he doubts a little whether to let him in or no. They say the Duke of Somerset is advised by his friends to let his wife stay with the Queen; I am sorry for it. I dined with the Secretary to-day, with mixed company; I don't love it. Our Society does not meet till Friday, because Thursday will be a busy day in the House of Commons, for then the Duke of Marlborough's bribery is to be examined into about the pension paid him by those that furnished bread to the army.

21. I have been five times with the Duke of Ormond about a perfect trifle, and he forgets it: I used him like a dog this morning for it. I was asked to-day by several in the Court of Requests whether it was true that the author of the *Examiner* was taken up in an action of twenty thousand pounds by the Duke of Marlborough? I dined in the City, where my printer showed me a pamphlet, called *Advice to the October Club*, which he said was sent him by an unknown hand: I commended it mightily; he never suspected me; 'tis a twopenny pamphlet. I came home and got timely to bed; but about eleven one of the Secretary's servants came to me to let me know that Lord Treasurer would immediately speak to me at Lord Masham's upon earnest business, and that, if I was

abed, I should rise and come. I did so: Lord Treasurer was above with the Queen; and when he came down he laughed, and said it was not he that sent for me: the business was of no great importance, only to give me a paper, which might have been done to-morrow. I stayed with them till past one, and then got to bed again. Pize take their frolics. I thought to have answered your letter.

22. Dr. Gastrell was to see me this morning: he is an eminent divine, one of the canons of Christ Church, and one I love very well: he said he was glad to find I was not with James Broad. I asked what he meant. "Why," says he, "have you not seen the Grub Street paper, that says Dr. Swift was taken up as author of the *Examiner*, on an action of twenty thousand pounds, and was now at James Broad's?" who, I suppose, is some bailiff. I knew of this; but at the Court of Requests twenty people told me they heard I had been taken up. Lord Lansdowne observed to the Secretary and me that the Whigs spread three lies yesterday; that about me; and another, that Maccartney, who was turned out last summer, is again restored to his places in the army; and the third, that Jack Hill's commission for Lieutenant of the Tower is stopped, and that Cadogan is to continue. Lansdowne thinks they have some design by these reports; I cannot guess it. Did I tell you that Sacheverell has desired mightily to come and see me? but I have put it off: he has heard that I have spoken to the Secretary in behalf of a brother whom he maintains, and who desires an employment. T'other day at the Court of Requests Dr. Yalden saluted me by name: Sacheverell, who was just by, came up to me, and made me many acknowledgment and compliments. Last night I desired Lord Treasurer to do something for that brother of Sacheverell's: he said he never knew he had a brother, but thanked me for telling him, and immediately put his name in his table-book. I will let Sacheverell know this, that he may take his measures accordingly, but he shall be none of my acquaintance. I dined to-day privately with the Secretary, left him at six, paid a visit or two, and came home.

23. I dined again to-day with the Secretary, but could not despatch some business I had with him, he has so much besides upon his hands at this juncture, and preparing against the great business to-morrow, which we are top full of. The Minister's design is that the Duke of Marlborough shall be censured as gently as possible, provided his friends will not make head to defend him, but if they do, it may end in some severer

votes. A gentleman, who was just now with him, tells me he is much cast down, and fallen away; but he is positive, if he has but ten friends in the House, that they shall defend him to the utmost, and endeavour to prevent the least censure upon him, which I think cannot be, since the bribery is manifest. Sir Solomon Medina paid him six thousand pounds a year to have the employment of providing bread for the army, and the Duke owns it in his letter to the Commissioners of Accounts. I was to-night at Lord Masham's: Lord Dupplin took out my new little pamphlet, and the Secretary read a great deal of it to Lord Treasurer: they all commended it to the skies, and so did I, and they began a health to the author. But I doubt Lord Treasurer suspected; for he said, "This is Mr. Davenant's style," which is his cant when he suspects me. But I carried the matter very well. Lord Treasurer put the pamphlet in his pocket to read at home. I'll answer your letter to-morrow.

24. The Secretary made me promise to dine with him to-day, after the Parliament was up: I said I would come; but I dined at my usual time, knowing the House would sit late on this great affair. I dined at a tavern with Mr. Domville and another gentleman; I have not done so before these many months. At ten this evening I went to the Secretary, but he was not come home: I sat with his lady till twelve, then came away; and he just came as I was gone, and he sent to my lodgings, but I would not go back; and so I know not how things have passed, but hope all is well; and I will tell you to-morrow day. It is late, etc.

25. The Secretary sent to me this morning to know whether we should dine together. I went to him, and there I learned that the question went against the Duke of Marlborough, by a majority of a hundred; so the Ministry is mighty well satisfied, and the Duke will now be able to do no hurt. The Secretary and I, and Lord Masham, etc., dined with Lieutenant-General Withers, who is just going to look after the army in Flanders: the Secretary and I left them a little after seven, and I am come home, and will now answer your letter, because this goes to-morrow: let me see—The box at Chester; oh, burn that box, and hang that Sterne; I have desired one to inquire for it who went toward Ireland last Monday, but I am in utter despair of it. No, I was not splenetic; you see what plunges the Court has been at to set all right again. And that Duchess is not out yet, and may one day cause more mischief. Somerset shows all about a letter from the Queen, desiring

him to let his wife continue with her. Is not that rare! I find Dingley smelled a rat; because the Whigs are *upish*; but if ever I hear that word again, I'll *uppish* you. I am glad you got your rasp safe and sound; does Stella like her apron? Your critics about guarantees of succession are puppies; that's an answer to the objection. The answerers here made the same objection, but it is wholly wrong. I am of your opinion that Lord Marlborough is used too hardly: I have often scratched out passages from papers and pamphlets sent me, before they were printed, because I thought them too severe. But he is certainly a vile man, and has no sort of merit beside the military. The *Examiners* are good for little: I would fain have hindered the severity of the two or three last, but could not. I will either bring your papers over, or leave them with Tooke, for whose honesty I will engage. And I think it is best not to venture them with me at sea. Stella is a prophet, by foretelling so very positively that all would be well. Duke of Ormond speak against peace? No, simpleton, he is one of the staunchest we have for the Ministry. Neither trouble yourself about the printer: he appeared the first day of the term, and is to appear when summoned again; but nothing else will come of it. Lord Chief-Justice is cooled since this new settlement. No; I will not split my journals in half; I will write but once a fortnight: but you may do as you will; which is, read only half at once, and t'other half next week. So now your letter is answered. (P—on these blots.) What must I say more? I will set out in March, if there be a fit of fine weather; unless the Ministry desire me to stay till the end of the session, which may be a month longer; but I believe they will not: for I suppose the peace will be made, and they will have no further service for me. I must make my canal fine this summer, as fine as I can. I am afraid I shall see great neglects among my quicksets. I hope the cherry-trees on the river walk are fine things now. But no more of this.

26. I forgot to finish this letter this morning, and am come home so late I must give it to the bellman; but I would have it go to-night, lest you should think there is anything in the story of my being arrested in an action of twenty thousand pounds by Lord Marlborough, which I hear is in Dyer's Letter, and, consequently, I suppose, gone to Ireland. Farewell, dearest MD, etc. etc.

LETTER XL

I have no gilt paper left of this size, so you must be content with plain. Our Society dined together to-day, for it was put off, as I told you, upon Lord Marlborough's business on Thursday. The Duke of Ormond dined with us to-day, the first time: we were thirteen at table; and Lord Lansdowne came in after dinner, so that we wanted but three. The Secretary proposed the Duke of Beaufort, who desires to be one of our Society; but I stopped it, because the Duke of Ormond doubts a little about it; and he was gone before it was proposed. I left them at seven, and sat this evening with poor Mrs. Wesley, who has been mightily ill to-day with a fainting fit; she has often convulsions, too: she takes a mixture with asafoetida, which I have now in my nose, and everything smells of it. I never smelt it before; 'tis abominable. We have eight packets, they say, due from Ireland.

27. I could not see Prince Eugene at Court to-day, the crowd was so great. The Whigs contrive to have a crowd always about him, and employ the rabble to give the word, when he sets out from any place. When the Duchess of Hamilton came from the Queen after church, she whispered me that she was going to pay me a visit. I went to Lady Oglethorpe's, the place appointed; for ladies always visit me in third places; and she kept me till near four: she talks too much, is a plaguy detractor, and I believe I shall not much like her. I was engaged to dine with Lord Masham: they stayed as long as they could, yet had almost dined, and were going in anger to pull down the brass peg for my hat, but Lady Masham saved it. At eight I went again to Lord Masham's; Lord Treasurer is generally there at night: we sat up till almost two. Lord Treasurer has engaged me to contrive some way to keep the Archbishop of York from being seduced by Lord Nottingham. I will do what I can in it to-morrow. 'Tis very late, so I must go sleep.

28. Poor Mrs. Manley, the author, is very ill of a dropsy and sore leg: the printer tells me he is afraid she cannot live long. I am heartily sorry for her: she has very generous principles for one of her sort, and a great deal of good sense and invention: she is about forty, very homely, and very fat. Mrs. Van made me dine with her to-day. I was this morning with

the Duke of Ormond and the Prolocutor about what Lord Treasurer spoke to me yesterday; I know not what will be the issue. There is but a slender majority in the House of Lords, and we want more. We are sadly mortified at the news of the French taking the town in Brazil from the Portuguese. The sixth edition of three thousand of the *Conduct of the Allies* is sold, and the printer talks of a seventh: eleven thousand of them have been sold, which is a most prodigious run. The little twopenny *Letter of Advice to the October Club* does not sell: I know not the reason, for it is finely written, I assure you; and, like a true author, I grow fond of it, because it does not sell: you know that it is usual to writers to condemn the judgment of the world: if I had hinted it to be mine, everybody would have bought it, but it is a great secret.

29. I borrowed one or two idle books of *Contes des Fées*, and have been reading them these two days, although I have much business upon my hands. I loitered till one at home; then went to Mr. Lewis at his office; and the Vice-Chamberlain told me that Lady Rialton had yesterday resigned her employment of lady of the bed-chamber, and that Lady Jane Hyde, Lord Rochester's daughter, a mighty pretty girl, is to succeed. He said, too, that Lady Sunderland would resign in a day or two. I dined with Lewis, and then went to see Mrs. Wesley, who is better to-day. But you must know that Mr. Lewis gave me two letters, one from the Bishop of Cloyne, with an enclosed from Lord Inchiquin to Lord Treasurer, which he desires I would deliver and recommend. I am told that lord was much in with Lord Wharton, and I remember he was to have been one of the Lords Justices by his recommendation; yet the Bishop recommends him as a great friend to the Church, etc. I'll do what I think proper. T'other letter was from little saucy MD, N. 26. O Lord, never saw the like, under a cover, too, and by way of journal; we shall never have done. Sirrahs, how durst you write so soon, sirrahs? I won't answer it yet.

30. I was this morning with the Secretary, who was sick, and out of humour: he would needs drink champagne some days ago, on purpose to spite me, because I advised him against it, and now he pays for it. Stella used to do such tricks formerly; he put me in mind of her. Lady Sunderland has resigned her place too. It is Lady Catherine Hyde that succeeds Lady Rialton, and not Lady Jane. Lady Catherine is the late Earl of Rochester's daughter. I dined with the Secretary, then visited

his lady; and sat this evening with Lady Masham: the Secretary came to us; but Lord Treasurer did not; he dined with the Master of the Rolls, and stayed late with him. Our Society does not meet till to-morrow se'nnight, because we think the Parliament will be very busy to-morrow upon the state of the war, and the Secretary, who is to treat as President, must be in the House. I fancy my talking of persons and things here must be very tedious to you, because you know nothing of them, and I talk as if you did. You know Kevin's Street, and Werburgh Street, and (what do you call the street where Mrs. Walls lives?) and Ingoldsby, and Higgins, and Lord Santry; but what care you for Lady Catherine Hyde? Why do you say nothing of your health, sirrah? I hope it is well.

31. Trimnel, Bishop of Norwich, who was with this Lord Sunderland at Moor Park in their travels, preached yesterday before the House of Lords; and to-day the question was put to thank him, and print his sermon; but passed against him; for it was a terrible Whig sermon. The Bill to repeal the Act for naturalising Protestant foreigners passed the House of Lords to-day by a majority of twenty, though the Scotch lords went out, and would vote neither way, in discontent about the Duke of Hamilton's patent, if you know anything of it. A poem is come out to-day inscribed to me, by way of a flirt; for it is a Whiggish poem, and good for nothing. They plagued me with it in the Court of Requests. I dined with Lord Treasurer at five alone, only with one Dutchman. Prior is now a Commissioner of the Customs. I told you so before, I suppose. When I came home to-night, I found a letter from Dr. Sacheverell, thanking me for recommending his brother to Lord Treasurer and Mr. Secretary for a place. Lord Treasurer sent to him about it: so good a solicitor was I, although I once hardly thought I should be a solicitor for Sacheverell.

Feb. 1. Has not your Dean of St. Patrick received my letter? you say nothing of it, although I writ above a month ago. My printer has got the gout, and I was forced to go to him to-day, and there I dined. It was a most delicious day: why don't you observe whether the same days be fine with you? To-night, at six, Dr. Atterbury, and Prior, and I, and Dr. Freind, met at Dr. Robert Freind's house at Westminster, who is master of the school: there we sat till one, and were good enough company. I here take leave to tell politic Dingley that the passage in the *Conduct of the Allies* is so far from being blamable that the Secretary designs to insist upon it in the House of Commons, when the Treaty of Barrier is debated there, as it now shortly will, for they have ordered it to be laid before them. The pamphlet of Advice to the October Club begins now to sell; but I believe its fame will hardly reach Ireland: 'tis finely written, I assure you. I long to answer your letter, but won't yet; you know, 'tis late, etc.

2. This ends Christmas, and what care I? I have neither seen, nor felt, nor heard any Christmas this year. I passed a lazy dull day. I was this morning with Lord Treasurer, to get some papers from him, which he will remember as much as a cat, although it be his own business. It threatened rain, but did not much; and Prior and I walked an hour in the Park, which quite put me out of my measures. I dined with a friend hard by; and in the evening sat with Lord Masham till twelve. Lord Treasurer did not come; this is an idle dining-day usually with him. We want to hear from Holland how our peace goes on; for we are afraid of those scoundrels the Dutch, lest they should play us tricks. Lord Mar, a Scotch earl, was with us at Lord Masham's: I was arguing with him about the stubbornness and folly of his countrymen; they are so angry about the affair of the Duke of Hamilton, whom the Queen has made a duke of England, and the House of Lords will not admit him. He swears he would vote for us, but dare not, because all Scotland would detest him if he did: he should never be chosen again, nor be able to live there.

3. I was at Court to-day to look for a dinner, but did not like any that were offered me; and I dined with Lord Mountjoy. The Queen has the gout in her knee, and was not at chapel. I hear we have a Dutch mail, but I know not what news, although I was with the Secretary this morning. He showed me a letter from the Hanover Envoy, Mr. Bothmar, complaining that the Barrier Treaty is laid before the House of Commons; and desiring that no infringement may be made in the guarantee of the succession; but the Secretary has written him a peppering answer. I fancy you understand all this, and are able states-girls, since you have read the *Conduct of the Allies*. We are all preparing against the Birthday; I think it is Wednesday next. If the Queen's gout increases, it will spoil sport. Prince Eugene has two fine suits made against it; and the Queen is to give him a sword worth four thousand pounds, the diamonds set transparent.

4. I was this morning soliciting at the House of Commons' door for Mr. Vesey, a son of the Archbishop of Tuam, who has petitioned for a Bill to relieve him in some difficulty about his estate: I secured him above fifty members. I dined with Lady Masham. We have no packet from Holland, as I was told yesterday: and this wind will hinder many people from appearing at the Birthday, who expected clothes from Holland. I appointed to meet a gentleman at the Secretary's to-night, and they both failed. The House of Commons have this day made many severe votes about our being abused by our Allies. Those who spoke drew all their arguments from my book, and their votes confirm all I writ; the Court had a majority of a hundred and fifty: all agree that it was my book that spirited them to these resolutions; I long to see them in print. My head has not been as well as I could wish it for some days past, but I have not had any giddy fit, and I hope it will go over.

5. The Secretary turned me out of his room this morning, and showed me fifty guineas rolled up, which he was going to give some French spy. I dined with four Irishmen at a tavern to-day: I thought I had resolved against it before, but I broke it. I played at cards this evening at Lady Masham's, but I only played for her while she was waiting; and I won her a pool, and supped there. Lord Treasurer was with us, but went away before twelve. The ladies and lords have all their clothes ready against to-morrow: I saw several mighty fine, and I hope there will be a great appearance, in spite of that spiteful French fashion of the Whiggish ladies not to come, which they have all resolved to a woman; and I hope it will more spirit the Queen against them for ever.

6. I went to dine at Lord Masham's at three, and met all the company just coming out of Court; a mighty crowd: they stayed long for their coaches: I had an opportunity of seeing several lords and ladies of my acquaintance in their fineries. Lady Ashburnham looked the best in my eyes. They say the Court was never fuller nor finer. Lord Treasurer, his lady, and two daughters and Mrs. Hill, dined with Lord and Lady Masham; the five ladies were monstrous fine. The Queen gave Prince Eugene the diamond sword to-day; but nobody was by when she gave it except my Lord Chamberlain. There was an entertainment of opera songs at night, and the Queen was at all the entertainment, and is very well after it. I saw Lady Wharton, as ugly as the devil, coming out in the crowd all in an undress; she has been with the Marlborough

daughters and Lady Bridgewater in St. James's, looking out of the window all undressed to see the sight. I do not hear that one Whig lady was there, except those of the bed-chamber. Nothing has made so great a noise as one Kelson's chariot, that cost nine hundred and thirty pounds, the finest was ever seen. The rabble huzzaed him as much as they did Prince Eugene. This is Birthday chat.

7. Our Society met to-day: the Duke of Ormond was not with us; we have lessened our dinners, which were grown so extravagant that Lord Treasurer and everybody else cried shame. I left them at seven, visited for an hour, and then came home, like a good boy. The Queen is much better after yesterday's exercise: her friends wish she would use a little more. I opposed Lord Jersey's election into our Society, and he is refused: I likewise opposed the Duke of Beaufort; but I believe he will be chosen in spite of me: I don't much care; I shall not be with them above two months; for I resolve to set out for Ireland the beginning of April next (before I treat them again), and see my willows.

8. I dined to-day in the City. This morning a scoundrel dog, one of the Queen's music, a German, whom I had never seen, got access to me in my chamber by Patrick's folly, and gravely desired me to get an employment in the Customs for a friend of his, who would be very grateful; and likewise to forward a project of his own, for raising ten thousand pounds a year upon operas: I used him civiller than he deserved; but it vexed me to the pluck. He was told I had a mighty interest with Lord Treasurer, and one word of mine, etc. Well; I got home early on purpose to answer MD's letter, N. 26; for this goes to-morrow.—Well; I never saw such a letter in all my life; so saucy, so journalish, so sanguine, so pretending, so everything. I satisfied all your fears in my last: all is gone well, as you say; yet you are an impudent slut to be so positive; you will swagger so upon your sagacity that we shall never have done. Pray don't mislay your reply; I would certainly print it, if I had it here: how long is it? I suppose half a sheet: was the answer written in Ireland? Yes, yes, you shall have a letter when you come from Ballygall. I need not tell you again who's out and who's in: we can never get out the Duchess of Somerset.—So, they say Presto writ the *Conduct*, etc. Do they like it? I don't care whether they do or no; but the resolutions printed t'other day in the Votes are almost quotations from it, and would never have passed if that book had not

been written. I will not meddle with the Spectator, let him fair-sex it to the world's end. My disorder is over, but blood was not from the p-les.—Well, Madam Dingley, the frost; why, we had a great frost, but I forget how long ago; it lasted above a week or ten days: I believe about six weeks ago; but it did not break so soon with us, I think, as December 29; yet I think it was about that time, on second thoughts. MD can have no letter from Presto, says you; and yet four days before you own you had my thirty-seventh, unreasonable sluts! The Bishop of Gloucester is not dead, and I am as likely to succeed the Duke of Marlborough as him if he were; there's enough for that now. It is not unlikely that the Duke of Shrewsbury will be your Governor; at least I believe the Duke of Ormond will not return.—Well, Stella again: why, really three editions of the *Conduct*, etc., is very much for Ireland; it is a sign you have some honest among you. Well; I will do Mr. Manley all the service I can; but he will ruin himself. What business had he to engage at all about the City? Can't he wish his cause well, and be quiet, when he finds that stirring will do it no good, and himself a great deal of hurt? I cannot imagine who should open my letter: it must be done at your side.—If I hear of any thoughts of turning out Mr. Manley, I will endeavour to prevent it. I have already had all the gentlemen of Ireland here upon my back often, for defending him. So now I have answered your saucy letter. My humble service to Goody Stoyte and Catherine; I will come soon for my dinner.

9. Morning. My cold goes off at last; but I think I have got a small new one. I have no news since last. They say we hear by the way of Calais, that peace is very near concluding. I hope it may be true. I'll go and seal up my letter, and give it myself to-night into the post-office; and so I bid my dearest MD farewell till to-night. I heartily wish myself with them, as hope saved. My willows, and quicksets, and trees, will be finely improved, I hope, this year. It has been fine hard frosty weather yesterday and to-day. Farewell, etc. etc. etc.

LONDON, *Feb.* 9, 1711–12

When my letter is gone, and I have none of yours to answer, my conscience is so clear, and my shoulder so light, and I go on with such courage to prate upon nothing to deerichar MD, oo would wonder. I dined with Sir Matthew Dudley, who is newly turned out of Commission of the Customs. He affects a good heart, and talks in the extremity of Whiggery, which was always his principle, though he was gentle a little, while he kept in employment. We can yet get no packets from Holland. I have not been with any of the Ministry these two or three days. I keep out of their way on purpose, for a certain reason, for some time, though I must dine with the Secretary to-morrow, the choosing of the company being left to me. I have engaged Lord Anglesea and Lord Carteret, and have promised to get three more; but I have a mind that none else should be admitted: however, if I like anybody at Court to-morrow, I may perhaps invite them. I have got another cold, but not very bad. Nite. . . MD.

10. I saw Prince Eugene at Court to-day very plain; he's plaguy yellow, and tolerably ugly besides. The Court was very full, and people had their Birthday clothes. I dined with the Secretary to-day. I was to invite five, but I only invited two, Lord Anglesea and Lord Carteret. Pshaw, I told you this but yesterday. We have no packets from Holland yet. Here are a parcel of drunken Whiggish lords, like your Lord Santry, who come into chocolate-houses and rail aloud at the Tories, and have challenges sent them, and the next morning come and beg pardon. General Ross was like to swinge the Marquis of Winchester for this trick t'other day; and we have nothing else now to talk of till the Parliament has had another bout with the state of the war, as they intended in a few days. They have ordered the Barrier Treaty to be laid before them; and it was talked some time ago, as if there was a design to impeach Lord Townshend, who made it. I have no more politics now. Nite dee MD.

11. I dined with Lord Anglesea to-day, who had seven Irishmen to be my companions, of which two only were coxcombs; one I did not know, and t'other was young Blith, who is a puppy of figure here, with a fine chariot. He asked me one day at Court, when I had been just talking with some lords who stood near me, "Doctor, when shall we see you in

the county of Meath?" I whispered him to take care what he said, for the people would think he was some barbarian. He never would speak to me since, till we met to-day. I went to Lady Masham's to-night, and sat with Lord Treasurer and the Secretary there till past two o'clock; and when I came home, found some letters from Ireland, which I read, but can say nothing of them till to-morrow, 'tis so very late; but I must always be. . . , late or early. Nite deelest sollahs.

12. One letter was from the Bishop of Clogher last night, and t'other from Walls, about Mrs. South's salary, and his own pension of £18 for his tithe of the park. I will do nothing in either; the first I cannot serve in, and the other is a trifle; only you may tell him I had his letter, and will speak to Ned Southwell about what he desires me. You say nothing of your Dean's receiving my letter. I find Clements, whom I recommended to Lord Anglesea last year, at Walls's desire, or rather the Bishop of Clogher's, is mightily in Lord Anglesea's favour. You may tell the Bishop and Walls so; I said to Lord Anglesea that I was (glad) I had the good luck to recommend him, etc. I dined in the City with my printer, to consult with him about some papers Lord Treasurer gave me last night, as he always does, too late; however, I will do something with them. My third cold is a little better; I never had anything like it before, three colds successively; I hope I shall have the fourth. Those messengers come from Holland to-day, and they brought over the six packets that were due. I know not the particulars yet, for when I was with the Secretary at noon they were just opening; but one thing I find, that the Dutch are playing us tricks, and tampering with the French; they are dogs; I shall know more tomollow. . . MD.

13. I dined to-day privately with my friend Lewis, at his lodgings, to consult about some observations on the Barrier Treaty. Our news from Holland is not good. The French raise difficulties, and make such offers to the Allies as cannot be accepted. And the Dutch are uneasy that we are likely to get anything for ourselves; and the Whigs are glad at all this. I came home early, and have been very busy three or four hours. I had a letter from Dr. Pratt to-day by a private hand, recommending the bearer to me, for something that I shall not trouble myself about. Wesley writ to recommend the same fellow to me. His expression is that, hearing I am acquainted with my Lord Treasurer, he desires I would do so and so: a matter of nothing. What puppies are mankind!

I hope I shall be wiser when I have once done with Courts. I think you han't troubled me much with your recommendations. I would do you all the saavis I could.

Pray have you got your aplon, maram Ppt? I paid for it but yesterday; that puts me in mind of it. I writ an inventory of what things I sent by Leigh in one of my letters; did you compare it with what you got? I hear nothing of your cards now; do you never play? Yes, at Ballygall. Go to bed. Nite, deelest MD.

14. Our Society dined to-day at Mr. Secretary's house. I went there at four; but hearing the House of Commons would sit late upon the Barrier Treaty, I went for an hour to Kensington, to see Lord Masham's children. My young nephew, his son of six months old, has got a swelling in his neck; I fear it is the evil. We did not go to dinner till eight at night, and I left them at ten. The Commons have been very severe on the Barrier Treaty, as you will find by their votes. A Whig member took out the *Conduct of the Allies*, and read that passage about the succession with great resentment; but none seconded him. The Church party carried every vote by a great majority. The A.B. Dublin is so railed at by all who come from Ireland that I can defend him no longer. Lord Anglesea assured me that the story of applying Piso out of Tacitus to Lord Treasurer's being wounded is true. I believe the Duke of Beaufort will be admitted to our Society next meeting. To-day I published the *Fable of Midas*, a poem, printed in a loose half-sheet of paper. I know not how it will sell; but it passed wonderfully at our Society to-night; and Mr. Secretary read it before me the other night to Lord Treasurer, at Lord Masham's, where they equally approved of it. Tell me how it passes with you. I think this paper is larger than ordinary; for here is six days' journal, and no nearer the bottom. I fear these journals are very dull. Nite my deelest lives.

15. Mr. Lewis and I dined by invitation with a Scotch acquaintance, after I had been very busy in my chamber till two afternoon. My third cold is now very troublesome on my breast, especially in the morning. This is a great revolution in my health; colds never used to return so soon with me, or last so long. 'Tis very surprising this news to-day of the Dauphin and Dauphiness both dying within six days. They say the old King is almost heart-broke. He has had prodigious mortifications in his family. The Dauphin has left two little sons, of four and two

years old; the eldest is sick. There is a foolish story got about the town that Lord Strafford, one of our Plenipotentiaries, is in the interests of France; and it has been a good while said that Lord Privy Seal and he do not agree very well. They are both long practised in business, but neither of them of much parts. Strafford has some life and spirit, but is infinitely proud, and wholly illiterate. Nite, MD.

16. I dined to-day in the City with my printer, to finish something I am doing about the Barrier Treaty; but it is not quite done. I went this evening to Lord Masham's, where Lord Treasurer sat with us till past twelve. The Lords have voted an Address to the Queen, to tell her they are not satisfied with the King of France's offers. The Whigs brought it in of a sudden; and the Court could not prevent it, and therefore did not oppose it. The House of Lords is too strong in Whigs, notwithstanding the new creations; for they are very diligent, and the Tories as lazy: the side that is down has always most industry. The Whigs intended to have made a vote that would reflect on Lord Treasurer; but their project was not ripe. I hit my face such a rap by calling the coach to stop to-night, that it is plaguy sore, the bone beneath the eye. Nite dee logues.

17. The Court was mighty full to-day, and has been these many Sundays; but the Queen was not at chapel. She has got a little fit of the gout in her foot. The good of going to Court is that one sees all one's acquaintance, whom otherwise I should hardly meet twice a year. Prince Eugene dines with the Secretary to-day, with about seven or eight General Officers, or foreign Ministers. They will be all drunk, I am sure. I never was in company with this Prince: I have proposed to some lords that we should have a sober meal with him; but I can't compass it. It is come over in the Dutch news prints that I was arrested on an action of twenty thousand pounds by the Duke of Marlborough. I did not like my Court invitation to-day; so Sir Andrew Fountaine and I went and dined with Mrs. Van. I came home at six, and have been very busy till this minute, and it is past twelve. So I got into bed to write to MD. . . MD. We reckon the Dauphin's death will put forward the peace a good deal. Pray is Dr. Griffith reconciled to me yet? Have I done enough to soften him? . . . Nite deelest logues.

18. Lewis had Guiscard's picture: he bought it, and offered it to Lord Treasurer, who promised to send for it, but never did; so I made Lewis

give it me, and I have it in my room; and now Lord Treasurer says he will take it from me: is that fair? He designs to have it at length in the clothes he was when he did the action, and a penknife in his hand; and Kneller is to copy it from this that I have. I intended to dine with Lord Treasurer to-day, but he has put me off till to-morrow; so I dined with Lord Dupplin. You know Lord Dupplin very well; he is a brother of the Society. Well, but I have received a letter from the Bishop of Cloyne, to solicit an affair for him with Lord Treasurer, and with the Parliament, which I will do as soon as fly. I am not near so keen about other people's affairs as. . . Ppt used to reproach me about; it was a judgment on me. Harkee, idle dearees both, meetinks I begin to want a rettle flom MD: faith, and so I do. I doubt you have been in pain about the report of my being arrested. The pamphleteers have let me alone this month, which is a great wonder: only the third part of the *Answer to the Conduct*, which is lately come out. (Did I tell you of it already?) The House of Commons goes on in mauling the late Ministry and their proceedings. Nite deelest MD.

19. I dined with Lord Treasurer to-day, and sat with him till ten, in spite of my teeth, though my printer waited for me to correct a sheet. I told him of four lines I writ extempore with my pencil, on a bit of paper in his house, while he lay wounded. Some of the servants, I suppose, made waste-paper of them, and he never had heard of them. Shall I tell them you? They were inscribed to Mr. Harley's physician. Thus

> *On Britain Europe's safety lies;*
> *Britain is lost, if Harley dies.*
> *Harley depends upon your skill:*
> *Think what you save, or what you kill.*

Are not they well enough to be done off-hand; for that is the meaning of the word extempore, which you did not know, did you? I proposed that some company should dine with him on the 8th of March, which was the day he was wounded, but he says he designs that the Lords of the Cabinet, who then sat with him, should dine that day with him: however, he has invited me too. I am not got rid of my cold; it plagues me in the morning chiefly. Nite, MD.

20. After waiting to catch the Secretary coming out from Sir Thomas Hanmer, for two hours, in vain, about some business, I went into the

City to my printer, to correct some sheets of the *Barrier Treaty and Remarks*, which must be finished to-morrow: I have been horrible busy for some days past, with this and some other things; and I wanted some very necessary papers, which the Secretary was to give me, and the pamphlet must now be published without them. But they are all busy too. Sir Thomas Hanmer is Chairman of the Committee for drawing up a Representation of the state of the nation to the Queen, where all the wrong steps of the Allies and late Ministry about the war will be mentioned. The Secretary, I suppose, was helping him about it to-day; I believe it will be a pepperer. Nite, deel MD.

21. I have been six hours to-day morning writing nineteen pages of a letter to Lord Treasurer, about forming a Society or Academy to correct and fix the English language. (Is English a speech or a language?) It will not be above five or six more. I will send it to him to-morrow, and will print it, if he desires me. I dined, you know, with our Society to-day: Thursday is our day. We had a new member admitted; it was the Duke of Beaufort. We had thirteen met: brother Ormond was not there, but sent his excuse that Prince Eugene dined with him. I left them at seven, being engaged to go to Sir Thomas Hanmer, who desired I would see him at that hour. His business was that I would *hoenlbp ihainm itavoi dsroanws ubpl tohne sroegporaensiepnotlastoigobn*, which I consented to do; but know not whether I shall succeed, because it is a little out of my way. However, I have taken my share. Nite, MD.

22. I finished the rest of my letter to Lord Treasurer to-day, and sent it to him about one o'clock; and then dined privately with my friend Mr. Lewis, to talk over some affairs of moment. I had gotten the thirteenth volume of Rymer's Collection of the Records of the Tower for the University of Dublin. I have two volumes now. I will write to the Provost, to know how I shall send them to him; no, I won't, for I will bring them myself among my own books. I was with Hanmer this morning, and there were the Secretary and Chancellor of the Exchequer very busy with him, laying their heads together about the representation. I went to Lord Masham's to-night, and Lady Masham made me read to her a pretty twopenny pamphlet, called *The St. Albans Ghost*. I thought I had writ it myself; so did they; but I did not. Lord Treasurer came down to us from the Queen, and we stayed till two o'clock. That is the best night-place I have. The usual company are Lord and Lady Masham,

Lord Treasurer, Dr. Arbuthnot, and I; sometimes the Secretary, and sometimes Mrs. Hill of the bed-chamber, Lady Masham's sister. I assure oo, it im vely rate now; but zis goes to-morrow: and I must have time to converse with own richar MD. Nite, deelest sollahs.

23. I have no news to tell you this last day, nor do I know where I shall dine. I hear the Secretary is a little out of order; perhaps I may dine there, perhaps not. I sent Hanmer what he wanted from me, I know not how he will approve of it. I was to do more of the same sort; I am going out, and must carry zis in my pottick to give it at some general post-house. I will talk further with oo at night. I suppose in my next I shall answer a letter from MD that will be sent me. On Tuesday it will be four weeks since I had your last, N. 26. This day se'nnight I expect one, for that will be something more than a full month. Farewell, MD. . . deelest. . . MD MD MD. . . ME ME ME. . . logues. . . lele.

LONDON, *Feb.* 23, 1711–12

After having disposed my last letter in the post-office, I am now to begin this with telling MD that I dined with the Secretary to-day, who is much out of order with a cold, and feverish; yet he went to the Cabinet Council to-night at six, against my will. The Secretary is much the greatest commoner in England, and turns the whole Parliament, who can do nothing without him; and if he lives and has his health, will, I believe, be one day at the head of affairs. I have told him sometimes that, if I were a dozen years younger, I would cultivate his favour, and trust my fortune with his. But what care oo for all this? I am sorry when I came first acquainted with this Ministry that I did not send you their names and characters, and then you would have relished what I would have writ, especially if I had let you into the particulars of affairs: but enough of this. Nite, deelest logues.

24. I went early this morning to the Secretary, who is not yet well. Sir Thomas Hanmer and the Chancellor of the Exchequer came while I was there, and he would not let me stir; so I did not go to church, but was busy with them till noon, about the affair I told you in my last. The other two went away; and I dined with the Secretary, and found my head very much out of order, but no absolute fit; and I have not been well all this day. It has shook me a little. I sometimes sit up very late at Lord Masham's, and have writ much for several days past: but I will amend both; for I have now very little business, and hope I shall have no more, and I am resolved to be a great rider this summer in Ireland. I was to see Mrs. Wesley this evening, who has been somewhat better for this month past, and talks of returning to the Bath in a few weeks. Our peace goes on but slowly; the Dutch are playing tricks, and we do not push it strongly as we ought. The fault of our Court is delay, of which the Queen has a great deal; and Lord Treasurer is not without his share. But pay richar MD ret us know a little of your life and tonvelsasens. Do you play at ombre, or visit the Dean, and Goody Walls and Stoytes and Manleys, as usual? I must have a letter from oo, to fill the other side of this sheet. Let me know what you do. Is my aunt alive yet?

Oh, pray, now I think of it, be so kind to step to my aunt, and take notice of my great-grandfather's picture; you know he has a ring on his finger, with a seal of an anchor and dolphin about it; but I think there is besides, at the bottom of the picture, the same coat of arms quartered with another, which I suppose was my great-grandmother's. If this be so, it is a stronger argument than the seal. And pray see whether you think that coat of arms was drawn at the same time with the picture, or whether it be of a later hand; and ask my aunt what she knows about it. But perhaps there is no such coat of arms on the picture, and I only dreamed it. My reason is, because I would ask some herald here, whether I should choose that coat, or one in Guillim's large folio of heraldry, where my uncle Godwin is named with another coat of arms of three stags. This is sad stuff to rite; so nite, MD.

25. I was this morning again with the Secretary, and we were two hours busy; and then went together to the Park, Hyde Park, I mean; and he walked to cure his cold, and we were looking at two Arabian horses sent some time ago to Lord Treasurer. The Duke of Marlborough's coach overtook us, with his Grace and Lord Godolphin in it; but they did not see us, to our great satisfaction; for neither of us desired that either of those two lords should see us together. There was half a dozen ladies riding like cavaliers to take the air. My head is better to-day. I dined with the Secretary; but we did no business after dinner, and at six I walked into the fields; the days are grown pure and long; then I went to visit Perceval and his family, whom I had seen but twice since they came to town. They too are going to the Bath next month. Countess Doll of Meath is such an owl that, wherever I visit, people are asking me whether I know such an Irish lady, and her figure and her foppery? I came home early, and have been amusing myself with looking into one of Rymer's volumes of the Records of the Tower, and am mighty easy to think I have no urgent business upon my hands. My third cold is not yet off; I sometimes cough, and am not right with it in the morning. Did I tell you that I believe it is Lady Masham's hot room that gives it me? I never knew such a stove; and in my conscience I believe both my lord and she, my Lord Treasurer, Mr. Secretary, and myself have all suffered by it. We have all had colds together, but I walk home on foot. Nite dee logues.

26. I was again busy with the Secretary. We read over some papers, and did a good deal of business; and I dined with him, and we were to do more business after dinner; but after dinner is after dinner—an old

saying and a true, "much drinking, little thinking." We had company with us, and nothing could be done, and I am to go there again to-morrow. I have now nothing to do; and the Parliament, by the Queen's recommendation, is to take some method for preventing libels, etc., which will include pamphlets, I suppose. I don't know what method they will take, but it comes on in a day or two. To-day in the morning I visited upwards: first I saw the Duke of Ormond below stairs, and gave him joy of his being declared General in Flanders; then I went up one pair of stairs, and sat with the Duchess; then I went up another pair of stairs, and paid a visit to Lady Betty; and desired her woman to go up to the garret, that I might pass half an hour with her, but she was young and handsome, and would not. The Duke is our President this week, and I have bespoke a small dinner on purpose, for good example. Nite mi deelest logues.

27. I was again with the Secretary this morning; but we only read over some papers with Sir Thomas Hanmer; then I called at Lord Treasurer's; it was his levee-day, but I went up to his bed-chamber, and said what I had to say. I came down and peeped in at the chamber, where a hundred fools were waiting, and two streets were full of coaches. I dined in the City with my printer, and came back at six to Lord Treasurer, who had invited me to dinner, but I refused him. I sat there an hour or two, and then went to Lord Masham's. They were all abroad: so truly I came, and read whatever stuff was next me. I can sit and be idle now, which I have not been above a year past. However, I will stay out the session, to see if they have any further commands for me, and that, I suppose, will end in April. But I may go somewhat before, for I hope all will be ended by then, and we shall have either a certain peace, or certain war. The Ministry is contriving new funds for money by lotteries, and we go on as if the war were to continue, but I believe it will not. 'Tis pretty late now, ung oomens; so I bid oo nite, own dee dallars.

28. I have been packing up some books in a great box I have bought, and must buy another for clothes and luggage. This is a beginning towards a removal. I have sent to Holland for a dozen shirts, and design to buy another new gown and hat. I will come over like a zinkerman, and lay out nothing in clothes in Ireland this good while. I have writ this night to the Provost. Our Society met to-day as usual, and we were fourteen, beside the Earl of Arran, whom his brother, the Duke

of Ormond, brought among us against all order. We were mightily shocked; but, after some whispers, it ended in choosing Lord Arran one of our Society, which I opposed to his face, but it was carried by all the rest against me.

29. This is leap year, and this is leap day. Prince George was born on this day. People are mistaken; and some here think it is St. David's Day; but they do not understand the virtue of leap year. I have nothing to do now, boys, and have been reading all this day like Gumdragon; and yet I was dictating some trifles this morning to a printer. I dined with a friend hard by, and the weather was so discouraging I could not walk. I came home early, and have read two hundred pages of Arran. Alexander the Great is just dead: I do not think he was poisoned; betwixt you and me, all those are but idle stories: it is certain that neither Ptolemy nor Aristobulus thought so, and they were both with him when he died. It is a pity we have not their histories. The Bill for limiting Members of Parliament to have but so many places passed the House of Commons, and will pass the House of Lords, in spite of the Ministry, which you know is a great lessening of the Queen's power. Four of the new lords voted against the Court in this point. It is certainly a good Bill in the reign of an ill prince, but I think things are not settled enough for it at present. And the Court may want a majority upon a pinch. Nite deelest logues. Rove Pdfr.

March 1. I went into the City to inquire after poor Stratford, who has put himself a prisoner into the Queen's Bench, for which his friends blame him much, because his creditors designed to be very easy with him. He grasped at too many things together, and that was his ruin. There is one circumstance relative to Lieutenant-General Meredith that is very melancholy: Meredith was turned out of all his employments last year, and had about £10,000 left to live on. Stratford, upon friendship, desired he might have the management of it for Meredith, to put it into the stocks and funds for the best advantage, and now he has lost it all. You have heard me often talk of Stratford; we were class-fellows at school and university. I dined with some merchants, his friends, to-day, and they said they expected his breaking this good while. I gave him notice of a treaty of peace, while it was a secret, of which he might have made good use, but that helped to ruin him; for he gave money, reckoning there would be actually a peace by this time, and consequently stocks rise high. Ford narrowly 'scaped losing £500 by him, and so did I too. Nite, my two deelest rives MD.

2. Morning. I was wakened at three this morning, my man and the people of the house telling me of a great fire in the Haymarket. I slept again, and two hours after my man came in again, and told me it was my poor brother Sir William Wyndham's house burnt, and that two maids, leaping out of an upper room to avoid the fire, both fell on their heads, one of them upon the iron spikes before the door, and both lay dead in the streets. It is supposed to have been some carelessness of one or both those maids. The Duke of Ormond was there helping to put out the fire. Brother Wyndham gave £6,000 but a few months ago for that house, as he told me, and it was very richly furnished. I shall know more particulars at night. He married Lady Catherine Seymour, the Duke of Somerset's daughter; you know her, I believe.—At night. Wyndham's young child escaped very narrowly; Lady Catherine escaped barefoot; they all went to Northumberland House. Mr. Brydges's house, at next door, is damaged much, and was like to be burnt. Wyndham has lost above £10,000 by this accident; his lady above a thousand pounds worth of clothes. It was a terrible accident. He was not at Court to-day. I dined with Lord Masham. The Queen was not at church. Nite, MD.

3. Pray tell Walls that I spoke to the Duke of Ormond and Mr. Southwell about his friend's affair, who, I find, needed not me for a solicitor, for they both told me the thing would be done. I likewise mentioned his own affair to Mr. Southwell, and I hope that will be done too, for Southwell seems to think it reasonable, and I will mind him of it again. Tell him this nakedly. You need not know the particulars. They are secrets: one of them is about Mrs. South having a pension; the other about his salary from the Government for the tithes of the park that lie in his parish, to be put upon the establishment, but oo must not know zees sings, zey are secrets; and we must keep them flom nauty dallars. I dined in the City with my printer, with whom I had some small affair; but I have no large work on my hands now. I was with Lord Treasurer this morning, and hat care oo for zat? Oo dined with the Dean to-day. Monday is parson's holiday, and oo lost oo money at cards and dice; ze Givars device. So I'll go to bed. Nite, my two deelest logues.

4. I sat to-day with poor Mrs. Wesley, who made me dine with her. She is much better than she was. I heartily pray for her health, out of the entire love I bear to her worthy husband. This day has passed very insignificantly. But it is a great comfort to me now that I can come home and read, and have nothing upon my hands to write. I was at Lord Masham's to-night, and stayed there till one. Lord Treasurer was there; but I thought, I thought he looked melancholy, just as he did at the beginning of the session, and he was not so merry as usual. In short, the majority in the House of Lords is a very weak one: and he has much ado to keep it up; and he is not able to make those removes he would, and oblige his friends; and I doubt too he does not take care enough about it, or rather cannot do all himself, and will not employ others: which is his great fault, as I have often told you. 'Tis late. Nite, MD.

5. I wish you a merry Lent. I hate Lent; I hate different diets, and furmity and butter, and herb porridge; and sour devout faces of people who only put on religion for seven weeks. I was at the Secretary's office this morning; and there a gentleman brought me two letters, dated last October; one from the Bishop of Clogher, t'other from Walls. The gentleman is called Colonel Newburgh. I think you mentioned him to me some time ago; he has business in the House of Lords. I will do him what service I can. The Representation of the House of Commons is printed: I have not seen it yet; it is plaguy severe, they say. I dined with Dr. Arbuthnot, and had a true Lenten dinner, not in point of victuals, but spleen; for his wife and a child or two were sick in the house, and that was full as mortifying as fish. We have had fine mighty cold frosty weather for some days past. I hope you take the advantage of it, and walk now and then. You never answer that part of my letters where I desire you to walk. I must keep my breath to cool my Lenten porridge. Tell Jemmy Leigh that his boy that robbed him now appears about the town: Patrick has seen him once or twice. I knew nothing of his being robbed till Patrick told me he had seen the boy. I wish it had been Sterne that had been robbed, to be revenged for the box that he lost, and be p-xed to him. Nite, MD.

6. I hear Mr. Prior has suffered by Stratford's breaking. I was yesterday to see Prior, who is not well, and I thought he looked melancholy. He can ill afford to lose money. I walked before dinner in the Mall a good

while with Lord Arran and Lord Dupplin, two of my brothers, and then we went to dinner, where the Duke of Beaufort was our President. We were but eleven to-day. We are now in all nine lords and ten commoners. The Duke of Beaufort had the confidence to propose his brother-in-law, the Earl of Danby, to be a member; but I opposed it so warmly that it was waived. Danby is not above twenty, and we will have no more boys, and we want but two to make up our number. I stayed till eight, and then we all went away soberly. The Duke of Ormond's treat last week cost £20, though it was only four dishes and four, without a dessert; and I bespoke it in order to be cheap. Yet I could not prevail to change the house. Lord Treasurer is in a rage with us for being so extravagant: and the wine was not reckoned neither; for that is always brought by him that is President. Lord Orrery is to be President next week; and I will see whether it cannot be cheaper; or else we will leave the house. . . Lord Masham made me go home with him to-night to eat boiled oysters. Take oysters, wash them clean; that is, wash their shells clean; then put your oysters into an earthen pot, with their hollow sides down, then put this pot into a great kettle with water, and so let them boil. Your oysters are boiled in their own liquor, and not mixed water. Lord Treasurer was not with us; he was very ill to-day with a swimming in the head, and is gone home to be cupped, and sent to desire Lady Masham to excuse him to the Queen. Nite, dee MD.

7. I was to-day at the House of Lords about a friend's Bill. Then I crossed the water at Westminster Stairs to Southwark, went through St. George's Fields to the Mint, which is the dominion of the King's Bench Prison, where Stratford lodges in a blind alley, and writ to me to come to him; but he was gone to the 'Change. I thought he had something to say to me about his own affairs. I found him at his usual coffee-house, and went to his own lodgings, and dined with him and his wife, and other company. His business was only to desire I would intercede with the Ministry about his brother-in-law, Ben Burton, of Dublin, the banker, who is likely to come into trouble, as we hear, about spreading false Whiggish news. I hate Burton, and told Stratford so; and I will advise the Duke of Ormond to make use of it, to keep the rogue in awe. Mrs. Stratford tells me her husband's creditors have consented to give him liberty to get up his debts abroad; and she hopes he will pay them all. He was cheerfuller than I have seen him this great while. I have walked much to-day.—Night, deelest logues.

8. This day twelvemonth Mr. Harley was stabbed; but he is ill, and takes physic to-day, I hear ('tis now morning), and cannot have the Cabinet Council with him, as he intended, nor me to say grace. I am going to see him. Pray read the Representation; 'tis the finest that ever was writ. Some of it is Pdfr's style, but not very much. This is the day of the Queen's accession to the Crown; so it is a great day. I am going to Court, and will dine with Lord Masham; but I must go this moment to see the Secretary about some businesses; so I will seal up this, and put it in the post my own self. Farewell, deelest hearts and souls, MD. Farewell MD MD MD FW FW FW ME ME Lele Lele Lele Sollahs lele.

Letter XLIII

I carried my forty-second letter in my pocket till evening, and then put it in the general post.—I went in the morning to see Lord Treasurer, who had taken physic, and was drinking his broth. I had been with the Secretary before, to recommend a friend, one Dr. Freind, to be Physician-General; and the Secretary promised to mention it to the Queen. I can serve everybody but myself. Then I went to Court, and carried Lord Keeper and the Secretary to dine with Lord Masham, when we drank the Queen and Lord Treasurer with every health, because this was the day of his stabbing.—Then I went and played pools at picquet with Lady Masham and Mrs. Hill; won ten shillings, gave a crown to the box, and came home. I met at my lodgings a letter from Joe, with a bit annexed from Ppt. What Joe asks is entirely out of my way, and I take it for a foolish whim in him. Besides, I know not who is to give a patent: if the Duke of Ormond, I would speak to him; and if it come in my head I will mention it to Ned Southwell. They have no patents that I know of for such things here, but good security is all; and to think that I would speak to Lord Treasurer for any such matter at random is a jest. Did I tell you of a race of rakes, called the Mohocks, that play the devil about this town every night, slit people's noses, and beat them, etc.? Nite, sollahs, and rove Pdfr. Nite, MD.

9. I was at Court to-day, and nobody invited me to dinner, except one or two, whom I did not care to dine with; so I dined with Mrs. Van. Young Davenant was telling us at Court how he was set upon by the Mohocks, and how they ran his chair through with a sword. It is not safe being in the streets at night for them. The Bishop of Salisbury's son is said to be of the gang. They are all Whigs; and a great lady sent to me, to speak to her father and to Lord Treasurer, to have a care of them, and to be careful likewise of myself; for she heard they had malicious intentions against the Ministers and their friends. I know not whether there be anything in this, though others are of the same opinion. The weather still continues very fine and frosty. I walked in the Park this evening, and came home early to avoid the Mohocks. Lord Treasurer is better. Nite, my own two deelest MD.

10. I went this morning again to the Lord Treasurer, who is quite recovered; and I stayed till he went out. I dined with a friend in the City, about a little business of printing; but not my own. You must buy a small twopenny pamphlet, called *Law is a Bottomless Pit*. 'Tis very prettily written, and there will be a Second Part. The Commons are very slow in bringing in their Bill to limit the press, and the pamphleteers make good use of their time; for there come out three or four every day. Well, but is not it time, methinks, to have a letter from MD? 'Tis now six weeks since I had your Number 26. I can assure oo I expect one before this goes; and I'll make shorter day's journals than usual, 'cause I hope to fill up a good deal of t'other side with my answer. Our fine weather lasts yet, but grows a little windy. We shall have rain soon, I dispose. Go to cards, sollahs, and I to seep. Nite, MD.

11. Lord Treasurer has lent the long letter I writ him to Prior, and I can't get Prior to return it. I want to have it printed, and to make up this Academy for the improvement of our language. Faith, we never shall improve it so much as FW has done; sall we? No, faith, ourrichar gangridge. I dined privately with my friend Lewis, and then went to see Ned Southwell, and talk with him about Walls's business, and Mrs. South's. The latter will be done; but his own not. Southwell tells me that it must be laid before Lord Treasurer, and the nature of it explained, and a great deal of clutter, which is not worth the while; and maybe Lord Treasurer won't do it (at) last; and it is, as Walls says himself, not above forty shillings a year difference. You must tell Walls this, unless he would have the business a secret from you: in that case only say I did all I could with Ned Southwell, and it can't be done; for it must be laid before Lord Treasurer, etc., who will not do it; and besides, it is not worth troubling his lordship. So nite, my two deelest nuntyes nine MD.

12. Here is the D—and all to do with these Mohocks. Grub Street papers about them fly like lightning, and a list printed of near eighty put into several prisons, and all a lie; and I begin almost to think there is no truth, or very little, in the whole story. He that abused Davenant was a drunken gentleman; none of that gang. My man tells me that one of the lodgers heard in a coffee-house, publicly, that one design of the Mohocks was upon me, if they could catch me; and though I believe nothing of it, I forbear walking late, and they have put me to the

charge of some shillings already. I dined to-day with Lord Treasurer and two gentlemen of the Highlands of Scotland, yet very polite men. I sat there till nine, and then went to Lord Masham's, where Lord Treasurer followed me, and we sat till twelve; and I came home in a chair for fear of the Mohocks, and I have given him warning of it too. Little Harrison, whom I sent to Holland, is now actually made Queen's Secretary at The Hague. It will be in the *Gazette* to-morrow. 'Tis worth twelve hundred pounds a year. Here is a young fellow has writ some Sea Eclogues, poems of Mermen, resembling pastorals of shepherds, and they are very pretty, and the thought is new. Mermen are he-mermaids; Tritons, natives of the sea. Do you understand me? I think to recommend him to our Society to-morrow. His name is Diaper. P—on him, I must do something for him, and get him out of the way. I hate to have any new wits rise, but when they do rise I would encourage them; but they tread on our heels and thrust us off the stage. Nite deelest MD.

13. You would laugh to see our printer constantly attending our Society after dinner, and bringing us whatever new thing he has printed, which he seldom fails to do. Yet he had nothing to-day. Lord Lansdowne, one of our Society, was offended at a passage in this day's *Examiner*, which he thinks reflects on him, as I believe it does, though in a mighty civil way. 'Tis only that his underlings cheat; but that he is a very fine gentleman every way, etc. Lord Orrery was President to-day; but both our dukes were absent. Brother Wyndham recommended Diaper to the Society. I believe we shall make a contribution among ourselves, which I don't like. Lord Treasurer has yet done nothing for us, but we shall try him soon. The company parted early, but Freind, and Prior, and I, sat a while longer and reformed the State, and found fault with the Ministry. Prior hates his Commission of the Customs, because it spoils his wit. He says he dreams of nothing but cockets, and dockets, and drawbacks, and other jargon words of the custom-house. Our good weather went away yesterday, and the nights are now dark, and I came home before ten. Night nown. . . deelest sollahs.

14. I have been plagued this morning with solicitors, and with nobody more than my brother, Dr. Freind, who must needs have to get old Dr. Lawrence, the Physician-General, turned out and himself in. He has argued with me so long upon the reasonableness of it, that I am fully convinced it is very unreasonable; and so I would tell the Secretary,

if I had not already made him speak to the Queen. Besides, I know not but my friend Dr. Arbuthnot would be content to have it himself, and I love him ten times better than Freind. What's all this to you? but I must talk of things as they happen in the day, whether you know anything of them or no. I dined in the City, and, coming back, one Parson Richardson of Ireland overtook me. He was here last summer upon a project of converting the Irish and printing Bibles, etc., in that language, and is now returned to pursue it on. He tells me Dr. Coghill came last night (to) town. I will send to see how he does to-morrow. He gave me a letter from Walls about his old business. Nite, deelest MD.

15. I had intended to be early with the Secretary this morning, when my man admitted upstairs one Mr. Newcomb, an officer, who brought me a letter from the Bishop of Clogher, with four lines added by Mrs. Ashe, all about that Newcomb. I think, indeed, his case is hard, but God knows whether I shall be able to do him any service. People will not understand: I am a very good second, but I care not to begin a recommendation, unless it be for an intimate friend. However, I will do what I can. I missed the Secretary, and then walked to Chelsea to dine with the Dean of Christ Church, who was engaged to Lord Orrery with some other Christ Church men. He made me go with him whether I would or not, for they have this long time admitted me a Christ Church man. Lord Orrery, generally every winter, gives his old acquaintance of that college a dinner. There were nine clergymen at table, and four laymen. The Dean and I soon left them, and after a visit or two, I went to Lord Masham's, and Lord Treasurer, Arbuthnot and I sat till twelve. And now I am come home and got to bed. I came afoot, but had my man with me. Lord Treasurer advised me not to go in a chair, because the Mohocks insult chairs more than they do those on foot. They think there is some mischievous design in those villains. Several of them, Lord Treasurer told me, are actually taken up. I heard at dinner that one of them was killed last night. We shall know more in a little time. I don't like them, as the men said. Nite MD.

16. This morning, at the Secretary's, I met General Ross, and recommended Newcomb's case to him, who promises to join with me in working up the Duke of Ormond to do something for him. Lord Winchelsea told me to-day at Court that two of the Mohocks caught a maid of old Lady Winchelsea's, at the door of their house in the

Park, where she was with a candle, and had just lighted out somebody. They cut all her face, and beat her without any provocation. I hear my friend Lewis has got a Mohock in one of the messenger's hands. The Queen was at church to-day, but was carried in an open chair. She has got an ugly cough, Arbuthnot, her physician, says. I dined with Crowe, late Governor of Barbados; an acquaintance of Sterne's. After dinner I asked him whether he had heard of Sterne. "Here he is," said he, "at the door in a coach:" and in came Sterne. He has been here this week. He is buying a captainship in his cousin Sterne's regiment. He told me he left Jemmy Leigh playing at cards with you. He is to give 800 guineas for his commission. I suppose you know all this better than I. How shall I have room to answer oo rettle hen I get it, I have gone so far already? Nite, deelest logues MD.

17. Dr. Sacheverell came this morning to give me thanks for getting his brother an employment. It was but six or seven weeks since I spoke to Lord Treasurer for him. Sacheverell brought Trapp along with him. We dined together at my printer's, and I sat with them till seven. I little thought, and I believe so did he, that ever I should be his solicitor to the present Ministry, when I left Ireland. This is the seventh I have now provided for since I came, and can do nothing for myself. I don't care; I shall have Ministries and other people obliged to me. Trapp is a coxcomb, and the t'other is not very deep; and their judgment in things of wit or sense is miraculous. The Second *Part of Law is a Bottomless Pit* is just now printed, and better, I think, than the first. Night, my two deel saucy dallars.

18. There is a proclamation out against the Mohocks. One of those that are taken is a baronet. I dined with poor Mrs. Wesley, who is returning to the Bath. Mrs. Perceval's young daughter has got the smallpox, but will do well. I walked this evening in the Park, and met Prior, who made me go home with him, where I stayed till past twelve, and could not get a coach, and was alone, and was afraid enough of the Mohocks. I will do so no more, though I got home safe. Prior and I were talking discontentedly of some managements, that no more people are turned out, which get Lord Treasurer many enemies: but whether the fault be in him, or the Queen, I know not; I doubt, in both. Ung omens, it is now seven weeks since I received your last; but I expect one next Irish packet, to fill the rest of this paper; but if it

don't come, I'll do without it: so I wish oo good luck at ombre with the Dean. Nite, nuntyes nine.

19. Newcomb came to me this morning, and I went to the Duke of Ormond to speak for him; but the Duke was just going out to take the oaths for General. The Duke of Shrewsbury is to be Lord Lieutenant of Ireland. I walked with Domville and Ford to Kensington, where we dined, and it cost me above a crown. I don't like it, as the man said. It was very windy walking. I saw there Lord Masham's children. The youngest, my nephew, I fear, has got the king's evil; the other two are daughters of three and four years old. 'Twas very windy walking. The gardens there are mighty fine. I passed the evening at Lord Masham's with Lord Treasurer and Arbuthnot, as usual, and we stayed till past one; but I had my man to come with me, and at home I found three letters; one from one Fetherston, a parson, with a postscript of Tisdall's to recommend him: and Fetherston, whom I never saw, has been so kind to give me a letter of attorney to recover a debt for him. Another from Lord Abercorn, to get him the dukedom of Chatelherault from the King of France; in which I will do what I can, for his pretensions are very just. The third, I warrant you, from our MD. 'Tis a great stir this, of getting a dukedom from the King of France: but it is only to speak to the Secretary, and get the Duke of Ormond to engage in it, and mention the case to Lord Treasurer, etc., and this I shall do. Nite deelest richar MD.

20. I was with the Duke of Ormond this morning, about Lord Abercorn, Dr. Freind, and Newcomb. Some will do, and some will not do; that's wise, marams. The Duke of Shrewsbury is certainly to be your Governor. I will go in a day or two, and give the Duchess joy, and recommend the Archbishop of Dublin to her. I writ to the Archbishop, some months ago, that it would be so, and told him I would speak a good word for him to the Duchess; and he says he has a great respect for her, etc. I made our Society change their house, and we met to-day at the Star and Garter in the Pall Mall. Lord Arran was President. The other dog was so extravagant in his bills, that for four dishes and four, first and second course, without wine or dessert, he charged twenty-one pounds, six shillings, and eightpence, to the Duke of Ormond. We design, when all have been Presidents this turn, to turn it into a reckoning of so much a head; but we shall break up when the session ends. Nite deelest MD.

21. Morning. Now I will answer MD's rettle, N. 27; you that are adding to your number and grumbling, had made it 26, and then altered it to 27. I believe it is above a month since your last; yes, it is above seven weeks since I had your last: but I ought to consider that this was twelve days right, so that makes it pretty even. O, the sirry zade, with her excuses of a fortnight at Ballygall, seeing their friends, and landlord running away. O Rold, hot a cruttle and a bustle!—No—if you will have it—I am not Dean of Wells, nor know anything of being so; nor is there anything in the story; and that's enough. It was not Roper sent that news: Roper is my humble slave.—Yes, I heard of your resolves, and that Burton was embroiled. Stratford spoke to me in his behalf; but I said I hated the rascal. Poor Catherine gone to Wales? But she will come back again, I hope. I would see her in my journey, if she were near the road; and bring her over. Joe is a fool; that sort of business is not at all in my way, pray put him off it. People laugh when I mention it. Bed ee paadon, Maram; I'm drad oo rike ee aplon: no harm, I hope. And so. . . DD wonders she has not a letter at the day; oo'll have it soon. . . The D—he is! married to that vengeance! Men are not to be believed. I don't think her a fool. Who would have her? Dilly will be governed like an ass; and she will govern like a lion. Is not that true, Ppt? Why, Sterne told me he left you at ombre with Leigh; and yet you never saw him. I know nothing of his wife being here: it may cost her a c—(I don't care to write that word plain). He is a little in doubt about buying his commission. Yes, I will bring oo over all the little papers I can think on. I thought I sent you, by Leigh, all that were good at that time. The author of the *Sea Eclogues* sent books to the Society yesterday, and we gave him guineas apiece; and, maybe, will do further from him (for him, I mean). So the Bishop of Clogher, and lady, were your guests for a night or two. Why, Ppt, you are grown a great gamester and company keeper. I did say to myself, when I read those names, just what you guess; and you clear up the matter wonderfully. You may converse with those two nymphs if you please, but the—take me if ever I do. Iss, fais, it is delightful to hear that Ppt is every way Ppt now, in health, and looks, and all. Pray God keep her so, many, many, many years. I doubt the session will not be over till the end of April; however, I shall not wait for it, if the Ministry will let me go sooner. I wish I were just now in my garden at Laracor. I would set out for Dublin early on Monday, and bring you an account of my young trees, which you are better acquainted with than the Ministry, and so am I. Oh, now you have got Number 41, have you so? Why,

perhaps, I forgot, and kept it to next post in my pocket: I have done such tricks. My cold is better, but not gone. I want air and riding. Hold ee tongue, oo Ppt, about colds at Moor Park! the case is quite different. I will do what you desire me for Tisdall, when I next see Lord Anglesea. Pray give him my service. The weather is warm these three or four days, and rainy. I am to dine to-day with Lewis and Darteneuf at Somers's, the Clerk of the Kitchen at Court. Darteneuf loves good bits and good sups. Good mollows richar sollohs.—At night. I dined, as I said; and it cost me a shilling for a chair. It has rained all day, and is very warm. Lady Masham's young son, my nephew, is very ill; and she is out of mind with grief. I pity her mightily. I am got home early, and going to write to the Bishop of Clogher, but have no politics to send him. Nite my own two deelest saucy d(ear) ones.

22. I am going into the City this morning with a friend about some business; so I will immediately seal up this, and keep it in my pottick till evening, and zen put it in the post. The weather continues warm and gloomy. I have heard no news since I went to bed, so can say no more. Pray send. . . that I may have time to write to. . . about it. I have here underneath given order for forty shillings to Mrs. Brent, which you will send to Parvisol. Farewell, deelest deel MD, and rove Pdfr dearly dearly. Farewell, MD, MD, FW, FW, FW, ME, ME, ME, Lele lele lele lele lele lele, and lele aden.

LETTER XLIV

Ugly, nasty weather. I was in the City to-day with Mrs. Wesley and Mrs. Perceval, to get money from a banker for Mrs. Wesley, who goes to Bath on Thursday. I left them there, and dined with a friend, and went to see Lord Treasurer; but he had people with him I did not know: so I went to Lady Masham's, and lost a crown with her at picquet, and then sat with Lord Masham and Lord Treasurer, etc., there till past one; but I had my man with me, to come home. I gave in my forty-third, and one for the Bishop of Clogher, to the post-office, as I came from the City; and so oo know 'tis late now, and I have nothing to say for this day. Our Mohocks are all vanished; however, I shall take care of my person. Nite my own two deelest nuntyes MD.

23. I was this morning, before church, with the Secretary, about Lord Abercorn's business, and some others. My soliciting season is come, and will last as long as the session. I went late to Court, and the company was almost gone. The Court serves me for a coffee-house; once a week I meet acquaintance there, that I should not otherwise see in a quarter. There is a flying report that the French have offered a cessation of arms, and to give us Dunkirk, and the Dutch Namur, for security, till the peace is made. The Duke of Ormond, they say, goes in a week. Abundance of his equipage is already gone. His friends are afraid the expense of this employment will ruin him, since he must lose the government of Ireland. I dined privately with a friend, and refused all dinners offered me at Court; which, however, were but two, and I did not like either. Did I tell you of a scoundrel about the Court that sells employments to ignorant people, and cheats them of their money? He lately made a bargain for the Vice-Chamberlain's place, for seven thousand pounds, and had received some guineas earnest; but the whole thing was discovered t'other day, and examination taken of it by Lord Dartmouth, and I hope he will be swinged. The Vice-Chamberlain told me several particulars of it last night at Lord Masham's. Can DD play at ombre yet, enough to hold the cards while Ppt steps into the next room? Nite deelest sollahs.

24. This morning I recommended Newcomb again to the Duke of Ormond, and left Dick Stewart to do it further. Then I went to visit the

Duchess of Hamilton, who was not awake. So I went to the Duchess of Shrewsbury, and sat an hour at her toilet. I talked to her about the Duke's being Lord Lieutenant. She said she knew nothing of it; but I rallied her out of that, and she resolves not to stay behind the Duke. I intend to recommend the Bishop of Clogher to her for an acquaintance. He will like her very well: she is, indeed, a most agreeable woman, and a great favourite of mine. I know not whether the ladies in Ireland will like her. I was at the Court of Requests, to get some lords to be at a committee to-morrow, about a friend's Bill: and then the Duke of Beaufort gave me a poem, finely bound in folio, printed at Stamford, and writ by a country squire. Lord Exeter desired the Duke to give it the Queen, because the author is his friend; but the Duke desired I would let him know whether it was good for anything. I brought it home, and will return it to-morrow, as the dullest thing I ever read; and advise the Duke not to present it. I dined with Domville at his lodgings, by invitation; for he goes in a few days for Ireland. Nite dee MD.

25. There is a mighty feast at a Tory sheriff's to-day in the City: twelve hundred dishes of meat.—Above five lords, and several hundred gentlemen, will be there, and give four or five guineas apiece, according to custom. Dr. Coghill and I dined, by invitation, at Mrs. Van's. It has rained or mizzled all day, as my pockets feel. There are two new answers come out to the *Conduct of the Allies*. The last year's *Examiners*, printed together in a small volume, go off but slowly. The printer over-printed himself by at least a thousand; so soon out of fashion are party papers, however so well writ. The *Medleys* are coming out in the same volume, and perhaps may sell better. Our news about a cessation of arms begins to flag, and I have not these three days seen anybody in business to ask them about it. We had a terrible fire last night in Drury Lane, or thereabouts, and three or four people destroyed. One of the maids of honour has the smallpox; but the best is, she can lose no beauty; and we have one new handsome maid of honour. Nite MD.

26. I forgot to tell you that on Sunday last, about seven at night, it lightened above fifty times as I walked the Mall, which I think is extraordinary at this time of the year, and the weather was very hot. Had you anything of this in Dublin? I intended to dine with Lord Treasurer to-day; but Lord Mansel and Mr. Lewis made me dine with them at Kit Musgrave's. I sat the evening with Mrs. Wesley, who goes to-morrow

morning to the Bath. She is much better than she was. The news of the French desiring a cessation of arms, etc., was but town talk. We shall know in a few days, as I am told, whether there will be a peace or not. The Duke of Ormond will go in a week for Flanders, they say. Our Mohocks go on still, and cut people's faces every night; fais, they shan't cut mine, I like it better as it is. The dogs will cost me at least a crown a week in chairs. I believe the souls of your houghers of cattle have got into them, and now they don't distinguish between a cow and a Christian. I forgot to wish you yesterday a happy New Year. You know the twenty-fifth of March is the first day of the year, and now you must leave off cards, and put out your fire. I'll put out mine the first of April, cold or not cold. I believe I shall lose credit with you by not coming over at the beginning of April; but I hoped the session would be ended, and I must stay till then; yet I would fain be at the beginning of my willows growing. Perceval tells me that the quicksets upon the flat in the garden do not grow so well as those famous ones on the ditch. They want digging about them. The cherry-trees, by the river-side, my heart is set upon. Nite MD.

27. Society day. You know that, I suppose. Dr. Arthburnett was President. His dinner was dressed in the Queen's kitchen, and was mighty fine. We ate it at Ozinda's Chocolate-house, just by St. James's. We were never merrier, nor better company, and did not part till after eleven. I did not summon Lord Lansdowne: he and I are fallen out. There was something in an *Examiner* a fortnight ago that he thought reflected on the abuses in his office (he is Secretary at War), and he writ to the Secretary that he heard I had inserted that paragraph. This I resented highly, that he should complain of me before he spoke to me. I sent him a peppering letter, and would not summon him by a note, as I did the rest; nor ever will have anything to say to him, till he begs my pardon. I met Lord Treasurer to-day at Lady Masham's. He would fain have carried me home to dinner, but I begged his pardon. What! upon a Society day! No, no. 'Tis rate, sollahs. I an't dlunk. Nite MD.

28. I was with my friend Lewis to-day, getting materials for a little mischief; and I dined with Lord Treasurer, and three or four fellows I never saw before. I left them at seven, and came home, and have been writing to the Archbishop of Dublin, and cousin Deane, in answer to one of his of four months old, that I spied by chance, routing among my papers. I have a pain these two days exactly upon the top of my

left shoulder. I fear it is something rheumatic; it winches now and then. Shall I put flannel to it? Domville is going to Ireland; he came here this morning to take leave of me, but I shall dine with him to-morrow. Does the Bishop of Clogher talk of coming for England this summer? I think Lord Molesworth told me so about two months ago. The weather is bad again; rainy and very cold this evening. Do you know what the longitude is? A projector has been applying himself to me, to recommend him to the Ministry, because he pretends to have found out the longitude. I believe he has no more found it out than he has found out mine. . . However, I will gravely hear what he says, and discover him a knave or fool. Nite MD.

29. I am plagued with these pains in my shoulder; I believe it is rheumatic; I will do something for it to-night. Mr. Lewis and I dined with Mr. Domville, to take our leave of him. I drank three or four glasses of champagne by perfect teasing, though it is bad for my pain; but if it continue, I will not drink any wine without water till I am well. The weather is abominably cold and wet. I am got into bed, and have put some old flannel, for want of new, to my shoulder, and rubbed it with Hungary water. It is plaguy hard. I never would drink any wine, if it were not for my head, and drinking has given me this pain. I will try abstemiousness for a while. How does MD do now; how does DD and Ppt? You must know I hate pain, as the old woman said. But I'll try to go seep. My flesh sucks up Hungary water rarely. My man is an awkward rascal, and makes me peevish. Do you know that t'other day he was forced to beg my pardon, that he could not shave my head, his hand shook so? He is drunk every day, and I design to turn him off soon as ever I get to Ireland. I'll write no more now, but go to sleep, and see whether sleep and flannel will cure my shoulder. Nite deelest MD.

30. I was not able to go to church or Court to-day for my shoulder. The pain has left my shoulder, and crept to my neck and collar-bone. It makes me think of poo Ppt's bladebone. Urge, urge, urge; dogs gnawing. I went in a chair at two, and dined with Mrs. Van, where I could be easy, and came back at seven. My Hungary water is gone; and to-night I use spirits of wine, which my landlady tells me is very good. It has rained terribly all day long, and is extremely cold. I am very uneasy, and such cruel twinges every moment! Nite deelest MD.

31. April 1, 2, 3, 4, 5, 6, 7, 8. All these days I have been extremely ill, though I twice crawled out a week ago; but am now recovering, though very weak. The violence of my pain abated the night before last: I will just tell you how I was, and then send away this letter, which ought to have gone Saturday last. The pain increased with mighty violence in my left shoulder and collar-bone, and that side my neck. On Thursday morning appeared great red spots in all those places where my pain was, and the violence of the pain was confined to my neck behind, a little on the left side; which was so violent that I had not a minute's ease, nor hardly a minute's sleep in three days and nights. The spots increased every day, and bred little pimples, which are now grown white, and full of corruption, though small. The red still continues too, and most prodigious hot and inflamed. The disease is the shingles. I eat nothing but water-gruel; am very weak; but out of all violent pain. The doctors say it would have ended in some violent disease if it had not come out thus. I shall now recover fast. I have been in no danger of life, but miserable torture. I must not write too much. So adieu, deelest MD MD MD FW FW, ME ME ME, Lele. I can say lele yet, oo see. Fais, I don't conceal a bit, as hope saved.

I must purge and clyster after this; and my next letter will not be in the old order of journal, till I have done with physic. An't oo surprised to see a letter want half a side?

Letter XLV

I had your twenty-eighth two or three days ago. I can hardly answer it now. Since my last I have been extremely ill. 'Tis this day just a month since I felt a small pain on the tip of my left shoulder, which grew worse, and spread for six days; then broke all out by my collar and left side of my neck in monstrous red spots inflamed, and these grew to small pimples. For four days I had no rest, nor nights, for a pain in my neck; then I grew a little better; afterward, where my pains were, a cruel itching seized me, beyond whatever I could imagine, and kept me awake several nights. I rubbed it vehemently, but did not scratch it: then it grew into three or four great sores like blisters, and run; at last I advised the doctor to use it like a blister, so I did with melilot plasters, which still run: and am now in pain enough, but am daily mending. I kept my chamber a fortnight, then went out a day or two, but then confined myself again. Two days ago I went to a neighbour to dine, but yesterday again kept at home. To-day I will venture abroad a little, and hope to be well in a week or ten days. I never suffered so much in my life. I have taken my breeches in above two inches, so I am leaner, which answers one question in your letter. The weather is mighty fine. I write in the morning, because I am better then. I will go and try to walk a little. I will give DD's certificate to Tooke to-morrow. Farewell, MD MD MD, ME ME, FW FW ME ME.

LONDON, *May* 10, 1712

I have not yet ease or humour enough to go on in my journal method, though I have left my chamber these ten days. My pain continues still in my shoulder and collar: I keep flannel on it, and rub it with brandy, and take a nasty diet drink. I still itch terribly, and have some few pimples; I am weak, and sweat; and then the flannel makes me mad with itching; but I think my pain lessens. A journal, while I was sick, would have been a noble thing, made up of pain and physic, visits, and messages; the two last were almost as troublesome as the two first. One good circumstance is that I am grown much leaner. I believe I told you that I have taken in my breeches two inches. I had your N. 29 last night. In answer to your good opinion of my disease, the doctors said they never saw anything so odd of the kind; they were not properly shingles, but *herpes miliaris*, and twenty other hard names. I can never be sick like other people, but always something out of the common way; and as for your notion of its coming without pain, it neither came, nor stayed, nor went without pain, and the most pain I ever bore in my life. Medemeris is retired in the country, with the beast her husband, long ago. I thank the Bishop of Clogher for his proxy; I will write to him soon. Here is Dilly's wife in town; but I have not seen her yet. No, sinkerton: 'tis not a sign of health, but a sign that, if it had not come out, some terrible fit of sickness would have followed. I was at our Society last Thursday, to receive a new member, the Chancellor of the Exchequer; but I drink nothing above wine and water. We shall have a peace, I hope, soon, or at least entirely broke; but I believe the first. My *Letter to Lord Treasurer*, about the English tongue, is now printing; and I suffer my name to be put at the end of it, which I never did before in my life. *The Appendix to the Third Part of John Bull* was published yesterday; it is equal to the rest. I hope you read *John Bull*. It was a Scotch gentleman, a friend of mine, that writ it; but they put it upon me. The Parliament will hardly be up till June. We were like to be undone some days ago with a tack; but we carried it bravely, and the Whigs came in to help us. Poor Lady Masham, I am afraid, will lose her only son, about a twelvemonth old, with the king's evil. I never would let Mrs. Fenton see me during my illness, though she often came; but she has been once here since I recovered. Bernage has been twice to see me of late. His regiment will be broke, and he only upon half-pay; so perhaps he thinks he will want me again. I am told here the Bishop of Clogher and family are coming over, but he says nothing of it himself. I have been returning the visits of those that sent howdees in my sickness; particularly the Duchess of Hamilton, who came and sat with me two hours. I make bargains with all people that I dine with, to let me scrub my back against a chair; and the Duchess of Ormond was forced to bear it the other day. Many of my friends are gone to Kensington, where the Queen has been removed for some time. This is a long letter for a kick body. I will begin the next in the journal way, though my journals will be sorry ones. My left hand is very weak, and trembles; but my right side has not been touched.

> *This is a pitiful letter*
> *For want of a better;*
> *But plagued with a tetter,*
> *My fancy does fetter.*

Ah! my poor willows and quicksets! Well, but you must read *John Bull*. Do you understand it all? Did I tell you that young Parson Gery is going to be married, and asked my advice when it was too late to break off? He tells me Elwick has purchased forty pounds a year in land adjoining to his living. Ppt does not say one word of her own little health. I am angry almost; but I won't, 'cause see im a dood dallar in odle sings; iss, and so im DD too. God bless MD, and FW, and ME, ay and Pdfr too. Farewell, MD, MD, MD, FW, FW, FW. ME, ME Lele. I can say lele it, ung oomens, iss I tan, well as oo.

Letter XLVII

I cannot yet arrive to my journal letters, my pains continuing still, though with less violence; but I don't love to write journals while I am in pain; and above all, not journals to MD. But, however, I am so much mended, that I intend my next shall be in the old way; and yet I shall, perhaps, break my resolution when I feel pain. I believe I have lost credit with you, in relation to my coming over; but I protest it is impossible for one who has anything to do with this Ministry to be certain when he fixes any time. There is a business which, till it take some turn or other, I cannot leave this place in prudence or honour. And I never wished so much as now that I had stayed in Ireland; but the die is cast, and is now a spinning, and till it settles, I cannot tell whether it be an ace or a sise. I am confident by what you know yourselves, that you will justify me in all this. The moment I am used ill, I will leave them; but know not how to do it while things are in suspense. The session will soon be over (I believe in a fortnight), and the peace, we hope, will be made in a short time; and there will be no further occasion for me; nor have I anything to trust to but Court gratitude, so that I expect to see my willows a month after the Parliament is up: but I will take MD in my way, and not go to Laracor like an unmannerly spraenekich ferrow. Have you seen my *Letter to Lord Treasurer*? There are two answers come out to it already; though it is no politics, but a harmless proposal about the improvement of the English Tongue. I believe if I writ an essay upon a straw some fool would answer it. About ten days hence I expect a letter from MD; N. 30.—You are now writing it, near the end, as I guess.—I have not received DD's money; but I will give you a note for it on Parvisol, and bed oo paadon I have not done it before. I am just now thinking to go lodge at Kensington for the air. Lady Masham has teased me to do it, but business has hindered me; but now Lord Treasurer has removed thither. Fifteen of our Society dined together under a canopy in an arbour at Parson's Green last Thursday: I never saw anything so fine and romantic. We got a great victory last Wednesday in the House of Lords by a majority, I think, of twenty-eight; and the Whigs had desired their friends to bespeak places to see Lord Treasurer carried to the Tower. I met your Higgins here yesterday: he roars at the insolence of the Whigs in Ireland, talks much of his own sufferings and expenses in asserting the cause of the Church; and I find he would fain plead merit enough to desire that his fortune should be mended. I believe he designs to make as much noise as he can in order to preferment. Pray let the Provost, when he sees you, give you ten English shillings, and I will give as much here to the man who delivered me Rymer's books: he knows the meaning. Tell him I will not trust him, but that you can order it to be paid me here; and I will trust you till I see you. Have I told you that the rogue Patrick has left me these two months, to my great satisfaction? I have got another, who seems to be much better, if he continues it. I am printing a threepenny pamphlet, and shall print another in a fortnight, and then I have done, unless some new occasion starts. Is my curate Warburton married to Mrs. Melthrop in my parish? so I hear. Or is it a lie? Has Raymond got to his new house? Do you see Joe now and then? What luck have you at ombre? How stands it with the Dean? . . . My service to Mrs. Stoyte, and Catherine, if she be come from Wales. I have not yet seen Dilly Ashe's wife. I called once, but she was not at home: I think she is under the doctor's hand. . . I believe the news of the Duke of Ormond producing letters in the council of war, with orders not to fight, will surprise you in Ireland. Lord Treasurer said in the House of Lords that in a few days the treaty of peace should be laid before them; and our Court thought it wrong to hazard a battle, and sacrifice many lives in such a juncture. If the peace holds, all will do well, otherwise I know not how we shall weather it. And it was reckoned as a wrong step in politics for Lord Treasurer to open himself so much. The Secretary would not go so far to satisfy the Whigs in the House of Commons; but there all went swimmingly. I'll say no more to oo to-nite, sellohs, because I must send away the letter, not by the bell, but early: and besides, I have not much more to say at zis plesent liting. Does MD never read at all now, pee? But oo walk plodigiousry, I suppose; oo make nothing of walking to, to, to, ay, to Donnybrook. I walk too as much as I can, because sweating is good; but I'll walk more if I go to Kensington. I suppose I shall have no apples this year neither, for I dined t'other day with Lord Rivers, who is sick at his country-house, and he showed me all his cherries blasted. Nite deelest sollahs; farewell deelest rives; rove poo poo Pdfr. Farewell deelest richar MD, MD, MD, FW, FW, FW, FW, FW, ME, ME, Lele, ME, Lele, Lele, richar MD.

Letter XLVIII

I have been so tosticated about since my last, that I could not go on in my journal manner, though my shoulder is a great deal better; however, I feel constant pain in it, but I think it diminishes, and I have cut off some slices from my flannel. I have lodged here near a fortnight, partly for the air and exercise, partly to be near the Court, where dinners are to be found. I generally get a lift in a coach to town, and in the evening I walk back. On Saturday I dined with the Duchess of Ormond at her lodge near Sheen, and thought to get a boat back as usual. I walked by the bank to Cue (Kew), but no boat, then to Mortlake, but no boat, and it was nine o'clock. At last a little sculler called, full of nasty people. I made him set me down at Hammersmith, so walked two miles to this place, and got here by eleven. Last night I had another such difficulty. I was in the City till past ten at night; it rained hard, but no coach to be had. It gave over a little, and I walked all the way here, and got home by twelve. I love these shabby difficulties when they are over; but I hate them, because they arise from not having a thousand pound a year. I had your N. 30 about three days ago, which I will now answer. And first, I did not relapse, but found I came out before I ought; and so, and so, as I have told you in some of my last. The first coming abroad made people think I was quite recovered, and I had no more messages afterwards. Well, but *John Bull* is not writ by the person you imagine, as hope! It is too good for another to own. Had it been Grub Street, I would have let people think as they please; and I think that's right: is not it now? so flap ee hand, and make wry mouth oo-self, sauci doxi. Now comes DD. Why sollah, I did write in a fortnight my 47th; and if it did not come in due time, can I help wind and weather? am I a Laplander? am I a witch? can I work miracles? can I make easterly winds? Now I am against Dr. Smith. I drink little water with my wine, yet I believe he is right. Yet Dr. Cockburn told me a little wine would not hurt me; but it is so hot and dry, and water is so dangerous. The worst thing here is my evenings at Lord Masham's, where Lord Treasurer comes, and we sit till after twelve. But it is convenient I should be among them for a while as much as possible. I need not tell oo why. But I hope that will be at an end in a month or two, one way or other, and I am resolved it shall. But I can't go to Tunbridge, or anywhere else out of the way, in this juncture.

So Ppt designs for Templeoag (what a name is that!). Whereabouts is that place? I hope not very far from Dublin. Higgins is here, roaring that all is wrong in Ireland, and would have me get him an audience of Lord Treasurer to tell him so; but I will have nothing to do in it, no, not I, faith. We have had no thunder till last night, and till then we were dead for want of rain; but there fell a great deal: no field looked green. I reckon the Queen will go to Windsor in three or four weeks: and if the Secretary takes a house there, I shall be sometimes with him. But how affectedly Ppt talks of my being here all the summer; which I do not intend: nor to stay one minute longer in England than becomes the circumstances I am in. I wish you would go soon into the country, and take a good deal of it; and where better than Trim? Joe will be your humble servant, Parvisol your slave, and Raymond at your command, for he piques himself on good manners. I have seen Dilly's wife—and I have seen once or twice old Bradley here. He is very well, very old, and very wise: I believe I must go see his wife, when I have leisure. I should be glad to see Goody Stoyte and her husband; pray give them my humble service, and to Catherine, and to Mrs. Walls—I am not the least bit in love with Mrs. Walls—I suppose the cares of the husband increase with the fruitfulness of the wife. I am grad at halt to hear of Ppt's good health: pray let her finish it by drinking waters. I hope DD had her bill, and has her money. Remember to write a due time before ME money is wanted, and be good galls, dood dallars, I mean, and no crying dallars. I heard somebody coming upstairs, and forgot I was in the country; and I was afraid of a visitor: that is one advantage of being here, that I am not teased with solicitors. Molt, the chemist, is my acquaintance. My service to Dr. Smith. I sent the question to him about Sir Walter Raleigh's cordial, and the answer he returned is in these words: "It is directly after Mr. Boyle's receipt." That commission is performed; if he wants any of it, Molt shall use him fairly. I suppose Smith is one of your physicians. So, now your letter is fully and impartially answered; not as rascals answer me: I believe, if I writ an essay upon a straw, I should have a shoal of answerers: but no matter for that; you see I can answer without making any reflections, as becomes men of learning. Well, but now for the peace: why, we expect it daily; but the French have the staff in their own hands, and we trust to their honesty. I wish it were otherwise. Things are now in the way of being soon in the extremes of well or ill. I hope and believe the first. Lord Wharton is gone out of town in a rage, and curses himself

JONATHAN SWIFT

and friends for ruining themselves in defending Lord Marlborough and Godolphin, and taking Nottingham into their favour. He swears he will meddle no more during this reign; a pretty speech at sixty-six, and the Queen is near twenty years younger, and now in very good health; for you must know her health is fixed by a certain reason, that she has done with braces (I must use the expression), and nothing ill is happened to her since; so she has a new lease of her life. Read the *Letter to a Whig Lord*. Do you ever read? Why don't you say so? I mean does DD read to Ppt? Do you walk? I think Ppt should walk to DD; as DD reads to Ppt, for Ppt oo must know is a good walker; but not so good as Pdfr. I intend to dine to-day with Mr. Lewis, but it threatens rain; and I shall be too late to get a lift; and I must write to the Bishop of Clogher. 'Tis now ten in the morning; and this is all writ at a heat. Farewell deelest. . . deelest MD, MD, MD, MD, MD, FW, FW, FW, ME, ME, ME, Lele, ME, Lele, ME, Lele, ME, Lele, Lele, Lele, ME.

LETTER XLIX

I never was in a worse station for writing letters than this, especially for writing to MD, since I left off my journals. For I go to town early; and when I come home at night, I generally go to Lord Masham, where Lord Treasurer comes, and we stay till past twelve. But I am now resolved to write journals again, though my shoulder is not yet well; for I have still a few itching pimples, and a little pain now and then. It is now high cherry-time with us; take notice, is it so soon with you? And we have early apricots, and gooseberries are ripe. On Sunday Archdeacon Parnell came here to see me. It seems he has been ill for grief of his wife's death, and has been two months at the Bath. He has a mind to go to Dunkirk with Jack Hill, and I persuade him to it, and have spoke to Hill to receive him; but I doubt he won't have spirit to go. I have made Ford Gazetteer, and got two hundred pounds a year settled on the employment by the Secretary of State, beside the perquisites. It is the prettiest employment in England of its bigness; yet the puppy does not seem satisfied with it. I think people keep some follies to themselves, till they have occasion to produce them. He thinks it not genteel enough, and makes twenty difficulties. 'Tis impossible to make any man easy. His salary is paid him every week, if he pleases, without taxes or abatements. He has little to do for it. He has a pretty office, with coals, candles, papers, etc.; can frank what letters he will; and his perquisites, if he takes care, may be worth one hundred pounds more. I hear the Bishop of Clogher is landing, or landed, in England; and I hope to see him in a few days. I was to see Mrs. Bradley on Sunday night. Her youngest son is married to somebody worth nothing, and her daughter was forced to leave Lady Giffard, because she was striking up an intrigue with a footman, who played well upon the flute. This is the mother's account of it. Yesterday the old Bishop of Worcester, who pretends to be a prophet, went to the Queen, by appointment, to prove to Her Majesty, out of Daniel and the Revelations, that four years hence there would be a war of religion; that the King of France would be a Protestant, and fight on their side; that the Popedom would be destroyed, etc.; and declared that he would be content to give up his bishopric if it were not true. Lord Treasurer, who told it me, was by, and some others; and I am told Lord Treasurer confounded him sadly in his own learning, which made the old fool very quarrelsome. He is near ninety years old. Old Bradley is fat and lusty, and has lost his palsy. Have you seen *Toland's Invitation to Dismal*? How do you like it? But it is an imitation of Horace, and perhaps you don't understand Horace. Here has been a great sweep of employments, and we expect still more removals. The Court seems resolved to make thorough work. Mr. Hill intended to set out to-morrow for Dunkirk, of which he is appointed Governor; but he tells me to-day that he cannot go till Thursday or Friday. I wish it were over. Mr. Secretary tells me he is (in) no fear at all that France will play tricks with us. If we have Dunkirk once, all is safe. We rail now all against the Dutch, who, indeed, have acted like knaves, fools, and madmen. Mr. Secretary is soon to be made a viscount. He desired I would draw the preamble of his patent; but I excused myself from a work that might lose me a great deal of reputation, and get me very little. We would fain have the Court make him an earl, but it would not be; and therefore he will not take the title of Bullenbrook, which is lately extinct in the elder branch of his family. I have advised him to be called Lord Pomfret; but he thinks that title is already in some other family; and, besides, he objects that it is in Yorkshire, where he has no estate; but there is nothing in that, and I love Pomfret. Don't you love Pomfret? Why? 'Tis in all our histories; they are full of Pomfret Castle. But what's all this to you? You don't care for this. Is Goody Stoyte come to London? I have not heard of her yet. The Dean of St. Patrick's never had the manners to answer my letter. I was t'other day to see Sterne and his wife. She is not half so handsome as when I saw her with you at Dublin. They design to pass the summer at a house near Lord Somers's, about a dozen miles off. You never told me how my *Letter to Lord Treasurer* passes in Ireland. I suppose you are drinking at this time Temple-something's waters. Steele was arrested the other day for making a lottery directly against an Act of Parliament. He is now under prosecution; but they think it will be dropped out of pity. I believe he will very soon lose his employment, for he has been mighty impertinent of late in his *Spectators*; and I will never offer a word in his behalf. Raymond writes me word that the Bishop of Meath was going to summon me, in order to suspension, for absence, if the Provost had not prevented him. I am prettily rewarded for getting them their First-Fruits, with a p—. We have had very little hot weather during the whole month of June; and for a week past we have had a great deal of rain, though not every day. I am just now told that the Governor of

Dunkirk has not orders yet to deliver up the town to Jack Hill and his forces, but expects them daily. This must put off Hill's journey a while, and I don't like these stoppings in such an affair. Go, get oo gone, and drink oo waters, if this rain has not spoiled them, sauci doxi. I have no more to say to oo at plesent; but rove Pdfr, and MD, and ME. And Podefr will rove Pdfr, and MD and ME. I wish you had taken any account when I sent money to Mrs. Brent. I believe I han't done it a great while. And pray send me notice when ME. . . to have it when it is due. Farewell, dearest MD FW FW FW ME ME ME.

LETTER L

I am weary of living in this place, and glad to leave it soon. The Queen goes on Tuesday to Windsor, and I shall follow in three or four days after. I can do nothing here, going early to London, and coming late from it, and supping at Lady Masham's. I dined to-day with the Duke of Argyle at Cue (Kew), and would not go to the Court to-night, because of writing to MD. The Bishop of Clogher has been here this fortnight: I see him as often as I can. Poor Master Ashe has a sad redness in his face; it is St. Anthony's fire; his face all swelled, and will break in his cheek, but no danger. Since Dunkirk has been in our hands, Grub Street has been very fruitful. Pdfr has writ five or six Grub Street papers this last week. Have you seen *Toland's Invitation to Dismal*, *or Hue and Cry after Dismal*, *or Ballad on Dunkirk*, *or Argument that Dunkirk is not in our Hands*? Poh! you have seen nothing. I am dead here with the hot weather; yet I walk every night home, and believe it does me good: but my shoulder is not yet right; itchings, and scratchings, and small achings. Did I tell you I had made Ford Gazetteer, with two hundred pounds a year salary, beside perquisites? I had a letter lately from Parvisol, who says my canal looks very finely; I long to see it; but no apples; all blasted again. He tells me there will be a triennial visitation in August. I must send Raymond another proxy. So now I will answer oo rettle N. 33, dated June 17. Ppt writes as well as ever, for all her waters. I wish I had never come here, as often and as heartily as Ppt. What had I to do here? I have heard of the Bishop's making me uneasy, but I did not think it was because I never writ to him. A little would make me write to him, but I don't know what to say. I find I am obliged to the Provost for keeping the Bishop from being impertinent. Yes, Maram DD, but oo would not be content with letters flom Pdfr of six lines, or twelve either, fais. I hope Ppt will have done with the waters soon, and find benefit by them. I believe, if they were as far off as Wexford, they would do as much good; for I take the journey to contribute as much as anything. I can assure you the Bishop of Clogher's being here does not in the least affect my staying or going. I never talked to Higgins but once in my life in the street, and I believe he and I shall hardly meet but by chance. What care I whether my *Letter to Lord Treasurer* be commended there or no? Why does not somebody among you answer it, as three or four have done here? (I am now sitting with nothing but my nightgown, for heat.) Ppt shall have a great Bible. I have put it down in my memlandums just now. And DD shall be repaid her t'other book; but patience, all in good time: you are so hasty, a dog would, etc. So Ppt has neither won nor lost. Why, mun, I play sometimes too at picket, that is picquet, I mean; but very seldom.—Out late? why, 'tis only at Lady Masham's, and that is in our town; but I never come late here from London, except once in rain, when I could not get a coach. We have had very little thunder here; none these two months. Why, pray, madam philosopher, how did the rain hinder the thunder from doing any harm? I suppose it ssquenched it. So here comes Ppt aden with her little watery postscript. O Rold, dlunken srut! drink Pdfr's health ten times in a morning! you are a whetter, fais; I sup MD's fifteen times evly molning in milk porridge. Lele's fol oo now—and lele's fol oo rettle, and evly kind of sing—and now I must say something else. You hear Secretary St. John is made Viscount Bullinbrook. I can hardly persuade him to take that title, because the eldest branch of his family had it in an earldom, and it was last year extinct. If he did not take it, I advised him to be Lord Pomfret, which I think is a noble title. You hear of it often in the *Chronicles*, Pomfret Castle: but we believed it was among the titles of some other lord. Jack Hill sent his sister a pattern of a head-dress from Dunkirk; it was like our fashion twenty years ago, only not quite so high, and looked very ugly. I have made Trapp chaplain to Lord Bullinbroke, and he is mighty happy and thankful for it. Mr. Addison returned me my visit this morning. He lives in our town. I shall be mighty retired, and mighty busy for a while at Windsor. Pray why don't MD go to Trim, and see Laracor, and give me an account of the garden, and the river, and the holly and the cherry-trees on the river-walk?

19. I could not send this letter last post, being called away before I could fold or finish it. I dined yesterday with Lord Treasurer; sat with him till ten at night; yet could not find a minute for some business I had with him. He brought me to Kensington, and Lord Bulingbrook would not let me go away till two; and I am now in bed, very lazy and sleepy at nine. I must shave head and face, and meet Lord Bullinbrook at eleven, and dine again with Lord Treasurer. To-day there will be another Grub, *A Letter from the Pretender to a Whig Lord*. Grub Street has but ten days to live; then an Act of Parliament takes place that ruins it, by taxing every half-sheet at a halfpenny. We have news just

come, but not the particulars, that the Earl of Albemarle, at the head of eight thousand Dutch, is beaten, lost the greatest part of his men, and himself a prisoner. This perhaps may cool their courage, and make them think of a peace. The Duke of Ormond has got abundance of credit by his good conduct of affairs in Flanders. We had a good deal of rain last night, very refreshing. 'Tis late, and I must rise. Don't play at ombre in your waters, sollah. Farewell, deelest MD, MD MD MD FW FW ME ME ME Lele Lele Lele.

London, *Aug.* 7, 1712

I had your N. 32 at Windsor: I just read it, and immediately sealed it up again, and shall read it no more this twelvemonth at least. The reason of my resentment at it is, because you talk as glibly of a thing as if it were done, which, for aught I know, is farther from being done than ever, since I hear not a word of it, though the town is full of it, and the Court always giving me joy and vexation. You might be sure I would have let you know as soon as it was done; but I believe you fancied I would affect not to tell it you, but let you learn it from newspapers and reports. I remember only there was something in your letter about ME's money, and that shall be taken care of on the other side. I left Windsor on Monday last, upon Lord Bolingbroke's being gone to France, and somebody's being here that I ought often to consult with in an affair I am upon: but that person talks of returning to Windsor again, and I believe I shall follow him. I am now in a hedge-lodging very busy, as I am every day till noon: so that this letter is like to be short, and you are not to blame me these two months; for I protest, if I study ever so hard, I cannot in that time compass what I am upon. We have a fever both here and at Windsor, which hardly anybody misses; but it lasts not above three or four days, and kills nobody. The Queen has forty servants down of it at once. I dined yesterday with Treasurer, but could do no business, though he sent for me, I thought, on purpose; but he desires I will dine with him again to-day. Windsor is a most delightful place, and at this time abounds in dinners. My lodgings there look upon Eton and the Thames. I wish I was owner of them; they belong to a prebend. God knows what was in your letter; and if it be not answered, whose fault is it, sauci dallars?—Do you know that Grub Street is dead and gone last week? No more ghosts or murders now for love or money. I plied it pretty close the last fortnight, and published at least seven penny papers of my own, besides some of other people's: but now every single half-sheet pays a halfpenny to the Queen. The *Observator* is fallen; the *Medleys* are jumbled together with the *Flying Post*; the *Examiner* is deadly sick; the *Spectator* keeps up, and doubles its price; I know not how long it will hold. Have you seen the red stamp the papers are marked with? Methinks it is worth a halfpenny, the stamping it. Lord Bolingbroke and Prior set out for France last Saturday. My lord's business is to hasten the peace before the Dutch are too much mauled, and hinder France from carrying the jest of beating them too far. Have you seen the Fourth Part of *John Bull*? It is equal to the rest, and extremely good. The Bishop of Clogher's son has been ill of St. Anthony's fire, but is now quite well. I was afraid his face would be spoiled, but it is not. Dilly is just as he used to be, and puns as plentifully and as bad. The two brothers see one another; but I think not the two sisters. Raymond writ to me that he intended to invite you to Trim. Are you, have you, will you be there? Won't oo see pool Laratol? Parvisol says I shall have no fruit. Blasts have taken away all. Pray observe the cherry-trees on the river-walk; but oo are too lazy to take such a journey. If you have not your letters in due time for two months hence, impute it to my being tosticated between this and Windsor. And pray send me again the state of ME's money; for I will not look into your letter for it. Poor Lord Winchelsea is dead, to my great grief. He was a worthy honest gentleman, and particular friend of mine: and, what is yet worse, my old acquaintance, Mrs. Finch, is now Countess of Winchelsea, the title being fallen to her husband, but without much estate. I have been poring my eyes all this morning, and it is now past two afternoon, so I shall take a little walk in the Park. Do you play at ombre still? Or is that off by Mr. Stoyte's absence, and Mrs. Manley's grief? Somebody was telling me of a strange sister that Mrs. Manley has got in Ireland, who disappointed you all about her being handsome. My service to Mrs. Walls. Farewell, deelest MD MD MD, FW FW FW, ME ME ME ME ME. Lele, logues both; rove poo Pdfr.

LETTER LII

I never was so long without writing to MD as now, since I left them, nor ever will again while I am able to write. I have expected from one week to another that something would be done in my own affairs; but nothing at all is, nor I don't know when anything will, or whether ever at all, so slow are people at doing favours. I have been much out of order of late with the old giddiness in my head. I took a vomit for it two days ago, and will take another about a day or two hence. I have eat mighty little fruit; yet I impute my disorder to that little, and shall henceforth wholly forbear it. I am engaged in a long work, and have done all I can of it, and wait for some papers from the Ministry for materials for the rest; and they delay me, as if it were a favour I asked of them; so that I have been idle here this good while, and it happened in a right time, when I was too much out of order to study. One is kept constantly out of humour by a thousand unaccountable things in public proceedings; and when I reason with some friends, we cannot conceive how affairs can last as they are. God only knows, but it is a very melancholy subject for those who have any near concern in it. I am again endeavouring, as I was last year, to keep people from breaking to pieces upon a hundred misunderstandings. One cannot withhold them from drawing different ways, while the enemy is watching to destroy both. See how my style is altered, by living and thinking and talking among these people, instead of my canal and river-walk and willows. I lose all my money here among the ladies; so that I never play when I can help it, being sure to lose. I have lost five pounds the five weeks I have been here. I hope Ppt is luckier at picquet with the Dean and Mrs. Walls. The Dean never answered my letter, though. I have clearly forgot whether I sent a bill for ME in any of my last letters. I think I did; pray let me know, and always give me timely notice. I wait here but to see what they will do for me; and whenever preferments are given from me, as hope saved, I will come over.

18. I have taken a vomit to-day, and hope I shall be better. I have been very giddy since I writ what is before, yet not as I used to be: more frequent, but not so violent. Yesterday we were alarmed with the Queen's being ill: she had an aguish and feverish fit; and you never

saw such countenances as we all had, such dismal melancholy. Her physicians from town were sent for, but towards night she grew better; to-day she missed her fit, and was up: we are not now in any fear; it will be at worst but an ague, and we hope even that will not return. Lord Treasurer would not come here from London, because it would make a noise if he came before his usual time, which is Saturday, and he goes away on Mondays. The Whigs have lost a great support in the Earl of Godolphin. It is a good jest to hear the Ministers talk of him now with humanity and pity, because he is dead, and can do them no more hurt. Lady Orkney, the late King's mistress (who lives at a fine place, five miles from hence, called Cliffden), and I, are grown mighty acquaintance. She is the wisest woman I ever saw; and Lord Treasurer made great use of her advice in the late change of affairs. I heard Lord Marlborough is growing ill of his diabetes; which, if it be true, may soon carry him off; and then the Ministry will be something more at ease. MD has been a long time without writing to Pdfr, though they have not the same cause: it is seven weeks since your last came to my hands, which was N. 32, that you may not be mistaken. I hope Ppt has not wanted her health. You were then drinking waters. The doctor tells me I must go into a course of steel, though I have not the spleen; for that they can never give me, though I have as much provocation to it as any man alive. Bernage's regiment is broke; but he is upon half-pay. I have not seen him this long time; but I suppose he is overrun with melancholy. My Lord Shrewsbury is certainly designed to be Governor of Ireland; and I believe the Duchess will please the people there mightily. The Irish Whig leaders promise great things to themselves from his government; but care shall be taken, if possible, to prevent them. Mrs. Fenton has writ to me that she has been forced to leave Lady Giffard, and come to town, for a rheumatism: that lady does not love to be troubled with sick people. Mrs. Fenton writes to me as one dying, and desires I would think of her son: I have not answered her letter. She is retired to Mrs. Povey's. Is my aunt alive yet? and do you ever see her? I suppose she has forgot the loss of her son. Is Raymond's new house quite finished? and does he squander as he used to do? Has he yet spent all his wife's fortune? I hear there are five or six people putting strongly in for my livings; God help them! But if ever the Court should give me anything, I would recommend Raymond to the Duke of Ormond; not for any particular friendship to him, but because it would be proper for the minister of Trim to have Laracor. You may keep the gold-studded snuff-box now; for my brother Hill, Governor of Dunkirk, has sent me the finest that ever you saw. It is allowed at Court that none in England comes near it, though it did not cost above twenty pounds. And the Duchess of Hamilton has made me pockets for (it) like a woman's, with a belt and buckle (for, you know, I wear no waistcoat in summer), and there are several divisions, and one on purpose for my box, oh ho!—We have had most delightful weather this whole week; but illness and vomiting have hindered me from sharing in a great part of it. Lady Masham made the Queen send to Kensington for some of her preserved ginger for me, which I take in the morning, and hope it will do me good. Mrs. Brent sent me a letter by a young fellow, a printer, desiring I would recommend him here, which you may tell her I have done: but I cannot promise what will come of it, for it is necessary they should be made free here before they can be employed. I remember I put the boy prentice to Brent. I hope Parvisol has set my tithes well this year: he has writ nothing to me about it; pray talk to him of it when you see him, and let him give me an account how things are. I suppose the corn is now off the ground. I hope he has sold that great ugly horse. Why don't you sell to him? He keeps me at charges for horses that I never ride: yours is lame, and will never be good for anything. The Queen will stay here about a month longer, I suppose; but Lady Masham will go in ten days to lie in at Kensington. Poor creature, she fell down in the court here t'other day. She would needs walk across it upon some displeasure with her chairmen, and was likely to be spoiled so near her time; but we hope all is over for a black eye and a sore side: though I shall not be at ease till she is brought to bed. I find I can fill up a letter, some way or other, without a journal. If I had not a spirit naturally cheerful, I should be very much discontented at a thousand things. Pray God preserve MD's health, and Pdfr's, and that I may live far from the envy and discontent that attends those who are thought to have more favour at Courts than they really possess. Love Pdfr, who loves MD above all things. Farewell, deelest, ten thousand times deelest, MD MD MD, FW FW, ME ME ME ME. Lele, Lele, Lele, Lele.

Letter LIII

I have left Windsor these ten days, and am deep in pills with asafoetida, and a steel bitter drink; and I find my head much better than it was. I was very much discouraged; for I used to be ill for three or four days together, ready to totter as I walked. I take eight pills a day, and have taken, I believe, a hundred and fifty already. The Queen, Lord Treasurer, Lady Masham, and I, were all ill together, but are now all better; only Lady Masham expects every day to lie in at Kensington. There was never such a lump of lies spread about the town together as now. I doubt not but you will have them in Dublin before this comes to you, and all without the least grounds of truth. I have been mightily put backward in something I am writing by my illness, but hope to fetch it up, so as to be ready when the Parliament meets. Lord Treasurer has had an ugly fit of the rheumatism, but is now near quite well. I was playing at one-and-thirty with him and his family t'other night. He gave us all twelvepence apiece to begin with: it put me in mind of Sir William Temple. I asked both him and Lady Masham seriously whether the Queen were at all inclined to a dropsy, and they positively assured me she was not: so did her physician Arbuthnot, who always attends her. Yet these devils have spread that she has holes in her legs, and runs at her navel, and I know not what. Arbuthnot has sent me from Windsor a pretty Discourse upon Lying, and I have ordered the printer to come for it. It is a proposal for publishing a curious piece, called *The Art of Political Lying*, in two volumes, etc. And then there is an abstract of the first volume, just like those pamphlets which they call *The Works of the Learned*. Pray get it when it comes out. The Queen has a little of the gout in one of her hands. I believe she will stay a month still at Windsor. Lord Treasurer showed me the kindest letter from her in the world, by which I picked out one secret, that there will be soon made some Knights of the Garter. You know another is fallen by Lord Godolphin's death: he will be buried in a day or two at Westminster Abbey. I saw Tom Leigh in town once. The Bishop of Clogher has taken his lodging for the winter; they are all well. I hear there are in town abundance of people from Ireland; half a dozen bishops at least. The poor old Bishop of London, at past fourscore, fell down backward going upstairs, and I think broke or cracked his skull;

yet is now recovering. The town is as empty as at midsummer; and if I had not occasion for physic, I would be at Windsor still. Did I tell you of Lord Rivers's will? He has left legacies to about twenty paltry old whores by name, and not a farthing to any friend, dependent, or relation: he has left from his only child, Lady Barrymore, her mother's estate, and given the whole to his heir-male, a popish priest, a second cousin, who is now Earl Rivers, and whom he used in his life like a footman. After him it goes to his chief wench and bastard. Lord Treasurer and Lord Chamberlain are executors of this hopeful will. I loved the man, and detest his memory. We hear nothing of peace yet: I believe verily the Dutch are so wilful, because they are told the Queen cannot live. I had poor MD's letter, N. 3, at Windsor: but I could not answer it then; poor Pdfr was vely kick then: and, besides, it was a very inconvenient place to send letters from. Oo thought to come home the same day, and stayed a month: that was a sign the place was agreeable. I should love such a sort of jaunt. Is that lad Swanton a little more fixed than he used to be? I think you like the girl very well. She has left off her grave airs, I suppose. I am now told Lord Godolphin was buried last night.—O poo Ppt! lay down oo head aden, fais I. . . ; I always reckon if oo are ill I shall hear it, and therefore hen oo are silent I reckon all is well. I believe I 'scaped the new fever for the same reason that Ppt did, because I am not well; but why should DD 'scape it, pray? She is melthigal, oo know, and ought to have the fever; but I hope it is now too late, and she won't have it at all. Some physicians here talk very melancholy, and think it foreruns the plague, which is actually at Hamburg. I hoped Ppt would have done with her illness; but I think we both have that faculty never to part with a disorder for ever; we are very constant. I have had my giddiness twenty-three years by fits. Will Mrs. Raymond never have done lying-in? He intends to leave beggars enough; for I daresay he has squandered away the best part of his fortune already, and is not out of debt. I had a letter from him lately.

Oct. 11. Lord Treasurer sent for me yesterday and the day before to sit with him, because he is not yet quite well enough to go abroad; and I could not finish my letter. How the deuce come I to be so exact in ME money? Just seventeen shillings and eightpence more than due; I believe you cheat me. If Hawkshaw does not pay the interest I will have the principal; pray speak to Parvisol and have his advice what I should do about it. Service to Mrs. Stoyte and Catherine and Mrs. Walls. Ppt makes a petition with many apologies. John Danvers, you know, is Lady Giffard's friend. The rest I never heard of. I tell you what, as things are at present, I cannot possibly speak to Lord Treasurer for anybody. I need tell you no more. Something or nothing will be done in my own affairs: if the former, I will be a solicitor for your sister; if the latter, I have done with Courts for ever. Opportunities will often fall in my way, if I am used well, and I will then make it my business. It is my delight to do good offices for people who want and deserve, and a tenfold delight to do it to a relation of Ppt, whose affairs she has so at heart. I have taken down his name and his case (not *her* case), and whenever a proper time comes, I will do all I can; zat's enough to say when I can do no more; and I beg oo pardon a sousand times, that I cannot do better. I hope the Dean of St. P(atrick's) is well of his fever: he has never writ to me: I am glad of it; pray don't desire him to write. I have dated your bill late, because it must not commence, ung oomens, till the first of November next. O, fais, I must be ise; iss, fais, must I; else ME will cheat Pdfr. Are you good housewives and readers? Are you walkers? I know you are gamesters. Are you drinkers? Are you—O Rold, I must go no further, for fear of abusing fine radies. Parvisol has never sent me one word how he set this year's tithes. Pray ask whether tithes set well or ill this year. The Bishop of Killaloe tells me wool bears a good rate in Ireland: but how is corn? I dined yesterday with Lady Orkney, and we sat alone from two till eleven at night.—You have heard of her, I suppose. I have twenty letters upon my hands, and am so lazy and so busy, I cannot answer them, and they grow upon me for several months. Have I any apples at Laracor? It is strange every year should blast them, when I took so much care for shelter. Lord Bolingbroke has been idle at his country-house this fortnight, which puts me backward in a business I have. I am got into an ordinary room two pair of stairs, and see nobody, if I can help it; yet some puppies have found me out, and my man is not such an artist as Patrick at denying me. Patrick has been soliciting to come to me again, but in vain. The printer has been here with some of the new whims printed, and has taken up my time. I am just going out, and can only bid oo farewell. Farewell, deelest ickle MD, MD MD MD FW FW FW FW ME ME ME ME. Lele deel ME. Lele lele lele sollahs bose.

Letter LIV

I have been in physic this month, and have been better these three weeks. I stop my physic, by the doctor's orders, till he sends me further directions. DD grows politician, and longs to hear the peace is proclaimed. I hope we shall have it soon, for the Dutch are fully humbled; and Prior is just come over from France for a few days; I suppose upon some important affair. I saw him last night, but had no private talk with him. Stocks rise upon his coming. As for my stay in England, it cannot be long now, so tell my friends. The Parliament will not meet till after Christmas, and by that time the work I am doing will be over, and then nothing shall keep me. I am very much discontented at Parvisol, about neglecting to sell my horses, etc.

Lady Masham is not yet brought to bed; but we expect it daily. I dined with her to-day. Lord Bolingbroke returned about two months ago, and Prior about a week; and goes back (Prior I mean) in a few days. Who told you of my snuff-box and pocket? Did I? I had a letter to-day from Dr. Coghill, desiring me to get Raphoe for Dean Sterne, and the deanery for myself. I shall indeed, I have such obligations to Sterne. But however, if I am asked who will make a good bishop, I shall name him before anybody. Then comes another letter, desiring I would recommend a Provost, supposing that Pratt (who has been here about a week) will certainly be promoted; but I believe he will not. I presented Pratt to Lord Treasurer, and truly young Molyneux would have had me present him too; but I directly answered him I would not, unless he had business with him. He is the son of one Mr. Molyneux of Ireland. His father wrote a book; I suppose you know it. Here is the Duke of Marlborough going out of England (Lord knows why), which causes many speculations. Some say he is conscious of guilt, and dare not stand it. Others think he has a mind to fling an odium on the Government, as who should say that one who has done such great services to his country cannot live quietly in it, by reason of the malice of his enemies. I have helped to patch up these people together once more. God knows how long it may last. I was to-day at a trial between Lord Lansdowne and Lord Carteret, two friends of mine. It was in the Queen's Bench, for about six thousand a year (or nine, I think). I sat under Lord Chief-Justice Parker, and his pen falling down I reached it up. He made me a low bow; and I was going to whisper him that *I had done good for evil; for he would have taken mine from me*. I told it Lord Treasurer and Bolingbroke. Parker would not have known me, if several lords on the bench, and in the court, bowing, had not turned everybody's eyes, and set them a whispering. I owe the dog a spite, and will pay him in two months at furthest, if I can. So much for that. But you must have chat, and I must say every sorry thing that comes into my head. They say the Queen will stay a month longer at Windsor. These devils of Grub Street rogues, that write the *Flying Post* and *Medley* in one paper, will not be quiet. They are always mauling Lord Treasurer, Lord Bolingbroke, and me. We have the dog under prosecution, but Bolingbroke is not active enough; but I hope to swinge him. He is a Scotch rogue, one Ridpath. They get out upon bail, and write on. We take them again, and get fresh bail; so it goes round. They say some learned Dutchman has wrote a book, proving by civil law that we do them wrong by this peace; but I shall show by plain reason that we have suffered the wrong, and not they. I toil like a horse, and have hundreds of letters still to read and squeeze a line out of each, or at least the seeds of a line. Strafford goes back to Holland in a day or two, and I hope our peace is very near. I have about thirty pages more to write (that is, to be extracted), which will be sixty in print. It is the most troublesome part of all, and I cannot keep myself private, though I stole into a room up two pair of stairs, when I came from Windsor; but my present man has not yet learned his lesson of denying me discreetly.

30. The Duchess of Ormond found me out to-day, and made me dine with her. Lady Masham is still expecting. She has had a cruel cold. I could not finish my letter last post for the soul of me. Lord Bolingbroke has had my papers these six weeks, and done nothing to them. Is Tisdall yet in the world? I propose writing controversies, to get a name with posterity. The Duke of Ormond will not be over these three or four days. I desire to make him join with me in settling all right among our people. I have ordered the Duchess to let me have an hour with the Duke at his first coming, to give him a true state of persons and things. I believe the Duke of Shrewsbury will hardly be declared your Governor yet; at least, I think so now; but resolutions alter very often. The Duke of Hamilton gave me a pound of snuff to-day, admirable good. I wish DD had it, and Ppt too, if she likes it. It cost me a quarter of an hour of his politics, which I was forced to hear. Lady Orkney is making me

a writing-table of her own contrivance, and a bed nightgown. She is perfectly kind, like a mother. I think the devil was in it the other day, that I should talk to her of an ugly squinting cousin of hers, and the poor lady herself, you know, squints like a dragon. The other day we had a long discourse with her about love; and she told us a saying of her sister Fitz-Hardinge, which I thought excellent, that in men, desire begets love, and in women, love begets desire. We have abundance of our old criers still hereabouts. I hear every morning your women with the old satin and taffeta, etc., the fellow with old coats, suits or cloaks. Our weather is abominable of late. We have not two tolerable days in twenty. I have lost money again at ombre, with Lord Orkney and others; yet, after all, this year I have lost but three-and-twenty shillings; so that, considering card money, I am no loser.

Our Society hath not yet renewed their meetings. I hope we shall continue to do some good this winter; and Lord Treasurer promises the Academy for reforming our language shall soon go forward. I must now go hunt those dry letter for materials. You will see something very notable, I hope. So much for that. God Almighty bless you.

Letter LV

Before this comes to your hands, you will have heard of the most terrible accident that hath almost ever happened. This morning, at eight, my man brought me word that the Duke of Hamilton had fought with Lord Mohun, and killed him, and was brought home wounded. I immediately sent him to the Duke's house, in St. James's Square; but the porter could hardly answer for tears, and a great rabble was about the house. In short, they fought at seven this morning. The dog Mohun was killed on the spot; and while the Duke was over him, Mohun, shortening his sword, stabbed him in at the shoulder to the heart. The Duke was helped toward the cake-house by the Ring in Hyde Park (where they fought), and died on the grass, before he could reach the house; and was brought home in his coach by eight, while the poor Duchess was asleep. Maccartney, and one Hamilton, were the seconds, who fought likewise, and are both fled. I am told that a footman of Lord Mohun's stabbed the Duke of Hamilton; and some say Maccartney did so too. Mohun gave the affront, and yet sent the challenge. I am infinitely concerned for the poor Duke, who was a frank, honest, good-natured man. I loved him very well, and I think he loved me better. He had the greatest mind in the world to have me go with him to France, but durst not tell it me; and those he did, said I could not be spared, which was true. They have removed the poor Duchess to a lodging in the neighbourhood, where I have been with her two hours, and am just come away. I never saw so melancholy a scene; for indeed all reasons for real grief belong to her; nor is it possible for anybody to be a greater loser in all regards. She has moved my very soul. The lodging was inconvenient, and they would have removed her to another; but I would not suffer it, because it had no room backward, and she must have been tortured with the noise of the Grub Street screamers mention(ing) her husband's murder to her ears.

I believe you have heard the story of my escape, in opening the bandbox sent to Lord Treasurer. The prints have told a thousand lies of it; but at last we gave them a true account of it at length, printed in the evening; only I would not suffer them to name me, having been so often named before, and teased to death with questions. I wonder how I came to have so much presence of mind, which is usually not my talent;

but so it pleased God, and I saved myself and him; for there was a bullet apiece. A gentleman told me that if I had been killed, the Whigs would have called it a judgment, because the barrels were of inkhorns, with which I had done them so much mischief. There was a pure Grub Street of it, full of lies and inconsistencies. I do not like these things at all, and I wish myself more and more among my willows. There is a devilish spirit among people, and the Ministry must exert themselves, or sink. Nite dee sollahs, I'll go seep.

16. I thought to have finished this yesterday; but was too much disturbed. I sent a letter early this morning to Lady Masham, to beg her to write some comforting words to the poor Duchess. I dined to-(day) with Lady Masham at Kensington, where she is expecting these two months to lie in. She has promised me to get the Queen to write to the Duchess kindly on this occasion; and to-morrow I will beg Lord Treasurer to visit and comfort her. I have been with her two hours again, and find her worse: her violences not so frequent, but her melancholy more formal and settled. She has abundance of wit and spirit; about thirty-three years old; handsome and airy, and seldom spared anybody that gave her the least provocation; by which she had many enemies and few friends. Lady Orkney, her sister-in-law, is come to town on this occasion, and has been to see her, and behaved herself with great humanity. They have been always very ill together, and the poor Duchess could not have patience when people told her I went often to Lady Orkney's. But I am resolved to make them friends; for the Duchess is now no more the object of envy, and must learn humility from the severest master, Affliction. I design to make the Ministry put out a proclamation (if it can be found proper) against that villain Maccartney. What shall we do with these murderers? I cannot end this letter to-night, and there is no occasion; for I cannot send it till Tuesday, and the crowner's inquest on the Duke's body is to be to-morrow, and I shall know more. But what care oo for all this? Iss, poo MD im sorry for poo Pdfr's friends; and this is a very surprising event. 'Tis late, and I'll go to bed. This looks like journals. Nite.

17. I was to-day at noon with the Duchess of Hamilton again, after I had been with Lady Orkney, and charged her to be kind to her sister in her affliction. The Duchess told me Lady Orkney had been with her, and that she did not treat her as gently as she ought. They hate one another,

but I will try to patch it up. I have been drawing up a paragraph for the *Postboy*, to be out to-morrow, and as malicious as possible, and very proper for Abel Roper, the printer of it. I dined at Lord Treasurer's at six in the evening, which is his usual hour of returning from Windsor: he promises to visit the Duchess to-morrow, and says he has a message to her from the Queen. Thank God. I have stayed till past one with him. So nite deelest MD.

18. The Committee of Council is to sit this afternoon upon the affair of the Duke of Hamilton's murder, and I hope a proclamation will be out against Maccartney. I was just now ('tis now noon) with the Duchess, to let her know Lord Treasurer will see her. She is mightily out of order. The jury have not yet brought in their verdict upon the crowner's inquest. We suspect Maccartney stabbed the Duke while he was fighting. The Queen and Lord Treasurer are in great concern at this event. I dine to-day again with Lord Treasurer; but must send this to the post-office before, because else I shall not have time; he usually keeping me so late. Ben Tooke bid me write to DD to send her certificate, for it is high time it should be sent, he says. Pray make Parvisol write to me, and send me a general account of my affairs; and let him know I shall be over in spring, and that by all means he sells the horses. Prior has kissed the Queen's hand, and will return to France in a few days, and Lord Strafford to Holland; and now the King of Spain has renounced his pretensions to France, the peace must follow very soon unavoidably. You must no more call Philip, Duke of Anjou, for we now acknowledge him King of Spain. Dr. Pratt tells me you are all mad in Ireland with your playhouse frolics and prologues, and I know not what. The Bishop of Clogher and family are well: they have heard from you, or you from them, lately, I have forgot which: I dined there t'other day, but the Bishop came not till after dinner; and our meat and drink was very so so. Mr. Vedeau was with me yesterday, and inquired after you. He was a lieutenant, and is now broke, and upon half-pay. He asked me nothing for himself; but wanted an employment for a friend, who would give a handsome pair of gloves. One Hales sent me up a letter t'other day, which said you lodged in his house, and therefore desired I would get him a civil employment. I would not be within, and have directed my man to give him an answer, that I never open letters brought me by the writers, etc. I was complaining to a lady that I wanted to mend an employment from forty to sixty pounds a year, in

the Salt Office, and thought it hard I could not do it. She told me one Mr. Griffin should do it. And afterward I met Griffin at her lodgings; and he was, as I found, one I had been acquainted with. I named Filby to him, and his abode somewhere near Nantwich. He said frankly he had formerly examined the man, and found he understood very little of his business; but if he heard he mended, he would do what I desired. I will let it rest a while, and then resume it; and if Ppt writes to Filby, she may advise him to diligence, etc. I told Griffin positively I would have it done, if the man mended. This is an account of poo Ppt's commission to her most humble servant Pdfr. I have a world of writing to finish, and little time; these toads of Ministers are so slow in their helps. This makes me sometimes steal a week from the exactness I used to write to MD. Farewell, dee logues, deelest MD MD MD, . . . FW FW FW ME ME ME Lele.

Smoke the folding of my letters of late.

LETTER LVI

Here is now a stlange ting; a rettle flom MD unanswered: never was
before. I am slower, and MD is faster: but the last was owing to DD's
certificate. Why could it not be sent before, pay now? Is it so hard for
DD to prove she is alive? I protest solemnly I am not able to write to
MD for other business, but I will resume my journal method next time.
I find it is easier, though it contains nothing but where I dine, and the
occurrences of the day. I will write now but once in three weeks till
this business is off my hands, which must be in six, I think, at farthest.
O Ppt, I remember your reprimanding me for meddling in other people's
affairs: I have enough of it now, with a wanion. Two women have been
here six times apiece; I never saw them yet. The first I have despatched
with a letter; the other I must see, and tell her I can do nothing for her:
she is wife of one Connor, an old college acquaintance, and comes on
a foolish errand, for some old pretensions, that will succeed when I am
Lord Treasurer. I am got (up) two pair of stairs, in a private lodging,
and have ordered all my friends not to discover where I am; yet every
morning two or three sots are plaguing me, and my present servant has
not yet his lesson perfect of denying me. I have written a hundred and
thirty pages in folio, to be printed, and must write thirty more, which
will make a large book of four shillings. I wish I knew an opportunity
of sending you some snuff. I will watch who goes to Ireland, and do it if
possible. I had a letter from Parvisol, and find he has set my livings very
low. Colonel Hamilton, who was second to the Duke of Hamilton, is
tried to-day. I suppose he is come off, but have not heard. I dined with
Lord Treasurer, but left him by nine, and visited some people. Lady
Betty, his daughter, will be married on Monday next (as I suppose) to
the Marquis of Caermarthen. I did not know your country place had
been Portraine, till you told me so in your last. Has Swanton taken it
of Wallis? That Wallis was a grave, wise coxcomb. God be thanked that
Ppt im better of her disoddles. Pray God keep her so. The pamphlet of
Political Lying is written by Dr. Arbuthnot, the author of *John Bull*; 'tis
very pretty, but not so obvious to be understood. Higgins, first chaplain
to the Duke of Hamilton? Why, the Duke of Hamilton never dreamt
of a chaplain, nor I believe ever heard of Higgins. You are glorious
newsmongers in Ireland—Dean Francis, Sir R. Levinge, stuff stuff: and

Pratt, more stuff. We have lost our fine frost here; and Abel Roper tells as you have had floods in Dublin; ho, brave you! Oh ho! Swanton seized Portraine, now I understand oo. Ay, ay, now I see Portraune at the top of your letter. I never minded it before. Now to your second, N. 36. So, you read one of the Grub Streets about the bandbox. The Whig papers have abused me about the bandbox. God help me, what could I do? I fairly ventured my life. There is a particular account of it in the *Postboy*, and Evening Post of that day. Lord Treasurer has had the seal sent him that sealed the box, and directions where to find the other pistol in a tree in St. James's Park, which Lord Bolingbroke's messenger found accordingly; but who sent the present is not yet known. The Duke of Hamilton avoided the quarrel as much as possible, according to the foppish rules of honour in practice. What signified your writing angry to Filby? I hope you said nothing of hearing anything from me. Heigh! do oo write by sandlelight! nauti, nauti, nauti dallar, a hundred times, fol doing so. O, fais, DD, I'll take care of myself! The Queen is in town, and Lady Masham's month of lying-in is within two days of being out. I was at the christening on Monday. I could not get the child named Robin, after Lord Treasurer; it is Samuel, after the father. My brother Ormond sent me some chocolate to-day. I wish you had share of it: but they say 'tis good for me, and I design to drink some in a morning. Our Society meets next Thursday, now the Queen is in town; and Lord Treasurer assures me that the Society for reforming the language shall soon be established. I have given away ten shillings to-day to servants; 'tan't be help if one should cry one's eyes out. Hot a stir is here about your company and visits! Charming company, no doubt; now I keep no company at all, nor have I any desire to keep any. I never go to a coffee-house nor a tavern, nor have touched a card since I left Windsor. I make few visits, nor go to levees; my only debauching is sitting late where I dine, if I like the company. I have almost dropped the Duchesses of Shrewsbury and Hamilton, and several others. Lord Treasurer, the Duke of Ormond, and Lady Orkney are all that I see very often. Oh yes, and Lady Masham and Lord Bolingbroke, and one or two private friends. I make no figure but at Court, where I affect to turn from a lord to the meanest of my acquaintance, and I love to go there on Sundays to see the world. But, to say the truth, I am growing weary of it. I dislike a million of things in the course of public affairs; and if I were to stay here much longer, I am sure I should ruin myself with endeavouring to mend them. I am every day invited into schemes of doing this, but

I cannot find any that will probably succeed. It is impossible to save people against their own will; and I have been too much engaged in patchwork already. Do you understand all this stuff? No. Well zen, you are now returned to ombre and the Dean, and Christmas; I wish oo a very merry one; and pray don't lose oo money, nor play upon Watt Welch's game. Nite, sollahs, 'tis rate I'll go to seep; I don't seep well, and therefore never dare to drink coffee or tea after dinner: but I am very seepy in a molning. This is the effect of time and years. Nite deelest MD.

18. Morn. I am so very seepy in the morning that my man wakens me above ten times; and now I can tell oo no news of this day. (Here is a restless dog, crying cabbages and savoys, plagues me every morning about this time; he is now at it. I wish his largest cabbage were sticking in his throat.) I lodge over against the house in Little Rider Street, where DD lodged. Don't oo lememble, maram? To-night I must see the Abbé Gaultier, to get some particulars for my History. It was he who was first employed by France in the overtures of peace, and I have not had time this month to see him; he is but a puppy too. Lady Orkney has just sent to invite me to dinner; she has not given me the bed-nightgown; besides, I am come very much off from writing in bed, though I am doing it this minute; but I stay till my fire is burnt up. My grate is very large; two bushels of coals in a week: but I save it in lodgings. Lord Abercorn is come to London, and will plague me, and I can do him no service. The Duke of Shrewsbury goes in a day or two for France, perhaps to-day. We shall have a peace very soon; the Dutch are almost entirely agreed, and if they stop we shall make it without them; that has been long resolved. One Squire Jones, a scoundrel in my parish, has writ to me to desire I would engage Joe Beaumont to give him his interest for Parliament-man for Trim: pray tell Joe this; and if he designed to vote for him already, then he may tell Jones that I received his letter, and that I writ to Joe to do it. If Joe be engaged for any other, then he may do what he will: and Parvisol may say he spoke to Joe, but Joe's engaged, etc. I received three pair of fine thread stockings from Joe lately. Pray thank him when you see him, and that I say they are very fine and good. (I never looked at them yet, but that's no matter.) This is a fine day. I am ruined with coaches and chairs this twelvepenny weather. I must see my brother Ormond at eleven, and then the Duchess of Hamilton, with whom I doubt I am in disgrace, not having seen her these ten days. I

send this to-day, and must finish it now; and perhaps some people may come and hinder me; for it im ten o'clock (but not shaving-day), and I must be abroad at eleven. Abbé Gaultier sends me word I can't see him to-night; pots cake him! I don't value anything but one letter he has of Petecum's, showing the roguery of the Dutch. Did not the *Conduct of the Allies* make you great politicians? Fais, I believe you are not quite so ignorant as I thought you. I am glad to hear oo walked so much in the country. Does DD ever read to you, ung ooman? O, fais! I shall find strange doings hen I tum ole! Here is somebody coming that I must see that wants a little place; the son of cousin Rooke's eldest daughter, that died many years ago. He's here. Farewell, deelest MD MD MD ME ME ME FW FW FW, Lele.

LETTER LVII

Our Society was to meet to-day; but Lord Harley, who was President this week, could not attend, being gone to Wimbledon with his new brother-in-law, the young Marquis of Caermarthen, who married Lady Betty Harley on Monday last; and Lord Treasurer is at Wimbledon too. However, half a dozen of us met, and I propose our meetings should be once a fortnight; for, between you and me, we do no good. It cost me nineteen shillings to-day for my Club at dinner; I don't like it, fais. We have terrible snowy slobbery weather. Lord Abercorn is come to town, and will see me, whether I will or no. You know he has a pretence to a dukedom in France, which the Duke of Hamilton was soliciting for; but Abercorn resolves to spoil their title, if they will not allow him a fourth part; and I have advised the Duchess to compound with him, and have made the Ministry of my opinion. Night, dee sollahs, MD, MD.

19. Ay mally zis is sumsing rike, for Pdfr to write journals again! 'Tis as natural as mother's milk, now I am got into it. Lord Treasurer is returned from Wimbledon ('tis not above eight miles off), and sent for me to dine with him at five; but I had the grace to be abroad, and dined with some others, with honest Ben Tooke, by invitation. The Duchess of Ormond promised me her picture, and coming home to-night, I found hers and the Duke's both in my chamber. Was not that a pretty civil surprise? Yes, and they are in fine gilded frames, too. I am writing a letter to thank her, which I will send to-morrow morning. I'll tell her she is such a prude that she will not let so much as her picture be alone in a room with *a man*, unless the Duke's be with it; and so forth. We are full of snow, and dabbling. Lady Masham has come abroad these three days, and seen the Queen. I dined with her t'other day at her sister Hill's. I hope she will remove in a few days to her new lodgings at St. James's from Kensington. Nite, dee logues MD.

20. I lodge (up) two pair of stairs, have but one room, and deny myself to everybody almost, yet I cannot be quiet; and all my mornings are lost with people, who will not take answers below stairs; such as Dilly, and the Bishop, and Provost, etc. Lady Orkney invited me to dinner

to-day, which hindered me from dining with Lord Treasurer. This is his day that his chief friends in the Ministry dine with him. However, I went there about six, and sat with them till past nine, when they all went off; but he kept me back, and told me the circumstances of Lady Betty's match. The young fellow has £60,000 ready money, three great houses furnished, £7,000 a year at present, and about five more after his father and mother die. I think Lady Betty's portion is not above £8,000. I remember either Tisdall writ to me in somebody's letter, or you did it for him, that I should mention him on occasion to Lord Anglesea, with whom, he said, he had some little acquaintance. Lord Anglesea was with me to-night at Lord Treasurer's; and then I asked him about Tisdall, and described him. He said he never saw him, but that he had sent him his book. See what it is to be a puppy. Pray tell Mr. Walls that Lord Anglesea thanked me for recommending Clements to him; that he says he is £20,000 the better for knowing Clements. But pray don't let Clements go and write a letter of thanks, and tell my lord that he hears so and so, etc. Why, 'tis but like an Irish understanding to do so. Sad weather; two shillings in coaches to-day, and yet I am dirty. I am now going to read over something and correct it. So, nite.

21. Puppies have got a new way of plaguing me. I find letters directed for me at Lord Treasurer's, sometimes with enclosed ones to him, and sometimes with projects, and some times with libels. I usually keep them three or four days without opening. I was at Court to-day, as I always am on Sundays, instead of a coffee-house, to see my acquaintance. This day se'nnight, after I had been talking at Court with Sir William Wyndham, the Spanish Ambassador came to him and said he heard that was Dr. Swift, and desired him to tell me that his master, and the King of France, and the Queen, were more obliged to me than any man in Europe; so we bowed, and shook hands, etc. I took it very well of him. I dined with Lord Treasurer, and must again to-morrow, though I had rather not (as DD says); but now the Queen is in town, he does not keep me so late. I have not had time to see Fanny Manley since she came, but intend it one of these days. Her uncle, Jack Manley, I hear, cannot live a month, which will be a great loss to her father in Ireland, for I believe he is one of his chief supports. Our peace now will soon be determined; for Lord Bolingbroke tells me this morning that four provinces of Holland have complied with the Queen, and we expect the rest will do so immediately. Nite MD.

22. Lord Keeper promised me yesterday the first convenient living to poor Mr. Gery, who is married, and wants some addition to what he has. He is a very worthy creature. I had a letter some weeks ago from Elwick, who married Betty Gery. It seems the poor woman died some time last summer. Elwick grows rich, and purchases lands. I dined with Lord Treasurer to-day, who has engaged me to come again to-morrow. I gave Lord Bolingbroke a poem of Parnell's. I made Parnell insert some compliments in it to his lordship. He is extremely pleased with it, and read some parts of it to-day to Lord Treasurer, who liked it as much. And indeed he outdoes all our poets here a bar's length. Lord Bolingbroke has ordered me to bring him to dinner on Christmas Day, and I made Lord Treasurer promise to see him; and it may one day do Parnell a kindness. You know Parnell. I believe I have told you of that poem. Nite, deel MD.

23. This morning I presented one Diaper, a poet, to Lord Bolingbroke, with a new poem, which is a very good one; and I am to give him a sum of money from my lord; and I have contrived to make a parson of him, for he is half one already, being in deacon's orders, and serves a small cure in the country; but has a sword at his a—here in town. 'Tis a poor little short wretch, but will do best in a gown, and we will make Lord Keeper give him a living. Lord Bolingbroke writ to Lord Treasurer to excuse me to-day; so I dined with the former, and Monteleon, the Spanish Ambassador, who made me many compliments. I stayed till nine, and now it is past ten, and my man has locked me up, and I have just called to mind that I shall be in disgrace with Tom Leigh. That coxcomb had got into acquaintance with one Eckershall, Clerk of the Kitchen to the Queen, who was civil to him at Windsor on my account; for I had done some service to Eckershall. Leigh teases me to pass an evening at his lodgings with Eckershall. I put it off several times, but was forced at last to promise I would come to-night; and it never was in my head till I was locked up, and I have called and called, but my man is gone to bed; so I will write an excuse to-morrow. I detest that Tom Leigh, and am as formal to him as I can when I happen to meet him in the Park. The rogue frets me, if he knew it. He asked me why I did not wait on the Bishop of Dromore. I answered I had not the honour to be acquainted with him, and would not presume, etc. He takes me seriously, and says the Bishop is no proud man, etc. He tells me of a judge in Ireland that has done ill things. I ask why he is not

out? Says he, "I think the bishops, and you, and I, and the rest of the clergy, should meet and consult about it." I beg his pardon, and say, "I cannot be serviceable that way." He answers, "Yes, everybody may help something."—Don't you see how curiously he contrives to vex me; for the dog knows that with half a word I could do more than all of them together. But he only does it from the pride and envy of his own heart, and not out of a humorous design of teasing. He is one of those that would rather a service should not be done, than done by a private man, and of his own country. You take all this, don't you? Nite dee sollahs, I'll go seep a dozey.

24. I dined to-day with the Chancellor of the Exchequer, in order to look over some of my papers; but nothing was done. I have been also mediating between the Hamilton family and Lord Abercorn, to have them compound with him; and I believe they will do it. Lord Selkirk, the late Duke's brother, is to be in town, in order to go to France, to make the demands; and the Ministry are of opinion they will get some satisfaction, and they empowered me to advise the Hamilton side to agree with Abercorn, who asks a fourth part, and will go to France and spoil all if they won't yield it. Nite sollahs.

25. All melly Titmasses—melly Titmasses—I said it first—I wish it a souzand (times) zoth with halt and soul. I carried Parnell to dine at Lord Bolingbroke's, and he behaved himself very well; and Lord Bolingbroke is mightily pleased with him. I was at St. James's Chapel by eight this morning; and church and sacrament were done by ten. The Queen has the gout in her hand, and did not come to church to-day; and I stayed so long in my chamber that I missed going to Court. Did I tell you that the Queen designs to have a Drawing-room and company every day? Nite dee logues.

26. I was to wish the Duke of Ormond a happy Christmas, and give half a crown to his porter. It will cost me a dozen half-crowns among such fellows. I dined with Lord Treasurer, who chid me for being absent three days. Mighty kind, with a p—; less of civility, and more of his interest! We hear Maccartney is gone over to Ireland. Was it not comical for a gentleman to be set upon by highwaymen, and to tell them he was Maccartney? Upon which they brought him to a justice of peace, in hopes of the reward, and the rogues were sent to gaol. Was it

not great presence of mind? But maybe you heard this already; for there was a Grub Street of it. Lord Bolingbroke told me I must walk away to-day when dinner was done, because Lord Treasurer, and he, and another, were to enter upon business; but I said it was as fit I should know their business as anybody, for I was to justify (it). So the rest went, and I stayed, and it was so important, I was like to sleep over it. I left them at nine, and it is now twelve. Nite, MD.

27. I dined to-day with General Hill, Governor of Dunkirk. Lady Masham and Mrs. Hill, his two sisters, were of the company, and there have I been sitting this evening till eleven, looking over others at play; for I have left off loving play myself; and I think Ppt is now a great gamester. I have a great cold on me, not quite at its height. I have them seldom, and therefore ought to be patient. I met Mr. Addison and Pastoral Philips on the Mall to-day, and took a turn with them; but they both looked terrible dry and cold. A curse of party! And do you know I have taken more pains to recommend the Whig wits to the favour and mercy of the Ministers than any other people. Steele I have kept in his place. Congreve I have got to be used kindly, and secured. Rowe I have recommended, and got a promise of a place. Philips I could certainly have provided for, if he had not run party mad, and made me withdraw my recommendation; and I set Addison so right at first that he might have been employed, and have partly secured him the place he has; yet I am worse used by that faction than any man. Well, go to cards, sollah Ppt, and dress the wine and olange, sollah MD, and I'll go seep. 'Tis rate. Nite MD.

28. My cold is so bad that I could not go to church to-day, nor to Court; but I was engaged to Lord Orkney's with the Duke of Ormond, at dinner; and ventured, because I could cough and spit there as I pleased. The Duke and Lord Arran left us, and I have been sitting ever since with Lord and Lady Orkney till past eleven: and my cold is worse, and makes me giddy. I hope it is only my cold. Oh, says Ppt, everybody is giddy with a cold; I hope it is no more; but I'll go to bed, for the fellow has bawled "Past twelve." Night, deels.

29. I got out early to-day, and escaped all my duns. I went to see Lord Bolingbroke about some business, and truly he was gone out too. I dined in the City upon the broiled leg of a goose and a bit of brawn,

with my printer. Did I tell you that I forbear printing what I have in hand, till the Court decides something about me? I will contract no more enemies, at least I will not embitter worse those I have already, till I have got under shelter; and the Ministers know my resolution, so that you may be disappointed in seeing this thing as soon as you expected. I hear Lord Treasurer is out of order. My cold is very bad. Every(body) has one. Nite two dee logues.

30. I suppose this will be full by Saturday; zen it sall go. Duke of Ormond, Lord Arran, and I, dined privately to-day at an old servant's house of his. The Council made us part at six. One Mrs. Ramsay dined with us; an old lady of about fifty-five, that we are all very fond of. I called this evening at Lord Treasurer's, and sat with him two hours. He has been cupped for a cold, and has been very ill. He cannot dine with Parnell and me at Lord Bolingbroke's to-morrow, but says he will see Parnell some other time. I hoise up Parnell partly to spite the envious Irish folks here, particularly Tom Leigh. I saw the Bishop of Clogher's family to-day; Miss is mighty ill of a cold, coughs incessantly. Nite MD.

31. To-day Parnell and I dined with Lord Bolingbroke, to correct Parnell's poem. I made him show all the places he disliked; and when Parnell has corrected it fully he shall print it. I went this evening to sit with Lord Treasurer. He is better, and will be out in a day or two. I sat with him while the young folks went to supper; and then went down, and there were the young folks merry together, having turned Lady Oxford up to my lord, and I stayed with them till twelve. There was the young couple, Lord and Lady Caermarthen, and Lord and Lady Dupplin, and Lord Harley and I; and the old folks were together above. It looked like what I have formerly done so often; stealing together from the old folks, though indeed it was not from poor Lord Treasurer, who is as young a fellow as any of us: but Lady Oxford is a silly mere old woman. My cold is still so bad that I have not the least smelling. I am just got home, and 'tis past twelve; and I'll go to bed, and settle my head, heavy as lead. Nite MD.

Jan. 1, 1712–13. A sousand melly new eels to deelest richar MD. Pray God Almighty bless you, and send you ever happy! I forgot to tell you that yesterday Lord Abercorn was here, teasing me about his French duchy, and suspecting my partiality to the Hamilton family in such a whimsical manner that Dr. Pratt, who was by, thought he was mad. He was no sooner gone but Lord Orkney sent to know whether he might come and sit with me half an hour upon some business. I returned answer that I would wait on him; which I did. We discoursed a while, and he left me with Lady Orkney; and in came the Earl of Selkirk, whom I had never seen before. He is another brother of the Duke of Hamilton, and is going to France, by a power from his mother, the old Duchess, to negotiate their pretensions to the duchy of Chatelherault. He teased me for two hours in spite of my teeth, and held my hand when I offered to stir; would have had me engage the Ministry to favour him against Lord Abercorn, and to convince them that Lord Abercorn had no pretensions; and desired I would also convince Lord Abercorn himself so; and concluded he was sorry I was a greater friend to Abercorn than Hamilton. I had no patience, and used him with some plainness. Am not I purely handled between a couple of puppies? Ay, says Ppt, you must be meddling in other folks' affairs. I appeal to the Bishop of Clogher whether Abercorn did not complain that I would not let him see me last year, and that he swore he would take no denial from my servant when he came again. The Ministers gave me leave to tell the Hamilton family it was their opinion that they ought to agree with Abercorn. Lord Anglesea was then by, and told Abercorn; upon which he gravely tells me I was commissioned by the Ministers, and ought to perform my commission, etc.—But I'll have done with them. I have warned Lord Treasurer and Lord Bolingbroke to beware of Selkirk's teasing,—x on him! Yet Abercorn vexes me more. The whelp owes to me all the kind receptions he has had from the Ministry. I dined to-day at Lord Treasurer's with the young folks, and sat with Lord Treasurer till nine, and then was forced to Lady Masham's, and sat there till twelve, talking of affairs, till I am out of humour, as everyone must that knows them inwardly. A thousand things wrong, most of them easy to mend; yet our schemes availing at best but little, and sometimes nothing at all. One evil, which I twice patched up with the hazard of all the credit I had, is now spread more than ever. But burn politics, and send me from Courts and Ministers! Nite deelest richar MD.

2. I sauntered about this morning, and went with Dr. Pratt to a picture auction, where I had like to be drawn in to buy a picture that I was fond of, but, it seems, was good for nothing. Pratt was there to buy some pictures for the Bishop of Clogher, who resolves to lay out ten pounds to furnish his house with curious pieces. We dined with the Bishop,

I being by chance disengaged. And this evening I sat with the Bishop of Ossory, who is laid up with the gout. The French Ambassador, Duke d'Aumont, came to town to-night; and the rabble conducted him home with shouts. I cannot smell yet, though my cold begins to break. It continues cruel hard frosty weather. Go and be melly, . . . sollahs.

3. Lord Dupplin and I went with Lord and Lady Orkney this morning at ten to Wimbledon, six miles off, to see Lord and Lady Caermarthen. It is much the finest place about this town. Did oo never see it? I was once there before, about five years ago. You know Lady Caermarthen is Lord Treasurer's daughter, married about three weeks ago. I hope the young fellow will be a good husband.—I must send this away now. I came back just by nightfall, cruel cold weather; I have no smell yet, but my cold something better. Nite (?) sollahs; I'll take my reeve. I forget how MD's accounts are. Pray let me know always timely before MD wants; and pray give the bill on t'other side to Mrs. Brent as usual. I believe I have not paid her this great while. Go, play cards, and. . . rove Pdfr. Nite richar MD. . . roves Pdfr. FW lele. . . MD MD MD MD MD FW FW FW FW MD MD Lele. . .

The six odd shillings, tell Mrs. Brent, are for her new year's gift.

I AM JUST NOW TOLD that poor dear Lady Ashburnham, the Duke of Ormond's daughter, died yesterday at her country house. The poor creature was with child. She was my greatest favourite, and I am in excessive concern for her loss. I hardly knew a more valuable person on all accounts. You must have heard me talk of her. I am afraid to see the Duke and Duchess. She was naturally very healthy; I am afraid she has been thrown away for want of care. Pray condole with me. 'Tis extremely moving. Her lord's a puppy; and I shall never think it worth my while to be troubled with him, now he has lost all that was valuable in his possession; yet I think he used her pretty well. I hate life when I think it exposed to such accidents; and to see so many thousand wretches burdening the earth, while such as her die, makes me think God did never intend life for a blessing. Farewell.

LETTER LVIII

I ended my last with the melancholy news of poor Lady Ashburnham's death. The Bishop of Clogher and Dr. Pratt made me dine with them to-day at Lord Mountjoy's, pursuant to an engagement, which I had forgot. Lady Mountjoy told me that Maccartney was got safe out of our clutches, for she had spoke with one who had a letter from him from Holland. Others say the same thing. 'Tis hard such a dog should escape.—As I left Lord Mountjoy's I saw the Duke d'Aumont, the French Ambassador, going from Lord Bolingbroke's, where he dined, to have a private audience of the Queen. I followed, and went up to Court, where there was a great crowd. I was talking with the Duke of Argyle by the fireside in the bed-chamber, when the Ambassador came out from the Queen. Argyle presented me to him, and Lord Bolingbroke and we talked together a while. He is a fine gentleman, something like the Duke of Ormond, and just such an expensive man. After church to-day I showed the Bishop of Clogher, at Court, who was who. Nite my two dee logues, and. . .

5. Our frost is broke, but it is bloody cold. Lord Treasurer is recovered, and went out this evening to the Queen. I dined with Lady Oxford, and then sat with Lord Treasurer while he went out. He gave me a letter from an unknown hand, relating to Dr. Brown, Bishop of Cork, recommending him to a better bishopric, as a person who opposed Lord Wharton, and was made a bishop on that account, celebrating him for a great politician, etc.: in short, all directly contrary to his character, which I made bold to explain. What dogs there are in the world! I was to see the poor Duke and Duchess of Ormond this morning. The Duke was in his public room, with Mr. Southwell and two more gentlemen. When Southwell and I were alone with him, he talked something of Lord Ashburnham, that he was afraid the Whigs would get him again. He bore up as well as he could, but something falling accidentally in discourse, the tears were just falling out of his eyes, and I looked off to give him an opportunity (which he took) of wiping them with his handkerchief. I never saw anything so moving, nor such a mixture of greatness of mind, and tenderness, and discretion. Nite MD.

6. Lord Bolingbroke and Parnell and I dined, by invitation, with my friend Darteneuf, whom you have heard me talk of. Lord Bolingbroke likes Parnell mightily; and it is pleasant to see that one who hardly passed for anything in Ireland makes his way here with a little friendly forwarding. It is scurvy rainy weather, and I have hardly been abroad to-day, nor know anything that passes.—Lord Treasurer is quite recovered, and I hope will be careful to keep himself well. The Duchess of Marlborough is leaving England to go to her Duke, and makes presents of rings to several friends, they say worth two hundred pounds apiece. I am sure she ought to give me one, though the Duke pretended to think me his greatest enemy, and got people to tell me so, and very mildly to let me know how gladly he would have me softened toward him. I bid a lady of his acquaintance and mine let him know that I had hindered many a bitter thing against him; not for his own sake, but because I thought it looked base; and I desired everything should be left him, except power. Nite MD.

7. I dined with Lord and Lady Masham to-day, and this evening played at ombre with Mrs. Vanhom, merely for amusement. The Ministers have got my papers, and will neither read them nor give them to me; and I can hardly do anything. Very warm slabby weather, but I made a shift to get a walk; yet I lost half of it, by shaking off Lord Rochester, who is a good, civil, simple man. The Bishop of Ossory will not be Bishop of Hereford, to the great grief of himself and his wife. And hat is MD doing now, I wonder? Playing at cards with the Dean and Mrs. Walls? I think it is not certain yet that Maccartney is escaped. I am plagued with bad authors, verse and prose, who send me their books and poems, the vilest trash I ever saw; but I have given their names to my man, never to let them see me. I have got new ink, and 'tis very white; and I don't see that it turns black at all. I'll go to seep; 'tis past twelve.—Nite, MD.

8. Oo must understand that I am in my geers, and have got a chocolate-pot, a present from Mrs. Ashe of Clogher, and some chocolate from my brother Ormond, and I treat folks sometimes. I dined with Lord Treasurer at five o'clock to-day, and was by while he and Lord Bolingbroke were at business; for it is fit I should know all that passes now, because, etc. The Duke of Ormond employed me to speak to Lord Treasurer to-day about an affair, and I did so; and the Duke had spoke

himself two hours before, which vexed me, and I will chide the Duke about it. I'll tell you a good thing; there is not one of the Ministry but what will employ me as gravely to speak for them to Lord Treasurer as if I were their brother or his; and I do it as gravely: though I know they do it only because they will not make themselves uneasy, or had rather I should be denied than they. I believe our peace will not be finished these two months; for I think we must have a return from Spain by a messenger, who will not go till Sunday next. Lord Treasurer has invited me to dine with him again to-morrow. Your Commissioner, Keatley, is to be there. Nite dee richar MD.

9. Dr. Pratt drank chocolate with me this morning, and then we walked. I was yesterday with him to see Lady Betty Butler, grieving for her sister Ashburnham. The jade was in bed in form, and she did so cant, she made me sick. I meet Tom Leigh every day in the Park, to preserve his health. He is as ruddy as a rose, and tells me his Bishop of Dromore recovers very much. That Bishop has been very near dying. This day's *Examiner* talks of the play of "What is it like?" and you will think it to be mine, and be bit; for I have no hand in these papers at all. I dined with Lord Treasurer, and shall again to-morrow, which is his day when all the Ministers dine with him. He calls it whipping-day. It is always on Saturday, and we do indeed usually rally him about his faults on that day. I was of the original Club, when only poor Lord Rivers, Lord Keeper, and Lord Bolingbroke came; but now Ormond, Anglesea, Lord Steward, Dartmouth, and other rabble intrude, and I scold at it; but now they pretend as good a title as I; and, indeed, many Saturdays I am not there. The company being too many, I don't love it. Nite MD.

10. At seven this evening, as we sat after dinner at Lord Treasurer's, a servant said Lord Peterborow was at the door. Lord Treasurer and Lord Bolingbroke went out to meet him, and brought him in. He was just returned from abroad, where he has been above a year. Soon as he saw me, he left the Duke of Ormond and other lords, and ran and kissed me before he spoke to them; but chid me terribly for not writing to him, which I never did this last time he was abroad, not knowing where he was; and he changed places so often, it was impossible a letter should overtake him. He left England with a bruise, by his coach overturning, that made him spit blood, and was so ill, we expected every post to hear of his death; but he outrode it or outdrank it, or something, and

is come home lustier than ever. He is at least sixty, and has more spirits than any young fellow I know in England. He has got the old Oxford regiment of horse, and I believe will have a Garter. I love the hang-dog dearly. Nite dee MD.

11. The Court was crammed to-day to see the French Ambassador; but he did not come. Did I never tell you that I go to Court on Sundays as to a coffee-house, to see acquaintance, whom I should otherwise not see twice a year? The Provost and I dined with Ned Southwell, by appointment, in order to settle your kingdom, if my scheme can be followed; but I doubt our Ministry will be too tedious. You must certainly have a new Parliament; but they would have that a secret yet. Our Parliament here will be prorogued for three weeks. Those puppies the Dutch will not yet come in, though they pretend to submit to the Queen in everything; but they would fain try first how our session begins, in hopes to embroil us in the House of Lords: and if my advice had been taken, the session should have begun, and we would have trusted the Parliament to approve the steps already made toward the peace, and had an Address perhaps from them to conclude without the Dutch, if they would not agree.—Others are of my mind, but it is not reckoned so safe, it seems; yet I doubt whether the peace will be ready so soon as three weeks, but that is a secret. Nite MD.

12. Pratt and I walked into the City to one Bateman's, a famous bookseller, for old books. There I laid out four pounds like a fool, and we dined at a hedge ale-house, for two shillings and twopence, like emperors. Let me see, I bought Plutarch, two volumes, for thirty shillings, etc. Well, I'll tell you no more; oo don't understand Greek. We have no news, and I have nothing more to say to-day, and I can't finish my work. These Ministers will not find time to do what I would have them. So nite, nown dee dallars.

13. I was to have dined to-day with Lord Keeper, but would not, because that brute Sir John Walter was to be one of the company. You may remember he railed at me last summer was twelvemonth at Windsor, and has never begged my pardon, though he promised to do it; and Lord Mansel, who was one of the company, would certainly have set us together by the ears, out of pure roguish mischief. So I dined with Lord Treasurer, where there was none but Lord Bolingbroke. I stayed

till eight, and then went to Lady Orkney's, who has been sick, and sat with her till twelve, from whence you may consider it is late, sollahs. The Parliament was prorogued to-day, as I told you, for three weeks. Our weather is very bad and slobbery, and I shall spoil my new hat (I have bought a new hat), or empty my pockets. Does Hawkshaw pay the interest he owes? Lord Abercorn plagues me to death. I have now not above six people to provide for, and about as many to do good offices to; and thrice as many that I will do nothing for; nor can I if I would. Nite dee MD.

14. To-day I took the circle of morning visits. I went to the Duchess of Ormond, and there was she, and Lady Betty, and Lord Ashburnham together: this was the first time the mother and daughter saw each other since Lady Ashburnham's death. They were both in tears, and I chid them for being together, and made Lady Betty go to her own chamber; then sat a while with the Duchess, and went after Lady Betty, and all was well. There is something of farce in all these mournings, let them be ever so serious. People will pretend to grieve more than they really do, and that takes off from their true grief. I then went to the Duchess of Hamilton, who never grieved, but raged, and stormed, and railed. She is pretty quiet now, but has a diabolical temper. Lord Keeper and his son, and their two ladies, and I, dined to-day with Mr. Cæsar, Treasurer of the Navy, at his house in the City, where he keeps his office. We happened to talk of Brutus, and I said something in his praise, when it struck me immediately that I had made a blunder in doing so; and, therefore, I recollected myself, and said, "Mr. Cæsar, I beg your pardon." So we laughed, etc. Nite, my own deelest richar logues, MD.

15. I forgot to tell you that last night I had a present sent me (I found it, when I came home, in my chamber) of the finest wild fowl I ever saw, with the vilest letter, and from the vilest poet in the world, who sent it me as a bribe to get him an employment. I knew not where the scoundrel lived, so I could not send them back, and therefore I gave them away as freely as I got them, and have ordered my man never to let up the poet when he comes. The rogue should have kept the wings at least for his muse. One of his fowls was a large capon pheasant, as fat as a pullet. I ate share of it to-day with a friend. We have now a Drawing-room every Wednesday, Thursday, and Saturday at one o'clock. The Queen does not come out; but all her Ministers, foreigners, and persons of

quality are at it. I was there to-day; and as Lord Treasurer came towards me, I avoided him, and he hunted me thrice about the room. I affect never to take notice of him at church or Court. He knows it, for I have told him so; and to-night, at Lord Masham's, he gave an account of it to the company; but my reasons are, that people seeing me speak to him causes a great deal of teasing. I tell you what comes into my head, that I never knew whether MD were Whigs or Tories, and I value our conversation the more that it never turned on that subject. I have a fancy that Ppt is a Tory, and a violent one. I don't know why; but methinks she looks like one, and DD a sort of a Trimmer. Am I right? I gave the Examiner a hint about this prorogation, and to praise the Queen for her tenderness to the Dutch in giving them still more time to submit. It fitted the occasions at present. Nite MD.

16. I was busy to-day at the Secretary's office, and stayed till past three. The Duke of Ormond and I were to dine at Lord Orkney's. The Duke was at the Committee, so I thought all was safe. When I went there, they had almost dined; for the Duke had sent to excuse himself, which I never knew. I came home at seven, and began a little whim, which just came into my head; and will make a threepenny pamphlet. It shall be finished and out in a week; and if it succeeds, you shall know what it is; otherwise, not. I cannot send this to-morrow, and will put it off till next Saturday, because I have much business. So my journals shall be short, and Ppt must have patience. So nite, dee sollahs.

17. This rogue Parnell has not yet corrected his poem, and I would fain have it out. I dined to-day with Lord Treasurer, and his Saturday company, nine of us in all. They went away at seven, and Lord Treasurer and I sat talking an hour after. After dinner he was talking to the lords about the speech the Queen must make when the Parliament meets. He asked me how I would make it. I was going to be serious, because it was seriously put; but I turned it to a jest. And because they had been speaking of the Duchess of Marlborough going to Flanders after the Duke, I said the speech should begin thus: "My Lords and Gentlemen, In order to my own quiet, and that of my subjects, I have thought fit to send the Duchess of Marlborough abroad after the Duke." This took well, and turned off the discourse. I must tell you I do not at all like the present situation of affairs, and remember I tell you so. Things must be on another foot, or we are all undone. I hate this driving always to an inch. Nite MD.

18. We had a mighty full Court to-day. Dilly was with me at the French church, and edified mightily. The Duke of Ormond and I dined at Lord Orkney's; but I left them at seven, and came home to my whim. I have made a great progress. My large Treatise stands stock still. Some think it too dangerous to publish, and would have me print only what relates to the peace. I cannot tell what I shall do.—The Bishop of Dromore is dying. They thought yesterday he could not live two hours; yet he is still alive, but is utterly past all hopes. Go to cards, sollahs, and nite.

19. I was this morning to see the Duke and Duchess of Ormond. The Duke d'Aumont came in while I was with the Duke of Ormond, and we complimented each other like dragons. A poor fellow called at the door where I lodge, with a parcel of oranges for a present for me. I bid my man know what his name was, and whence he came. He sent word his name was Bun, and that I knew him very well. I bid my man tell him I was busy, and he could not speak to me; and not to let him leave his oranges. I know no more of it, but I am sure I never heard the name, and I shall take no such presents from strangers. Perhaps he might be only some beggar, who wanted a little money. Perhaps it might be something worse. Let them keep their poison for their rats. I don't love it. That blot is a blunder. Nite dee MD. . .

20. A Committee of our Society dined to-day with the Chancellor of the Exchequer. Our Society does not meet now as usual, for which I am blamed: but till Lord Treasurer will agree to give us money and employments to bestow, I am averse to it; and he gives us nothing but promises. The Bishop of Dromore is still alive, and that is all. We expect every day he will die, and then Tom Leigh must go back, which is one good thing to the town. I believe Pratt will drive at one of these bishoprics. Our English bishopric is not yet disposed of. I believe the peace will not be ready by the session. Nite MD.

21. I was to-day with my printer, to give him a little pamphlet I have written, but not politics. It will be out by Monday. If it succeeds, I will tell you of it; otherwise, not. We had a prodigious thaw to-day, as bad as rain; yet I walked like a good boy all the way. The Bishop of Dromore still draws breath, but cannot live two days longer. My large book lies flat. Some people think a great part of it ought not to be now printed. I

believe I told you so before. This letter shall not go till Saturday, which makes up the three weeks exactly; and I allow MD six weeks, which are now almost out; so oo must know I expect a rettle vely soon, and that MD is vely werr; and so nite, dee MD.

22. This is one of our Court days, and I was there. I told you there is a Drawing-room, Wednesday, Thursday, and Saturday. The Hamiltons and Abercorns have done teasing me. The latter, I hear, is actually going to France. Lord Treasurer quarrelled with me at Court for being four days without dining with him; so I dined there to-day, and he has at last fallen in with my project (as he calls it) of coining halfpence and farthings, with devices, like medals, in honour of the Queen, every year changing the device. I wish it may be done. Nite MD.

23. The Duke of Ormond and I appointed to dine with Ned Southwell to-day, to talk of settling your affairs of Parliament in Ireland, but there was a mixture of company, and the Duke of Ormond was in haste, and nothing was done. If your Parliament meets this summer, it must be a new one; but I find some are of opinion there should be none at all these two years. I will trouble myself no more about it. My design was to serve the Duke of Ormond. Dr. Pratt and I sat this evening with the Bishop of Clogher, and played at ombre for threepences. That, I suppose, is but low with you. I found, at coming home, a letter from MD, N. 37. I shall not answer it zis bout, but will the next. I am sorry for poo poo Ppt. Pray walk hen oo can. I have got a terrible new cold before my old one was quite gone, and don't know how. Pay. . . I shall have DD's money soon from the Exchequer. The Bishop of Dromore is dead now at last. Nite, dee MD.

24. I was at Court to-day, and it was comical to see Lord Abercorn bowing to me, but not speaking, and Lord Selkirk the same. I dined with Lord Treasurer and his Saturday Club, and sat with him two hours after the rest were gone, and spoke freer to him of affairs than I am afraid others do, who might do more good. All his friends repine, and shrug their shoulders; but will not deal with him so freely as they ought. It is an odd business; the Parliament just going to sit, and no employments given. They say they will give them in a few days. There is a new bishop made of Hereford; so Ossory is disappointed. I hinted so to his friends two months ago, to make him leave off deluding himself,

and being indiscreet, as he was. I have just time to send this, without giving to the bellman. Nite deelest richar MD. . . dee MD MD MD FW FW FW ME ME ME Lele Lele Lele.

My second cold is better now. Lele lele lele lele.

We had such a terrible storm to-day, that, going to Lord Bolingbroke's, I saw a hundred tiles fallen down; and one swinger fell about forty yards before me, that would have killed a horse: so, after church and Court, I walked through the Park, and took a chair to Lord Treasurer's. Next door to his house, a tin chimneytop had fallen down, with a hundred bricks. It is grown calm this evening. I wonder had you such a wind to-day? I hate it as much as any hog does. Lord Treasurer has engaged me to dine again with him to-morrow. He has those tricks sometimes of inviting me from day to day, which I am forced to break through. My little pamphlet is out: 'tis not politics. If it takes, I say again you shall hear of it. Nite dee logues.

26. This morning I felt a little touch of giddiness, which has disordered and weakened me with its ugly remains all this day. Pity Pdfr. After dinner at Lord Treasurer's, the French Ambassador, Duke d'Aumont, sent Lord Treasurer word that his house was burnt down to the ground. It took fire in the upper rooms, while he was at dinner with Monteleon, the Spanish Ambassador, and other persons; and soon after Lord Bolingbroke came to us with the same story. We are full of speculations upon it, but I believe it was the carelessness of his French rascally servants. 'Tis odd that this very day Lord Somers, Wharton, Sunderland, Halifax, and the whole club of Whig lords, dined at Pontack's in the City, as I received private notice. They have some damned design. I tell you another odd thing; I was observing it to Lord Treasurer, that he was stabbed on the day King William died; and the day I saved his life, by opening the bandbox, was King William's birthday. My friend Mr. Lewis has had a lie spread on him by the mistake of a man, who went to another of his name, to give him thanks for passing his Privy Seal to come from France. That other Lewis spread about that the man brought him thanks from Lord Perth and Lord Melfort (two lords with the Pretender), for his great services, etc. The Lords will examine that t'other Lewis to-morrow in council; and I believe you will hear of it in the prints, for I will make Abel Roper give a relation of it. Pray tell me if it be necessary to write a little plainer; for I looked over a bit of my last letter, and could

hardly read it. I'll mend my hand, if oo please: but you are more used to it nor I, as Mr. Raymond says. Nite MD.

27. I dined to-day with Lord Treasurer: this makes four days together; and he has invited me again to-morrow, but I absolutely refused him. I was this evening at a christening with him of Lord Dupplin's daughter. He went away at ten; but they kept me and some others till past twelve; so you may be sure 'tis late, as they say. We have now stronger suspicions that the Duke d'Aumont's house was set on fire by malice. I was to-day to see Lord Keeper, who has quite lost his voice with a cold. There Dr. Radcliffe told me that it was the Ambassador's confectioner set the house on fire by boiling sugar, and going down and letting it boil over. Yet others still think differently; so I know not what to judge. Nite my own deelest MD, rove Pdfr.

28. I was to-day at Court, where the Spanish Ambassador talked to me as if he did not suspect any design in burning d'Aumont's house: but Abbé Gaultier, Secretary for France here, said quite otherwise; and that d'Aumont had a letter the very same day to let him know his house should be burnt, and they tell several other circumstances too tedious to write. One is, that a fellow mending the tiles just when the fire broke out, saw a pot with wildfire in the room. I dined with Lord Orkney. Neither Lord Abercorn nor Selkirk will now speak with me. I have disobliged both sides. Nite dear MD.

29. Our Society met to-day, fourteen of us, and at a tavern. We now resolve to meet but once a fortnight, and have a Committee every other week of six or seven, to consult about doing some good. I proposed another message to Lord Treasurer by three principal members, to give a hundred guineas to a certain person, and they are to urge it as well as they can. We also raised sixty guineas upon our own Society; but I made them do it by sessors, and I was one of them, and we fitted our tax to the several estates. The Duke of Ormond pays ten guineas, and I the third part of a guinea; at that rate, they may tax as often as they please. Well, but I must answer oor rettle, ung oomens: not yet; 'tis rate now, and I can't tind it. Nite deelest MD.

30. I have drank Spa waters this two or three days; but they do not pass, and make me very giddy. I an't well; faith, I'll take them no more. I

sauntered after church with the Provost to-day to see a library to be sold, and dined at five with Lord Orkney. We still think there was malice in burning d'Aumont's house. I hear little Harrison is come over; it was he I sent to Utrecht. He is now Queen's Secretary to the Embassy, and has brought with him the Barrier Treaty, as it is now corrected by us, and yielded to by the Dutch, which was the greatest difficulty to retard the peace. I hope he will bring over the peace a month hence, for we will send him back as soon as possible. I long to see the little brat, my own creature. His pay is in all a thousand pounds a year, and they have never paid him a groat, though I have teased their hearts out. He must be three or four hundred pounds in debt at least, the brat! Let me go to bed, sollahs.—Nite dee richar MD.

31. Harrison was with me this morning: we talked three hours, and then I carried him to Court. When we went down to the door of my lodging, I found a coach waited for him. I chid him for it; but he whispered me it was impossible to do otherwise; and in the coach he told me he had not one farthing in his pocket to pay it; and therefore took the coach for the whole day, and intended to borrow money somewhere or other. So there was the Queen's Minister entrusted in affairs of the greatest importance, without a shilling in his pocket to pay a coach! I paid him while he was with me seven guineas, in part of a dozen of shirts he bought me in Holland. I presented him to the Duke of Ormond, and several lords at Court; and I contrived it so that Lord Treasurer came to me and asked (I had Parnell by me) whether that was Dr. Parnell, and came up and spoke to him with great kindness, and invited him to his house. I value myself upon making the Ministry desire to be acquainted with Parnell, and not Parnell with the Ministry. His poem is almost fully corrected, and shall soon be out. Here's enough for to-day: only to tell you that I was in the City with my printer to alter an *Examiner* about my friend Lewis's story, which will be told with remarks. Nite MD.

Feb. 1. I could do nothing till to-day about the *Examiner*, but the printer came this morning, and I dictated to him what was fit to be said, and then Mr. Lewis came, and corrected it as he would have it; so I was neither at church nor Court. The Duke of Ormond and I dined at Lord Orkney's. I left them at seven, and sat with Sir Andrew Fountaine, who has a very bad sore leg, for which he designs to go to France. Fais, here's a week gone, and one side of this letter not finished. Oh, but I write now but once in three weeks; iss, fais, this shall go sooner. The Parliament is to sit on the third, but will adjourn for three or four days; for the Queen is laid up with the gout, and both Speakers out of order, though one of them, the Lord Keeper, is almost well. I spoke to the Duke of Ormond a good deal about Ireland. We do not altogether agree, nor am I judge enough of Irish affairs; but I will speak to Lord Treasurer to-morrow, that we three may settle them some way or other. Nite sollahs both, rove Pdfr.

2. I had a letter some days ago from Moll Gery; her name is now Wigmore, and her husband has turned parson. She desires nothing but that I would get Lord Keeper to give him a living; but I will send her no answer, though she desires it much. She still makes mantuas at Farnham. It rained all this day, and Dilly came to me, and was coaching it into the City; so I went with him for a shaking, because it would not cost me a farthing. There I met my friend Stratford, the merchant, who is going abroad to gather up his debts, and be clear in the world. He begged that I would dine with some merchant friends of ours there, because it was the last time I should see him: so I did, and thought to have seen Lord Treasurer in the evening, but he happened to go out at five; so I visited some friends, and came home. And now I have the greatest part of your letter to answer; and yet I will not do it to-night, say what oo please. The Parliament meets to-morrow, but will be prorogued for a fortnight; which disappointment will, I believe, vex abundance of them, though they are not Whigs; for they are forced to be in town at expense for nothing: but we want an answer from Spain, before we are sure of everything being right for the peace; and God knows whether we can have that answer this month. It is a most ticklish juncture of affairs; we are always driving to an inch: I am weary of it. Nite MD.

3. The Parliament met, and was prorogued, as I said, and I found some cloudy faces, and heard some grumbling. We have got over all our difficulties with France, I think. They have now settled all the articles of commerce between us and them, wherein they were very much disposed to play the rogue if we had not held them to (it); and this business we wait from Spain is to prevent some other rogueries of the French, who are finding an evasion to trade to the Spanish West Indies; but I hope we shall prevent it. I dined with Lord Treasurer, and

he was in good humour enough. I gave him that part of my book in manuscript to read where his character was, and drawn pretty freely. He was reading and correcting it with his pencil, when the Bishop of St. David's (now removing to Hereford) came in and interrupted us. I left him at eight, and sat till twelve with the Provost and Bishop of Clogher at the Provost's. Nite MD.

4. I was to-day at Court, but kept out of Lord Treasurer's way, because I was engaged to the Duke of Ormond, where I dined, and, I think, ate and drank too much. I sat this evening with Lady Masham, and then with Lord Masham and Lord Treasurer at Lord Masham's. It was last year, you may remember, my constant evening place. I saw Lady Jersey with Lady Masham, who has been laying out for my acquaintance, and has forced a promise for me to drink chocolate with her in a day or two, which I know not whether I shall perform (I have just mended my pen, you see), for I do not much like her character; but she is very malicious, and therefore I think I must keep fair with her. I cannot send this letter till Saturday next, I find; so I will answer oors now. I see no different days of the month; yet it is dated January 3: so it was long a coming. I did not write to Dr. Coghill that I would have nothing in Ireland, but that I was soliciting nothing anywhere, and that is true. I have named Dr. Sterne to Lord Treasurer, Lord Bolingbroke, and the Duke of Ormond, for a bishopric, and I did it heartily. I know not what will come of it; but I tell you as a great secret that I have made the Duke of Ormond promise me to recommend nobody till he tells me, and this for some reasons too long to mention. My head is still in no good order. I am heartily sorry for poo Ppt, I'm sure. Her head is good for. . . I'll answer more to-mollow. Nite, dearest MD; nite dee sollahs, MD.

5. I must go on with oo letter. I dined to-day with Sir Andrew Fountaine and the Provost, and I played at ombre with him all the afternoon. I won, yet Sir Andrew is an admirable player. Lord Pembroke came in, and I gave him three or four scurvy Dilly puns, that begin with an IF. Well, but oor letter, well, ret me see.—No; I believe I shall write no more this good while, nor publish what I have done. Nauty (?) Ppt, oo are vely tempegant. I did not suspect oo would tell Filby. Oo are so. . . Turns and visitations—what are these? I'll preach and visit as much for Mr. Walls. Pray God mend poopt's health; mine is but very indifferent. I have left off Spa water; it makes my leg swell. Nite deelest MD.

6. This is the Queen's Birthday, and I never saw it celebrated with so much luxury and fine clothes. I went to Court to see them, and I dined with Lord Keeper, where the ladies were fine to admiration. I passed the evening at Mrs. Vanhomrigh's, and came home pretty early, to answer oo rettle again. Pray God keep the Queen. She was very ill about ten days ago, and had the gout in her stomach. When I came from Lord Keeper's, I called at Lord Treasurer's, because I heard he was very fine, and that was a new thing; and it was true, for his coat and waistcoat were embroidered. I have seen the Provost often since, and never spoke to him to speak to the Temples about Daniel Carr, nor will; I don't care to do it. I have writ lately to Parvisol. Oo did well to let him make up his accounts. All things grow dear in Ireland, but corn to the parsons; for my livings are fallen much this year by Parvisol's account. Nite dee logues, MD.

7. I was at Court to-day, but saw no Birthday clothes; the great folks never wear them above once or twice. I dined with Lord Orkney, and sat the evening with Sir Andrew Fountaine, whose leg is in a very dubious condition. Pray let me know when DD's money is near due: always let me know it beforehand. This, I believe, will hardly go till Saturday; for I tell you what, being not very well, I dare not study much: so I let company come in a morning, and the afternoon pass in dining and sitting somewhere. Lord Treasurer is angry if I don't dine with him every second day, and I cannot part with him till late: he kept me last night till near twelve. Our weather is constant rain above these two months, which hinders walking, so that our spring is not like yours. I have not seen Fanny Manley yet; I cannot find time. I am in rebellion with all my acquaintance, but I will mend with my health and the weather. Clogher make a figure! Clogher make a—. Colds! why, we have been all dying with colds; but now they are a little over, and my second is almost off. I can do nothing for Swanton indeed. It is a thing impossible, and wholly out of my way. If he buys, he must buy. So now I have answered oo rettle; and there's an end of that now; and I'll say no more, but bid oo nite, dee MD.

8. It was terrible rainy to-day from morning till night. I intended to have dined with Lord Treasurer, but went to see Sir Andrew Fountaine, and he kept me to dinner, which saved coach-hire; and I stayed with him all the afternoon, and lost thirteen shillings and sixpence at ombre.

There was management! and Lord Treasurer will chide; but I'll dine with him to-morrow. The Bishop of Clogher's daughter has been ill some days, and it proves the smallpox. She is very full; but it comes out well, and they apprehend no danger. Lady Orkney has given me her picture; a very fine original of Sir Godfrey Kneller's; it is now a mending. He has favoured her squint admirably; and you know I love a cast in the eye. I was to see Lady Worsley to-day, who is just come to town; she is full of rheumatic pains. All my acquaintance grow old and sickly. She lodges in the very house in King Street, between St. James's Street and St. James's Square, where DD's brother bought the sweetbread, when I lodged there, and MD came to see me. Short sighs. Nite MD.

9. I thought to have dined with Lord Treasurer to-day, but he dined abroad at Tom Harley's; so I dined at Lord Masham's, and was winning all I had lost playing with Lady Masham at crown picquet, when we went to pools, and I lost it again. Lord Treasurer came in to us, and chid me for not following him to Tom Harley's. Miss Ashe is still the same, and they think her not in danger; my man calls there daily after I am gone out, and tells me at night. I was this morning to see Lady Jersey, and we have made twenty parties about dining together, and I shall hardly keep one of them. She is reduced after all her greatness to seven servants, and a small house, and no coach. I like her tolerably as yet. Nite MD.

10. I made visits this morning to the Duke and Duchess of Ormond, and Lady Betty, and the Duchess of Hamilton. (When I was writing this near twelve o'clock, the Duchess of Hamilton sent to have me dine with her to-morrow. I am forced to give my answer through the door, for my man has got the key, and is gone to bed; but I cannot obey her, for our Society meets to-morrow.) I stole away from Lord Treasurer by eight, and intended to have passed the evening with Sir Thomas Clarges and his lady; but met them in another place, and have there sat till now. My head has not been ill to-day. I was at Court, and made Lord Mansel walk with me in the Park before we went to dinner.— Yesterday and to-day have been fair, but yet it rained all last night. I saw Sterne staring at Court to-day. He has been often to see me, he says: but my man has not yet let him up. He is in deep mourning; I hope it is not for his wife. I did not ask him. Nite MD.

12. I have reckoned days wrong all this while; for this is the twelfth. I do not know when I lost it. I dined to-day with our Society, the greatest dinner I have ever seen. It was at Jack Hill's, the Governor of Dunkirk. I gave an account of sixty guineas I had collected, and am to give them away to two authors to-morrow; and Lord Treasurer has promised us a hundred pounds to reward some others. I found a letter on my table last night to tell me that poor little Harrison, the Queen's Secretary, that came lately from Utrecht with the Barrier Treaty, was ill, and desired to see me at night; but it was late, and I could not go till to-day. I have often mentioned him in my letters, you may remember. . . I went in the morning, and found him mighty ill, and got thirty guineas for him from Lord Bolingbroke, and an order for a hundred pounds from the Treasury to be paid him to-morrow; and I have got him removed to Knightsbridge for air. He has a fever and inflammation on his lungs; but I hope will do well. Nite.

13. I was to see a poor poet, one Mr. Diaper, in a nasty garret, very sick. I gave him twenty guineas from Lord Bolingbroke, and disposed the other sixty to two other authors, and desired a friend to receive the hundred pounds for poor Harrison, and will carry it to him to-morrow morning. I sent to see how he did, and he is extremely ill; and I very much afflicted for him, for he is my own creature, and in a very honourable post, and very worthy of it. I dined in the City. I am in much concern for this poor lad. His mother and sister attend him, and he wants nothing. Nite poo dee MD.

14. I took Parnell this morning, and we walked to see poor Harrison. I had the hundred pounds in my pocket. I told Parnell I was afraid to knock at the door; my mind misgave me. I knocked, and his man in tears told me his master was dead an hour before. Think what grief this is to me! I went to his mother, and have been ordering things for his funeral with as little cost as possible, to-morrow at ten at night. Lord Treasurer was much concerned when I told him. I could not dine with Lord Treasurer, nor anywhere else; but got a bit of meat toward evening. No loss ever grieved me so much: poor creature! Pray God Almighty bless poor MD. Adieu.

I send this away to-night, and am sorry it must go while I am in so much grief.

Letter LX

I dined to-day with Mr. Rowe and a projector, who has been teasing me with twenty schemes to get grants; and I don't like one of them; and, besides, I was out of humour for the loss of poor Harrison. At ten this night I was at his funeral, which I ordered to be as private as possible. We had but one coach with four of us; and when it was carrying us home after the funeral, the braces broke; and we were forced to sit in it, and have it held up, till my man went for chairs, at eleven at night in terrible rain. I am come home very melancholy, and will go to bed. Nite. . . MD.

16. I dined to-day with Lord Dupplin and some company to divert me; but left them early, and have been reading a foolish book for amusement. I shall never have courage again to care for making anybody's fortune. The Parliament meets to-morrow, and will be prorogued another fortnight, at which several of both parties were angry; but it cannot be helped, though everything about the peace is past all danger. I never saw such a continuance of rainy weather. We have not had two fair days together these ten weeks. I have not dined with Lord Treasurer these four days, nor can I till Saturday; for I have several engagements till then, and he will chide me to some purpose. I am perplexed with this hundred pounds of poor Harrison's, what to do with it. I cannot pay his relations till they administer, for he is much in debt; but I will have the staff in my own hands, and venture nothing. Nite poo dee MD.

17. Lady Jersey and I dined by appointment to-day with Lord Bolingbroke. He is sending his brother to succeed Mr. Harrison. It is the prettiest post in Europe for a young gentleman. I lose my money at ombre sadly; I make a thousand blunders. I play but threepenny ombre; but it is what you call running ombre. Lady Clarges, and a drab I hate, won a dozen shillings of me last night. The Parliament was prorogued to-day; and people grumble; and the good of it is the peace cannot be finished by the time they meet, there are so many fiddling things to do. Is Ppt an ombre lady yet? You know all the tricks of it now, I suppose. I reckon you have all your cards from France, for ours pay sixpence a pack taxes, which goes deep to the box. I have given away all my Spa

water, and take some nasty steel drops, and my head has been better this week past. I send every day to see how Miss Ashe does: she is very full, they say, but in no danger. I fear she will lose some of her beauty. The son lies out of the house. I wish he had them too, while he is so young.—Nite MD.

18. The Earl of Abingdon has been teasing me these three months to dine with him; and this day was appointed about a week ago, and I named my company; Lord Stawel, Colonel Disney, and Dr. Arbuthnot; but the two last slipped out their necks, and left Stawell and me to dine there. We did not dine till seven, because it is Ash Wednesday. We had nothing but fish, which Lord Stawell could not eat, and got a broiled leg of a turkey. Our wine was poison; yet the puppy has twelve thousand pound a year. His carps were raw, and his candles tallow. He shall not catch me in haste again, and everybody has laughed at me for dining with him. I was to-day to let Harrison's mother know I could not pay till she administers; which she will do. I believe she is an old bawd, and her daughter a—. There were more Whigs to-day at Court than Tories. I believe they think the peace must be made, and so come to please the Queen. She is still lame with the gout. Nite MD.

19. I was at Court to-day, to speak to Lord Bolingbroke to look over Parnell's poem since it is corrected; and Parnell and I dined with him, and he has shown him three or four more places to alter a little. Lady Bolingbroke came down to us while we were at dinner, and Parnell stared at her as if she were a goddess. I thought she was like Parnell's wife, and he thought so too. Parnell is much pleased with Lord Bolingbroke's favour to him, and I hope it may one day turn to his advantage. His poem will be printed in a few days. Our weather continues as fresh raining as if it had not rained at all. I sat to-night at Lady Masham's, where Lord Treasurer came and scolded me for not dining with him. I told him I could not till Saturday. I have stayed there till past twelve. So nite dee sollahs, nite.

20. Lady Jersey, Lady Catherine Hyde, the Spanish Ambassador, the Duke d'Atree, another Spaniard, and I, dined to-day by appointment with Lord Bolingbroke; but they fell a drinking so many Spanish healths in champagne that I stole away to the ladies, and drank tea till eight; and then went and lost my money at ombre with Sir Andrew

Fountaine, who has a very bad leg. Miss Ashe is past all danger; and her eye, which was lately bad (I suppose one effect of her distemper), is now better. I do not let the Bishop see me, nor shall this good while. Good luck! when I came home, I warrant, I found a letter from MD, No.38; and oo write so small nowadays, I hope oo poor eyes are better. Well, this shall go to-morrow se'nnight, with a bill for MD. I will speak to Mr. Griffin to-morrow about Ppt's brother Filby, and desire, whether he deserves or no, that his employment may be mended; that is to say, if I can see Griffin; otherwise not; and I'll answer oo rettle hen I Pdfr think fit. Nite MD.

21. Methinks I writ a little saucy last night. I mean the last. . . I saw Griffin at Court. He says he knows nothing of a salt-work at Recton; but that he will give Filby a better employment, and desires Filby will write to him. If I knew how to write to Filby, I would; but pray do you. Bid him make no mention of you; but only let Mr. Griffin know that he has the honour to be recommended by Dr. S—, etc.; that he will endeavour to deserve, etc.; and if you dictated a whole letter for him, it would be better; I hope he can write and spell well. I'll inquire for a direction to Griffin before I finish this. I dined with Lord Treasurer and seven lords to-day. You know Saturday is his great day, but I sat with them alone till eight, and then came home, and have been writing a letter to Mrs. Davis, at York. She took care to have a letter delivered for me at Lord Treasurer's; for I would not own one she sent by post. She reproaches me for not writing to her these four years; and I have honestly told her it was my way never to write to those whom I am never likely to see, unless I can serve them, which I cannot her, etc. Davis the schoolmaster's widow. Nite MD.

22. I dined to-day at Lord Orkney's, with the Duke of Ormond and Sir Thomas Hanmer. Have you ever heard of the latter? He married the Duchess of Grafton in his youth (she dined with us too). He is the most considerable man in the House of Commons. He went last spring to Flanders, with the Duke of Ormond; from thence to France, and was going to Italy; but the Ministry sent for him, and he has been come over about ten days. He is much out of humour with things: he thinks the peace is kept off too long, and is full of fears and doubts. It is thought he is designed for Secretary of State, instead of Lord Dartmouth. We have been acquainted these two years; and I intend, in a day or two, to

have an hour's talk with him on affairs. I saw the Bishop of Clogher at Court; Miss is recovering. I know not how much she will be marked. The Queen is slowly mending of her gout, and intends to be brought in a chair to Parliament when it meets, which will be March 3; for I suppose they will prorogue no more; yet the peace will not be signed then, and we apprehend the Tories themselves will many of them be discontented. Nite dee MD.

23. It was ill weather to-day, and I dined with Sir Andrew Fountaine, and in the evening played at ombre with him and the Provost, and won twenty-five shillings; so I have recovered myself pretty well. Dilly has been dunning me to see Fanny Manley; but I have not yet been able to do it. Miss Ashe is now quite out of danger; and hope will not be much marked. I cannot tell how to direct to Griffin; and think he lives in Bury Street, near St. James's Street, hard by me; but I suppose your brother may direct to him to the Salt Office, and, as I remember, he knows his Christian name, because he sent it me in the list of the Commissioners. Nite dee MD.

24. I walked this morning to Chelsea, to see Dr. Atterbury, Dean of Christ Church. I had business with him about entering Mr. Fitzmaurice, my Lord Kerry's son, into his College; and Lady Kerry is a great favourite of mine. Lord Harley, Lord Dupplin, young Bromley the Speaker's son, and I, dined with Dr. Stratford and some other clergymen; but I left them at seven to go to Lady Jersey, to see Monteleon the Spanish Ambassador play at ombre. Lady Jersey was abroad, and I chid the servants, and made a rattle; but since I came home she sent me a message that I was mistaken, and that the meeting is to be to-morrow. I have a worse memory than when I left you, and every day forget appointments; but here my memory was by chance too good. But I'll go to-morrow; for Lady Catherine Hyde and Lady Bolingbroke are to be there by appointment, and I listed up my periwig, and all, to make a figure. Well, who can help it? Not I, vow to. . . ! Nite MD.

25. Lord Treasurer met me last night at Lord Masham's, and thanked me for my company in a jeer, because I had not dined with him in three days. He chides me if I stay away but two days together. What will this come to? Nothing. My grandmother used to say, "More of your lining, and less of your dining." However, I dined with him, and

could hardly leave him at eight, to go to Lady Jersey's, where five or six foreign Ministers were, and as many ladies. Monteleon played like the English, and cried "gacco," and knocked his knuckles for trump, and played at small games like Ppt. Lady Jersey whispered me to stay and sup with the ladies when the fellows were gone; but they played till eleven, and I would not stay. I think this letter must go on Saturday; that's certain; and it is not half full yet. Lady Catherine Hyde had a mighty mind I should be acquainted with Lady Dalkeith, her sister, the Duke of Monmouth's eldest son's widow, who was of the company to-night; but I did not like her; she paints too much. Nite MD.

26. This day our Society met at the Duke of Ormond's, but I had business that called me another way; so I sent my excuses, and dined privately with a friend. Besides, Sir Thomas Hanmer whispered me last night at Lady Jersey's that I must attend Lord Treasurer and Duke of Ormond at supper at his house to-night; which I did at eleven, and stayed till one, so oo may be sure 'tis late enough. There was the Duchess of Grafton, and the Duke her son; nine of us in all. The Duke of Ormond chid me for not being at the Society to-day, and said sixteen were there. I said I never knew sixteen people good company in my life; no, fais, nor eight either. We have no news in this town at all. I wonder why I don't write you news. I know less of what passes than anybody, because I go to no coffee-house, nor see any but Ministers, and such people; and Ministers never talk politics in conversation. The Whigs are forming great schemes against the meeting of Parliament, which will be next Tuesday, I still think, without fail; and we hope to hear by then that the peace is ready to sign. The Queen's gout mends daily. Nite MD.

27. I passed a very insipid day, and dined privately with a friend in the neighbourhood. Did I tell you that I have a very fine picture of Lady Orkney, an original, by Sir Godfrey Kneller, three-quarters length? I have it now at home, with a fine frame. Lord Bolingbroke and Lady Masham have promised to sit for me; but I despair of Lord Treasurer; only I hope he will give me a copy, and then I shall have all the pictures of those I really love here; just half a dozen; only I'll make Lord Keeper give me his print in a frame. This letter must go to-morrow, because of sending ME a bill; else it should not till next week, I assure oo. I have little to do now with my pen; for my grand business stops till they are more pressing, and till something or other happens; and I believe I

shall return with disgust to finish it, it is so very laborious. Sir Thomas Hanmer has my papers now. And hat is MD doing now? Oh, at ombre with the Dean always on Friday night, with Mrs. Walls. Pray don't play at small games. I stood by, t'other night, while the Duke d'Atree lost six times with manilio, basto, and three small trumps; and Lady Jersey won above twenty pounds. Nite dee richar MD.

28. I was at Court to-day, when the Abbé Gaultier whispered me that a courier was just come with an account that the French King had consented to all the Queen's demands, and his consent was carried to Utrecht, and the peace will be signed in a few days. I suppose the general peace cannot be so soon ready; but that is no matter. The news presently ran about the Court. I saw the Queen carried out in her chair, to take the air in the garden. I met Griffin at Court, and he told me that orders were sent to examine Filby; and, if he be fit, to make him (I think he called it) an assistant; I don't know what, Supervisor, I think; but it is some employment a good deal better than his own. The Parliament will have another short prorogation, though it is not known yet. I dined with Lord Treasurer and his Saturday company, and left him at eight to put this in the post-office time enough. And now I must bid oo farewell, deelest richar Ppt. God bless oo ever, and rove Pdfr. Farewell MD MD MD FW FW FW FW ME ME ME Lele Lele.

Letter LXI

'Tis out of my head whether I answered all your letter in my last yesterday or no. I think I was in haste, and could not: but now I see I answered a good deal of it; no, only about your brother, and ME's bill. I dined with Lady Orkney, and we talked politics till eleven at night; and, as usual, found everything wrong, and put ourselves out of humour. Yes, I have Lady Giffard's picture sent me by your mother. It is boxed up at a place where my other things are. I have goods in two or three places; and when I leave a lodging, I box up the books I get (for I always get some), and come naked into a new lodging; and so on. Talk not to me of deaneries; I know less of that than ever by much. Nite MD.

2. I went to-day into the City to see Pat Rolt, who lodges with a City cousin, a daughter of coz Cleve; (you are much the wiser). I had never been at her house before. My he-coz Thompson the butcher is dead, or dying. I dined with my printer, and walked home, and went to sit with Lady Clarges. I found four of them at whist; Lady Godolphin was one. I sat by her, and talked of her cards, etc., but she would not give me one look, nor say a word to me. She refused some time ago to be acquainted with me. You know she is Lord Marlborough's eldest daughter. She is a fool for her pains, and I'll pull her down. What can I do for Dr. Smith's daughter's husband? I have no personal credit with any of the Commissioners. I'll speak to Keatley; but I believe it will signify nothing. In the Customs people must rise by degrees, and he must at first take what is very low, if he be qualified for that. Ppt mistakes me; I am not angry at your recommending anyone to me, provided you will take my answer. Some things are in my way, and then I serve those I can. But people will not distinguish, but take things ill, when I have no power; but Ppt is wiser. And employments in general are very hard to be got. Nite MD.

3. I dined to-day with Lord Treasurer, who chid me for my absence, which was only from Saturday last. The Parliament was again prorogued for a week, and I suppose the peace will be ready by then, and the Queen will be able to be brought to the House, and make her speech. I saw Dr. Griffith two or three months ago, at a Latin play at Westminster;

but did not speak to him. I hope he will not die; I should be sorry for Ppt's sake; he is very tender of her. I have long lost all my colds, and the weather mends a little. I take some steel drops, and my head is pretty well. I walk when I can, but am grown very idle; and, not finishing my thing, I gamble abroad and play at ombre. I shall be more careful in my physic than Mrs. Price: 'tis not a farthing matter her death, I think; and so I say no more to-night, but will read a dull book, and go sleep. Nite dee MD.

4. Mr. Ford has been this half-year inviting me to dine at his lodgings: so I did to-day, and brought the Provost and Dr. Parnell with me, and my friend Lewis was there. Parnell went away, and the other three played at ombre, and I looked on; which I love, and would not play. Tisdall is a pretty fellow, as you say; and when I come back to Ireland with nothing, he will condole with me with abundance of secret pleasure. I believe I told you what he wrote to me, that I have saved England, and he Ireland; but I can bear that. I have learned to hear and see, and say nothing. I was to see the Duchess of Hamilton to-day, and met Blith of Ireland just going out of her house into his coach. I asked her how she came to receive young fellows. It seems he had a ball in the Duke of Hamilton's house when the Duke died; and the Duchess got an advertisement put in the *Postboy*, reflecting on the ball, because the Marlborough daughters were there; and Blith came to beg the Duchess's pardon, and clear himself. He's a sad dog. Nite poo dee deelest MD.

5. Lady Masham has miscarried; but is well almost again. I have many visits to-day. I met Blith at the Duke of Ormond's; and he begged me to carry him to the Duchess of Hamilton, to beg her pardon again. I did on purpose to see how the blunderbuss behaved himself; but I begged the Duchess to use him mercifully, for she is the devil of a teaser. The good of it is, she ought to beg his pardon, for he meant no harm; yet she would not allow him to put in an advertisement to clear himself from hers, though hers was all a lie. He appealed to me, and I gravely gave it against him. I was at Court to-day, and the foreign Ministers have got a trick of employing me to speak for them to Lord Treasurer and Lord Bolingbroke; which I do when the case is reasonable. The College need not fear; I will not be their Governor. I dined with Sir Thomas Hanmer and his Duchess. The Duke of Ormond was there, but we parted soon, and I went to visit Lord Pembroke for the first time; but it was to see

some curious books. Lord Cholmondeley came in; but I would not talk to him, though he made many advances. I hate the scoundrel for all he is your Griffith's friend.—Yes, yes, I am abused enough, if that be all. Nite sollahs.

6. I was to-day at an auction of pictures with Pratt, and laid out two pound five shillings for a picture of Titian, and if it were a Titian it would be worth twice as many pounds. If I am cheated, I'll part with it to Lord Masham: if it be a bargain, I'll keep it to myself. That's my conscience. But I made Pratt buy several pictures for Lord Masham. Pratt is a great virtuoso that way. I dined with Lord Treasurer, but made him go to Court at eight. I always tease him to be gone. I thought to have made Parnell dine with him, but he was ill; his head is out of order like mine, but more constant, poor boy!—I was at Lord Treasurer's levee with the Provost, to ask a book for the College.—I never go to his levee, unless to present somebody. For all oor rallying, saucy Ppt, as hope saved, I expected they would have decided about me long ago; and as hope saved, as soon as ever things are given away and I not provided for, I will be gone with the very first opportunity, and put up bag and baggage. But people are slower than can be thought. Nite MD.

7. Yes, I hope Leigh will soon be gone, a p—on him! I met him once, and he talked gravely to me of not seeing the Irish bishops here, and the Irish gentlemen; but I believe my answers fretted him enough. I would not dine with Lord Treasurer to-day, though it was Saturday (for he has engaged me for to-morrow), but went and dined with Lord Masham, and played at ombre, sixpenny running ombre, for three hours. There were three voles against me, and I was once a great loser, but came off for three shillings and sixpence. One may easily lose five guineas at it. Lady Orkney is gone out of town to-day, and I could not see her for laziness, but writ to her. She has left me some physic. Fais, I never knew MD's politics before, and I think it pretty extraordinary, and a great compliment to you, and I believe never three people conversed so much with so little politics. I avoid all conversation with the other party; it is not to be borne, and I am sorry for it. O yes, things (are) very dear. DD must come in at last with DD's two eggs a penny. There the proverb was well applied. Parvisol has sent me a bill of fifty pounds, as I ordered him, which, I hope, will serve me, and

bring me over. Pray God MD does not be delayed for it; but I have had very little from him this long time. I was not at Court to-day; a wonder! Nite sollahs. . . Pdfr.

8. Oo must know, I give chocolate almost every day to two or three people that I suffer to come to see me in a morning. My man begins to lie pretty well. 'Tis nothing for people to be denied ten times. My man knows all I will see, and denies me to everybody else. This is the day of the Queen's coming to the Crown, and the day Lord Treasurer was stabbed by Guiscard. I was at Court, where everybody had their Birthday clothes on, and I dined with Lord Treasurer, who was very fine. He showed me some of the Queen's speech, which I corrected in several places, and penned the vote of address of thanks for the speech; but I was of opinion the House should not sit on Tuesday next, unless they hear the peace is signed; that is, provided they are sure it will be signed the week after, and so have one scolding for all. Nite MD.

9. Lord Treasurer would have had me dine with him to-day; he desired me last night, but I refused, because he would not keep the day of his stabbing with all the Cabinet, as he intended: so I dined with my friend Lewis; and the Provost and Parnell, and Ford, was with us. I lost sixteen shillings at ombre; I don't like it, as etc. At night Lewis brought us word that the Parliament does not sit to-morrow. I hope they are sure of the peace by next week, and then they are right in my opinion: otherwise I think they have done wrong, and might have sat three weeks ago. People will grumble; but Lord Treasurer cares not a rush. Lord Keeper is suddenly taken ill of a quinsy, and some lords are commissioned, I think Lord Trevor, to prorogue the Parliament in his stead. You never saw a town so full of ferment and expectation. Mr. Pope has published a fine poem, called *Windsor Forest*. Read it. Nite.

10. I was early this morning to see Lord Bolingbroke. I find he was of opinion the Parliament should sit; and says they are not sure the peace will be signed next week. The prorogation is to this day se'nnight. I went to look on a library I am going to buy, if we can agree. I have offered a hundred and twenty pounds, and will give ten more. Lord Bolingbroke will lend me the money. I was two hours poring on the books. I will sell

some of them, and keep the rest; but I doubt they won't take the money. I dined in the City, and sat an hour in the evening with Lord Treasurer, who was in very good humour; but reproached me for not dining with him yesterday and to-day. What will all this come to? Lord Keeper had a pretty good night, and is better. I was in pain for him. How do oo do sollahs? . . . Nite MD.

11. I was this morning to visit the Duke and Duchess of Ormond, and the Duchess of Hamilton, and went with the Provost to an auction of pictures, and laid out fourteen shillings. I am in for it, if I had money; but I doubt I shall be undone; for Sir Andrew Fountaine invited the Provost and me to dine with him, and play at ombre, when I fairly lost fourteen shillings. Fais, it won't do; and I shall be out of conceit with play this good while. I am come home; and it is late, and my puppy let out my fire, and I am gone to bed and writing there, and it is past twelve a good while. Went out four matadores and a trump in black, and was bested. Vely bad, fais! Nite my deelest logues MD.

12. I was at another auction of pictures to-day, and a great auction it was. I made Lord Masham lay out forty pounds. There were pictures sold of twice as much value apiece. Our Society met to-day at the Duke of Beaufort's: a prodigious fine dinner, which I hate; but we did some business. Our printer was to attend us, as usual; and the Chancellor of the Exchequer sent the author of the *Examiner* twenty guineas. He is an ingenious fellow, but the most confounded vain coxcomb in the world, so that I dare not let him see me, nor am acquainted with him. I had much discourse with the Duke of Ormond this morning, and am driving some points to secure us all in case of accidents, etc. I left the Society at seven. I can't drink now at all with any pleasure. I love white Portugal wine better than claret, champagne, or burgundy. I have a sad vulgar appetite. I remember Ppt used to maunder, when I came from a great dinner, and DD had but a bit of mutton. I cannot endure above one dish; nor ever could since I was a boy, and loved stuffing. It was a fine day, which is a rarity with us, I assure (you). Never fair two days together. Nite dee MD.

13. I had a rabble of Irish parsons this morning drinking my chocolate. I cannot remember appointments. I was to have supped last night with the Swedish Envoy at his house, and some other company, but forgot

it; and he rallied me to-day at Lord Bolingbroke's, who excused me, saying, the Envoy ought not to be angry, because I serve Lord Treasurer and him the same way. For that reason, I very seldom promise to go anywhere. I dined with Lord Treasurer, who chid me for being absent so long, as he always does if I miss a day. I sat three hours this evening with Lady Jersey; but the first two hours she was at ombre with some company. I left Lord Treasurer at eight: I fancied he was a little thoughtful, for he was playing with an orange by fits, which, I told him, among common men looked like the spleen. This letter shall not go to-morrow; no haste, ung oomens; nothing that presses. I promised but once in three weeks, and I am better than my word. I wish the peace may be ready, I mean that we have notice it is signed, before Tuesday; otherwise the grumbling will much increase. Nite logues.

14. It was a lovely day this, and I took the advantage of walking a good deal in the Park, before I went to Court. Colonel Disney, one of our Society, is ill of a fever, and, we fear, in great danger. We all love him mightily, and he would be a great loss. I doubt I shall not buy the library; for a roguey bookseller has offered sixty pounds more than I designed to give; so you see I meant to have a good bargain. I dined with Lord Treasurer and his Saturday company; but there were but seven at table. Lord Peterborrow is ill, and spits blood, with a bruise he got before he left England; but, I believe, an Italian lady he has brought over is the cause that his illness returns. You know old Lady Bellasis is dead at last? She has left Lord Berkeley of Stratton one of her executors, and it will be of great advantage to him; they say above ten thousand pounds. I stayed with Lord Treasurer upon business, after the company was gone; but I dare not tell you upon what. My letters would be good memoirs, if I durst venture to say a thousand things that pass; but I hear so much of letters opening at your post-office that I am fearful, etc., and so good-nite, sollahs, rove Pdfr, MD.

15. Lord Treasurer engaged me to dine with him again to-day, and I had ready what he wanted; but he would not see it, but put me off till to-morrow. The Queen goes to chapel now. She is carried in an open chair, and will be well enough to go to Parliament on Tuesday, if the Houses meet, which is not yet certain; neither, indeed, can the Ministers themselves tell; for it depends on winds and weather, and circumstances of negotiation. However, we go on as if it was certainly to meet; and I am

to be at Lord Treasurer's to-morrow, upon that supposition, to settle some things relating that way. Ppt may understand me. The doctors tell me that if poor Colonel Disney does not get some sleep to-night, he must die. What care you? Ah! but I do care. He is one of our Society; a fellow of abundance of humour; an old battered rake, but very honest, not an old man, but an old rake. It was he that said of Jenny Kingdom, the maid of honour, who is a little old, that, since she could not get a husband, the Queen should give her a brevet to act as a married woman. You don't understand this. They give brevets to majors and captains to act as colonels in the army. Brevets are commissions. Ask soldiers, dull sollahs. Nite MD.

16. I was at Lord Treasurer's before he came; and, as he entered, he told me the Parliament was prorogued till Thursday se'nnight. They have had some expresses, by which they count that the peace may be signed by that time; at least, that France, Holland, and we, will sign some articles, by which we shall engage to sign the peace when it is ready: but Spain has no Minister there; for Monteleon, who is to be their Ambassador at Utrecht, is not yet gone from hence; and till he is there, the Spaniards can sign no peace: and (of) one thing take notice, that a general peace can hardly be finished these two months, so as to be proclaimed here; for, after signing, it must be ratified; that is, confirmed by the several princes at their Courts, which to Spain will cost a month; for we must have notice that it is ratified in all Courts before we can proclaim it. So be not in too much haste. Nite MD.

17. The Irish folks were disappointed that the Parliament did not meet to-day, because it was St. Patrick's Day; and the Mall was so full of crosses that I thought all the world was Irish. Miss Ashe is almost quite well, and I see the Bishop, but shall not yet go to his house. I dined again with Lord Treasurer; but the Parliament being prorogued, I must keep what I have till next week: for I believe he will not see it till just the evening before the session. He has engaged me to dine with him again to-morrow, though I did all I could to put it off; but I don't care to disoblige him. Nite dee sollahs 'tis late. Nite MD.

18. I have now dined six days successively with Lord Treasurer; but to-night I stole away while he was talking with somebody else, and so am at liberty to-morrow. There was a flying report of a general

cessation of arms: everybody had it at Court; but, I believe, there is nothing in it. I asked a certain French Minister how things went. And he whispered me in French, "Your Plenipotentiaries and ours play the fool." None of us, indeed, approve of the conduct of either at this time; but Lord Treasurer was in full good-humour for all that. He had invited a good many of his relations; and, of a dozen at table, they were all of the Harley family but myself. Disney is recovering, though you don't care a straw. Dilly murders us with his *if* puns. You know them. . . Nite MD.

19. The Bishop of Clogher has made an *if* pun that he is mighty proud of, and designs to send it over to his brother Tom. But Sir Andrew Fountaine has wrote to Tom Ashe last post, and told him the pun, and desired him to send it over to the Bishop as his own; and, if it succeeds, 'twill be a pure bite. The Bishop will tell it us as a wonder that he and his brother should jump so exactly. I'll tell you the pun:—If there was a hackney coach at Mr. Pooley's door, what town in Egypt would it be? Why, it would be Hecatompolis; *Hack at Tom Pooley's*. "Sillly," says Ppt. I dined with a private friend to-day; for our Society, I told you, meet but once a fortnight. I have not seen Fanny Manley yet; I can't help it. Lady Orkney is come to town: why, she was at her country house; hat care you? Nite darling (?) dee MD.

20. Dilly read me a letter to-day from Ppt. She seems to have scratched her head when she writ it. 'Tis a sad thing to write to people without tact. There you say, you hear I was going to Bath. No such thing; I am pretty well, I thank God. The town is now sending me to Savoy. Forty people have given me joy of it, yet there is not the least truth that I know in it. I was at an auction of pictures, but bought none. I was so glad of my liberty, that I would dine nowhere; but, the weather being fine, I sauntered into the City, and ate a bit about five, and then supped at Mr. Burke's your Accountant-General, who had been engaging me this month. The Bishop of Clogher was to have been there, but was hindered by Lord Paget's funeral. The Provost and I sat till one o'clock; and, if that be not late, I don't know what is late. Parnell's poem will be published on Monday, and to-morrow I design he shall present it to Lord Treasurer and Lord Bolingbroke at Court. The poor lad is almost always out of order with his head. Burke's wife is his sister. She has a little of the pert Irish way. Nite MD.

21. Morning. I will now finish my letter; for company will come, and a stir, and a clutter; and I'll keep the letter in my pottick, and give it into the post myself. I must go to Court, and you know on Saturdays I dine with Lord Treasurer, of course. Farewell, deelest MD MD MD, FW FW FW, MD ME ME ME Lele sollahs.

Letter LXII

I gave your letter in this night. I dined with Lord Treasurer to-day, and find he has been at a meeting at Lord Halifax's house, with four principal Whigs; but he is resolved to begin a speech against them when the Parliament sits; and I have begged that the Ministers may have a meeting on purpose to settle that matter, and let us be the attackers; and I believe it will come to something, for the Whigs intend to attack the Ministers: and if, instead of that, the Ministers attack the Whigs, it will be better: and farther, I believe we shall attack them on those very points they intend to attack us. The Parliament will be again prorogued for a fortnight, because of Passion Week. I forgot to tell you that Mr. Griffin has given Ppt's brother a new employment, about ten pounds a year better than his former; but more remote, and consequently cheaper. I wish I could have done better, and hope oo will take what can be done in good part, and that oo brother will not dislike it.—Nite own dear. . . MD.

22. I dined to-day with Lord Steward. There Frank Annesley (a Parliament-man) told me he had heard that I had wrote to my friends in Ireland to keep firm to the Whig interest; for that Lord Treasurer would certainly declare for it after the peace. Annesley said twenty people had told him this. You must know this is what they endeavour to report of Lord Treasurer, that he designs to declare for the Whigs; and a Scotch fellow has wrote the same to Scotland; and his meeting with those lords gives occasion to such reports. Let me henceforth call Lord Treasurer Eltee, because possibly my letters may be opened. Pray remember Eltee. You know the reason; L. T. and Eltee pronounced the same way. Stay, 'tis five weeks since I had a letter from MD. I allow you six. You see why I cannot come over the beginning of April; whoever has to do with this Ministry can fix no time: but as hope saved, it is not Pdfr's fault. Pay don't blame poo Pdfr. Nite deelest logues MD.

23. I dined to-day at Sir Thomas Hanmer's, by an old appointment: there was the Duke of Ormond, and Lord and Lady Orkney. I left them at six. Everybody is as sour as vinegar. I endeavour to keep a firm friendship between the Duke of Ormond and Eltee. (Oo know

who Eltee is, or have oo fordot already?) I have great designs, if I can compass them; but delay is rooted in Eltee's heart; yet the fault is not altogether there, that things are no better. Here is the cursedest libel in verse come out that ever was seen, called *The Ambassadress*; it is very dull, too; it has been printed three or four different ways, and is handed about, but not sold. It abuses the Queen horribly. The *Examiner* has cleared me to-day of being author of his paper, and done it with great civilities to me. I hope it will stop people's mouths; if not, they must go on and be hanged, I care not. 'Tis terribly rainy weather, I'll go sleep. Nite deelest MD.

24. It rained all this day, and ruined me in coach-hire. I went to Colonel Disney, who is past danger. Then I visited Lord Keeper, who was at dinner; but I would not dine with him, but drove to Lord Treasurer (Eltee I mean), paid the coachman, and went in; but he dined abroad: so I was forced to call the coachman again, and went to Lord Bolingbroke's. He dined abroad too; and at Lord Dupplin's I alighted, and by good luck got a dinner there, and then went to the Latin play at Westminster School, acted by the boys; and Lord Treasurer (Eltee I mean again) honoured them with his presence. Lady Masham's eldest son, about two years old, is ill, and I am afraid will not live: she is full of grief, and I pity and am angry with her. Four shillings to-day in coach-hire; fais, it won't do. Our peace will certainly be ready by Thursday fortnight; but our Plenipotentiaries were to blame that it was not done already. They thought their powers were not full enough to sign the peace, unless every Prince was ready, which cannot yet be; for Spain has no Minister yet at Utrecht; but now ours have new orders. Nite MD.

25. Weather worse than ever; terrible rain all day, but I was resolved I would spend no more money. I went to an auction of pictures with Dr. Pratt, and there met the Duke of Beaufort, who promised to come with me to Court, but did not. So a coach I got, and went to Court, and did some little business there, but was forced to go home; for oo must understand I take a little physic over-night, which works me next day. Lady Orkney is my physician. It is hiera picra, two spoonfuls, devilish stuff! I thought to have dined with Eltee, but would not, merely to save a shilling; but I dined privately with a friend, and played at ombre, and won six shillings. Here are several people of quality lately dead of the smallpox. I have not yet seen Miss Ashe, but hear she is well. The

Bishop of Clogher has bought abundance of pictures, and Dr. Pratt has got him very good pennyworths. I can get no walks, the weather is so bad. Is it so with oo, sollahs? . . .

26. Though it was shaving-day, head and beard, yet I was out early to see Lord Bolingbroke, and talk over affairs with him; and then I went to the Duke of Ormond's, and so to Court, where the Ministers did not come, because the Parliament was prorogued till this day fortnight. We had terrible rain and hail to-day. Our Society met this day, but I left them before seven, and went to Sir A(ndrew) F(ountaine), and played at ombre with him and Sir Thomas Clarges, till ten, and then went to Sir Thomas Hanmer. His wife, the Duchess of Grafton, left us after a little while, and I stayed with him about an hour, upon some affairs, etc. Lord Bolingbroke left us at the Society before I went; for there is an express from Utrecht, but I know not yet what it contains; only I know the Ministers expect the peace will be signed in a week, which is a week before the session. Nite, MD.

27. Parnell's poem is mightily esteemed; but poetry sells ill. I am plagued with that. . . poor Harrison's mother; you would laugh to see how cautious I am of paying her the £100 I received for her son from the Treasury. I have asked every creature I know whether I may do it safely, yet durst not venture, till my Lord Keeper assured me there was no danger. I have not paid her, but will in a day or two: though I have a great mind to stay till Ppt sends me her opinion, because Ppt is a great lawyer. I dined to-day with a mixture of people at a Scotchman's, who made the invitation to Mr. Lewis and me, and has some design upon us, which we know very well. I went afterwards to see a famous moving picture, and I never saw anything so pretty. You see a sea ten miles wide, a town on t'other end, and ships sailing in the sea, and discharging their cannon. You see a great sky, with moon and stars, etc. I'm a fool. Nite, dee MD.

28. I had a mighty levee to-day. I deny myself to everybody, except about half a dozen, and they were all here, and Mr. Addison was one, and I had chocolate twice, which I don't like. Our rainy weather continues. Coach-hire goes deep. I dined with Eltee and his Saturday company, as usual, and could not get away till nine. Lord Peterborow was making long harangues, and Eltee kept me in spite. Then I went to see the

Bishop of Ossory, who had engaged me in the morning; he is going to Ireland. The Bishop of Killaloe and Tom Leigh was with us. The latter had wholly changed his style, by seeing how the bishops behaved themselves, and he seemed to think me one of more importance than I really am. I put the ill conduct of the bishops about the First-Fruits, with relation to Eltee and me, strongly upon Killaloe, and showed how it had hindered me from getting a better thing for them, called the Crown rents, which the Queen had promised. He had nothing to say, but was humble, and desired my interest in that and some other things. This letter is half done in a week: I believe oo will have it next. Nite MD.

29. I have been employed in endeavouring to save one of your junior Fellows, who came over here for a dispensation from taking orders, and, in soliciting it, has run out his time, and now his fellowship is void, if the College pleases, unless the Queen suspends the execution, and gives him time to take orders. I spoke to all the Ministers yesterday about it; but they say the Queen is angry, and thought it was a trick to deceive her; and she is positive, and so the man must be ruined, for I cannot help him. I never saw him in my life; but the case was so hard, I could not forbear interposing. Your Government recommended him to the Duke of Ormond, and he thought they would grant it; and by the time it was refused, the fellowship by rigour is forfeited. I dined with Dr. Arbuthnot (one of my brothers) at his lodgings in Chelsea, and was there at chapel; and the altar put me in mind of Tisdall's outlandish would at your hospital for the soldiers. I was not at Court to-day, and I hear the Queen was not at church. Perhaps the gout has seized her again. Terrible rain all day. Have oo such weather? Nite MD.

30. Morning. I was naming some time ago, to a certain person, another certain person, that was very deserving, and poor and sickly; and t'other, that first certain person, gave me a hundred pounds to give the other, which I have not yet done. The person who is to have it never saw the giver, nor expects one farthing, nor has the least knowledge or imagination of it; so I believe it will be a very agreeable surprise; for I think it is a handsome present enough. At night I dined in the City, at Pontack's, with Lord Dupplin, and some others. We were treated by one Colonel Cleland, who has a mind to be Governor of Barbados, and is laying these long traps for me and others, to engage our interests for him. He is a true Scotchman. I paid the hundred pounds this evening,

and it was an agreeable surprise to the receiver. We reckon the peace is now signed, and that we shall have it in three days. I believe it is pretty sure. Nite MD.

31. I thought to-day on Ppt when she told me she suppose(d) I was acquainted with the steward, when I was giving myself airs of being at some lord's house. Sir Andrew Fountaine invited the Bishop of Clogher and me, and some others, to dine where he did; and he carried us to the Duke of Kent's, who was gone out of town; but the steward treated us nobly, and showed us the fine pictures, etc. I have not yet seen Miss Ashe. I wait till she has been abroad, and taken the air. This evening Lady Masham, Dr. Arbuthnot, and I, were contriving a lie for to-morrow, that Mr. Noble, who was hanged last Saturday, was recovered by his friends, and then seized again by the sheriff, and is now in a messenger's hands at the Black Swan in Holborn. We are all to send to our friends, to know whether they have heard anything of it, and so we hope it will spread. However, we shall do our endeavours; nothing shall be wanting on our parts, and leave the rest to fortune. Nite MD.

April 1. We had no success in our story, though I sent my man to several houses, to inquire among the footmen, without letting him into the secret; but I doubt my colleagues did not contribute as they ought. Parnell and I dined with Darteneuf to-day. You have heard of Darteneuf: I have told you of Darteneuf. After dinner we all went to Lord Bolingbroke's, who had desired me to dine with him; but I would not, because I heard it was to look over a dull poem of one parson Trapp upon the peace. The Swedish Envoy told me to-day at Court that he was in great apprehensions about his master; and indeed we are afraid that prince has died among those Turkish dogs. I prevailed on Lord Bolingbroke to invite Mr. Addison to dine with him on Good Friday. I suppose we shall be mighty mannerly. Addison is to have a play of his acted on Friday in Easter Week: 'tis a tragedy, called *Cato*; I saw it unfinished some years ago. Did I tell you that Steele has begun a new daily paper, called the *Guardian*? they say good for nothing. I have not seen it. Nite dee MD.

2. I was this morning with Lord Bolingbroke, and he tells me a Spanish courier is just come, with the news that the King of Spain has agreed to everything that the Queen desires; and the Duke d'Ossuna has left

Paris in order to his journey to Utrecht. I was prevailed on to come home with Trapp, and read his poem and correct it; but it was good for nothing. While I was thus employed, Sir Thomas Hanmer came up to my chamber, and balked me of a journey he and I intended this week to Lord Orkney's at Cliffden; but he is not well, and his physician will not let him undertake such a journey. I intended to dine with Lord Treasurer; but going to see Colonel Disney, who lives with General Withers, I liked the General's little dinner so well, that I stayed and took share of it, and did not go to Lord Treasurer till six, where I found Dr. Sacheverell, who told us that the bookseller had given him £100 for his sermon, preached last Sunday, and intended to print 30,000: I believe he will be confoundedly bit, and will hardly sell above half. I have fires still, though April has begun, against my old maxim; but the weather is wet and cold. I never saw such a long run of ill weather in my life. Nite dee logues MD.

3. I was at the Queen's chapel to-day, but she was not there. Mr. St. John, Lord Bolingbroke's brother, came this day at noon with an express from Utrecht, that the peace is signed by all the Ministers there, but those of the Emperor, who will likewise sign in a few days; so that now the great work is in effect done, and I believe it will appear a most excellent peace for Europe, particularly for England. Addison and I, and some others, dined with Lord Bolingbroke, and sat with him till twelve. We were very civil, but yet when we grew warm, we talked in a friendly manner of party. Addison raised his objections, and Lord Bolingbroke answered them with great complaisance. Addison began Lord Somers's health, which went about; but I bid him not name Lord Wharton's, for I would not pledge it; and I told Lord Bolingbroke frankly that Addison loved Lord Wharton as little as I did: so we laughed, etc. Well, but you are glad of the peace, you Ppt the Trimmer, are not you? As for DD I don't doubt her. Why, now, if I did not think Ppt had been a violent Tory, and DD the greater Whig of the two! 'Tis late. Nite MD.

4. This Passion Week, people are so demure, especially this last day, that I told Dilly, who called here, that I would dine with him, and so I did, faith; and had a small shoulder of mutton of my own bespeaking. It rained all day. I came home at seven, and have never stirred out, but have been reading Sacheverell's long dull sermon, which he sent me.

It is the first sermon since his suspension is expired; but not a word in it upon the occasion, except two or three remote hints. The Bishop of Clogher has been sadly bit by Tom Ashe, who sent him a pun, which the Bishop had made, and designed to send to him, but delayed it; and Lord Pembroke and I made Sir Andrew Fountaine write it to Tom. I believe I told you of it in my last; it succeeded right, and the Bishop was wondering to Lord Pembroke how he and his brother could hit on the same thing. I'll go to bed soon, for I must be at church by eight to-morrow, Easter Day. Nite dee MD.

5. Warburton wrote to me two letters about a living of one Foulkes, who is lately dead in the county of Meath. My answer is, that before I received the first letter, General Gorges had recommended a friend of his to the Duke of Ormond, which was the first time I heard of its vacancy, and it was the Provost told me of it. I believe verily that Foulkes was not dead when Gorges recommended the other: for Warburton's last letter said that Foulkes was dead the day before the date.—This has prevented me from serving Warburton, as I would have done, if I had received early notice enough. Pray say or write this to Warburton, to justify me to him. I was at church at eight this morning, and dressed and shaved after I came back, but was too late at Court; and Lord Abingdon was like to have snapped me for dinner, and I believe will fall out with me for refusing him; but I hate dining with them, and I dined with a private friend, and took two or three good walks; for it was a very fine day, the first we have had a great while. Remember, was Easter Day a fine day with you? I have sat with Lady Worsley till now. Nite dee MD.

6. I was this morning at ten at the rehearsal of Mr. Addison's play, called Cato, which is to be acted on Friday. There were not above half a score of us to see it. We stood on the stage, and it was foolish enough to see the actors prompted every moment, and the poet directing them; and the drab that acts Cato's daughter, out in the midst of a passionate part, and then calling out, "What's next?" The Bishop of Clogher was there too; but he stood privately in a gallery. I went to dine with Lord Treasurer, but he was gone to Wimbledon, his daughter Caermarthen's country seat, seven miles off. So I went back, and dined privately with Mr. Addison, whom I had left to go to Lord Treasurer. I keep fires yet; I am very extravagant. I sat this evening with

Sir A. Fountaine, and we amused ourselves with making *ifs* for Dilly. It is rainy weather again; nevle saw ze rike. This letter shall go to-morrow; remember, ung oomens, it is seven weeks since oor last, and I allow oo but five weeks; but oo have been galloping into the country to Swanton's. O pray tell Swanton I had his letter, but cannot contrive how to serve him. If a Governor were to go over, I would recommend him as far as lay in my power, but I can do no more: and you know all employments in Ireland, at least almost all, are engaged in reversions. If I were on the spot, and had credit with a Lord Lieutenant, I would very heartily recommend him; but employments here are no more in my power than the monarchy itself. Nite, dee MD.

7. Morning. I have had a visitor here, that has taken up my time. I have not been abroad, oo may be sure; so I can say nothing to-day, but that I rove MD bettle zan ever, if possibbere. I will put this in the post-office; so I say no more. I write by this post to the Dean, but it is not above two lines; and one enclosed to you, but that enclosed to you is not above three lines; and then one enclosed to the Dean, which he must not have but upon condition of burning it immediately after reading, and that before your eyes; for there are some things in it I would not have liable to accident. You shall only know in general that it is an account of what I have done to serve him in his pretensions on these vacancies, etc. But he must not know that you know so much. Does this perplex you? Hat care I? But rove Pdfr, saucy Pdfr. Farewell, deelest MD MD MD FW FW FW, . . . ME, MD Lele.

Letter LXIII

I fancy I marked my last, which I sent this day, wrong; only 61, and it ought to be 62. I dined with Lord Treasurer, and though the business I had with him is something against Thursday, when the Parliament is to meet, and this is Tuesday, yet he put it off till to-morrow. I dare not tell you what it is, lest this letter should miscarry or be opened; but I never saw his fellow for delays. The Parliament will now certainly sit, and everybody's expectations are ready to burst. At a Council to-night the Lord Chief-Justice Parker, a Whig, spoke against the peace; so did Lord Chomley, another Whig, who is Treasurer of the Household. My Lord Keeper was this night made Lord Chancellor. We hope there will soon be some removes. Nite, dee sollahs; Late. Rove Pdfr.

8. Lord Chomley (the right name is Cholmondeley) is this day removed from his employment, for his last night's speech; and Sir Richard Temple, Lieutenant-General, the greatest Whig in the army, is turned out; and Lieutenant-General Palmes will be obliged to sell his regiment. This is the first-fruits of a friendship I have established between two great men. I dined with Lord Treasurer, and did the business I had for him to his satisfaction. I won't tell MD what it was... for zat. The Parliament sits to-morrow for certain. Here is a letter printed in Maccartney's name, vindicating himself from the murder of the Duke of Hamilton. I must give some hints to have it answered; 'tis full of lies, and will give an opportunity of exposing that party. To morrow will be a very important day. All the world will be at Westminster. Lord Treasurer is as easy as a lamb. They are mustering up the proxies of the absent lords; but they are not in any fear of wanting a majority, which death and accidents have increased this year. Nite MD.

9. I was this morning with Lord Treasurer, to present to him a young son of the late Earl of Jersey, at the desire of the widow. There I saw the mace and great coach ready for Lord Treasurer, who was going to Parliament. Our Society met to-day; but I expected the Houses would sit longer than I cared to fast; so I dined with a friend, and never inquired how matters went till eight this evening, when I went

to Lord Orkney's, where I found Sir Thomas Hanmer. The Queen delivered her speech very well, but a little weaker in her voice. The crowd was vast. The order for the Address was moved, and opposed by Lord Nottingham, Halifax, and Cowper. Lord Treasurer spoke with great spirit and resolution; Lord Peterborow flirted against the Duke of Marlborough (who is in Germany, you know), but it was in answer to one of Halifax's impertinences. The order for an Address passed by a majority of thirty-three, and the Houses rose before six. This is the account I heard at Lord Orkney's. The Bishop of Chester, a high Tory, was against the Court. The Duchess of Marlborough sent for him some months ago, to justify herself to him in relation to the Queen, and showed him letters, and told him stories, which the weak man believed, and was perverted. Nite MD.

10. I dined with a cousin in the City, and poor Pat Rolt was there. I have got her rogue of a husband leave to come to England from Port-Mahon. The Whigs are much down; but I reckon they have some scheme in agitation. This Parliament-time hinders our Court meetings on Wednesdays, Thursdays, and Saturdays. I had a great deal of business to-night, which gave me a temptation to be idle, and I lost a dozen shillings at ombre, with Dr. Pratt and another. I have been to see t'other day the Bishop of Clogher and lady, but did not see Miss. It rains every day, and yet we are all over dust. Lady Masham's eldest boy is very ill: I doubt he will not live, and she stays at Kensington to nurse him, which vexes us all. She is so excessively fond, it makes me mad. She should never leave the Queen, but leave everything, to stick to what is so much the interest of the public, as well as her own. This I tell her; but talk to the winds. Nite MD.

11. I dined at Lord Treasurer's, with his Saturday company. We had ten at table, all lords but myself and the Chancellor of the Exchequer. Argyle went off at six, and was in very indifferent humour as usual. Duke of Ormond and Lord Bolingbroke were absent. I stayed till near ten. Lord Treasurer showed us a small picture, enamelled work, and set in gold, worth about twenty pounds; a picture, I mean, of the Queen, which she gave to the Duchess of Marlborough, set in diamonds. When the Duchess was leaving England, she took off all the diamonds, and gave the picture to one Mrs. Higgins (an old intriguing woman, whom everybody knows), bidding her make the best of it she could. Lord

Treasurer sent to Mrs. Higgins for this picture, and gave her a hundred pounds for it. Was ever such an ungrateful beast as that Duchess? or did you ever hear such a story? I suppose the Whigs will not believe it. Pray, try them. Takes off the diamonds, and gives away the picture to an insignificant woman, as a thing of no consequence: and gives it to her to sell, like a piece of old-fashioned plate. Is she not a detestable slut? Nite deelest MD.

12. I went to Court to-day, on purpose to present Mr. Berkeley, one of your Fellows of Dublin College, to Lord Berkeley of Stratton. That Mr. Berkeley is a very ingenious man, and great philosopher, and I have mentioned him to all the Ministers, and given them some of his writings; and I will favour him as much as I can. This I think I am bound to, in honour and conscience, to use all my little credit toward helping forward men of worth in the world. The Queen was at chapel to-day, and looks well. I dined at Lord Orkney's with the Duke of Ormond, Lord Arran, and Sir Thomas Hanmer. Mr. St. John, Secretary at Utrecht, expects every moment to return there with the ratification of the peace. Did I tell you in my last of Addison's play called Cato, and that I was at the rehearsal of it? Nite MD.

13. This morning my friend, Mr. Lewis, came to me, and showed me an order for a warrant for the three vacant deaneries; but none of them to me. This was what I always foresaw, and received the notice of it better, I believe, than he expected. I bid Mr. Lewis tell Lord Treasurer that I took nothing ill of him but his not giving me timely notice, as he promised to do, if he found the Queen would do nothing for me. At noon, Lord Treasurer hearing I was in Mr. Lewis's office, came to me, and said many things too long to repeat. I told him I had nothing to do but go to Ireland immediately; for I could not, with any reputation, stay longer here, unless I had something honourable immediately given to me. We dined together at the Duke of Ormond's. He there told me he had stopped the warrants for the deans, that what was done for me might be at the same time, and he hoped to compass it to-night; but I believe him not. I told the Duke of Ormond my intentions. He is content Sterne should be a bishop, and I have St. Patrick's; but I believe nothing will come of it, for stay I will not; and so I believe for all oo. . . oo may see me in Dublin before April ends. I am less out of humour than you would imagine: and if it were not that impertinent people will

condole with me, as they used to give me joy, I would value it less. But I will avoid company, and muster up my baggage, and send them next Monday by the carrier to Chester, and come and see my willows, against the expectation of all the world.—Hat care I? Nite deelest logues, MD.

14. I dined in the City to-day, and ordered a lodging to be got ready for me against I came to pack up my things; for I will leave this end of the town as soon as ever the warrants for the deaneries are out, which are yet stopped. Lord Treasurer told Mr. Lewis that it should be determined to-night: and so he will for a hundred nights. So he said yesterday, but I value it not. My daily journals shall be but short till I get into the City, and then I will send away this, and follow it myself; and design to walk it all the way to Chester, my man and I, by ten miles a day. It will do my health a great deal of good. I shall do it in fourteen days. Nite dee MD.

15. Lord Bolingbroke made me dine with him to-day; he was as good company as ever; and told me the Queen would determine something for me to-night. The dispute is, Windsor or St. Patrick's. I told him I would not stay for their disputes, and he thought I was in the right. Lord Masham told me that Lady Masham is angry I have not been to see her since this business, and desires I will come to-morrow. Nite deelest MD.

16. I was this noon at Lady Masham's, who was just come from Kensington, where her eldest son is sick. She said much to me of what she had talked to the Queen and Lord Treasurer. The poor lady fell a shedding tears openly. She could not bear to think of my having St. Patrick's, etc. I was never more moved than to see so much friendship. I would not stay with her, but went and dined with Dr. Arbuthnot, with Mr. Berkeley, one of your Fellows, whom I have recommended to the Doctor, and to Lord Berkeley of Stratton. Mr. Lewis tells me that the Duke of Ormond has been to-day with the Queen; and she was content that Dr. Sterne should be Bishop of Dromore, and I Dean of St. Patrick's; but then out came Lord Treasurer, and said he would not be satisfied but that I must be Prebend(ary) of Windsor. Thus he perplexes things. I expect neither; but I confess, as much as I love England, I am so angry at this treatment that, if I had my choice, I would rather have St. Patrick's. Lady Masham says she will speak to purpose to the Queen to-morrow. Nite, . . . dee MD.

17. I went to dine at Lady Masham's to-day, and she was taken ill of a sore throat, and aguish. She spoke to the Queen last night, but had not much time. The Queen says she will determine to-morrow with Lord Treasurer. The warrants for the deaneries are still stopped, for fear I should be gone. Do you think anything will be done? I don't care whether it is or no. In the meantime, I prepare for my journey, and see no great people, nor will see Lord Treasurer any more, if I go. Lord Treasurer told Mr. Lewis it should be done to-night; so he said five nights ago. Nite MD.

18. This morning Mr. Lewis sent me word that Lord Treasurer told him the Queen would determine at noon. At three Lord Treasurer sent to me to come to his lodgings at St. James's, and told me the Queen was at last resolved that Dr. Sterne should be Bishop of Dromore, and I Dean of St. Patrick's; and that Sterne's warrant should be drawn immediately. You know the deanery is in the Duke of Ormond's gift; but this is concerted between the Queen, Lord Treasurer, and the Duke of Ormond, to make room for me. I do not know whether it will yet be done; some unlucky accident may yet come. Neither can I feel joy at passing my days in Ireland; and I confess I thought the Ministry would not let me go; but perhaps they can't help it. Nite MD.

19. I forgot to tell you that Lord Treasurer forced me to dine with him yesterday as usual, with his Saturday company; which I did after frequent refusals. To-day I dined with a private friend, and was not at Court. After dinner Mr. Lewis sent me a note, that the Queen stayed till she knew whether the Duke of Ormond approved of Sterne for Bishop. I went this evening, and found the Duke of Ormond at the Cock-pit, and told him, and desired he would go to the Queen, and approve of Sterne. He made objections, desired I would name any other deanery, for he did not like Sterne; that Sterne never went to see him; that he was influenced by the Archbishop of Dublin, etc.; so all now is broken again. I sent out for Lord Treasurer, and told him this. He says all will do well; but I value not what he says. This suspense vexes me worse than anything else. Nite MD.

20. I went to-day, by appointment, to the Cock-pit, to talk with the Duke of Ormond. He repeated the same proposals of any other deanery, etc. I desired he would put me out of the case, and do as he pleased. Then, with

great kindness, he said he would consent; but would do it for no man alive but me, etc. And he will speak to the Queen to-day or to-morrow; so, perhaps, something will come of it. I can't tell. Nite dee dee logues, MD.

21. The Duke of Ormond has told the Queen he is satisfied that Sterne should be Bishop, and she consents I shall be Dean; and I suppose the warrants will be drawn in a day or two. I dined at an ale-house with Parnell and Berkeley; for I am not in humour to go among the Ministers, though Lord Dartmouth invited me to dine with him to-day, and Lord Treasurer was to be there. I said I would, if I were out of suspense. Nite deelest MD.

22. The Queen says warrants shall be drawn, but she will dispose of all in England and Ireland at once, to be teased no more. This will delay it some time; and, while it is delayed, I am not sure of the Queen, my enemies being busy. I hate this suspense. Nite deelest MD.

23. I dined yesterday with General Hamilton. I forgot to tell oo. I write short journals now. I have eggs on the spit. This night the Queen has signed all the warrants, among which Sterne is Bishop of Dromore, and the Duke of Ormond is to send over an order for making me Dean of St. Patrick's. I have no doubt of him at all. I think 'tis now passed. And I suppose MD is malicious enough to be glad, and rather have it than Wells. But you see what a condition I am in. I thought I was to pay but six hundred pounds for the house; but the Bishop of Clogher says eight hundred pounds; first-fruits one hundred and fifty pounds, and so, with patent, a thousand pounds in all; so that I shall not be the better for the deanery these three years. I hope in some time they will be persuaded here to give me some money to pay off these debts. I must finish the book I am writing, before I can go over; and they expect I shall pass next winter here, and then I will dun them to give me a sum of money. However, I hope to pass four or five months with MD, and whatever comes on it. MD's allowance must be increased, and shall be too, fais. . . I received oor rettle No. 39 to-night; just ten weeks since I had your last. I shall write next post to Bishop Sterne. Never man had so many enemies of Ireland as he. I carried it with the strongest hand possible. If he does not use me well and gently in what dealings I shall have with him, he will be the most ungrateful of mankind. The Archbishop of York, my mortal enemy, has sent, by a third hand, that

he would be glad to see me. Shall I see him, or not? I hope to be over in a month, and that MD, with their raillery, will be mistaken, that I shall make it three years. I will answer oo rettle soon; but no more journals. I shall be very busy. Short letters from hence forward. I shall not part with Laracor. That is all I have to live on, except the deanery be worth more than four hundred pounds a year. Is it? If it be, the overplus shall be divided between MD and FW beside usual allowance of MD. . . Pray write to me a good-humoured letter immediately, let it be ever so short. This affair was carried with great difficulty, which vexes me. But they say here 'tis much to my reputation that I have made a bishop, in spite of all the world, to get the best deanery in Ireland. Nite dee sollahs.

24. I forgot to tell you I had Sterne's letter yesterday, in answer to mine. Oo performed oor commission well, dood dallars both. I made mistakes the three last days, and am forced to alter the number. I dined in the City to-day with my printer, and came home early, and am going to (be) busy with my work. I will send this to-morrow, and I suppose the warrants will go then. I wrote to Dr. Coghill, to take care of passing my patent; and to Parvisol, to attend him with money, if he has any, or to borrow some where he can. Nite MD.

25. Morning. I know not whether my warrant be yet ready from the Duke of Ormond. I suppose it will by to-night. I am going abroad, and will keep this unsealed, till I know whether all be finished. Mollow, sollahs.

I had this letter all day in my pocket, waiting till I heard the warrants were gone over. Mr. Lewis sent to Southwell's clerk at ten; and he said the Bishop of Killaloe had desired they should be stopped till next post. He sent again, that the Bishop of Killaloe's business had nothing to do with ours. Then I went myself, but it was past eleven, and asked the reason. Killaloe is removed to Raphoe, and he has a mind to have an order for the rents of Raphoe, that have fallen due since the vacancy, and he would have all stop till he has gotten that. A pretty request! But the clerk, at Mr. Lewis's message, sent the warrants for Sterne and me; but then it was too late to send this, which frets me heartily, that MD should not have intelligence first from Pdfr. I think to take a hundred pounds a year out of the deanery, and divide it between MD and Pr, and so be one year longer in paying the debt; but we'll talk of zis hen I come over. So nite dear sollahs. Lele.

26. I was at Court to-day, and a thousand people gave me joy; so I ran out. I dined with Lady Orkney. Yesterday I dined with Lord Treasurer and his Saturday people as usual; and was so bedeaned! The Archbishop of York says he will never more speak against me. Pray see that Parvisol stirs about getting my patent. I have given Tooke DD's note to prove she is alive. I'll answer oo rettle. . . Nite.

27. Nothing new to-day. I dined with Tom Harley, etc. I'll seal up this to-night. Pray write soon. . . MD MD MD FW FW FW ME ME ME Lele, lele.

LETTER LXIV

LONDON, *May* 16, 1713

I had yours, No. 40, yesterday. Your new Bishop acts very ungratefully. I cannot say so bad of it as he deserved. I begged at the same post his warrant and mine went over, that he would leave those livings to my disposal. I shall write this post to him to let him know how ill I take it. I have letters to tell me that I ought to think of employing some body to set the tithes of the deanery. I know not what to do at this distance. I cannot be in Ireland under a month. I will write two orders; one to Parvisol, and t'other to Parvisol, and a blank for whatever fellow it is whom the last Dean employed; and I would desire you to advise with friends which to make use of: and if the latter, let the fellow's name be inserted, and both act by commission. If the former, then speak to Parvisol, and know whether he can undertake it. I doubt it is hardly to be done by a perfect stranger alone, as Parvisol is. He may perhaps venture at all, to keep up his interest with me; but that is needless, for I am willing to do him any good, that will do me no harm. Pray advise with Walls and Raymond, and a little with Bishop Sterne for form. Tell Raymond I cannot succeed for him to get that living of Moimed. It is represented here as a great sinecure. Several chaplains have solicited for it; and it has vexed me so, that, if I live, I will make it my business to serve him better in something else. I am heartily sorry for his illness, and that of the other two. If it be not necessary to let the tithes till a month hence, you may keep the two papers, and advise well in the meantime; and whenever it is absolutely necessary, then give that paper which you are most advised to. I thank Mr. Walls for his letter. Tell him that must serve for an answer, with my service to him and her. I shall buy Bishop Sterne's hair as soon as his household goods. I shall be ruined, or at least sadly cramped, unless the Queen will give me a thousand pounds. I am sure she owes me a great deal more. Lord Treasurer rallies me upon it, and I believe intends it; but, quando? I am advised to hasten over as soon as possible, and so I will, and hope to set out the beginning of June. Take no lodging for me. What? at your old tricks again? I can lie somewhere after I land, and I care not where, nor how. I will buy your eggs and bacon, DD. . . your caps and Bible; and pray think immediately, and give me some commissions, and I will perform them as far as oo poo Pdfr can. The letter I sent before this was

A JOURNAL TO STELLA

to have gone a post before; but an accident hindered it; and, I assure oo, I wam very akkree MD did not write to Dean Pdfr, and I think oo might have had a Dean under your girdle for the superscription. I have just finished my Treatise, and must be ten days correcting it. Farewell, deelest MD, MD, MD, FW, FW, FW, ME, ME, ME, Lele.

You'll seal the two papers after my name.

LONDON, *May* 16, 1713

I appoint Mr. Isaiah Parvisol and Mr. . . to set and let the tithes of the Deanery of St. Patrick's for this present year. In witness whereof, I hereunto set my hand and seal, the day and year above written.

JONAT. SWIFT

* * * * *

LONDON, *May* 16, 1713

I do hereby appoint Mr. Isaiah Parvisol my proctor, to set and let the tithes of the Deanery of St. Patrick's. In witness whereof, I have hereunto set my hand and seal, the day and year above written.

JONAT. SWIFT

LETTER LXV

I am come here after six days. I set out on Monday last, and got here to-day about eleven in the morning. A noble rider, fais! and all the ships and people went off yesterday with a rare wind. This was told me, to my comfort, upon my arrival. Having not used riding these three years, made me terrible weary; yet I resolve on Monday to set out for Holyhead, as weary as I am. 'Tis good for my health, mam. When I came here, I found MD's letter of the 26th of May sent down to me. Had you writ a post sooner I might have brought some pins: but you were lazy, and would not write your orders immediately, as I desired you. I will come when God pleases; perhaps I may be with you in a week. I will be three days going to Holyhead; I cannot ride faster, say hat oo will. I am upon Stay-behind's mare. I have the whole inn to myself. I would fain 'scape this Holyhead journey; but I have no prospect of ships, and it will be almost necessary I should be in Dublin before the 25th instant, to take the oaths; otherwise I must wait to a quarter sessions. I will lodge as I can; therefore take no lodgings for me, to pay in my absence. The poor Dean can't afford it. I spoke again to the Duke of Ormond about Moimed for Raymond, and hope he may yet have it, for I laid it strongly to the Duke, and gave him the Bishop of Meath's memorial. I am sorry for Raymond's fistula; tell him so. I will speak to Lord Treasurer about Mrs. South to-morrow. Odso! I forgot; I thought I had been in London. Mrs. Tisdall is very big, ready to lie down. Her husband is a puppy. Do his feet stink still? The letters to Ireland go at so uncertain an hour, that I am forced to conclude. Farewell, MD, MD MD FW FW FW ME ME ME ME.

Lele lele
lele logues and
Ladies bose fair
and slender.

(*On flyleaf.*)
I mightily approve Ppt's project of hanging the blind parson. When I read that passage upon Chester walls, as I was coming into town, and just received your letter, I said aloud—Agreeable B—tch.

A Note About the Author

Jonathan Swift (1667–1745) was an Irish poet and satirical writer. When the spread of Catholicism in Ireland became prevalent, Swift moved to England, where he lived and worked as a writer. Due to the controversial nature of his work, Swift often wrote under pseudonyms. In addition to his poetry and satirical prose, Swift also wrote for political pamphlets and since many of his works provided political commentary this was a fitting career stop for Swift. When he returned to Ireland, he was ordained as a priest in the Anglican church. Despite this, his writings stirred controversy about religion and prevented him from advancing in the clergy.

A Note from the Publisher

Spanning many genres, from non-fiction essays to literature classics to children's books and lyric poetry, Mint Edition books showcase the master works of our time in a modern new package. The text is freshly typeset, is clean and easy to read, and features a new note about the author in each volume. Many books also include exclusive new introductory material. Every book boasts a striking new cover, which makes it as appropriate for collecting as it is for gift giving. Mint Edition books are only printed when a reader orders them, so natural resources are not wasted. We're proud that our books are never manufactured in excess and exist only in the exact quantity they need to be read and enjoyed.

Discover more of your favorite classics with Bookfinity™.

- Track your reading with custom book lists.
- Get great book recommendations for your personalized Reader Type.
- Add reviews for your favorite books.
- AND MUCH MORE!

Visit **bookfinity.com** and take the fun Reader Type quiz to get started.

Enjoy our classic and modern companion pairings!

Classic & Modern